John Doe Chinaman

JOHN DOE CHINAMAN

A Forgotten History of Chinese Life under American Racial Law

BETH LEW-WILLIAMS

THE BELKNAP PRESS OF
HARVARD UNIVERSITY PRESS
Cambridge, Massachusetts
London, England
2025

Copyright © 2025 by the President and Fellows of Harvard College
All rights reserved

Printed in the United States of America

First printing

EU GPSR Authorised Representative
LOGOS EUROPE, 9 rue Nicolas Poussin,
17000, LA ROCHELLE, France E-mail: Contact@logoseurope.eu

Credit for frontispiece: Jesse Brown Cook Scrapbooks Documenting San Francisco History and Law Enforcement, BANC PIC 1996.003: Volume 21:033—fALB, The Bancroft Library, University of California, Berkeley.

Library of Congress Cataloging-in-Publication Data
Names: Lew-Williams, Beth, author.
Title: John Doe Chinaman : A forgotten history of Chinese life under American racial law / Beth Lew-Williams.
Description: Cambridge : The Belknap Press of Harvard University Press, 2025. | Includes index.
Identifiers: LCCN 2024060251 | ISBN 9780674294110 (cloth)
Subjects: LCSH: Chinese Americans—Legal status, laws, etc.—West (U.S.)—History—19th century. | Race discrimination—Law and legislation—West (U.S.)—History. | Law—West (U.S.)—History. | Chinese—West (U.S.)—History—19th century.
Classification: LCC KF4757.5.C47 L49 2025 | DDC 342.7308/73—dc23/eng/20250305
LC record available at https://lccn.loc.gov/2024060251

For Casey

CONTENTS

	Introduction	1
1	The "Coolie" and the Threat of Chinese Labor	26
2	The "Criminal" and the Fear of a Chinese Underclass	59
3	The "Alien" and the Reconstruction of Chinese Rights	97
4	The "Chinawoman" and the Search for Runaways	130
5	The "Invader" and the Entrenchment of Chinese Segregation	166
6	The "Predator" and the Problem of Interracial Intimacy	205
7	The "Immigrant" and the Meaning of Chinese Exclusion	233
	Epilogue	269
	Appendix: Selected Sections of Statutes Regulating Chinese Residents	283
	Abbreviations	295
	Notes	297
	Acknowledgments	345
	Index	349

John Doe Chinaman

2700 — Chinese Boy Babies of San Francisco China Town in 1889

INTRODUCTION

It takes a moment for the photograph to come into focus. When it does, black and white dots suddenly clarify into hundreds of faces, maybe thousands. They belong to infants and young children, most of them old enough to sit but not to run, some nude with their legs spread to display their sex, and others fully dressed in ornamental clothing. The children were individually photographed, then their images were cut out and pasted into a photo collage, which was photographed again. The result is not exactly artistic, but neither is it haphazard. At the center of the collage is an oversized photograph of a child sitting alert and unclothed, his head shaved in a classic style of the Qing dynasty.[1]

The caption reads: "2700 Chinese Boy Babies of San Francisco China Town in 1889." The words appear in the scrawling hand of Jesse Brown Cook. Cook worked at police stations in Houston and San Diego before coming to San Francisco as a sergeant in the 1880s. He led the Chinatown Squad in the 1890s and eventually became chief of police. Years later he spent his retirement compiling as many as fifty scrapbooks, which included more than 12,000 items in no apparent order, documenting his police work, the history of the force, and the city of San Francisco itself. On page 33 of scrapbook 21, he pasted this unsettling image of Chinese American children.[2]

Who made the collage is not known. Cook was no photographer, and there are no indications that the photographs, costly to produce, were taken by police.[3] The tender age of the subjects, their nudity, and their calm demeanor suggest these may be family photos rather

Detail of "2700 Chinese Boy Babies of San Francisco China Town in 1889." This haunting photo collage was preserved in a scrapbook belonging to Jesse Brown Cook, onetime leader of the Chinatown Squad. An unknown photographer collected Chinese baby portraits and assembled them into an anonymous horde. (Jesse Brown Cook Scrapbooks Documenting San Francisco History and Law Enforcement, BANC PIC 1996.003:Volume 21:033—fALB, The Bancroft Library, University of California, Berkeley)

than mug shots. After all, the Chinese community in San Francisco had taken a liking to American studio photography in the 1870s, and may have been particularly eager to purchase photographs of their newborn sons. American studio photographers, in turn, could increase their profits by reprinting Chinese portraits and selling them to white people as curiosities. A photographer likely crafted this collage in secret, without customers' knowledge or consent, since few would have approved of the inauspicious practice of cutting family photographs. Likely, these families did not know that the faces of their cherished children had been compiled into an anonymous mass and then sold to strangers. Certainly they had no idea that their pictures would end up in a policeman's scrapbook, alongside images of criminals.⁴

For white Americans in the late nineteenth century, such as Cook, the collage's effect was ominous, and the nature of the threat would have been immediately clear. To them, these infants represented the contamination of the American citizenry. A few years earlier, in 1882, the United States had declared the Chinese an undesirable race and barred most immigrants from China from entering the nation. In subsequent decades the federal government passed a series of Chinese exclusion laws, which pledged (but frequently failed) to keep out new Chinese arrivals. Border control only addressed part of the problem, however. What about the Chinese who were already present? What about these infants, their parents, and the wider Chinese diaspora in the American West?

While many white westerners declared "the Chinese Must Go" and fought for Chinese exclusion, men like Cook were more concerned with regulating the Chinese population already living in the United States. For them, it was the long-term presence of the Chinese in the city, rather than their imagined threat at the border, that provoked racial anxiety. We can see his outsized fears in his chosen caption, because he got the numbers wrong. There are not 2,700 babies in the picture; there were fewer than 2,700 Chinese babies in all of San Francisco Chinatown in 1889.⁵ But Chinese children loomed large in Cook's mind because to him they represented the culmination of an invasion. The enemy already stood within the city gates. At this point, border control seemed too little and too late.

If the photo collage captures the magnitude of white fears, for viewers today it also reveals the danger of historical erasure. When we look at this photograph, we see what many white Americans saw: a multitude of unknown Chinese children. Unfortunately this anonymity is common in the nineteenth-century American archive. Until recently, western archives failed to collect and preserve Chinese records, so traces of their lives can primarily be found in the writings of white people. As a result, we are left with tales of "John Doe Chinaman" and other nameless Chinese.⁶

The presence of "John Doe Chinaman" in the archive, in the absence of personal names, presents historical and methodological problems. What can we really know about the "John Doe Chinaman"

Legal complaint from *People v. John Doe Chinaman* (1862). Nineteenth-century American legal records failed to record Chinese names with any accuracy or consistency. Some officials did not even attempt to record Chinese names, and instead relied on racial monikers like "John Doe Chinaman." Past disregard for Chinese individuality continues to make historical recovery difficult. (County of Tuolumne Carlo di Ferrari Archive)

who stood accused of murder in Los Angeles? How can we tell the difference between the "John Doe Chinaman" who sat in a jail cell in Sacramento, and the "John Doe Chinaman (deceased)" who lay on the side of the road outside Sonora? Record keepers shortened the name of this enigmatic figure even further to "John Chinaman" or simply "Chinaman." The 1852 California census counted 2,581 Chinese residents in San Francisco, but listed only two dozen by name. The rest were simply anonymous, interchangeable, inscrutable "Chinamen" or, occasionally, "Chinawomen."[7]

At the time, few thought twice about the word "Chinaman."* In the nineteenth century, Americans used the term in newspapers,

---

* In this book I have made a number of imperfect choices concerning racial terminology. I use "white" to represent all people of European descent in the American West, because starting in the nineteenth century white people (despite their many differences) claimed a common racial identity when contrasting themselves with the Chinese. For Native people, I name their nations when possible and otherwise use the terms "Native," "Native American," or (when quoting or drawing upon original sources) "Indian." I use "Black," "African American," or

lawmaking, court trials, and everyday speech to denote a racial identity they believed to be innate.[8] When communicating with white people in English, Chinese residents also used the term "Chinaman." It was part of common parlance rather than an aggressive racial slur. (People who wanted to convey particular malice could deploy more insulting terms, like "John Doe Chink.") As the word "Chinaman" became ubiquitous, it grew into a powerful agent of racialization, one that forcibly stripped the Chinese of their individuality.

In the hands of American record keepers, some Chinese migrants became literal John Does, but far more became figurative ones. The men and women who were recorded as "Charley Chinaman," "Ah Sing," or "China Mary" had fallen victim to racial prejudice, bureaucratic disregard, and failures of transliteration. Like other John Does, their true names will be forever unknown. When reading early government records of the Chinese in America, it is difficult to see beyond the perspective of white Americans, just as it is hard to view the collage of babies without seeing what Cook saw.

But what happens if we attempt, instead, to see through the eyes of these children looking out at the world? This is no simple task. Chinese in the American West lived full and complicated lives, but often the only remaining evidence of their experiences comes from people who feared and reviled them. Cook is in that group, and it is important to understand how individuals like him viewed Chinese residents, and how the white community and the American state sought to regulate them. It is equally critical to ask what it meant for Chinese to live within these constraints.

To understand their experiences is to understand a lived reality of white supremacy. This is not the late nineteenth-century white supremacy we are more familiar with—the violent breed of anti-Black terror that followed the dismantling of chattel slavery.[9] The

---

(when quoting or drawing upon original sources) "Negro." I refer to people from China as "Chinese," although I recognize that these people belonged to multiple ethnic groups. I use "Chinese American" only when exclusively referring to US citizens of Chinese descent in order to highlight the legal bars to naturalization. I capitalize the terms "Black," "Native," and "Chinese," because each term reflects a shared sense of identity based, in part, on a history of oppression in America. I have chosen not to capitalize "white," because few in the modern era have claimed a shared sense of white identity except white supremacists. Finally, this book includes historical sources that use offensive racial terms. This language is uncomfortable, even painful, but it is essential for an accurate depiction of American history.

racial regime the Chinese encountered may have flowed from America's history of enslavement and settler colonialism that preceded their arrival and it may have helped to fuel the Jim Crow segregation and Native dispossession that followed. But while these strains of racism often crossed, they never merged into a single American color line. In other words, Chinese migrants encountered a form of white supremacy that was tailored just for them.[10]

The Chinese did not simply live in this racial regime, but acted within, against, and through it. When Cook led the Chinatown Squad in the 1890s, for example, a Chinese merchant named Lai Hock Yan filed a legal complaint against him. Lai alleged that Cook had "brutally assaulted, maimed and injured several Chinese" while enforcing city ordinances. "It is not so much that we want to make an example of Cook," Lai's lawyer explained to the press, but instead to "insist upon having Chinese treated like human beings."[11] The complaint held power: Cook faced a Police Commissioner's inquiry, criminal charges, a $500 bail, and the loss of his command—at least temporarily. Such moments of resistance mattered, even when fleeting, because they represented a renegotiation of the racial order. Following the complaint, the Chinatown Squad would think twice before throwing Chinese residents down staircases.

In the history of the Chinese in America, the border has caught our attention and held it. Chinese migrants' attempts to cross the border, and America's attempts to stop them, is the story historians have told and retold.[12] But long before the Chinese faced the first exclusion laws, and long afterward as well, they endured a racial regime within America every day. This book is the history of that racial regime and the lives it touched.

Arriving on California's shores in the 1850s, Chinese migrants entered a young nation with an old tradition of white dominance. White Californians did not agree on what to do with these "exotic" newcomers, but they were certain that the Chinese did not belong. Set apart by their race, religion, and supposed slavish tendencies, the Chinese could not be enfolded into the nation as others would be. Their inferior stock could contaminate the citizenry, their heathen beliefs could introduce immorality, and their inherent servility could undercut white workers. Perhaps these "heathen coolies" could be put to good work while they were here, but their stays must be temporary. They had no future in America, or at least that is what lawmakers hoped.

To make it so, western states, territories, and towns enacted anti-Chinese laws. Laws and legal customs regulated the ability of Chinese people to work, operate a business, own property, testify in court, seek education, and form families. For the Chinese, these laws were both more and less than they appeared on paper; more because of the unspoken level of violence that could lie behind them, less because many failed to withstand Chinese resistance.

The idea that Chinese faced discriminatory laws in nineteenth-century America is not new. This book owes much to scholars who have painstakingly documented western racial laws and prominent cases against them.[13] But only recently have "big data" methods made it possible to conduct a more comprehensive survey. I teamed up with Hannah Postel, a demographer and public policy researcher, to build a database of anti-Chinese measures. With the help of student research assistants and a keyword discovery algorithm, we surveyed state constitutions and laws in California, Oregon, and Washington, as well as available full-text charters, ordinances, and statutes from 133 municipalities in these states. We searched broadly for laws with discriminatory intent as well as those with discriminatory effect. A computer-assisted machine learning classifier enabled us to identify more than 5,000 laws and legal provisions that regulated Chinese residents, directly or indirectly, during 1850–1920.[14]

This book starts with our new finding—the little-known fact that Chinese faced thousands of discriminatory local and state laws—but it does not end there. I propose a framework to comprehend these laws, and in doing so I offer a new legal history of Chinese in the American West.

Existing historical narratives do not recognize the extent of these laws and the racial structures they helped to erect. Efforts to fit these laws under the history of Chinese exclusion, for example, miss the mark. Most of these laws did not have exclusionary aims, nor did they have exclusionary effects. They cannot be understood as steps on the path to Chinese exclusion, because many came after the advent of federal immigration control.

Likewise, attempts to describe these laws as mere variations on Jim Crow are inadequate.[15] Anti-Blackness was then, and still is today, a fundamental structuring force in American society, but its logic alone cannot explain the Chinese experience. If these western racial laws were milder versions of southern anti-Black statutes, then why were so many of them applied only to the Chinese? (In the 1880s, for example, California lawmakers chose to integrate Black students and segregate Chinese students.) And if Chinese regulations derived from Jim Crow laws, then why do some of them predate anti-Black equivalents? (For example, the earliest known examples of racial zoning laws and racial restrictive covenants targeted the Chinese.)

Local anti-Chinese laws were entwined in the structures of Chinese exclusion and Jim Crow, but were not subsumed by them. Racial regulation of Chinese inhabitants was a phenomenon unto itself, a phenomenon in need of a history.[16]

Although formal law was only one aspect of the anti-Chinese racial regime, comprehending and categorizing racial laws is a good place to start. Anti-Chinese laws came in three general forms: *identity-based laws, behavior-based laws,* and *general-outcast laws.*

Identity-based laws targeted Chinese based on their racial identity or alien status. Due to racial bars on naturalization, Chinese migrants' racial and alien status were both permanent fixtures in the eyes of American law. Some identity-based laws explicitly targeted only "Chinamen," "Chinese," "Mongolians," "Orientals," "Chinese quarters," or "Chinatown." Some named the Chinese alongside other races, including "Negros," "Mulattos," "Indians," and "Kanakas" or "South Sea Islanders." Others were more circumspect and (potentially) broad, outlining the legal disadvantages of "aliens," "foreigners," persons "ineligible to citizenship," or persons who had not declared their intent to naturalize.[17] Even broader measures outlined the special privileges of US "citizens."

Behavior-based laws regulated labor and cultural practices strongly associated with the Chinese, including the use of opium, the game fan tan, the practice of hanging baskets over the shoulder using poles, the use of firecrackers on days other than July Fourth, and particular fishing, shrimping, and laundry techniques. These behavior-based laws used race-neutral language but landed on the Chinese with unique force. Sometimes this was lawmakers' intent; they chose to regulate the Chinese through indirect means. But other times the culprits were the police; they

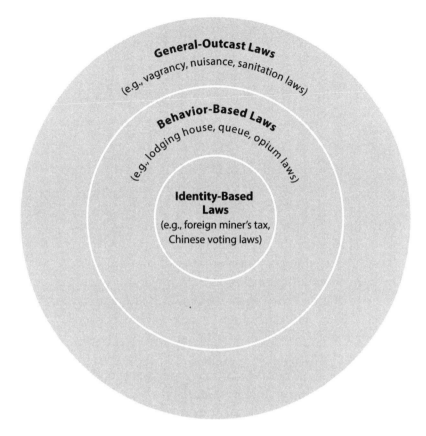

Anti-Chinese laws arranged by form. Chinese were regulated by thousands of discriminatory laws. This figure categorizes those laws by how they targeted the Chinese. Identity-based laws targeted Chinese based on their racial identity or alien status; behavior-based laws regulated labor and cultural practices strongly associated with the Chinese; and general-outcast laws regulated a broad group of "undesirables," of which the Chinese were a part. Chinese felt the cumulative effect of these laws. (See Appendix for additional racial laws.)

used their discretionary enforcement powers to transform racially neutral statutes into de facto anti-Chinese laws.

General-outcast laws regulated a broad group of "undesirables," of which the Chinese were a part. Arising from a long lineage of "poor laws," general-outcast laws regulated "nuisance," "lewdness," "prostitution," "gambling," "filth," "disease," "indecency," "disorder," and "vagrancy." General-outcast policies constitute approximately half of our sample. Previous historians have found these statutes to be a central element of Jim Crow despite their lack of explicit racial language.[18] In and beyond the West, lawmakers and police used these vague statutes to target racial outsiders, new immigrants, lower classes, migratory laborers, unmarried men, itinerants, sexual deviants, and strangers. Chinese migrants regularly fell within these categories and therefore felt the weight of these laws as well.

Racial laws can be categorized by their form—how they targeted the Chinese—but their form had limited relevance to daily life. Therefore, it is important to also understand them based on their impact—how they affected Chinese lives.[19] Together with social norms and racial violence, these laws defined rules for Chinese behavior, rules designed to ensure the impermanence and subordination of Chinese residents. These racial rules set the preconditions for Chinese life in the American West, underpinning a process that I call *conditional inclusion*.

The term "conditional inclusion" has previously been used to describe a twentieth-century phenomenon. In that context, conditional inclusion is what happened after Chinese exclusion ended. Scholars have argued that US policies—in domains as far-ranging as citizenship, immigration law, public education, real estate, and employment—shifted from logics of racial exclusion to policies of conditional inclusion. This scholarship maintains that, thanks to a newfound belief in racial liberalism, Chinese and other people of color were at least provisionally included in civil society by the late twentieth century. In its afterlife, racial exclusion became conditional inclusion.[20]

In contrast, I use "conditional inclusion" to describe an earlier time and I do so with a different purpose. My intent is to show how Chinese migrants were conditionally included in the United States as soon as they arrived in the 1850s, and continued to be included, conditionally, even during the period of federal exclusion laws.[21] Exclusion and inclusion coexisted, as federal systems of exclusion grew up alongside local systems of social control. American federalism allowed for, and at times encouraged, these seemingly contradictory projects, which operated at different scales.

When using the term "inclusion," I do not intend to suggest the Chinese were granted equality or belonging. Conditional inclusion simply meant that Chinese migrants were granted access to a highly stratified society in carefully controlled ways.[22] As local laws and legal customs proscribed many behaviors for the Chinese, they also quietly defined what was possible, detailing permissible occupations,

INTRODUCTION 11

neighborhoods, and even wives. If they followed the racial etiquette, Chinese could live in the American West, maybe even flourish. After all, western capitalists knew that some degree of inclusion would be necessary in order to profit from Chinese labor, and western lawmakers knew Chinese inclusion could generate tax revenue. Conditional inclusion was exploitative, even predatory.[23]

The terms of conditional inclusion, which governed all domains of Chinese life, can be understood as economic, political, cultural, and spatial in nature.

The terms of economic inclusion held that the Chinese would have unequal access to resources, including employment, property,

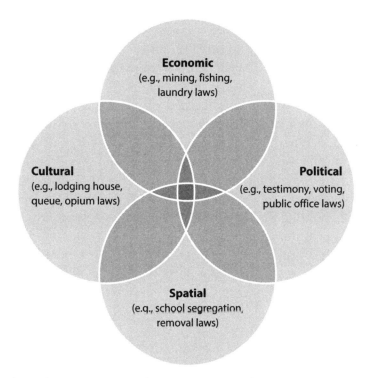

Anti-Chinese laws arranged by effect. Racial laws reinforced the racial etiquette of daily life by making explicit some of the prevailing rules for Chinese behavior. These racial norms—which I call the terms of conditional inclusion—regulated different domains of life: economic, cultural, political, and spatial. It is important to note that a single racial law could affect multiple domains of life. For example, school segregation laws directly affected the terms of spatial inclusion by separating Chinese from white students, but they also had profound implications for economic mobility, cultural maintenance, and political rights. (See Appendix for additional racial laws.)

and housing. Western states wished to limit Chinese earning power, but also to profit from it. Therefore, Chinese were allowed to work in the United States, but local laws and labor practices meant they could only work in certain sectors, at lower wages, with worse conditions, fewer prospects, and higher taxes. Generally, Chinese were allowed to own and rent property, especially within designated areas, but these rights were curtailed over time. In response to these constraints, Chinese workers and entrepreneurs turned inward to niche industries, ethnic businesses, and, at times, criminal activities.

The terms of political inclusion held that the Chinese would have unequal access to civic membership and governance. To deny the Chinese a direct role within American democracy, lawmakers barred their naturalization and their capacity to vote, hold public office, access public records, and serve on juries. Western states did what they could to silence the Chinese within the judicial system, which in turn limited their ability to challenge American governance. Nevertheless, Chinese migrants insisted on participating in American politics through petitions, negotiations, diplomacy, civil disobedience, and, at times, the ballot. They also went to court, despite racial restrictions on their testimony, and on occasion they prevailed.

The terms of cultural inclusion forced Chinese to endure debasement of their customs and endangerment of their lives. Under the banner of policing vice, lawmakers regulated Chinese leisure activities (including gambling, prostitution, opium, fireworks, and theaters), their living arrangements (in particular, single-sex boardinghouses and second wives), and burial practices (specifically, disinterment and repatriation of bones to China). These attempts to enforce American norms threatened Chinese social lives and put Chinese familial, cultural, and religious practices at risk. Chinese communities responded with flexibility and adaptation, finding creative ways to maintain cultural traditions, but they could not shield themselves entirely. Regulations not only criminalized Chinese ways of life but also endangered Chinese life itself. Some local officials tacitly endorsed racial violence of policemen, tax collectors, and vigilantes, and in doing so they threatened Chinese lives.

The terms of spatial inclusion held that the Chinese should be separated from white communities whenever possible. Although white and Chinese both inhabited the multiracial US West, the state and public worked to prevent incorporation of the Chinese into civil society. Residential segregation schemes explicitly drew the boundaries of Chinatowns, and in some areas segregated schools and public accommodations further confined Chinese residents. This racial segregation diminished Chinese access to healthy places to live and to education, and limited their upward socioeconomic mobility. Anti-miscegenation laws further worked to forestall social intimacy by distancing white women from Chinese men. But social distance could never be fully maintained. Proximity, familiarity, partnership, and cohabitation persisted despite these racial rules.

Enforced through law, custom, and violence, these terms of inclusion outlined how the Chinese were to behave. As white and Chinese people enacted and reenacted racial rules in daily life, those rules became an enduring part of the racial terrain. Like all codes of conduct, this racial etiquette changed based on one's class and circumstances, differed in rural and urban settings, and shifted over time.[24] Never did these terms of inclusion take on the uniformity of federal exclusion laws. Some protocols came in written form and others remained unspecified, and therefore Chinese migrants found it hard to understand the rules without testing them. But the consequences of even an unintentional violation could be harsh. When discovered, breaches could result in social ostracism, criminal accusations, or racial violence. As the racial rules became entrenched and punishments loomed large, overt enforcement became unnecessary. The Chinese learned to mind their racial manners and discipline themselves. At times the Chinese directly contested these racial rules, but more often they skirted, manipulated, or avoided them.

Having been granted only conditional inclusion, the Chinese fought for more. A few Chinese sought inclusion because they believed in racial equality and envisioned their future in America, but this was a rare and radical stance. Most Chinese migrants had more modest goals. They hoped to secure a foothold within America's racial regime, one that was above that of Black and Native people. They wished to lessen the conditional nature of their inclusion and to make the racial etiquette constraining their lives more permissive. They sought access to the privileges and rights that inclusion could provide, but few demanded full belonging. Most Chinese migrants in the nineteenth century understood their journey to America to be a temporary sojourn.[25] They came to work on behalf of their families back in China, and while they labored, they wanted dignity and security. They wanted protection from discrimination and violence, and some power over the course of their lives. They wanted to earn enough to go home and they wanted the opportunity to return to America one day. For those leading transpacific lives, inclusion was a means, not an end.

✷ ✷ ✷

Like all racial regimes, the one that governed the Chinese changed over time. While the conditional nature of Chinese inclusion remained constant, what that meant in practice shifted during the course of the nineteenth century. Change came from many directions: from across the Pacific, the Eastern Seaboard, the state capitol, the court's bench, and the streets. These forces pushed and pulled in different directions, but together they formed patterns and phases. This history can be understood in three periods: the emergence of an anti-Chinese regime (1850–1868); racial reconstruction and contestation (1868–1885); and racial retrenchment and Chinese exclusion (1885–1943).

Our story begins with the arrival of Chinese gold miners in California in the 1850s and the first attempts to regulate their earning power. In many ways, Chinese miners were no different from the prospectors from the eastern states, Europe, and South America who also poured into California in hope of striking it rich. But racial stereotypes set the Chinese apart and racial laws soon did as well. State and local governments began by enacting racialized taxes, criminalizing Chinese cultural practices, and banning the Chinese from participating in elections. During the emergence of the anti-Chinese regime, lawmakers blatantly targeted the Chinese based on their race, with little fear of judicial review. These identity-based laws helped to forge a wider racial etiquette that deeply constrained Chinese economic, cultural, political, and spatial behavior.

But then events of the 1860s tested this early anti-Chinese regime. Following a decades-long Black freedom struggle and a bloody Civil War, Americans sought to remake the nation without chattel slavery. In its efforts to rebuild the South and integrate formerly enslaved people into society, the federal government embarked on a project of reconstruction that would transform America and its legal landscape. Rejecting the tentative actions of the executive branch, Radical Republicans in Congress pushed forward constitutional amendments and civil rights laws to protect formerly enslaved people.[26] These events set in motion a postbellum restructuring of race in American law and society, which I refer to as "racial reconstruction."[27] Eventually the profound effects could be felt even on the Pacific Coast by the Chinese. Together, the Fourteenth Amendment (1868), the Burlingame Treaty with China (1868), and a series of civil rights laws pledged federal protection from state discrimination for all of America's inhabitants, including the Chinese.

At first this turn of events seemed to be a clear win for Chinese residents. Between 1868 and 1885, racial reconstruction challenged the anti-Chinese regime. Chinese litigants, with the help of their American lawyers, learned what rights they were due under the new Reconstruction Amendments. For them, equal protection became a newfound legal foothold from which to contest racial regulations. In court, Chinese litigants questioned the constitutionality of laws that curtailed their employment, cultural practices, and witness testimony. These legal challenges achieved remarkable success and, for a time, seemed to threaten the very existence of racial laws at the local and state level.

As racial reconstruction proceeded, however, Chinese losses began to pile up, as their vigorous battle against the racial laws inspired a devastating backlash. In their attempt to brace against Chinese litigation, American lawmakers began to construct a newly menacing racial regime. Policymakers found clever ways to bypass constitutional guarantees of equal protection and redouble their efforts to dictate the terms of Chinese inclusion.

At the local level, governments began enacting seemingly race-neutral ordinances designed to withstand Chinese legal challenges. Drawing on the "police powers" granted to them by the US Constitution, local and state governments passed behavior-based and general-outcast measures that ostensibly regulated health, safety, morality, and public order but in fact were applied to the Chinese with the utmost rigor. Local lawmakers also continued to target the Chinese based on alienage through carefully tailored identity-based laws. At the national level, Congress turned to immigration laws as a way to sidestep equal protection. First, the Page Act (1875) targeted "Oriental" women, and then the Chinese Restriction Act (1882) temporarily barred new Chinese laborers.

Emergence of Anti-Chinese Laws
1850-1868

Civil war
(1861-1865)

- Foreign miner's tax
  (CA, 1852)
- Chinese fishing law
  (OR, 1859)
- Anti-miscegenation law
  (NV, 1861)
- Chinese, Negro & Kanaka poll tax
  (OR, 1862)
- Chinese prostitution law
  (San Francisco, 1865)

Racial Reconstruction & Contestation
1868-1885

Fourteenth amendment &
Burlingame treaty
(1868)
Page act
(1875)
Chinese restriction act
(1882)

- Lodging house law
  (San Francisco, 1870)
- Chinese public employment law
  (OR, 1872)
- Laundry law
  (San Francisco, 1873)
- Opium den law
  (Sacramento, 1873)
- Ineligible aliens fishing law
  (CA, 1880)

Racial Retrenchment & Chinese Exclusion
1885-1943

Anti-Chinese expulsions
(1885-1886)
Chinese exclusion act
(1888)
Geary act
(1892)

- Alien land law
  (WT, 1886)
- Racial restrictive covenants
  (CA, 1886)
- Ineligible aliens public employment law
  (WY, 1889)
- Chinese removal law
  (San Francisco, 1890)
- Chinatown quarantine order
  (Honolulu, 1899)

Chinese exclusion repealer
(1943)

Racial reconstruction gave way to racial retrenchment in the mid-1880s. As a white counter-revolution swept the South and ushered in a new period of Jim Crow, white westerners also intensified their efforts to establish white supremacy. Amid cyclical national recessions and a growing white workforce, economic and racial anxieties reached new peaks. In 1885 and 1886, anti-Chinese racism erupted into an expulsion campaign that roiled the West, touching more than 168 communities, killing scores of Chinese migrants, and dislocating tens of thousands. In response, Congress first passed the Chinese Exclusion Act (1888), which unilaterally barred all Chinese laborers from entering the United States, and then the Geary Act (1892), which required that all Chinese aliens residing in the country register with the government. Constitutional guarantees of due process and equal protection, which had partially shielded the Chinese from local racial laws, could do little to restrain draconian federal immigration laws.

But it is important to recognize that even after the advent of Chinese exclusion, the Pacific states continued to grant conditional inclusion to Chinese residents. That is, western communities continued to use law, custom, and violence to incorporate the Chinese in limited ways. State and local governments deployed scattershot legal strategies to enforce the terms of inclusion. Some policies targeted the Chinese based on alienage rather than race, some continued to target race but deployed the legal doctrine of "separate but equal," and some relied on collaboration between public and private actors. When strategies worked, they quickly spread to other localities.

Conditional inclusion continued during the era of Chinese exclusion. In fact, the exclusion laws became yet another form of social control that constrained the lives of Chinese residents. As federal agents fought to close the gates on Chinese immigrants, they began in roundabout ways to police long-term residents as well. Federal immigration agents began to coordinate with local police, blurring

---

Left: Anti-Chinese laws arranged by first-known enactment. This timeline divides the history of anti-Chinese laws into three periods: the emergence of anti-Chinese laws (1850–1868); racial reconstruction and contestation (1868–1885); and racial retrenchment and Chinese exclusion (1885–1943). On the left are relevant national and regional events; on the right are examples of local and state anti-Chinese laws. Each law is listed by the place and date of the first-known instance, but all were subsequently copied elsewhere. (See Appendix for additional racial laws.)

the line between policing and border control. As the threat of deportation from the interior grew, Chinese residents had one more reason to adhere to racial rules.

Most of the events in this book took place in the Pacific West, specifically in California, Oregon, and Washington. Previous historians have shown that Chinese migration played an essential role in building these regions. Today we celebrate Chinese contributions to western development with tales of felling trees, blasting tunnels, and harvesting fruit. But with these triumphant stories of Chinese labor and ingenuity comes a truth worth mourning. Anti-Chinese laws also built the West. By denying the Chinese equal access to wages, advancement, and property, western racial laws and legal customs made possible a political economy based on the exploitation of Chinese labor. The anti-Chinese regime erected economic, legal, and cultural structures that were foundational to the American West.

When the United States claimed these western lands in 1848, the Native people who lived there numbered in the hundreds of thousands. Within a decade the Native population plummeted due to violence, dispossession, and disease. By the late 1860s, if not before, white settlers greatly outnumbered Native people on the West Coast, and the Chinese outnumbered all other people of color. Demographic

Table 1 Chinese population in California, Oregon, Washington, and United States, 1860–1920.

	1860	1870	1880	1890	1900	1910	1920
California	34,933	49,255	75,132	72,472	45,753	36,248	28,812
Oregon	425	3,330	9,510	9,540	10,397	7,363	3,090
Washington	1	234	3,186	3,260	3,629	2,709	2,363
Pacific West Total	35,359	52,819	87,828	85,272	59,779	46,320	34,265
National Total[1]	34,933[3]	63,199[4]	105,465	107,488	89,863	71,531	61,639
(percentage female)[2]	(5.1%)	(7.2%)	(4.5%)	(3.6%)	(5.0%)	(6.5%)	(12.6%)

Sources: Based on US Census Bureau, "Population of the United States in 1860, 1870, 1880, 1890, 1900, 1910, 1920," and US Census Bureau, "Chinese and Japanese in the United States," 1910.

1. National totals do not include the insular territories, including Hawaii and the Philippines.

2. Percentage female is based on US Census Bureau, "Population of the United States in 1920," table 36.

3. The 1860 national total excludes Oregon and Washington. It appears that Oregon and Washington Territory reported Chinese as part of the total white population. In 1860 the census designated only three possible racial categories (white, Black, and Mulatto), which led to inconsistencies. In California, census takers often wrote in "Mon[golian]."

4. Previous historians have sometimes included Japanese when reporting on Chinese in the 1870 census, but here totals do not include enumerated Japanese.

data from this period show that the Chinese population grew rapidly, the state of California was home to the most Chinese by far, and the vast majority of Chinese residents were men. Given these realities, it is not surprising that lawmakers in the Pacific West initially targeted Chinese men, that they developed a more extensive system to regulate Chinese than anywhere else in the nation, and that California pioneered many of these structures of social control.

In the nineteenth century, Black and Japanese populations were small compared to the Chinese population, but that had begun to change by 1900. At the turn of the century, there were 59,779 Chinese, 18,269 Japanese, and 14,664 Black people residing on the Pacific Coast.[28] Although my central concern is to map the parameters of the anti-Chinese regime, when this history intersects with the regulation of African Americans, Native Americans, or Japanese migrants I point toward these connections. It is beyond the scope of this book, however, to trace the distinct encounters of non-Chinese people with western racial laws.

Rather than attempt the impossible task of capturing this racial regime in its entirety, I have chosen to probe particular moments when Chinese residents encountered social control. I ask: What were the Chinese permitted to do in American society? To what extent were these racial rules determined by law and governance? How did Chinese residents endure, negotiate, and resist these rules?

To some extent these questions can be answered in the aggregate. In this introduction, I have categorized racial laws in terms of their form; I have grouped the constraints on Chinese lives into economic,

Table 2 Chinese, Black, Japanese, and white population in the Pacific West, 1860–1920.

	1860	1870	1880	1890	1900	1910	1920
Chinese	35,359	52,819	87,828	85,272	59,779	46,320	34,265
Black	4,421	4,648	6,830	14,110	14,664	29,195	47,790
Japanese	0	33	89	1,532	18,269	57,703	93,490
White	432,301	608,548	997,455	1,753,943	2,045,538	4,023,873	5,353,634

Sources: US Census Bureau, "Population of the United States in 1860, 1870, 1880, 1890, 1900, 1910, 1920," and US Census Bureau, "Chinese and Japanese in the United States," 1910. These figures are based on the US decennial federal censuses conducted in California, Oregon, and Washington. Native people have been omitted from this table, because the federal census did not reliably record their numbers. But in 1890, US census takers conducted an unusually comprehensive count of "Indians" (living within and outside white society) and reported 32,776 in the Pacific West.

political, cultural, and spatial terms; and I have sketched out three periods to describe how the regime changed over time. But in truth, this level of abstraction only gets us so far. Many of the answers to my questions can only be found in individual stories of everyday life: That time when a tax collector visited the Chinese barber and threatened to cut his queue. That time when Gan Que ran away, and then ran away again, and again, and again. That time when Ruby Tsang went to the theater and attempted to sit down. Then, as now, everyday life was made up of messy moments and chance encounters that defy simple categorization.

To uncover the heretofore obscure stories contained in this book, I journeyed to thirty-three archives in California, Oregon, and Washington in search of local legal records. I visited the urban centers of Seattle, Portland, Sacramento, Oakland, San Francisco, and Los Angeles; the California gold rush towns of Downieville, Sonora, Placerville, Auburn, and Nevada City; California's agricultural regions in Santa Clara, Ventura, and Colusa Counties; logging areas near Bellingham, Washington; and fishing hubs near Monterey, California. I found legal records in historical societies (often with the help of kind volunteers) and in operating courthouses (where clerks took a pause from the daily demands of court to locate dusty volumes). For counties where local records have been lost, I relied on the cases that made their way to the appellate courts and are now held by state or federal archives.

What I found in these archives was a remarkable and practically untapped collection of Chinese legal records, including criminal prosecutions, civil complaints, jail registers, prison records, and mugshots. Of particular note is the existence of Chinese legal testimony, some of which dates from the nineteenth century when such Chinese migrant "voices" are particularly rare. In the many periods and places where scholars have yet to find Chinese-language accounts, Chinese legal testimony offers an unparalleled view of daily life in the American West. This is especially the case for Chinese women and girls, who left behind virtually no written records.

The view offered by legal testimony, however, is still partially obscured. Most Chinese interactions with the law left no mark, and when they did, their impression was usually faint. Court transcripts that include detailed Chinese testimony are rare, in part because discriminatory testimony laws kept Chinese silent in most court proceedings for decades. And what Chinese testimony survives was mediated by outsiders, because the Chinese usually testified with the help of English-language translators and the legal guidance of their white attorneys. To make matters worse, the Chinese, like all witnesses, came to court to tell stories, not all of which were true.[29]

There is also the problem of Chinese names. Some legal records omit Chinese names entirely, but more often they include carelessly transliterated names. Admittedly, Chinese names were difficult for English-speaking officials. At the time there was no standard way to romanize Chinese characters, and differences of dialect led to wide variation in the pronunciation. For example, American officials recorded the surname 廖 in various ways, including "Leo," "Liao," "Liaw," "Liu," "Lu," "Luo," "Lau," "Law," and (in the case of my family) "Lew." To make matters worse, officials used the same romanization for multiple surnames. For example, "Lew" could refer to four possible surnames: 廖, 劉, 柳, or 呂. Moreover, many nineteenth-century American records of Chinese names do not include surnames at all; instead officials recorded only "Ah" (阿, a diminutive term that denotes familiarity) followed by the person's given name. For married Chinese women, officials frequently failed to record a given name; instead they recorded "Shi," "Shee," "Sea," "See," or "She" (氏, a term that means clan) followed by her maiden surname.[30] Whether due to confusion, disregard, or malice on the part of American officials, or obfuscation on the part of the Chinese, Chinese names were recorded haphazardly in US records. As a result, it is difficult to know more about the lives of Chinese plaintiffs, defendants, and witnesses beyond the few words they uttered in court.

Still, much can be learned from legal transcripts. Chinese migrants began going to court as soon as they arrived in the 1850s, negotiating the terms of their inclusion as complainants, plaintiffs, witnesses, and defendants. They carried with them knowledge of the Chinese legal system and soon adapted to the American system. Chinese resistance in the courts, and outside them, guaranteed that racial laws would not dictate reality. Scholars have shown that law and society are mutually constituted, that legal rights spill into social relations and flow from them.[31] The terms of conditional inclusion, then, were not simply determined by the rights due to the Chinese under the law; they were dependent on the rights the Chinese managed to exert in daily practice. This cut two ways. Sometimes the

Chinese managed to claim powers not granted to them by formal law, but at other times they were denied privileges they were guaranteed by formal law. Legal custom could be gentler than the law, or it could be harsher. Within the gaps between formal law and legal custom lie stories of both arbitrary state force and successful Chinese resistance.[32] More often than not, published court opinions and legal statutes smooth over this messy legal landscape, but trial transcripts can reveal more of the bumps and crevices.

I analyzed these transcripts in multiple ways. The existence of a court case reflects a belief that a rule has been violated and that its violation constitutes a private or public injury. Therefore, I use court cases to see the formal and informal rules of society, as well as the consequences of breaking them. Witness testimony also presents people's perspectives on events. When read carefully, I believe, testimony can expose what cultural assumptions historical actors held, what rights they claimed, and how they assigned meaning to their experiences. Finally, court opinions are decisions that carry consequences. But I also read them as value-laden narratives that granted recognition or refused it, all in the interest of instructing the population and the legal institution itself. I find that court transcripts, in all their complexity, can be best understood when situated in their local context and read alongside other historical sources.[33] Legal archives speak to the meaning of law, but so do other archives, if we are prepared to listen.

Many, many stories emerge from these sources. Some of these stories are myths, fearful tales about wily "Chinamen" and the threats they posed. These narratives provided powerful motivation and justification for racial policing, and I have chosen to organize my chapters around these stereotypes. There was the Chinese "coolie," who outcompeted white labor and sent his profits to China; the Chinese "criminal," who deceived his victims and the police; the Chinese "alien," who did not belong but demanded civil rights; the "Chinawoman," who represented the return of slavery; the Chinese "invader," who contaminated white neighborhoods; the Chinese "predator," who preyed on white girls; and the Chinese "immigrant," who threatened to overrun America. Across seven chapters I consider the regulations that emerged from these racial myths and helped to reinforce them.

Each chapter describes racial myths and regulations, but each chapter also includes the stories of real people: Chinese migrants who encountered, accommodated, and refused the preconditions for their inclusion. A few of these narratives may be familiar, because they resulted in landmark court cases. But most Chinese who went to court left little mark on American law, history, or memory. Instead, all that remains is a glimpse of their experiences.

As I sifted through extensive legal archives, I found that the volume of fragmentary stories tested my attention, my empathy, and my willingness to hold contradictions in my mind. You may be tested as well. I have tried to hear each voice above the din, but the cacophony can become overwhelming. I think that is okay. Even when distinct voices blur into noise, the sound can still move us.

Let us start with Pany Lowe. Perhaps we can see through his eyes. Lowe was not one of the "2700 boy babies of San Francisco Chinatown," but in many ways his experience resembled theirs. Born in Portland, Oregon, in 1873, Lowe journeyed to China for his education, and then returned to America, moving between major western cities, first San Francisco, then Denver, on to Portland and Seattle. By the time Lowe sat down with a researcher for an interview in 1924, he had acquired a lifetime of knowledge about the racial regime in the American West.[34]

He had learned, for example, that he could go to some restaurants and not others. *Once I go into restaurant, they refused to serve me. I no want to cause trouble so I just walk out. Whole lots of things like this happen but I forget. Now when I want to eat I go to chop house. No trouble th[ere].* He knew some restaurants did not want him, knew chop suey joints were safe, and made the choice to avoid possible humiliation.

He also learned he could go to some barbers and not others. *Lots of time people insult me. Once I remember I go barber shop. I sit one hour no ask me what I want. Pretty soon barber say what you want. I tell him I want hair cut, how much? He say $3.00. That make me mad but I make him cut my hair just the same. . . . I never go to white bastard again.* He knew that price gouging was a form of discrimination, but also that money could sometimes buy access.

Over time he learned that legal action could also open seemingly closed doors. *My second wife take my little girl born in this country to have her hair cut at Frederick & Nelson. They say they very sorry, no cut Chinese hair. Oh, my wife get mad. She go see my lawyer tell*

A Chinese family in Monterey, California (circa 1883). What did the American West look like in the eyes of these Chinese American children? (Chinese in California, FN-26239, California Historical Society)

him about it, Mr. Sullivan. He write letter to Frederick & Nelson. They write letter back and apologize. Lowe knew the pain of being refused service, he knew illegal discrimination when he saw it, but he also learned that avoidance was easier than confrontation. *All the time I tell my wife keep away from those swell places, only make trouble.* He knew how to mind racial rules and move on.

He learned he could live in some neighborhoods and not others. *When I in Portland I want to live in residential district but they make lots of trouble [if] you try to live outside China town.* He learned about the trouble from his friends. *One friend, he born in this country, he buy $6,000 house in rose city district. White people make hell lot trouble for him. They take it to court. He fight it. Just the same they kick him out. He can own house but no live here.*

Lowe knew the Chinese were supposed to be equally protected by American law. But he knew that, in practice, the law protected white neighborhoods from Chinese encroachment. *I think that very unjust. Those people very uncivilized, have no regard for humanity. So when my friend had so much trouble I decided to stay in China town. Nobody care there.* He knew some spaces were reserved for white people and chose not to test the line.

After the exclusion laws passed, Lowe also learned the consequences of border control. *My people be in this country long time. My grandfather come to this country. When I in China he tell me about work on railroad and work in laundry. Before when he go back they have the check system. Make Chinese carry paper tell who they are. Some inspector today make Chinaman show card. All same dog license. I say who the hell are you. He show me United States Secret man. I tell him I born in this country . . . He say all right, but he take some other men, lo[c]k them up for a day or two.* Lowe knew that exclusion made all Chinese residents vulnerable and a missing paper could mean deportation.

Finally, Lowe learned that American law held uncommon sway over his marriage prospects. He could marry some women and not others. *Not allowed marry white girl. Not enough American born Chinese to go around. China only place to get wife. Not allowed to bring them back. For Chinaman, very unjust. Not human. Very uncivilized.* He knew that anti-miscegenation and exclusion laws would forever mark his family. He knew that enduring such indignities was a condition of living in the American West.

Given all this, Pany Lowe knew that he would never belong. *When I was young fellow I felt that I American. I no Chinaman. Now I get more sense. I know I never be American, always Chinaman. I no care now anymore.* He lived at the margins of America society and didn't know if he should hope for more. *Very hard to tell whether people treat better now than before. Some time, I think so, some time I don't think so.* He did not know if there had been progress.

Still, he held out hope that white Americans could learn. *I hope this survey do lot of good for Chinese people. Make American people realize that Chinese people are humans . . .*

I think very few American people really know anything about Chinese.

{1}

The "COOLIE"

and the THREAT of CHINESE LABOR

IT TOOK LESS THAN a month on the job for Charles Egbert DeLong to have his first casualty. On Saturday, March 24, 1855, he penned in his diary: "shot a Chinaman."[1]

DeLong had come to California in 1850 at the age of seventeen in the company of his older brother, James. They had grown up on a farm in New York, but news of gold convinced them to make the six-month sea journey to California by way of Cape Horn. Landing in San Francisco, they headed inland to the hills surrounding Placerville. They acquired small claims in North San Juan along the Yuba River and farther north in Camptonville, but struggled to make a living on "the diggings" alone. James headed back to "the states" after a couple of years. Charles ("Charlie" to his brother) remained in Yuba County, trying his hand at storekeeping and other odd jobs.

In March 1855 he secured a job as a deputy sheriff, which seemed like a step up in the world even though he received no salary and had to pay out of pocket for his expenses. DeLong rented a horse (or, more often, a mule), paid for room and board on the road, and hired armed men to aid in his work. In return he received 15 percent of any money he collected, and his primary task was collecting fines and fees. The Foreign Miner's Act then in effect required that every person who was not a US citizen and had not declared their intent to become one must pay $4 monthly for a license to mine. In practice, this meant that every month DeLong would receive hundreds of blank foreign miner licenses and go in search of "Chinamen" to pay for them.

Together with his friend Frank, DeLong headed out for his first day of collecting on Thursday, March 15, 1855. Visiting the small mining encampments of Youngs Hill, Oak Valley, Woods Bridge, and Negro Slide, he was "met with ordinary success." Within two days of traversing the countryside, however, he was "worn down." It didn't help that during his day off on Saturday he "had a poor Ball and poorer accommodations," after which he declared he had "sworn off" dances. A Sunday spent at Oregon Bar, French Bar, Pittsburgh, and Missouri Bar was a "very hard days work." Monday at Sucker, Willow, Alabama, Mississippi, Wambos, and South Range ended with "no dinner."

Then his luck turned. On Tuesday he "collected all day" and reported that he had "done well." Upon returning home to Oregon Hill, he "met a drove" of Chinese whom he "searched and left." Thursday, he stopped "three Droves in town," but complained that "most all [were] broke." Friday was a bit more challenging. He went up the river to Bullards Bar, where he "had a time with the Chinese" and "stayed the night."

Then it was Saturday, March 24. DeLong recorded the barest outlines of the story in his diary:

> Went down to the little Yuba thence up
> shot a Chinaman
> had a hell of a time
> returned home by way of Fosters.[2]

DeLong did not record what happened to the "Chinaman." For him, the violence appears to be little more than a bad day at work.

One Chinese miner, later reflecting on his time in the California goldfields, remembered the violence of tax collectors differently. "Some poor [Chinese] men can not get any food," he recalled, "and when the collector comes they have no money to pay, and the collector search all over and knocks them down and whips them very badly, and in some instances, kill them."

The Chinese miner had a simple term for this practice: "This I call law robbing."³

※ ※ ※

Chinese labor in the American West generated significant profit, and many stood to benefit. Chinese migrants themselves, whether working the mines or employed in lumbering, agriculture, or manufacturing, could make more in a month in California than they would have made in a year back in Guangdong. Chinese elites, who were in the business of transporting, contracting, and provisioning Chinese laborers, earned appreciably more. Many American businessmen, industrialists, and developers also came to depend on the steady stream of Chinese laborers.⁴

Chinese labor also became a central source of state revenue. Over time, western municipalities, states, and territories enacted special taxes and fees targeting Chinese businessmen, laundrymen, fishermen, peddlers, and miners. In California the most lucrative of these taxes was the foreign miner's tax. Between 1854 and 1870, California collected nearly $5 million in foreign miner licenses; Chinese paid 99 percent of these fees. In most years the foreign miner's tax supplied at least 10 percent of total state revenue. During DeLong's short tenure as deputy collector, these license fees made up more than 25 percent. Half of this revenue stream went directly to the mining counties.⁵

Not everyone felt they benefited from Chinese labor, however. White miners and workingmen maintained, inaccurately, that Chinese migrants came as "coolies"—that is, that they were unfree, indentured laborers—and their presence would be ruinous to free white labor in the American West. They argued that the Chinese were racially predisposed to be servile and slavish, making them pliant tools for the greedy monopolists who sought to undercut white workingmen. The only solution, many white workingmen believed, was expulsion of the Chinese from mining regions and then from the West Coast entirely.⁶

While white miners and workers called for expulsion and exclusion, local governments more often turned to regulation and exploitation. Regulation, lawmakers hoped, could answer capitalists' desire for cheap labor while pacifying white workers' fears of competition. Lawmakers used identity-based tax and licensure laws to restrain Chinese earning power, reduce Chinese ability to compete with white workers, and steer the Chinese away from lucrative trades. Through taxes and fees, lawmakers helped make the Chinese into a pliant, cheap, and temporary workforce that could fuel western development. In other words, they helped to make the Chinese into the "coolies" they were imagined to be.

The government violently enforced the conditions of this economic inclusion. Taxes were what sent Deputy DeLong out for his fateful meeting in March 1855 with an unfortunate, unnamed "Chinaman." Taxation provided the pretext for violent policing of the Chinese in the goldfields of California, and soon thereafter in Oregon and Washington. Although lawmakers viewed the web of taxes, fees, and regulations that arose in the 1850s as a moderate approach, collectively these measures made the Chinese uniquely vulnerable to police violence while denying them equal access to economic resources in the Pacific West.[7]

Chinese migrants recognized both the benefits and the pitfalls of these laws. On the one hand, license laws clarified that the Chinese had the right to work, as other men did. The Chinese might be subject to special regulations and disabling fees, but their right to work remained. And they found that paying taxes gave them a certain degree of power. Most could not speak out as citizens or voters, but they could make demands as taxpayers who funded local and state governments.

But if taxes got too high, they would become an indirect means of exclusion and expulsion, so the Chinese community worked to restrain the government's ability to tax them. Chinese workers and their employers launched repeated legal challenges, establishing over time that the Chinese miner had a right to work his claim, the Chinese industrial worker had a right to collect his wage, and the Chinese entrepreneur had the right to open a laundry. Outside the courts, Chinese migrants also sought to restrain taxation through petitioning, lobbying, negotiation, and civil disobedience.

Some historians have assumed that racialized tax laws were simply Chinese exclusion measures in disguise.[8] But in fact these laws represent highly contested attempts to set the preconditions for Chinese inclusion, conditions that would ensure a racially stratified labor force. The regulation of Chinese miners in California was an early example of this effort, one that would set legal precedents and touch many lives.

ECONOMIC INCLUSION THROUGH TAXATION

Within a year of the discovery of gold at Sutter's Mill in California, more than 80,000 hopeful prospectors descended on the newly acquired American territory. Among the tens of thousands who arrived in 1849, a mere 325 men were from China. Another 450 Chinese followed in 1850, then 2,176 in 1851. In the early years of the California gold rush, the Chinese miner was regarded by most white settlers as a rare curiosity and an occasional annoyance. The Chinese community was overwhelmingly male, but at the time other communities were as well. It was not until their arrivals increased tenfold in 1852—to 20,026 migrants, or 20 percent of all new arrivals—that Chinese migration captured the attention of state officials.[9]

Upon assuming the governorship of California in 1852, John Bigler declared Chinese "coolies" to be an existential threat to the state and urged the legislature to take swift action. "I am deeply impressed with the conviction that, in order to enhance the prosperity and to preserve the tranquility of the State," he declared, "measures must be adopted to check this tide of Asiatic immigration, and prevent the exportation by them of the precious metals which they dig up from our soil without charge, and without assuming any of the obligations imposed upon citizens."[10] Chinese miners, in Governor Bigler's assessment, posed a multipronged economic threat to American workingmen: they competed with white American miners in the rush for gold and did so with an unfair advantage. While Bigler believed that all white miners were independent prospectors, he accused Chinese miners of being "coolies," working under term contracts that kept them temporarily enslaved. Formally barred from naturalization, and according to Bigler racially incapable of assimilation, the Chinese "coolie" would not become a productive part of American society. What gold Chinese miners managed to acquire, Bigler complained, they sent directly home to China. They did not bring their women. They did not form families.

THE "COOLIE" AND THE THREAT OF CHINESE LABOR 31

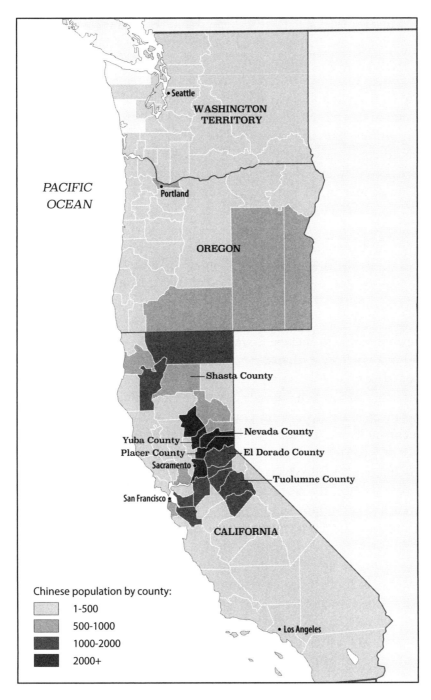

Chinese population by county in 1870. The map also highlights cities and counties that are critical to this history. (Data sources: U.S. Census Bureau, "Population of the United States in 1870"; Social Explorer)

Most California legislators agreed that the Chinese worker posed a problem, but they disagreed on the remedy. As they watched the steep increase in Chinese arrivals in 1852, policymakers considered four possible solutions. The distance between these solutions reveals the warring impulses to exclude or include. Would it be best to keep Chinese miners out altogether? Or should California include them in carefully prescribed ways? The answers to these questions had broad consequences. By 1860, 99 percent of Chinese in the United States resided in California, and approximately 70 percent of adult Chinese men in the state engaged in mining.[11]

First, lawmakers discussed the most radical response: barring all Chinese migrants from entering California. In the California Assembly, the Committee on Federal Relations discussed a proposal to "exclude all foreigners, except those of European nations or of European descent, from the state." They noted that such a plan would fulfill their primary objective—to protect the American miner in his rights, immunities, and interests—but the idea presented insurmountable problems. It was generally understood, the Committee acknowledged, that a racial bar at the state level would be unconstitutional. The committee remained "doubtful whether the State of California has power to prevent the immigration of aliens," believing instead that the power resided with the federal government under the commerce clause.[12] Moreover, Chinese exclusion would threaten California's economic future, which many believed lay in commercial expansion in the Pacific World.[13]

On its face, the second option the California legislature considered had the opposite intent. An "Act to Enforce Contracts and Obligations to Perform Work and Labor or Contracts for Foreign Laborers" (1852), known as the "Coolie Bill," proposed to import Chinese indentured workers in large numbers under five-year contracts. If the Chinese refused to work under these terms, they would be turned over to the jails and paroled as convict labor to toil on public works. The proposed bill may have been inspired by an already existing racial law, an "Act for the Government and Protection of Indians" (1850). Under the guise of "apprenticeship," this law authorized white men to lease Indian convicts and obtain custody of Indian children until they reached the age of fifteen (for girls) or eighteen (for boys). It had, in short, codified a system of unfree labor for Native children in California.[14]

The author of the "Coolie Bill," Senator George Tingley, wished to do the same for the Chinese. Tingley shared Governor Bigler's fears that most Chinese workers were already unfree laborers who sent their earnings out of the country. Rather than trying to bar the immigration of Chinese indentured labor, however, Tingley wished to legalize and promote the practice for the benefit of white men.[15] Detractors alleged that the Coolie Bill represented a new system of bondage, and like the existing slave system, would inevitably degrade the place of white labor. California was nominally a free state—despite the forced indenture of Native children—and many hoped to keep it that way.

Third, the California Senate considered a series of bills that sought to bar the Chinese from mining specifically. The Federal Relations Committee of the Assembly, for example, considered a bill that would have allowed only "Europeans and those of European descent" to work in the mines. In the Senate, a special committee formed to investigate Asiatic immigration also recommended a racial bar on Chinese miners. According to the committee, the Chinese "cannot become citizens. They cannot be slaves in the States, under the Constitution. We want no subordinate grades in a *free* State, where all men should be freemen." The solution was to "at once exclude all Chinamen from the mines, working on their own account, or for others."[16]

It was the fourth proposal, "An Act to Provide for the Protection of Foreigners and to Define Their Liabilities and Privileges," that made its way into law.[17] It was based on the first foreign miner's tax, of 1850, which had been repealed. In its first life, the foreign miner's tax was levied against foreigners generally. All miners who were not US citizens, Native California Indians, or former Mexican citizens had to pay $20 a month to be granted a license permitting them to mine in the State of California. Violations of the law, a misdemeanor, were punishable by arrest, three-month imprisonment, and a fine of up to $1,000. Although billed as a tax, the exorbitant fee of $240 a year amounted to an all-out ban on foreign miners, most of whom in 1850 where white and qualified for naturalization under US law. Resistance began almost immediately. An estimated 3,000 to 5,000 French, Chilean, and Mexican miners poured into the gold rush town of Sonora on May 19, 1850, to protest the ruinous effect of the new law. The opposition proved too much for state lawmakers. First the state legislature lowered the tax rate to $80 a year and then repealed it altogether.[18]

When the Senate considered bringing back the foreign miner's tax in 1852 to regulate the Chinese, it was at a much lower rate: $4 a month.[19] Like the first Foreign Miner's law, the second was race-neutral, targeting all foreigners alike; but unlike its predecessor, it was expressly touted as a solution to Chinese labor. An Assembly committee promised it would protect against Chinese competition and noted that the licensing fee had the potential to "raise an immense revenue for the State," because "a larger income will be derived from a moderate tax, which will be willingly paid, than will be yielded from exorbitant rates, which will in every possible manner be avoided."[20] The first foreign miner's tax presented an impossible hurdle to foreign mining. What the second foreign miner's tax would mean, at $48 a year, was not immediately clear.

Some policymakers suggested that the new tax would drive out Chinese miners and provide a roundabout means of expulsion, but many white miners feared it would do no such thing.[21] In comparison to other proposals—to exclude the Chinese, indenture them, or bar them from the mines—the tax appeared to be moderately inclusive. The legislature hoped this political compromise would satisfy multiple constituencies.

Chinese miners with above-average luck could pay the moderate tax and still have enough to subsist and send money back to their families. For a below-average earner, however, the tax could mean the difference between breaking even and struggling to survive.[22] But if Chinese miners could pay their monthly tax, the law promised to protect their access to the mines. Answering complaints that the Chinese would outcompete white miners and send their riches out of the country, policymakers had devised a way to reduce Chinese earning power and ensure California a share in their profit.

This strategy of social control was not entirely new. During the antebellum period, southern states implemented race-based poll taxes to discourage the presence of free Black people and reinforce a slave-based economy. Alabama, for example, implemented a yearly head tax in 1852, which demanded fifty cents from every white male and $2 from every "free negro" male. Southern cities implemented occupational taxes, requiring tradespeople to be licensed. Although these laws were race-neutral, enforcement practices revealed their discriminatory intent. Free Black people often had to wear badges as evidence that they had paid their fee, and no such standard existed for white tradespeople. Even where licensure laws did not distinguish by race, they had a disproportionate effect on the free Black community because of its relative poverty. California legislators, especially those from the southern states, knew that taxes could do more than raise revenue. They could also serve as means for indirect social control.[23]

Not everyone was satisfied with moderation, however. White miners in California recognized the Foreign Miner's Act as a form of economic inclusion, rather than the outright exclusion many had demanded. Angered, they showed their displeasure by attempting to expel the Chinese using other means. Days after the adoption of the foreign miner's tax on May 4, 1852, mass rallies against the Chinese spread from town to town. The *Sacramento Daily Union* reported "daily expulsions" along the North Fork of the American River.[24] In Centerville, El Dorado County, miners met and drew up resolutions "to prevent any more [Chinese] coming in our diggings, and likewise to expel those now among us."[25] Later in the summer, the *San Joaquin Republican* reported successful expulsions of the Chinese in "Oregon Bar, El Dorado Slide, and several places on the Middle Fork of the American River."[26]

Expulsion efforts in Columbia, Tuolumne County, were particularly effective. Following the passage of the tax, miners pledged to form a "Vigilance Committee" to "exclude all Chinse laborers from the district."[27] They continued their campaign to drive out the Chinese through the year,[28] and then formalized their bar on Chinese labor in the "Columbia Mining Laws" of 1853. These communal laws sought to formalize the exclusion of Chinese from the region: Article 10 declared that "none but Americans and Europeans who have or shall declare their intentions of becoming citizens shall hold claims in this district"; and Article 11 barred "Asiatics" and "South Sea Islanders" from mining in the district "for themselves or for others."[29] The mining committee in Columbia, however, was unusually organized, effective, and long-lasting. Elsewhere, extralegal attempts at expulsion diminished in a matter of months.

In the long run, the foreign miner's tax attracted the most ire from European immigrants, who complained that they should be exempt. The California legislature responded in 1854 by rewriting the law so it would only affect foreigners ineligible for citizenship. The rewrite targeted the Chinese, because lawmakers believed the Chinese to be racially barred from naturalization.[30] This solution did not stick for long, however. In April 1855, a few months into DeLong's job as tax collector, the legislature readjusted the law by introducing two separate rates. All aliens would be subject to a fee of $4 a month, but for aliens who were ineligible for citizenship (that is, Chinese miners), the licensure fee would increase each year. A Chinese miner who paid $4 a month in 1855 would have to pay $6 a month in 1856 and, in theory, $8 a month in 1857. The spiraling tax would become prohibitive for Chinese miners over time. What was currently a policy of social control would eventually transform into a de facto policy of exclusion.

While Californian lawmakers carefully chose race-neutral language, Oregon legislators did not attempt to hide the racially discriminatory purpose of their mining laws. The Oregon Constitution declared, "No chinaman, not a resident of the state at the adoption of this constitution, shall hold any real-estate or mining claim, or work any mining claim therein." However, the Oregon legislature did not enact laws to enforce this bar; instead it passed a Chinese mining tax. In addition, Oregon passed "An Act to Tax and Protect Chinamen Mining in Oregon" (1857), which required that able-bodied Chinese living in mining districts (who were not otherwise employed) pay $24 annually to gain "the right to their mining claim" and "the privileges that protect and govern American citizens." The total annual fee climbed to $48 in 1858.[31]

By the end of the 1850s, both California and Oregon had settled on a policy of identity-based regulation and taxation. As long as these taxes remained moderate, they functioned as forms of conditional inclusion. But the spiraling tax in California meant exclusion still stood on the horizon.

CHARLES DELONG AND THE VIOLENCE OF ECONOMIC INCLUSION

Charles DeLong began a letter to his brother with an apology: "I have been so confounded busy," he wrote on August 21, 1855, "that I have not written." The trouble was his new job. "I am on foot all

THE "COOLIE" AND THE THREAT OF CHINESE LABOR   37

the time travvelling [sic] from one end of the County to another collecting Taxes on Foreigners," he explained; "anyone that thinks it is fun will alter their minds after trying it once."³²

On paper, the foreign miner's tax mandated an orderly procedure. In 1855 it required every foreign miner in Yuba County to pay Deputy DeLong $4 once a month. Upon payment, DeLong was supposed to issue a receipt in the form of a license to mine, which designated the name of the payee and the date. But this is not how DeLong operated. Instead, every few weeks he would receive a bundle of blank licenses, about 400 at a time, and then spend an evening filling each one out to payee "Chinaman." The next day he would head out in search of men to pay for the receipts. He cared greatly about "selling" every receipt in his possession but had little concern for who was made to pay. Although the tax was written as a license fee, the law functioned as a bounty in the mining counties. For every Chinese miner DeLong located in a month, he could expect a reward.³³

At times his methods were careful and calculated. He learned, for example, the advantages of collecting in the dark. "Hunted Chinamen in the night," he noted in his diary on July 30, 1855. "Done very well collected about 80 Licenses."³⁴ DeLong dedicated only these one dozen words to describe what must have been hours of dark work. The details remain unspoken, but we can imagine the scene.

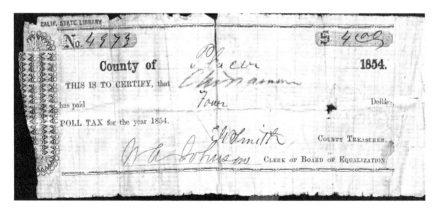

Receipt for payment of the foreign miner's tax (1854). Like Deputy Charles DeLong, this Placer County tax collector has made out the generic receipt to "Chinaman." (Reproduction courtesy of the California History Room, California State Library, Sacramento, California)

In the heart of summer, the hills around the Yuba River are dry, the oak trees crisp, the grass brown, the roads dusty. DeLong only had moonlight and his memory to guide him as he headed out from Fosters Bar, a town of 300 inhabitants, to the scattered mining encampments that rarely held more than a few dozen men.[35] He did not go alone; he never did. He brought a hired man with him because he needed to know that he would be in control. When DeLong suddenly emerged from the darkness of the woods into the light of a campfire, and when the Chinese stumbled awake and spotted his pistol, he needed to know they would obey. DeLong regularly described this work as "hunting," and the word seems apt. During these raids, he was a hunter in the dark, seeking, pursuing, and capturing his prey.

DeLong and his party did not always leave once he extracted payment. If he was too tired, hungry, or far from home, he would also demand that the Chinese camps feed and host him. On Thursday, August 16, 1855, he "had a China fight[,] knocked down some and drawed our tools on the rest and they put out." This violent confrontation ended with DeLong staying overnight at the Chinese camp and paying them for meals. The next day ended the same way. Arriving at Alabama Bar after dark, he "had another bit of a muss" with the Chinese, but then "made them keep us over night and in the morning paid them $6.00." Chinese miners could earn back a bit of their license fees by playing host to DeLong, but they had no choice in the matter.

Between his multi-night "hunting" trips, DeLong relied on chance to sell licenses. He spent Sunday, October 21, for example, "loafing around doing nothing." Even so, he managed to "pick up a few Chinamen whom their bad luck and my good threw in my way." When relying on chance alone, DeLong was more likely to demand payment from a wider cast of characters. "I collected around home off of Frenchmen, Niggers, Chinamen &c.," he noted.[36] Using derogatory language for Black people and subjecting them to a tax designed for "foreigners" reveals the racial assumptions that lay beneath DeLong's actions. The small number of Black miners in California were both free and born on American soil, but DeLong still considered them to be outsiders. The "Frenchmen" could escape the tax by declaring their intent to become US citizens, but in DeLong's

"The Heathen Chinee Prospecting" (1852). Chinese miners hoped to strike it rich just like other prospectors, but they faced racialized fears and identity-based taxes. (Chinese in California, FN-04470, California Historical Society)

view, both Chinese and Black miners were fair game because their race made them perpetual "foreigners."

If chance threw Black miners or newly arrived immigrants in his way, DeLong was happy to take their money, but he made it clear that the Chinese were his primary target. He was not the only one to see "foreign miner" as a pseudonym for "Chinaman." Local newspapers regularly referred to the law as the "Chinese tax," and to the deputy sheriff as the "Chinese tax" collector.[37] "The tax upon foreign miners," the *Nevada Journal* explained, "means simply Chinese miners, for the collectors, it is said, do not attempt to inflict it upon any other people."[38]

The job was lucrative. DeLong did not include a running total in his diary, but in a letter to his brother he noted, "I am doing very well." He offered to lend his brother money, if he should need it, and expressed his hope that the Democratic ticket would win the election so that he could keep the job for another two years. "If I get beat, thanks to my office I have got acquainted with almost everyone in the County," he assured his brother. "I will have no trouble in getting into something that will pay me." To further convince his brother of his newfound wealth, Charles tucked some gold into the letter with a brief note: "I send you some Goodyear Bar gold taken by me from a Chinaman for Tax, keep it for old acquaintance."[39]

It is possible that DeLong sometimes collected more than he was due. Although in his diary he never admitted to pocketing money, his vague accounting does not always add up. After four particularly lucrative days of collecting, for example, DeLong proudly declared that he had acquired a total of $1,800. The problem is that he only had 300 receipts when he began his "cruise collecting" and therefore should only have been able to collect $1,200. Where did the additional $600 come from? And did it end up in his pocket or the state's? The *Nevada Journal,* reporting in 1855, noted that the foreign miner's tax had made possible "a species of semilegalized robbery perpetrated" upon the Chinese. "Many of the collectors are gentlemen in every sense of the word," the editor assured readers, "but there are others who take advantage of their position to extort the last dollar from the poverty stricken Chinese. They date licenses back, exact pay in some instances for extra trouble in hunting up the terrified and fleeing Chinamen, and by various devices, fatten themselves upon the spoils thus obtained."[40]

Rampant corruption did not go unnoticed. In Tuolumne County, the grand jury repeatedly complained that their sheriff and his deputy were taking more than their fair share of the foreign miner's tax. The law stated that the sheriff was entitled to no more than 3 percent of funds collected, and his deputy collector could retain no more than 15 percent. In June 1858 the grand jury determined that the county had brought in $35,464 the previous year, but together the sheriff and deputy collector had pocketed 25 percent of the collections. When the grand jury convened again in February 1859, they

THE "COOLIE" AND THE THREAT OF CHINESE LABOR   41

found that this corruption continued and further complained about the sheriff's records. Since the collectors failed to register the names of those who paid, there was no way to keep track of delinquent taxpayers or fraudulent licenses. The jury observed that due to the "unchecked manner of issue," "spurious licenses may have been flooded upon this and other counties," and created a "great deficit from this service of revenue." In fact, the system offered "every inducement and facility to fraud."[41]

Although tax collectors pocketed a good share, they were not the primary beneficiaries of the tax. After DeLong and the local sheriff received their cut, California and the county divided the remainder in half. Between 1854 and 1870, California collected $1,967,814.70, the counties retained an additional $1,967,814.70, and collectors made $983,907.00. Chinese miners paid 99 percent of these fees, $4,908,416.29 in total.[42] Both the state government and the mining counties depended on the foreign miner's tax and therefore had a vested interest in the work of both Chinese miners and tax collectors.

The scale of funds involved gave tax collectors incentives to extract money from Chinese by any means necessary. If a Chinese miner did not have $4, the law gave DeLong the right to immediately seize and sell the miner's goods. His diary tells us that he did just that on Saturday, September 22, 1855. That morning he headed "down the River at Sunrise" to collect at Cherokee Bar. When he got there, he "had a Stand off with a John [Chinaman]." It appears the conflict was sparked by the man's inability to pay, because shortly after, DeLong "took breakfast at a Chilie Camp" and "had an Auction." In other words, he offered to sell the man's goods to the highest bidder. Seizing and auctioning goods was onerous work, so DeLong was pleased to report that he had better fortune after dinner. He "found a hell's grist of them at the lower end of the Bar."[43]

DeLong seemed to become more than accustomed to the violence of tax collecting. As summer turned to fall, his diary entries shift from descriptions of casual cruelty to open sadism. On October 23, after eight months on the job, DeLong ate supper at Hesse's Crossing and then "headed down the river in the night" collecting "all of the way." Then he scribbled two chilling incomplete sentences: "had a great time, Chinamen tails cut off." Whether or not he understood it, by cutting the men's hair DeLong not only inflicted bodily harm but also severed the men's ties to China. Chinese men wore their hair in a long braid as an act of deference to the Qing Court; without their queue, they would be outcasts in their native land.[44]

According to the *Sacramento Daily Union*, DeLong was not alone in using Chinese men's braids as the basis of racial violence. The proprietor of a sawmill, Captain Hall, wrote to the paper to complain that he had witnessed the Glen County Collector "seize one of these Chinese by the hair, holding at the same time a revolver in his hand, while another person searched his pockets." With this method, the collector searched ten or twelve men, but was only able to locate $2 in total. Horrified by this tactic, the captain inquired further about the collector's practices. A gentleman "informed him that he had seen the same Collector catch a lot of these Chinamen and tie them together by the hair, and then torture them by driving them like mules; and this punishment inflicted because these poor creatures refused to do what it was not in their power to do, viz: pay the tax." When threats did not produce the fee, some collectors turned to humiliation.[45]

Such creative tortures were not necessary to terrify the Chinese. DeLong could strike terror into the hearts of the Chinese by simply prolonging his encounter with them. When he found two "Johns" on November 15, he declined to collect their taxes on the spot. Instead he captured them and "made them come down the hill with me." "Like to have scared them out of their sense," he bragged in his diary.[46] In truth, it was a simple thing to terrorize Chinese miners, because they knew that tax collection could be deadly. DeLong may not have bothered to record what happened to the "Chinaman" he shot in his first month on the job, but even the California legislature admitted that taxation could be lethal for the Chinese. When California launched a special committee to study the Chinese in 1862, they reviewed a list of "eighty-eight Chinamen who are known to have been murdered by white people, eleven of which number are known to have been murdered by Collectors of Foreign Miner's License Tax—sworn officers of the law." "Generally," the report acknowledged, these murderers "have been allowed to escape without the slightest punishment."[47] Tax collectors appeared to act with impunity.

For a time it seemed that Deputy Collector Fountain Williams might be an exception to this rule. In Georgetown, El Dorado

County, Deputy Williams was implicated in the death of "one John Doe (alias) a Chinaman," and the resulting court case provides a view into both tax collector violence and impunity. On March 25, 1861, Deputy Williams and his partner, O. H. Hickok, entered the shop of a Chinese barber and demanded a tax payment. The barber, all witnesses agreed, refused to pay, claiming he "was barber & ought to be exempt." Williams claimed he was collecting road tax, rather than the usual miner's tax, and therefore "his being Barber would not let him off."[48]

What happened next was contested at trial in *People v. Williams* (1860). The primary witness for the state was an eleven-year-old boy, Shannon L. Knox, who described a harrowing scene. There were two Chinese men in the shop at the time: the unnamed barber and the man receiving a shave, "John Doe Chinaman." "It was the barber he wanted to pay his taxes," Knox testified. "When [the defendant] asked him to pay his taxes [the barber] said, No Sir. Def[endant] then said he wanted him to pay his taxes. Chinaman laughed." The barber's next response "was in China" and Knox could not understand the foreign language. Williams "went out & got whipstalk" and asked the child to "go out & get a club." Knox hurriedly complied. Now armed with a large board and whip, Deputy Williams again demanded payment.

According to Knox, the barber calmly finished shaving his client and set the razor down. That's when Williams struck the barber with the board, took out his pocketknife, and "told him if he did not pay the tax he'd cut off his cue." "John Doe Chinaman," who had been watching the scene from the barber's chair, caught hold of Williams arm to prevent the severing of the queue. Williams took out his pistol in response.

The child only witnessed the first shot, which hit the floor. By the time the second shot rang out—the one that would prove lethal for John Doe—Knox had already run away. He was still close enough, however, to hear the threat Williams made on his way out of the barber shop. "I heard him say he would shoot half a dozen more if they did not pay."[49]

Williams's partner, Hickok, was the primary witness for the defense. He agreed that Williams had shot "the Chinaman," but alleged it was an act of self-defense. According to Hickok, the John Doe had thrown "a tin Tea-Pot" and an "earthen bowl," or maybe two. Only because he feared for his own life did Williams wield his revolver. The defense also attempted to enter testimony from another El Dorado County tax collector who was not at the scene. Serving as an expert witness, the tax collector explained, "That it is a notorious fact that Chinese are in the habit of resisting forcibly the collection of taxes and that all collectors feel compelled to go armed for the purpose of resisting the assaults of the Chinese, and that it is a common practice for the Chinese to assault collectors without provocation." The judge, however, ruled this testimony to be irrelevant. And the Knox boy was returned to the stand to testify that he saw no brawl before he ran, and no "broken crackery [sic]" after he returned.

The judge's instructions to the jury were unequivocal: "The fact that the de[ceased] was a Chinaman gave [Williams] no more right to take his life than if he had been a white person." He continued, "Nor did the fact, if you so find, that the [defendant] was seeking to enforce the collection of taxes against another Chinaman," the judge continued, "give [Williams] any right to take his life. Our laws do not sanction the sacrifice of human life in order to encourage the collection of taxes or licenses." With these instructions in hand, the jury declined to convict Williams of murder, but found him guilty on the lesser charge of manslaughter. The judge sentenced him to five years in prison.

But Williams appealed and the California Supreme Court swiftly threw out the conviction. The judges cited multiple grounds: the lower court judge had erroneously dismissed a juror, excluded testimony on the violent proclivities of the Chinese race, and prejudiced the jury when he reminded them that collection of taxes should not entail loss of life. Furthermore, the California Supreme Court found the verdict to be "contrary to the evidence."[50]

Deputy Williams, in the end, would be just one more tax collector who shot a Chinese migrant "without the slightest punishment."

CHINESE CONTESTATION OF ECONOMIC INCLUSION

It is rare to find Chinese accounts of tax collection. The Chinese barber in *People v. Williams* (1860) not only lacked a name at trial, but also lacked a voice. An 1854 California Supreme Court ruling (followed by a criminal statute in 1863) barred Chinese from testifying against white people at trial in California (as will be discussed in Chapter 3). Therefore, Chinese testimony about tax collection only entered the historical record in circuitous ways, as in, for example, *People v. Ah Fa & Sing Chow* (1858). As defendants, Ah Fa and Sing Chow were allowed to testify in their own defense. Their testimony provides an account of what could happen when Chinese miners physically resisted tax collection.

That trial resulted from a confrontation on June 11, 1858, when Tuolumne County deputy collector David Hayes called on Ah Fa and Sing Chow at their home to demand money for a road tax. As Chinese men in a mining district, no doubt this was not their first encounter with an American tax collector. And yet they may or may not have understood what this particular tax entailed. "I did not understand much," testified Sing Chow at trial. "I told Mr. Hayes to come up in town to Wing Wo's Store and he would pay him." (It does seem likely that Wing Wo would have paid the tax had Hayes followed this suggestion, given that Wing Wo later offered a $500 security bond on Sing Chow's behalf.) Hayes, however, refused to wait for his payment and instead attempted to immediately confiscate Sing Chow's property, a pile of blankets. Forcible seizure of property in lieu of payment was permissible by law, as was sale of that property within the hour.

But Sing Chow and Ah Fa would not allow Hayes to take their blankets. At trial, all of the men involved agreed on the broad strokes of what occurred next but disagreed on the particulars. According to the collector, the Chinese men threatened him with a large butcher knife, grabbed him "by his private parts," and disarmed him. But according to Sing Chow, "Ah Fa caught hold of Mr. Hayes to stop him from taking the blankets. Mr. Hayes then drew his pistol on Ah Fa and seemed to be mad. I then took the pistol away from Hayes. After I had taken the pistol from Mr. Hayes, he (Hayes) took a butcher knife off the table. We then tried to take the knife from Mr. Hayes and succeeded in getting the knife away. I cut my hand badly. Then having the knife and the pistol both, we came out of the gate for the purposes of coming up town."

As they exited the house, Hayes shouted across the yard to several white men for help. Within minutes, Sing Chow and Ah Fa were disarmed and arrested, but not before Sing Chow bit Hayes's finger.

"Then Hayes kicked me in the mouth," Sing Chow testified. The tax collector's forcible confiscation of property fell within the scope of the law, but the Chinese men's defense of their property and safety did not. Therefore, it was Sing Chow and Ah Fa who were indicted for assault and battery.[51]

Physical resistance, as in the case of Ah Fa and Sing Chow, does not appear to have been a common response to tax collection. In fact, at least a few Chinese attempted the opposite: paying taxes in advance. When Chinese miners first arrived in the small mining town of Siskiyou in 1853, for example, they occasioned "quite a ferment." White miners greeted the thirty-five "pig-tailed gentry" with threats and calls for their expulsion. In response, the Chinese newcomers "promptly tendered the amount of the miner's tax for each one in advance." With no tax official to be found, the Chinese paid the agitators directly and were permitted to remain.[52] Somewhere between a down payment and a bribe, the $140 seemed to convince the townspeople that the Chinese would be worthwhile community members. Or at least they convinced the editors of the *Shasta Courier*. "Certain parties would chase the Chinamen from the diggings in which they were at work, violate the laws of their country, and perpetrate a great wrong upon a parcel of weak, peaceable, inoffensive, and industrious men," the editors complained. "Remember, too, that every one of them has promptly paid his tax of four dollars per month thus furnishing a very important source of revenue to the State."[53]

Like the Chinese miners in Siskiyou, Chinese elites saw the potential power embedded in the foreign miner's tax. Despite the rampant abuse involved in tax collection, Chinese leaders in San Francisco did not decry the law; instead they announced their endorsement of it in 1853. The State Assembly's Committee on Mines visited representatives of the four Chinese "companies": Sze Yup, Yeong Wo, Sam Yup, and Sun On Company. At the time, the Chinese government had no established consulate in the United States, but the committee believed that the leaders of these four Chinese "companies" represented the Chinese community as a whole. The only record of the meeting is the committee's report, which paraphrases the Chinese leaders' responses and offers encouraging commentary.

The four "companies" were huiguan, or district associations, formed by Chinese merchants in San Francisco around common dialects, native places, or ethnic origins. Huiguan in China had voluntary membership, but those in America were compulsory, which allowed them to prevent Chinese migrants from leaving California before settling their debts. In the face of rampant racism and legal discrimination, the priorities of the huiguan shifted over time from economic advancement to mutual aid and protection.[54]

Protection was on the forefront of the Chinese leaders' minds as they met with the California Mining Committee. They presented records of "unjust" treatment in mining disputes and complained that "the testimony and statements of their people have not been allowed before courts of justice, because . . . of the color of their skin." Apparently, the Mining Committee attempted to defend identity-based testimony laws "to inform them of the legal connection between the color of a man's skin and a complaint in court," but the Chinese pointedly failed to grasp their logic. The leaders of the huiguan then protested that "their people are taxed by the State for the privilege of working in the mines, while at the same time the State does not or cannot afford them that protection which is implied in the payment of taxes."[55]

Rather than arguing that discriminatory taxation should be abandoned, however, the huiguan suggested increasing the tax and giving the revenue directly to the county where it was collected. "This they believe," reported the Mining Committee, "would create them friends among the tax paying citizens of the mining counties, or those who would at least be willing to tolerate their people among them, in consideration of the benefit which the counties would derive." In return for this direct investment in local communities, the leaders wished protection, "that their persons and property may in *fact* as well as in law, occupy the same position as the persons and property of other foreigners." The Chinese leaders recognized that taxation provided a path to conditional inclusion, which both secured for the Chinese the legal right to mine and helped buy them good favor from local communities.[56] Unknowingly, they built on a long tradition of African Americans asserting rights based on their status as taxpayers.[57]

The "superintendents of the four Chinese houses" offered to do what they could to help, including furnishing an interpreter to accompany the tax collector in every county, encouraging Chinese miners to pay willingly, and attempting to redistribute Chinese miners more evenly among mining counties. An interpreter, the men explained, "would make known to the Chinese that the Tax Collector was a true officer, and not someone imposing upon them by pretending to be an officer."[58] (No doubt the interpreters would also keep a careful eye on the sheriff's use of force.) But California policymakers did not take them up on the offer.

Despite having won huiguan endorsement of the foreign miner's tax in 1853, the Mining Committee did not reach out to them again in subsequent years. Chinese leaders in San Francisco continued to make their voices heard in the state capital. In 1855, after Governor Bigler used his annual address to call for Chinese exclusion, a group of Chinese merchants published a public letter arguing for economic inclusion and fair treatment. The petitioners sought to remind policymakers and the public that Chinese "merchants paid freely their customs and taxes; and miners their licenses" even as these tax laws had "destroyed life and plundered property."[59] If California continued to harass miners, the petition implied, the state could not expect Chinese merchants and their lucrative businesses to remain.

And even though the huiguan had supported the foreign miner's tax in 1853, the Chinese community cried foul when California amended the law to create a spiraling tax, which threatened to become a form of de facto expulsion. Chinese leaders expressed their displeasure in the pages of *The Oriental* (*Tung-Ngai San-Luk* 東涯新錄), a bilingual newspaper printed in San Francisco from 1855 to 1857 under the guidance of Rev. William Speer. Only a few issues of the newspaper survive, but these suggest that the *Oriental* became a central organ for protesting the tax hike.

In October 1855 the front page of the *Oriental* reported (in English) that collectors had begun demanding $6 a month from Chinese miners. "As the Chinese are driven into the poorest, or exhausted diggings, and many make but a dollar or so a day ... they feel the burden to be intolerable," reported the editors. "The tide has now begun to set back from California. A few years will show our politicians their mistake." The *Oriental*'s Chinese-language reporting was more direct and aggrieved: "If we Chinese people tolerate these kinds of bullying and sufferings, we will suffer much without getting any benefits."[60]

In addition to vocal protests by Chinese merchants and sympathetic missionaries, there were rumors that the huiguan had launched a subscription campaign to oppose the higher tax. Several local California newspapers printed reports that "a number of men are traveling through the State, procuring the signatures of the Chinese miners to a paper, or power of attorney, authorizing the companies at San Francisco to which they belong to pay one dollar on each of their respective accounts, provided the incoming Legislature reduces the Foreign Miner's License Tax to $4 per month." The *Empire County Argus* declared the campaign "a new swindle" orchestrated by "rascals" who wished "to prey upon the Chinamen to the tune of $40,000 or 50,000, through their ignorance of how our laws are enacted."[61] The writer seemed amused by the idea that new laws could be bought and laughed at the Chinese who seemed so ready to part with their money.

However, this subscription campaign may have been an early example of what would become a common political tactic for the Chinese. In 1862 the huiguan organized themselves into a confederation of "Six Companies," later known as the Chinese Consolidated Benevolent Association, to better advocate as a collective. In the 1880s and 1890s the Six Companies raised funds for legal challenges to the Chinese exclusion laws by demanding $1 "donations" from all huiguan members.[62] It is possible that the huiguan had a similar plan to mount a legal challenge in 1855, or that they hoped to use the money to lobby (or bribe) state officials. If so, their plans remained behind closed doors and off the historical record.

In public, it was Rev. William Speer, the missionary founder of *The Oriental*, who took the issue directly to the California legislature in February 1856. His address, which he afterward published as "An Humble Plea for the Chinese," claimed to speak "in behalf of the immigrants from the Empire of China." Speer had served as a Presbyterian missionary in Guangzhou starting in 1847 and acquired fluency in Cantonese, but ill health and the death of his son had sent him back to the United States within four years. In 1852 the Presbyterian Board of Foreign Missions proposed opening a branch in San Francisco to reach newly arriving Chinese migrants and chose Speer to lead the effort. A year later he established the Chinese Mission Chapel, the first Chinese Church in North America. Speer found it difficult to win converts, but the Chinese community proved more receptive to his efforts to provide a Western education, print a newspaper, and advocate for racial harmony. Using the same publishing office as his newspaper, Speer printed copies of his "Humble Plea" and sent them to every legislator and newspaper editor in the state.[63]

The petition targeted two recent laws "calculated to exclude or debase Chinese immigration here"—namely, the spiraling foreign miner's tax and a $50 capitation tax upon arrival. First, Speer made a fervent case that the Chinese were not "coolies" and posed no threat to the morality of the state. He reserved the majority of his address, however, to argue that the Chinese could be a financial boon for the state—if California did not over-tax them.

Quoting newspapers from the mining regions, Speer reported that the $6 rate had caused a sudden drop in the number of Chinese paying the tax. According to the *Empire County Argus*, "The burden is more than they can bear [sic]. For several months past, the Chinese in most sections of the mines have not averaged six dollars a month, and if they are required to pay this to the collector, starvation is their portion. Aside the question of humanity, the increased tax is causing a depletion of the county treasuries."[64] Speer also complained of the treatment of the Chinese at the hands of collectors: "How often do you read of Chinamen shot, or stabbed, or whipped, or stripped and searched, or maltreated and insulted in some other way, by collectors[?]" If the legislature did not lower the rate and offer additional protections, Speer warned, the Chinese would simply leave and pay no tax at all.[65]

Speer's petition received favorable press, with many newspaper editors agreeing that "the State cannot afford to blot out so much capital."[66] Speer's sentiments were repeated in the Majority Report of the Committee on Mining in January 1856, as the legislature considered repealing the spiraling tax. Charles Westmoreland, committee chairman, lamented, "These people have always been willing to pay four dollars per month, but refuse to pay six."[67] He believed it was time for the law's repeal. But three members of the Mining Committee authored a scathing minority report in reply, pointing out that "the existing Chinese laws were passed in obedience to the almost unanimous demand of the laboring men of the country; That these laws operated, and are operating, precisely as their authors predicted."[68]

The majority report viewed the law as a form of conditional inclusion, but the minority saw it as a tacit form of expulsion. Both groups, however, agreed that the Chinese were not paying the higher tax. How exactly Chinese miners dodged the tax is unclear. Because the law enabled the collector to seize goods in lieu of payment, it was difficult for a miner to simply plead poverty. Instead, it seems likely that Chinese miners hid from the tax collector, left the trade, or vacated mining regions in large numbers. Whether this was a coordinated act of civil disobedience or a desperate act by impoverished individuals, nonpayment struck a death blow to tax hike.

Citing the drop in revenue, the California Senate amended the law to reduce the tax to $4 on March 21, and the Assembly followed a few weeks later. (In the years that followed, Oregon would also drop its rate, first to $24 annually in 1860 and then $16 annually in 1866, for fear of losing the revenue stream altogether.) It could not have been a coincidence that the California Assembly had an unusual visitor on the day it voted through the amendment.[69] The *Sacramento Daily Union* reported that a staff member invited an unnamed Chinese man and sat him next to the San Francisco delegation. Mr. Sharp, a San Francisco delegate, "appeared very much pleased at having one of his Chinese constituents so near him," but the House took "grave offense" at the man's presence and passed a censure against him.[70] The newspaper made no link between the nameless man and the reinstatement of the lower tax, but his presence hints that the Chinese elite had been in direct talks with policymakers.

Although it was a vote by California statesmen that ultimately repealed the tax hike in California, it was Chinese merchants in San Francisco, their white missionary advocates, and Chinese miners in the foothills of the Sierras who had rendered the law unpopular and unenforceable. Rejected en masse from the electorate and, apparently, subject to expulsion from the chambers of the State Assembly, Chinese migrants still managed to exert some power over California's first attempt to regulate their right to work in the state. They used their position as taxpayers to negotiate the terms of their economic inclusion.[71]

CHARLES DELONG AND THE EXCLUSION QUESTION

Charles DeLong did not remain a deputy sheriff and tax collector for long. The Know Nothings, a third party that based its bid on nativism, swept local elections in 1856, unseating the Democrat who had appointed DeLong. Out of a job, DeLong turned to other pursuits in which he could make use of his newly acquired familiarity with the criminal justice system. First he worked as a bounty hunter and then as an amateur lawyer while studying to pass the bar. As a lawyer, DeLong did not hesitate to represent a wide range of locals, including both "Negros" and "Chinamen."

But he had his eyes on bigger and better things. In September 1857, DeLong ran for state assemblyman representing Yuba County and won. In his diary, he closed the year with a poem celebrating his sudden political ascent.

> Six long years have mostly flown
> Since first I trod this mountain's brow.
> I came a stranger boy unknown;
> A lawyer, Legislator, and a man I leave it now.

When he moved to the state capital in Sacramento, DeLong brought his experiences with him, including his night rides hunting Chinese miners. In his first year as a lawmaker, DeLong made a name for himself as a charming dandy favored by the ladies and a brash politician who proposed bold racial laws. The *Daily Alta California* described him as the "shortest man in stature, but the greatest in his own estimation."[72]

DeLong first became a champion of "An Act to Restrict and Prevent the Immigration to and Residence in This State of Negroes and Mulattoes." The Negro Exclusion Bill proposed to bar Black people from entering California and force all current Black residents to register with the state. It would also have outlawed the practice of bringing enslaved persons to California with the intent to free them.

DeLong viewed Black people as inferior, but he wanted to exclude them rather than enslave them. Therefore, he expressed deep concern when a special committee attempted to add a new provision to his bill, which would have authorized a sheriff to force Black people to work to pay for their own deportations. "I cannot tolerate this proposition at all," he declared. "I am in favor of the passage of a bill which will properly restrict the immigration of negroes into this State, giving them due notice of its existence. If they come in after the passage of such a law, we may hang, or do any other reasonable thing with them." According to the papers, he paused to laugh at his own dark observation. "But I am most decidedly opposed to making slaves of them in this way."[73] He wished to make California into a free white republic and wanted nothing to do with the institution of slavery.

As the debate continued over Negro exclusion, DeLong noted in his diary that he "arose early in the morning" on Wednesday, March 31, "and drew up a bill to prevent Chinese and Mongolian's [sic] from emigrating to this state." The bill proposed that no Chinese person should be allowed to enter California and declared it a misdemeanor for anyone to aid their entry. The Negro Exclusion Bill passed the California State Assembly on April 7, followed by the Chinese Exclusion Bill the next day. A divided State Senate declined to bar Black people from California. But the Senate passed the racial bar on Chinese, and the bill received the governor's endorsement and became law on April 24, 1858. DeLong had gone from collecting taxes from Chinese in the dark of night to passing the first Chinese exclusion law in the nation.

His win would be short-lived. Even before the law could go into effect on October 1, many questioned its legality. When queried informally by San Francisco merchants, Judge M. H. McAllister of the US Circuit Court offered his opinion in July that the law was unconstitutional. He argued that California's attempt to prohibit Chinese immigrants "is not a police power" because it was not "necessary for the preservation of health, the morals, or the domestic peace of the state." Instead, it was a regulation of commerce, and under the Constitution, Congress alone retained the power to regulate commerce and intercourse with foreign nations.[74] Shortly after the law went into effect, Captain Joseph Hossack of the British vessel *Cyclone* was arrested for landing Chinese immigrants. He filed a writ of habeas corpus, and in an unwritten opinion the California Supreme Court struck down California's Chinese Exclusion Law of 1858.[75]

Not only did DeLong's bid to exclude the Chinese ultimately fail, but subsequent events would show that the state government was not about to make the foreign miner's tax into a means of indirect exclusion. To the contrary, California fought to protect Chinese miners against expulsion from Shasta County.

In February 1859, miners in Shasta began meeting to draft local Chinese exclusion laws and petition the state to follow suit. The miners hoped to enact local exclusion by passing communal "mining laws" that barred all Chinese from mining in Shasta County. But they knew that these customary mining laws carried little legal weight, so they also called upon California to prohibit Chinese immigration entirely. The petitioners waited less than two weeks for an answer from the state before taking the matter into their own hands. After declaring their local exclusion laws to be in effect, 300 armed men forcibly rounded up and attempted to expel all Chinese miners in the county.

The white miners claimed that the law was on their side, but others did as well. The sheriff of Shasta, H. C. Stockton, opposed the miners with full confidence that he acted in the right. Stockton raised a posse to prevent what he saw as an extralegal expulsion and wrote to the governor immediately, asking for ammunition to assist his enforcement of the law. "I know of no way to get at the matter, to effectually stop any further outrage, except to send the Chinese to the district from whence they have been expelled, and station a party of armed men, in each district, who will be present and prepared at all times to defend them," he explained to the governor. This would demonstrate to the mob that "if the laws can not be peaceably enforced, extreme measures will be used."[76]

A local paper, the *Daily National Democrat,* lauded the sheriff for his swift response. "As long as the Chinese are licensed to work in the mines, under the promised protection of the State Government," the editors opined, "it is a despicable Government that would refuse to protect them, and a despicable people that would not sustain the Government in its efforts to protect them." According to the sheriff and the paper, the foreign miner's tax had created a legal obligation to protect Chinese miners. The law's official name—"An Act to Provide for the Protection of Foreigners and to Define Their Liabilities and Privileges"—usually had the ring of irony. But not on this day.

Governor John B. Weller wrote clear instructions to Sheriff Stockton that "the law must be maintained, at all hazards." He sent 113 rifles (all that could be mustered) and 2,500 ball cartridges to aid the cause, and a colonel to help organize the posse. With this extra ammunition, the sheriff managed to prevent the expulsion of the Chinese from Shasta and similar movements in neighboring counties.[77] Through the force of arms, California had affirmed Chinese inclusion, defending Chinese miners and the stream of revenue their taxes provided. The foreign miner's tax, in this instance at least, had protected against expulsion.

Despite continued calls for Chinese exclusion from politicians like DeLong, western legislatures spent more time in the following decades establishing the terms of economic inclusion. The Foreign Miner's Act was one of the first laws to regulate Chinese work and enterprise, but it was joined by others in subsequent decades. Initially these identity-based regulations made their aims explicit. For example, in 1860 California passed a law that declared that "no Chinese or Mongolian shall be allowed to catch or take fish" without paying $4 a month for a license. That same year, Oregon instituted a license requirement on all Chinese merchants, charging them an exorbitant $600 a year to operate.[78]

The Pacific states also attempted to enact identity-based poll taxes, which demanded payment from Chinese migrants based solely on their race. In Oregon, lawmakers targeted Chinese along with other people of color in 1862, passing a poll tax of $5 a year on "each and every negro, Chinaman, Kanaka, and Mulatto." Any person who refused to pay could be "arrested and forced to work." In 1862 California passed a law known as the "Chinese Police Tax," which was copied by Washington Territory almost verbatim two years later. These laws levied an additional license fee. For those "Mongolians" not already paying for a foreign miner's license or another business license, these new laws demanded a monthly fee. In California, the rate was $2.50 a month; in Washington it was $6 per quarter. One California assemblyman explained, "The Chinese in the mountains were taxed already, and this was to tax Chinese in agricultural counties."[79]

Chinese plaintiffs turned to the courts in the 1860s to contest these identity-based tax laws. In *Lin Sing v. Washburn* (1862), for example, lawyers on behalf of the plaintiff made an impassioned case against all forms of discriminatory taxation. According to their brief on appeal, the California police tax meant that Chinese "are hunted everywhere . . . they are detained on steamboats and highways, and made prisoners till they pay; and in the mines they are tortured to discover gold dust which they do not possess; all this, to drive Chinamen out of the United States, in the face of an act of Congress which invites them in."[80] The appellant alleged that under the guise of taxation California lawmakers were attempting to exclude and expel Chinese immigrants, a right reserved for Congress under the foreign commerce clause of the US Constitution. The court agreed and sided with the appellant, eliminating one of many discriminatory taxes.

Chinese miners also used lawsuits to chip away at the foreign miner's tax. First came a challenge by Ah Hee. When he refused to pay the $4 tax in 1861, the sheriff of Mariposa County, Joshua Crippen, seized his $250 horse and threatened to sell it on the spot. Ah Hee produced the money to rescue his horse, but then sued Crippen to recover his $4 and won. *Ah Hee v. Crippen* (1861) found that Chinese miners working on private land could not be required to hold a foreign miner's license. This was not only a small victory for the Chinese, but a true triumph for white men who employed Chinese miners on their private lands.[81]

That same year California sought to extend the foreign miner's tax to all aliens ineligible for citizenship living in a "mining district," regardless of whether they engaged in mining. The law faced an immediate legal challenge. A tax collector in El Dorado County demanded payment from Chinese washerman Ah Pong, who refused to pay. The collector ordered Ah Pong to work the public roads to pay off the debt, but he refused. The county court sentenced Ah Pong to twenty days in jail, but he filed a writ of habeas corpus. In *Ex parte Ah Pong* (1861) the California Supreme Court ruled the new law unconstitutional. "The Legislature had the power to license or tax all foreigners who mined," the court ruled, but "it has not the power to tax for mining those who do not mine. A license is a permission to do a given act. No one shall be held responsible, civilly or criminally, for acts he does not do." The state could not make Chinese pay the foreign miner's tax simply because they lived in a mining county.

In the end, changes in both law and circumstance brought about the end of California's foreign miner's tax. By the late 1860s the goldfields were running dry, prospectors moved into other occupations, and mining licenses provided only a small proportion of state revenue. And as we will see in Chapter 3, the Civil War and Reconstruction had transformed American law. Through a series of constitutional amendments and federal civil rights laws, Congress provided new protections against racial discrimination.

It was in this context that a Chinese suit put an end to California's foreign miner's tax once and for all. Chinese miner Ah Koo made a complaint against John Jackson, sheriff and tax collector in Trinity County, based on the federal Enforcement Act of 1870. The Act declared that all persons "shall be subject to like punishment, pains, penalties, taxes, licenses and exactions of every kind and no other, any law, statute, ordinance, regulation or custom to the contrary notwithstanding."[82] Ah Koo alleged that the foreign miner's tax discriminated on the basis of race. In response to his complaint, a grand jury recognized the tax to be discriminatory and indicted Jackson for enforcing it.

As news of the case rippled across the state, tax collectors declared they were fearful to continue enforcing the law. The state's attorney complained, "In consequence . . . the collection of the Foreign Miner's License Tax has been discontinued, officers of our State concluding it better to disobey the laws of our State than to be punished for obeying them." Jackson was tried, convicted, and sentenced to pay a small fine, and the foreign miner's tax came to an end.[83]

During its seventeen-year life, the foreign miner's tax helped forge the economic conditions for Chinese inclusion. It was the first racial law to target Chinese profit, but it would not be the last. In response to the imagined threat of the Chinese "coolie," California lawmakers had built an elaborate regulatory structure and tacitly endorsed violent enforcement practices. These measures may have dissuaded some Chinese from gold mining, but they never succeeded in barring the Chinese entirely, in large part because of Chinese resistance. Chinese miners and merchants managed to keep the tax law in check and ultimately rendered it unenforceable.

※ ※ ※

As he aged, even Charles DeLong started to see things differently. His time in the California state legislature would turn out to be short. The Great Flood of Marysville in 1862 led to a crushing electoral defeat of Democrats, including DeLong. He moved to Nevada, where he set up a law practice but maintained his interest in politics. He served as a delegate in the third Nevada Constitutional Convention in 1864 and then ran for US senator representing the new state. He lost in 1864 and again in 1867; in 1868, now running as a Republican, he withdrew his bid in return for a political appointment.

That political appointment turned out to be US minister to the empire of Japan. The job matched DeLong's adventurous spirit, if not his experience, and he relished the luxury of traveling with three servants, three horses, and a $200 sewing machine. But after a few years he disliked dealing with a people "just waking from the barbarism of ages, who still detest the foreigner in their hearts, and only listen when they fear."[84] He served in Japan, first as minister and then as envoy, from 1869 to 1873.

When DeLong returned to the States, he turned to campaigning once again. He sought the support of the Republican Party in 1876, and in one of his stump speeches he "took up the Chinese Question." He recalled the 1850s when "the Chinese were blackening the land like swarms of flies." In his estimation, the Republicans had made one important stride, which was to "prohibit[] them from ever becoming citizens and thus preventing their hordes from controlling the ballot box."[85]

DeLong had been a champion of Chinese exclusion, but in the 1870s he reconsidered his position. Better to welcome the Chinese into "certain quarters in four or five of the chief cities of the Union, where they might live, but outside of which they must not sleep over night." Extreme segregation measures were the solution, he told his audience. "This would dispose of the whole question of coolie importation, and at the same time keep such relations with China as would continue our silver market there."[86] Why exclude the Chinese when one could profit from them?

By the end, DeLong had endorsed a new vision for conditional inclusion, albeit one that would never materialize. He died in October 1876 of typhoid fever at age forty-four.

{2}

The "CRIMINAL"
and the FEAR of a CHINESE UNDERCLASS

CONSIDER TWO MEN, Fou Sin and John Chinaman, both criminals. Taken together, their stories—one reported widely in vivid detail and the other concealed behind impenetrable anonymity—embody the history of the Chinese "criminal" in the nineteenth-century American West.

The first, Fou Sin, was born in Guangdong Province in a farming village wedged between the trading hubs of Hong Kong and Guangzhou (also known as Canton). Guangzhou was the only port in China where the Qing Court allowed Western merchants, so the riches and vices of British, French, and American trade flowed through the city and its environs. Opium was one of those vices, and when Fou Sin was only seven years old, China's attempt to ban the addictive drug was met by Britain's declaration of war. At the end of the First Opium War in 1842, China ceded the island of Hong Kong, agreed to pay a large indemnity, and opened additional ports to Western imperialists. Two years after the forcible opening of China, twelve-year-old Fou Sin climbed aboard a British brig and set sail for England. Fou Sin worked on that ship for over a year, but later could not name a single port where it had docked, no doubt owing to his youth and the fact that his captain would not permit him to go ashore. He better recalled his second voyage as a sixteen-year-old cabin boy aboard an American ship in 1848, as well as his third and fourth.

Over six years, he traveled from Singapore, around Cape Horn, via the South Sandwich Islands to New Bedford, Massachusetts, and back again. He spent a year as a cook for a wholesale merchant in Honolulu, before shipping out to Japan, Russia, and Panama, and then landing for what would be the last time in San Francisco in 1857. He got into a few scrapes in the city while working as a domestic servant. When a "drunken negro" called him a "Goddamn Chinaman," Fou Sin answered with a knife and ended up in court. By his second scrape, a fistfight in a Chinese brothel, he had learned to run before the police arrived. After a few months of unreliable work, Fou Sin left the city to head inland to Jackson, a mining boomtown in Amador County. There a Chinese stage agent gave him an introduction to Martin Van Buren Griswold, a forty-niner turned business manager who needed a cook.

Within months, Griswold was found dead.[1] According to his account, Fou Sin was in the backyard of Griswold's house splitting wood with his friend Chou Yee on the morning of November 7, 1857, when three Chinese men, who were known to him only by sight, stopped by. Fou Sin assumed the men were there to "get a little dust changed," since his employer was in the business of buying gold. But the men had other intentions. "Your master is very rich, ain't he?" asked one of the men, Coon See.

Fou Sin denied he was involved in the violence that followed, but he did take a cut of the profit. The others, he claimed, hit Griswold over the head with a board, choked him to death with a cord around his neck, took a key from his body, and searched his safe for gold dust and money, which they found in abundance. After hiding the body under Fou Sin's bed, Fou Sin and the other men split the money and fled.

As their names became known, they crisscrossed the Central Valley attempting to elude a growing state manhunt. By the time Fou Sin was apprehended, the reward for his capture had reached $3,000 (with California's governor, an unnamed group of "Chinamen," and Griswold's employer all contributing). At trial, the prosecution made the case that Fou Sin, the self-described innocent domestic servant, was in fact a criminal mastermind. Four of the men were charged, and all were found guilty and sentenced to hang. Coon See preemptively hanged himself in jail, but the others went to the gallows, accompanied by fifty cavalrymen of the Amador Rangers, fifty members of the Boynton Engine Company No. 1, and more than 5,000 spectators.[2]

Whatever the truth of Fou Sin's life, in death he became a symbol of Chinese criminality. A local newspaperman anticipated large crowds at the triple execution and published a commemorative pamphlet for the occasion. Fou Sin's face, drawn from an ambrotype, looks out from the cover of "Murder of M. V. B. Griswold, by Five Chinese Assassins." Inside, the pamphlet declares the murder "foul" but also "ingeniously conceived and dexterously executed." The pamphleteer explained that the Chinese were racially inferior, but that only aided their ability to catch their victim by surprise. It was Griswold's "utter contempt" for "the whole race" that made it difficult for him to see trouble coming. No one doubted that he could "have whipped in a fair open fight fifty or an [sic] hundred such men as the Chinamen," but Griswold did not encounter a fair fight. He was struck from behind, "a victim to Asiatic cunning and treachery." Griswold may not have seen what was coming, but the pamphleteer told his readers to know better: a docile Chinese cook could be an assassin in disguise.[3] This sinister description of Fou Sin fed emerging stereotypes of the Chinese as a criminal underclass.

But it is the story of a second criminal, John Chinaman, that hews more closely to the experience of Chinese residents in the Pacific West. We know much less about John Chinaman. Presumably John Chinaman was also born in China before he made his way to Sonora, another California mining town. Any particulars of when and where he was born or his path to the gold hills have been lost, however. The California census of 1852 recorded thirty-four men listed as "John Chinaman" in Tuolumne County alone and many more as simply "Chinaman."[4]

The record of John Chinaman's crime consists of only a few lines in the Sonora jail register. Arrested October 1, 1860, on the charge of "vagrancy," he was sentenced to thirty days and served in full. What made him a vagrant is unclear. According to California statute, he could have been a person "who roam[s] about from place to place without any lawful business," or a "lewd and dissolute" person, or a "common prostitute," or a "common drunkard."

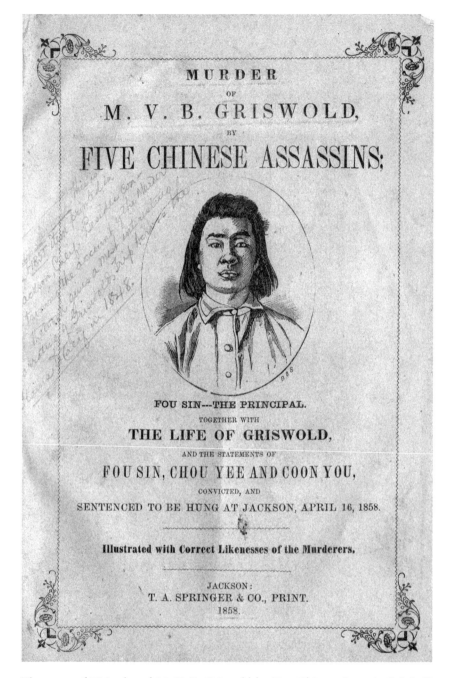

The cover of "Murder of M. V. B. Griswold by Five Chinese Assassins" (1858) shows an image of Fou Sin, an accused murderer. The pamphlet's gruesome depiction of the crime helped to feed emerging stereotypes of the Chinese as cunning criminals. (VAULT BIOG G889m, California Historical Society)

A page from the Tuolumne County census schedule (1852). In place of a name, the schedule lists one "John Chinaman" and forty-four "Chinaman." All are men who range in age from eighteen to forty-nine. Given the color categories "White, Black, or Mulatto," this census taker has marked them with a "W" for "white." (California Census of 1852, Schedule II Volume I, California State Archives, Office of the Secretary of State, Sacramento.)

It is also unclear if this was the only time he faced arrest. In the same jail register, a John Chinaman was arrested for selling liquor to the "Wallaws"; he was sentenced to $40 or twenty days in jail and chose the latter. There was also John Chinaman who "disturbed the peace" but was released without sentence; John Chinaman who was arrested for "insanity" and committed to the asylum; John Charley Chinaman who was arrested for petty larceny; and "Chinaman no. 7" who was declared a nuisance. Likely these were multiple men, each with his own life, his own accounting of love and loss, but in the lines of the jail register, and the eyes of the historian, they are indistinguishable.[5]

※ ※ ※

Although the experiences of Fou Sin and John Chinaman diverged greatly, the stereotype of the Chinese criminal mastermind and the experience of misdemeanor policing were tightly linked. Accused Chinese felons and petty criminals both encountered racial profiling, discrimination in court, disproportionate sentencing, and, as a result, unprecedented rates of incarceration. These forms of racial regulation endangered Chinese lives, devalued Chinese culture, and socially isolated the Chinese community. In other words, racialized policing of crime helped to construct the cultural terms of Chinese inclusion.

The criminalization of the Chinese did not happen all at once. The tale of "Five Chinese Assassins" foreshadowed what would become a pervasive image of Chinese criminality. But when Fou Sin met his end in 1857, there was not yet a consensus about the nature of the Chinese. Occasional alarmist rumors of Chinese cunning were countered by more frequent reports of their peaceable nature. Even early exclusionists who opposed Chinese immigration in the 1850s and 1860s complained more of their industriousness than any alleged criminality.

In these early decades the Chinese community was both over-policed and under-protected. Over-policing came in the form of vigilante justice and police violence—when racial anxieties fueled aggressive, sometimes lethal, regulation of the Chinese community. In urban Chinatowns, for example, police worked to entrap Chinese women, assuming that the small female population was a constant source of sexual vice. Under-protecting came in the form of neglect—

when local law enforcement expressed little to no concern about providing public safety for the Chinese community. San Francisco, for example, did not provide a publicly funded police force for Chinatown before 1878; instead the city expected the Chinese to pay for their own peace officers.

In response, the Chinese community came to rely on systems of self-policing. Chinese associations developed forms of vernacular law, which operated based on communal obligations and kinship relations. Chinese vernacular law had its own ethical norms, forms of regulation, and processes to administer justice. In the Pacific West, state regulation and vernacular law coexisted and comingled. Scholars have found that such blended legal systems, which rely on state and non-state social control, are ubiquitous around the world. But at the time, American lawmakers, policemen, and judges found rumors that the Chinese practiced alternative forms of justice to be strange and threatening. They came to view Chinese vernacular law as itself evidence of Chinese criminality.[6]

Starting in the 1870s, western lawmakers came to believe that the Chinese were inherently criminal. They helped to turn this stereotype into a reality by using discretionary policing to target Chinatowns and enacting behavior-based misdemeanor laws specifically tailored to practices associated with the Chinese. In California the state legislature did not stop at internal regulation; it went a step further, using Chinese criminality as a legal justification for border control measures. In this way, fears of the Chinese "criminal" came to dictate the terms of conditional inclusion and the campaign for exclusion.

POLICING THE PEACEABLE CHINAMAN

Reports of Chinese criminal activity date back to the 1850s, but so do laudatory accounts of the peaceable nature of the Chinese. Newspapers occasionally published scandalous rumors of Asiatic treachery, but they also commented on the lack of criminal activity among the Chinese. In December 1853, for example, the newspaper in a mining town noted that the Chinese rarely appeared in court. "It is a singular fact that there has been but one Chinaman arrested in this town on a criminal charge," noted the *Columbia Gazette*, "and he was discharged by request of the prosecutor." In San Francisco *The Daily Alta California* reported, "It is perfectly well known that they are the most peaceable, unmolesting and inoffensive class of adventurers that come among us, and that they are not easily provoked to angry deeds; preferring to suffer wrong rather than do wrong, and more sinned against than sinning." While the paper allowed that Chinese "coolieism" posed a danger to the white workingman, it denied the existence of Chinese criminality, at least in 1852.[7]

California lawmakers were quicker to label and police "Indians." Upon statehood in 1850, California passed laws that criminalized Native peoples and offered pretenses for arresting them. The Act for the Government and Protection of Indians (1850), for example, broadly defined "vagrancy" and allowed for the arrest, imprisonment, and indenture of Indian vagrants. In Los Angeles, city officials also used race-neutral "public order" laws to aggressively police the Native population. In the 1850s and 1860s, Natives crowded Los Angeles jails, labored in prison chain gangs, and faced auction as indentured laborers. At the same time, Natives living outside of white society faced state violence in the form of government-funded raids, assaults, and land grabs. The first governor of California described these acts as a "war of elimination" and indeed they contributed to the devastation of Native nations.[8]

As white westerners targeted Natives for incarceration, forced labor, and elimination, they did not immediately mark the Chinese for similar treatment. Rarely did California compile criminal statistics in its early years of statehood, but what survives reinforces the journalists' impressions. When a legislative committee investigated the Chinese population in California in 1862, they found no evidence of excessive criminality.[9] "The criminal statistics of the State show that the Chinese are less addicted to crime than any other foreign class," reported the *Sacramento Daily Union* in 1869. And according to the paper, nine-tenths of criminal complaints against Chinese migrants resulted from white prejudice rather than Chinese misdeeds. The editors opined, "If there be demoralization in their presence, it results from the want of laws and wholesome public opinion to restrain mean whites from exercising cruelty upon the weak and unoffending race."[10]

In the 1850s and 1860s, then, the Chinese did not encounter a pervasive stereotype of criminality. Still, they faced legal and extralegal policing that could turn violent. Justice that fell outside formal law could be particularly cruel. George Bancroft, the famed nineteenth-century historian of the American West, found ample evidence that western settlers frequently turned to "popular tribunals," rather than official court proceedings.

Racial profiling often initiated these extralegal actions, and racial violence was often the result. For example, Bancroft recounts the story of a "John Chinaman" who allegedly robbed a mining sluice in Butte County in 1857. "The heathen was detected by a watchman and shot, once, twice; notwithstanding the leaden increase of weight, John ran two hundred yards, when he fell and was captured. Semi-strangulation was resorted to in order to ascertain the whereabouts of plunder previously taken. John was firm. Off came the pride-sustaining queue; still John spoke no words." When "John" was unable to produce the stolen gold, "some were for hanging what remained of John upon a tree. But others said No; what advantage should accrue from extinguishing the little light left in that unhallowed lamp." Even under threat of lynching, the unnamed Chinese man maintained his innocence.[11]

Other accused Chinese did not survive such rough treatment. When a Chinese man known as "Whalebone" stood in court accused of killing a white man in 1858, a mob "burst into the court-room and took the trembling Whalebone and stoned him to death; then hanged the body to a limb of a tree." Having killed Whalebone, the mob "went through the Chinese camp and levelled every cabin to the ground. It was only by the utmost efforts of officers and the better portion of the community that a general destruction of all the Chinese property in the county was prevented." What began as a formal trial became an act of vigilante justice, followed by mob violence targeting the Chinese community at large.

In Bancroft's survey of popular tribunals in the American West, he found many accounts of Chinese who met their end in the hands of a mob, as well as numerous accounts of American, Native, Mexican, and European victims. Even within Bancroft's gruesome catalog of violence, however, tales of vigilante "justice" for the Chinese stand out for their specific racial undertones. In the account above, the crowd did not simply torture John Chinaman in hopes of a confession, they also cut off his queue. And the mob did not simply take Whalebone's life, they also leveled the Chinese quarters. Through these acts, vigilantes made these alleged criminals stand in for the Chinese race.[12]

Legal records also reveal the combined effects of popular tribunals and legal proceedings against the Chinese. In *People v. Ah Ki (Chinaman)* (1861), two witnesses attested to the extreme measures taken to force a confession from the defendant. Ah Ki stood accused of burglarizing his former employer, Nelson Mining Company, by a grand jury in Nevada County.

According to the head of the company, James Nelson, Ah Ki had abruptly quit in protest two weeks before the alleged burglary. Ah Ki was protesting because he had not been paid. "He went away we thought because his wages had been garnished for Road Tax," explained Nelson. Rather than pay the "Chinaman," Nelson had directly handed Ah Ki's wages to the tax collector. Two weeks later, when a silver watch, $20 in gold coin, and additional money went missing, Nelson immediately suspected the disgruntled Ah Ki. After a search, Nelson and men in his employ "arrested" Ah Ki, questioned him, and found the watch in his possession. Nelson described it to the court as an open and closed case.

Nelson's two employees, however, were more forthcoming about the tactics used to extract a confession and locate the watch. Mr. Manohan described a popular tribunal held at the scene of the crime, followed by a hanging: "When Ah Ki was arrested we took him to Nelson & Co's cabin where the property was stolen, called in the miners & had a Court, Judge Lynch presided. Court decided to hang [Defendant] until he confessed the crime, there was a rope tied around Ah Ki's neck & thrown over the limb of a tree near the Cabin; Ah Ki was strung up some 8 or 10 times; after hanging him up in this manner he confessed. . . . He told us nothing whatever until he was hung up." Although Manohan rhetorically evoked the law—describing an "arrest" and holding "court"—his reference to "Judge Lynch" makes it clear he knew these proceedings were better described as lynch law. Only following this forced confession was Ah Ki formally arrested, tried, and convicted (in just thirty minutes) by a jury in Nevada County.[13]

Proceedings did not need to be extralegal to be violent, but legal records tend to be circumspect about police violence. In a case against two alleged thieves in Tuolumne County in 1866, for example, Constable A. M. Hill testified that one of the prisoners "admitted to me that he had stolen the things" and "after some considerable persuasion" produced the stolen goods.[14] What methods of persuasion the constable used on the Chinese men remained unspoken.

Sometimes defense attorneys appealed convictions on the basis of a forced confession. In 1867, for example, H. Fellows, an attorney for Ah Kim, appealed his burglary conviction. At the time of his trial Ah Kim was suffering from a gunshot wound received during his arrest, and the pain was so great he had to lie down on the floor of the courtroom as he testified (without an attorney present). After this testimony was taken, Ah Kim was then released to the prosecutor's primary witness, C. Ambery, who was allowed to bring him to a separate room. There Ambery "interrogated" the defendant, without the aid of an interpreter or a lawyer, until Ah Kim allegedly confessed to the crime. Although Ambery claimed that "no threats were used," Ah Kim's appeal questioned how this could be considered a "free and voluntary" confession.[15]

Death inquests offer glimpses of how policing sometimes turned lethal. For example, the Nevada County coroner, J. G. Palmer, conducted an "inquest into the body of a Chinaman" in October 1871. Summoned by police officers, Palmer found the dead man lying in the middle of Pine Street in front of the Nevada City courthouse, a bullet wound in the back of his neck. He did not know the name of the deceased, but he had a pretty good idea of how the man had died because his assailant, Officer William Scott, had already confessed.

According to Officer Scott, at half past 9 o'clock the night before, he had been patrolling outside the courthouse when the Chinaman walked past. "I turned around to see what he held," Scott testified. "I saw a load under his arms that looked like blankets." The blankets, according the police officer, quickly raised his suspicion. A Mr. Hugh Feeney had reported that a pair of grey blankets had gone missing from his cabin a few days before, and he had told Scott that it was likely the work of "a Chinaman." Accordingly, Scott began to follow ten yards behind the blanket-carrying "Chinaman," but then his suspect broke into a run and dropped the blankets. Scott continued his chase, yelled, "stop, stop, stop," pulled his pistol, and then fired several shots, one of which landed in the back of the Chinese man's neck.

In front of a coroner's jury the next day, Scott's account was corroborated by two white men who had not been present: the sheriff who was called to the scene afterward and Mr. Feeney, who had complained of his missing blankets. Ah Sing, the only Chinese witness, made a one-sentence statement about the deceased, simply to give the John Doe an identity. "Says his name is A[h] Fat," reported his interpreter. The twelve-man jury determined that "Ah Fat came to his death by a pistol that [was] fired by officer William Scott in the discharge of his duty." Furthermore, they found, "that the act was justifiable and commendable." In truth, nothing in California's criminal code gave Officer Scott the right to shoot a man from behind based merely on suspicion of petty theft.[16]

There may not yet have been a consensus on their criminal nature before the 1870s, but the Chinese still suffered from aggressive, sometimes lethal, policing in the American West. Perhaps this was because when a Chinese migrant broke the law, he transgressed both the formal criminal code and unwritten racial etiquette. Such a double violation may have driven harsh police tactics and uncompromising punishments.

CHINESE VERNACULAR LAW

Not only did Chinese migrants have to contend with American law and justice, they also had to navigate evolving legal rules, norms, and institutions within the Chinese community. Starting in the 1850s, huiguan were the dominant force in determining these communal laws. Led and organized by Chinese merchants, these associations were designed to facilitate Chinese labor recruitments by arranging work, providing places to stay, offering mediation services, and guaranteeing care after death. Huiguan representatives negotiated on behalf of foreign miners, greeted each boat of new arrivals in San Francisco, and signed off on each Chinese departure, making sure laborers settled their debts before their voyage. The huiguan blended mutual aid and social control, with an eye toward keeping profits steady for the Chinese elite.[17]

In 1862, in an attempt to maintain harmony between different huiguan, community leaders formed the Chinese Six Companies (later known as the Chinese Consolidated Benevolent Association). The Six Companies, which was led by rotating representatives from the dominant huiguan, positioned itself as a powerful intermediary between kinship, trade, and native place associations, as well as the Chinese and US government. For Chinese workers, the Six Companies could be a powerful force for communal protection as well as a source of authoritarian rule. Although reliable records on the huiguan are scarce, there is no doubt that they policed the Chinese community, enforcing contracts, resolving disputes, and punishing offenders.

Abuse and neglect on the part of the American justice system facilitated this turn toward internal policing. In San Francisco, for example, the local government did not provide any police services in Chinatown before 1878. If the Chinese community wanted protection from crime, they had to pay for it themselves. Chinese business leaders hired Chinese guards to protect their businesses, and in what amounted to a special tax, they also paid city employees to act as "special police officers."

One such officer, George Duffield, explained the system in 1876. He described himself as "the same as any other police officer, only I am paid by the Chinese." How much he was paid, Duffield refused to disclose. He would only say that the Chinese pay him "as they see fit," as was the "custom" "ever since the Chinamen have been here." This peculiar arrangement had the potential to cut both ways. Huiguan could, in the light of day, pay the special police officers generously for favorable treatment. With this power came the potential to keep some lawbreakers out of jail. Special police officers could also be induced to enforce Chinese communal rules as well as American laws. But the arrangement also made the Chinese community uniquely vulnerable to officers' greed. "Could this arrangement be used as oppression?" Duffield was asked in his interview. "Yes, sir," he answered.[18]

Despite their peaceable reputation, Chinese had participated in their share of "vice" since their arrival in the American West, particularly gambling, prostitution, and opium smoking. All three trades were common in China, and while considered illicit by the educated elite there, were not subject to the same moral disapprobation as in American society. Some newly arrived Chinese businessmen pursued these illicit trades because of barriers to entry into more reputable industries. Conditional inclusion had granted them unequal access to economic resources, occupations, and property, and therefore they looked for opportunity in illicit trades and products. They hoped these trades would be beyond the watchful eyes of the police.

It was true that American policemen did not prioritize public safety for the Chinese community, and when they did pay attention to Chinese-on-Chinese crime, they found it difficult to distinguish wrongdoers from victims. Therefore, it fell to Chinese community leaders to keep crime in check. In the 1860s it was the huiguan and Six Companies that provided much of this internal regulation. But in the 1870s, when huiguan distanced themselves from the vice trades under pressure from the police, new organizations called "tongs" stepped in to take their place.

Tongs, or sworn brotherhood societies, got their name in the United States based on a romanization of the Chinese word for "hall." Tongs first emerged in 1852, but only became widespread on the West Coast during the 1870s. While the leaders of the huiguan were prominent merchants and their membership was determined by native place, men could voluntarily join tongs and become leaders through ritual oaths of loyalty. Portraying themselves as a workingman's alternative to the elitism of the merchant-run huiguan, tongs offered many of the same mutual aid and protection services as huiguan, including lodging, employment, mediation, and proper burial. But the tongs also demanded absolute loyalty and secrecy.

Tongs came to specialize in protecting the vice trades. They required steep payment for their services, forbade members from talking to American authorities, and commanded power through violence and fear. Although tong membership never numbered more than several thousand, their violent rivalries could terrorize the Chinese community. American officials depicted tongs as nothing more than criminal organizations of "highbinders" and "hatchet men," but for the Chinese community they were an additional form of vernacular law.

Through written by-laws, tongs established rules of protection, mediation, and punishment for those involved in the vice trades. By-laws for the Hop Sing Tong, for example, specified that huiguan would be held responsible if one of their members committed a crime at a gambling house. This policy of collective liability incentivized the associations to keep members in line. The Hop Sing Tong's by-laws also expressly forbid members from directly engaging with

American businessmen or American authorities without guidance, translation, and counsel provided by the tong. These customary laws had mixed results. No doubt the tongs' laws kept some Chinese outside the American justice system, but their violent tactics landed others in prison.[19]

Tongs' alternative forms of justice also fueled police distrust of the Chinese community. Accusations reached new heights on occasions when tongs and huiguan attempted to use American courts to enforce the internal rules of their community. Borrowing from legal customs in rural China, Chinese in America sometimes pursued both community mediation and legal proceedings simultaneously, strategically intertwining vernacular and formal law. In the Qing legal system, a legal complaint was frequently used to encourage communal mediation and an informal settlement could conclude a legal case. The back and forth between customary and formal law was so common that historian Philip C. C. Huang has argued that it created a "third realm" of Qing justice, which "successfully resolved disputes by attending to the twin considerations of peacemaking and of law, through the joint working of the two."[20] In the American context, however, this approach to law bred fear and misunderstanding. For example, if a Chinese defendant offered financial remuneration to settle a dispute and end court proceedings, they were more likely to be accused of bribery than to be seen as making peace.

Lem Schaum, a self-described "Christian Chinese," testified before a California state committee in 1876 on the internal workings of Chinese American justice. "When members of a company do anything against the rules of that company they are punished," he explained. "For instance, suppose I should march myself out and kill a Chinaman. I am brought before the company and made to pay a fine. They take the money and send it back to the family of the killed party to support his mother." Rather than inflict corporal punishment or incarceration, this vernacular law demanded financial redress. If he pays the fine, Lem Schaum went on to explain, "they will let the whole matter drop." If he should refuse to pay redress to the company, "I must go through the American Courts" where they will convict him.[21]

When the Chinese intertwined vernacular law and the American justice system, the results cast suspicion over the entire community. Problems arose, for example, from differing conceptions of guilt. In comparison to American law, Chinese American vernacular law deemphasized the guilt of an individual and emphasized the mutual responsibility of a family, tong, or huiguan. Although fraud was frowned upon in China, scholars have found that Chinese peasants there approached litigation in pragmatic ways. Chinese peasants would first turn to private retribution or mediation to settle disputes. But when cycles of revenge spiraled out of control, peasants went to court to help settle their differences. When crafting legal complaints against their adversaries, Chinese peasants sometimes approached litigation in a more utilitarian than literal manner. For instance, Chinese witnesses preferred to testify against the perpetrator of a crime, but if the guilty party was nowhere to be found, they might also be willing to testify against a member of his family. Scholars who have documented this legal practice note that it was not condoned by formal Chinese law and that incidents of false testimony in China and the United States may have been exaggerated by orientalist ideas of Chinese "lawlessness."[22]

Only occasionally did American courts find conclusive evidence of orchestrated fraud on the part of Chinese witnesses. In the case from a later period, *People v. Chew Sing Wing* (1890), the police stumbled upon a letter in Chinese that offered instructions on how to enter false testimony. Liu Him wrote to his brother, Liu Tang Fook, to inform him that "a man of our own family, Liu Jing, was violently killed, rendered lifeless, put out of existence," and they blamed the Chiu [Chew] family. In response, "the people of our family and friends sent the American policeman (Detective) Cox, to the brothel of [Chiu] Sin Wing, and had him arrest Chiu Sing Wing." The Liu family hoped that this false accusation would force the Chiu family to pay $300 in reparations for the death, an outcome that "would be satisfactory, and will constitute revenge." To apply pressure, Liu Him instructed his brother, in the name of family loyalty, to head to San Francisco to testify against Chiu Sing Wing. The brother's testimony helped to secure a conviction.[23]

In this way, internal disputes could spill into the American justice system in unpredictable, messy, and consequential ways. When police, judges, and juries glimpsed the workings of Chinese vernacular law, they reacted with confusion, concern, and allegations of wrongdoing. Ironically, the attempt to internally regulate the Chinese community, in the absence of public safety provided by the government, sometimes fueled accusations that the Chinese were a criminal underclass.

In 1870, California assemblyman E. A. Rockwell used growing concern over the tongs to argue that the Chinese community itself was a criminal enterprise. He proposed an inflammatory bill that would have created a special police force to regulate the Chinese community in California, levying a $5 monthly tax on all Chinese in the state. The additional $2.4 million in annual revenue would, in theory, have funded a special police force to "break up the Chinese imperium" and "bring them to punishment, whenever they coerce, oppress or in any manner maltreat their unfortunate and, at present, unprotected countrymen."[24]

Rockwell was not the only one to believe the Chinese community operated outside of the law. "So far as the Chinese are concerned," a special committee report on the bill declared, "[they are] wholly independent, outside and in derision of the authority of the State of California as well as that of the Government of the United States." The report alleged that the Six Companies in San Francisco held their own "tribunals," sponsored their own "Chino-California prisons," and had "flogged, beaten, otherwise maltreated" Chinese who opposed them. The power of the Six Companies "made it impossible for the ordinary civil force of the State . . . to break up this extraordinary, tyrannical and illegal organization."[25] The "Chinese imperium" threatened American sovereignty by operating outside US law. In the eyes of some lawmakers, Chinese attempts at internal regulation had become evidence of their inherent criminality.

CHINESE CRIMINALIZATION AND THE CAMPAIGN FOR EXCLUSION

As Assemblyman Rockwell was likely aware, there were legal advantages to classifying the entire Chinese community as a criminal enterprise. In 1862, when the California Supreme Court struck down the Police Tax Law, which bore the official title "An Act to Protect Free White Labor and to Discourage the Immigration of the Chinese into the State of California," the court pointed a way forward for California to regulate the Chinese. In *Lin Sing v. Washburn*, the court ruled that the racial tax amounted to immigration restriction—

this was explicit in the official title of the act—and that the states did not have the power to regulate immigration. But importantly, the majority opinion also noted an alternative approach, explaining that states retained "police powers" over the health, safety, and well-being of their populations. California did not have the power to exclude Chinese immigrants on the basis of race but retained the power to exclude criminals, paupers, vagrants, or "obnoxious person[s]." Likely, the California Supreme Court was reacting to the US Supreme Court's decision in the *Passenger Cases* (1848), which held that although Massachusetts and New York could not enact a head tax on new arrivals, the states' right to police power implied the ability to reject outsiders deemed harmful to general welfare.[26]

Chinese criminals may have posed a problem for local regulation, but this legal rationale meant they also provided a possible solution for those calling for California to enact Chinese exclusion. In California, Governor Henry H. Haight led the charge. Running as a Democrat in 1867, Haight based his campaign on his opposition to Reconstruction. In addition to opposing equality for African Americans, Haight announced that he would "try all powers of the state" to exclude Chinese immigrants.[27]

When Rockwell's bill to police the "Chinese imperium" was tabled in committee, Governor Haight urged the California legislature to move forward with two other bills focused on Chinese criminality. These bills targeted both Chinese men and women, and commanded wide support. On March 18, 1870, Governor Haight signed into law "An Act to Prevent the Kidnapping and Importation of Mongolian, Chinese and Japanese Females, for Criminal or Demoralizing Purposes" and "An Act to Prevent the Importation of Chinese Criminals and to Prevent the Establishment of Coolie Slavery."

The Anti-Kidnapping Law and Anti-Coolie Law, as they came to be known, made their legal justification clear in their preambles. The former claimed that "the business of importing into this state Chinese women for criminal and demoralizing purposes has been carried on extensively during the past year, to the scandal and injury of the people of this State"; the latter alleged that "criminals and malefactors are being constantly imported from Chinese seaports, whose depredations upon property entail burdensome expense upon the administration of criminal justice in this State." Both identity-based laws asserted that California was "in exercise of the police power appertaining to every state of the Union" by prohibiting criminal, immoral, or obnoxious Chinese.[28]

As California barred the arrival of Chinese criminals, policymakers also worked to broaden the definition of what constituted criminal behavior. Policies of social control could help feed policies of exclusion. Beginning in the 1870s, local and state governments showed a new interest in stamping out Chinese "vices." Most of these laws did not explicitly name the Chinese race or "aliens ineligible to citizenship"; instead, they were behavior-based laws that targeted cultural practices strongly associated with Chinese residents. San Francisco, for example, banned the use of firecrackers (1866), the carrying of baskets upon poles while walking on the sidewalk (1866 and again in 1870), the playing of gongs in theatrical productions (1873), and opium smoking (1878). In addition to behavior-based laws, cities used rigorous enforcement of general-outcast laws—including those regulating vagrancy, disease, prostitution, and gambling—to further regulate Chinese. Misdemeanor violations usually came with a fine or, in lieu of payment, a short jail sentence.[29]

State legislatures added to the layers of regulation. In 1878, for example, California targeted Chinese burial practices by requiring extensive paperwork and a $10 license fee for the exhumation of human remains. Chinese migrants, who traditionally returned the bones of the deceased to their native place, faced a penalty of $50 for failure to comply. In 1881 California also regulated the Chinese by prohibiting opium smoking, and similar laws followed in Nevada, Washington Territory, and Oregon. By building exemptions for "medicinal" uses of opium into these laws, the states tailored the law to Chinese users and found ways to exempt white ones.

Together these behavior-based laws defined key Chinese cultural practices as "nuisances," and invited local police and sheriffs to intervene at their discretion. These new efforts to police Chinese came after the precipitous decline of Native populations, before the arrival in the Pacific West of Black people in large numbers, and during a time when Mexicans were legally classified as white. All of these groups faced racialization and discriminatory policing, but the Chinese, as the largest and most visible racial minority group in most West Coast towns and cities, drew particular attention from local and state officials.

San Francisco continued to stand out in its enthusiasm to enforce behavior-based and general-outcast ordinances against Chinese residents. A shift toward aggressive regulation arrived with Mayor Andrew Jackson Bryant, a Democrat who served during a national economic downturn between 1875 and 1879. In his first address as mayor, Bryant declared his opposition to Chinese migration and his intent to pursue Chinese criminals. He proposed a separate Chinese prison "on the outskirts of the city" and Chinese convict labor "made to work upon our public squares." This would allow police officers to "eradicate" the Chinese "nuisance" through "wholesale arrests." Mass arrests, in turn, would slow Chinese migration and relieve "public indignation."[30]

With the newly aggressive campaign in the 1870s to police Chinese came a renewed effort to document their criminal nature and build the case for exclusion. In 1862 a California joint committee had found scant evidence of Chinese criminality, but when the legislature formed a new committee in 1876, the investigation came to a different conclusion. They found that most Chinese belonged to the "criminal classes." "This mass of aliens are not only not amenable to law," the committee found, "but they are governed by secret tribunals unrecognized and unauthorized by law." The legislators were concerned that Chinese "companies and guilds" were "recognized as legitimate authorities by the Chinese population" and held the power to "levy taxes, command masses of men, intimidate interpreters and witnesses, enforce perjury, regulate trade, punish the refractory, remove witnesses beyond the reach of our Courts, control liberty of action, and prevent the return of Chinese to their homes in China without their consent." In other words, the Chinese community had found ways to "nullify and supersede State and National Authorities."[31]

After painting the huiguan and tongs as criminal organizations, the 1876 Special Committee proceeded to confirm the criminality of the entire Chinese population. The committee treated San Francisco chief of police Henry Hiram Ellis with skepticism when he testified that out of the 30,000 Chinese living in San Francisco, only about 1,500 to 2,000 belonged to the criminal classes. These numbers aligned with city arrest statistics, but the committee was clearly dissatisfied. Members asked leading questions that pushed the chief to reconsider his estimation. If he included those "who violate the city

THE "CRIMINAL" AND THE FEAR OF A CHINESE UNDERCLASS 79

CALIFORNIA.—THE CRUSADE AGAINST THE CHINESE IN SAN FRANCISCO.—From Sketches by Geo. F. Kelly.—See Page 55.

Geo. F. Kelly's illustration "California—The Crusade Against the Chinese in San Francisco" (1882) appeared in *Frank Leslie's Illustrated Magazine*. It depicts the policing of Chinese in the city, including a police raid of a gambling den and health inspectors confronting a Chinese leper. The inset represents the threat of the next generation: a "Chinese lady and child." (Philip P. Choy Papers [M2521]. Department of Special Collections and University Archives, Stanford Libraries, Stanford, California.)

ordinances in relation to fires and health, and those who live off the wages of the criminal classes," the committee wanted to know, then how many of the Chinese were criminals? "I think almost the entire population," Ellis answered. By defining criminality broadly, the committee pushed Chief Ellis to inflate his estimate of the "criminal classes" from 6 percent of the Chinese population to 100 percent.[32]

The findings of the 1876 California Special Committee helped to justify aggressive policing on the local level and to demand exclusion at the federal level—two different solutions to be enacted at two different scales. The committee forwarded its findings to Congress under the banner "An Address to the People of the United States upon the Evils of Chinese Immigration." Warning that the "Pacific Coast has become a Botany Bay to which the criminal classes of China are brought in large numbers," the committee urged Congress to act. "Our police force, our constabulary, and the machinery of our judicial system, are overwhelmed." The only solution, the committee declared, was to exclude Chinese immigrants from America.[33]

Congress had already begun to act on allegations of Chinese criminality. When California's Kidnapping Law (1870, amended 1873) faced judicial scrutiny, Congress rushed to duplicate the law at the federal level. The resulting Page Act, adopted April 3, 1875, is best known for its bar on "oriental" "prostitutes" (which will be discussed in Chapter 4). But the law also contained elements of California's Anti-Coolie Law, making it a felony to knowingly and willingly import "any cooly" into the United States and barring all "persons who are undergoing a sentence for conviction in their own country of felonious crimes."[34] These provisions targeted contract laborers and criminal aliens, defining the latter in fairly narrow terms.

After expediting the passage of the Page Act without significant discussion, Congress launched a more thorough investigation in 1877, sending a Joint Special Committee of its own to San Francisco. The Special Committee invited local white officials and business leaders to testify, but it did not choose to interview a single Chinese resident. After gathering more than 900 pages of testimony, the congressional committee reported on Californians' "bitterly hostile feeling toward the Chinese, which has exhibited itself sometimes in laws and ordinances of very doubtful propriety and in the abuse of

THE "CRIMINAL" AND THE FEAR OF A CHINESE UNDERCLASS   81

individual Chinamen and sporadic cases of mob violence." Following this slight admonishment, the committee then essentially agreed with California's 1876 report, repeating allegations that "the Chinese have a quasi government among themselves independent of our laws," "there is a great want of veracity among Chinese witnesses," and "large numbers of them . . . occupy the State's prison and jails." Adding criminality to a long list of charges against the Chinese, the committee declared that Congress must "restrain the great Asiatic influx to this country" or lose the Pacific States to "a race alien in all its tendencies."[35]

Within five years, Congress would heed their warning. The Chinese Restriction Act of 1882 barred all new Chinese laborers from entering the United States for the following ten years.

CHINESE CRIMINALIZATION AND CONDITIONAL INCLUSION

Fear of the Chinese criminal not only helped drive the campaign for federal exclusion; it also dictated the cultural terms of their inclusion in the Pacific West. Aggressive policing of the Chinese, which began in the 1850s, culminated in high rates of arrest, conviction, and incarceration by the 1880s. At the time, lawmakers used crime statistics to argue that the Chinese were criminal by nature, but in fact the data reveal a far more complicated story. In hindsight, it is a story of an immigrant community, disproportionately male, that attempted to regulate itself through internal policing, but could not avoid the discriminatory criminal justice system.

Consider arrest statistics. Few towns and cities on the Pacific Coast preserved nineteenth-century jail registers, but in Portland, criminologist Charles A. Tracy found a complete run of registers for 1871–1885, which offers a telling picture of local policing. In Portland, Chinese did not constitute a disproportionate number of those arrested during this period, since they averaged 8 percent of the total population and 8 percent of arrests. In fact, their share of arrests is lower than we might expect, given the gender ratio of the community, and the fact that historically men are more likely to commit (and be arrested for) crimes. In 1880 there were eighteen Chinese males for every one Chinese female in the United States, a markedly uneven ratio that resulted from both Chinese cultural norms and discriminatory immigration laws. If Chinese residents were arrested at the same rate as white, despite the higher proportion of men, it seems likely that either Chinese men committed fewer crimes or Chinese internal regulation was working.[36]

Even if the rate of Chinese arrests was low overall, a closer look at the nature of arrests reveals racialized policing at work. Scholars represent arrest rates in terms of total arrests per a hypothetical 10,000 population. This approach accounts for the small Chinese population and reveals that Chinese were disproportionately arrested for misdemeanor vice crimes. It is important to note, however, that the same person may be arrested multiple times for the same offense.

For prostitution offenses, Chinese were arrested at a rate of 49 per 10,000 Chinese; non-Chinese were arrested at a rate of 6 per 10,000. The discrepancy was even larger for gambling (Chinese, 154 per 10,000; non-Chinese, 7) and opium (Chinese, 50 per 10,000; non-Chinese, 4). The notable exception was for public drunkenness (Chinese, 16 per 10,000; non-Chinese, 730).[37] While Chinese and whites were arrested at similar rates overall, Chinese were more likely to be arrested for vice crimes. The Chinese were also more likely to be arrested for violent crimes (Chinese, 56 per 10,000; non-Chinese, 19).[38]

Particularly telling is the enforcement of city health ordinances. Setting aside prostitution, gambling, opium, and alcohol offenses, the remaining "health and safety" city ordinances show an even higher rate of Chinese arrests in Portland (Chinese, 394 per 10,000; non-Chinese, 20). This was by design, because some health ordinances explicitly focused on disrupting Chinese cultural practices.

For example, Ordinance No. 1347 (1873) necessitated 550 cubic feet of air for each occupant (aiming at Chinatown's tight living quarters); Ordinance No. 2177 (1878) prohibited exhibiting animal parts deemed "offensive" (chicken feet, for example); Ordinance No. 3354 (1882) prohibited playing anything other than a stringed musical instrument in any theater after midnight (gongs, for example); and Ordinance No. 4539 (1885) required special licensing of wash-houses (a common Chinese trade).

At times, Portland city councilmen would pass a single ordinance that included provisions clearly aimed at the Chinese and ones that appeared race-neutral on their face. For example, Portland Ordinance No. 3983 (1883) prohibited carrying baskets suspended from poles or upon shoulders in a traditional Chinese style; smoking opium, keeping a resort for smoking opium, or simply being in a house where opium is being smoked; and playing fan tan, a Chinese game of chance. In addition to these racially coded infractions, Ordinance No. 3983 also barred prostitution; any "indecent or immoral act or practice"; roaming about the streets after midnight; employing persons to sing or dance; obstructing the sidewalk; and transporting swill at unapproved times (see Appendix). Given their placement within the same ordinance, it is possible that the latter group of infractions was also associated with the Chinese at the time.[39]

The city of San Francisco reported similar arrest statistics starting in 1875. That year, Chief of Police Ellis noted in his annual report, "Our Chinese inhabitants are more frequent violators of sanitary and police regulations than any others." Armed with the mayor's "cheerful and earnest support in enforcing these laws among the Chinese," Ellis stepped up his policing of Chinatown. The following year, Ellis declared that he had arrested 2,995 Chinese between July 1, 1875, and September 30, 1876. Among them were many victims of behavior-based laws, including 518 people arrested for living in crowded conditions, seventy-seven arrested for carrying baskets on a pole, and eleven arrested for playing fan tan.

There is no doubt that racial thinking infused policing practices in San Francisco. In most western cities, including San Francisco, Chinese migrants (as permanent aliens) were prohibited from serving in public office, including as sheriffs, police, and judges.[40] Therefore, when San Francisco denied the Chinese a regular city-funded police force in the 1860s and 1870s, the Chinese community was forced to hire white men to enforce public safety. And when San Francisco changed tactics in 1878, forming a specialized city-funded Chinatown Squad, white men again populated the force.

The premise of the specialized Chinatown Squad was clear, as was the effect. San Francisco believed the Chinese race to be uniquely criminal and made it so through arrests and convictions. Specialized policing communicated to white residents the racial danger posed by the Chinese, widening the social distance between races, and demarcated Chinatown as a distinct space separate from the rest of the city.[41] Once policemen in Chinatown received a city salary, they had less incentive to work with the Chinese community to resolve conflicts. Some members of the Chinatown Squad may have continued to receive payments from the tongs on the side, but others prided themselves on bringing newly forceful police tactics to Chinatown.

Chinese in San Francisco complained of mass arrests based on racial profiling, but surviving records of such police action are scarce. In Sacramento, however, daily arrest records from the nineteenth century have survived and show clear patterns. Sacramento jail registers reveal that police conducted mass arrests of Chinese for both misdemeanor violations and graver accusations. In the state capitol, more than half the Chinese arrested during 1867–1899 were swept up in groups of three or more. Many of these group arrests were for health and safety infractions. For example, on January 23, 1874, twenty-three Chinese residents were arrested for "washing clothes in the slough." Mass arrests could also occur with felonies. Following a suspicious death in 1892, Sacramento police arrested five Chinese on suspicion of murder, fifteen for concealed weapons, and sixteen for "threats against life."[42]

There are indications that public pressure could play a direct role in racialized policing in the West. In Portland, for example, white residents called for raids of Chinatown in the 1880s, sending repeated petitions to the city council complaining about Chinese residents and urging the rigorous enforcement of city ordinances.[43] One 1885 petition from the "Workingmen and Businessmen of the First Ward" called on the mayor to "instruct the chief of police to at once 'raid' those Chinese dens of prostitution . . . upon oak street within the shadow of the police building, and that the inmates of those dens be arrested and made to suffer the penalty provided by law."[44] And in 1887, twenty-three "taxpayers of the City of Portland" demanded the removal of the "longstanding nuisance" of the Chinese vegetable market on Alder Street, which had made the sidewalks impassable and produced "an offensive odor throughout the neighborhood."[45] Responding to (white) public pressure, Portland police vigorously enforced health and safety ordinances in Chinatown.

Chinese residents protested their unfair treatment at the time. In 1876, for example, huiguan representatives wrote to the San Francisco chief of police (copying the mayor and the governor) to object to the prevailing racial etiquette. "Frequent and unprovoked assaults" took place on "Chinese people walking peacefully the streets of this city," they reported. The assailants were "seldom arrested by your officers," but "if a Chinaman resists the assault he is frequently arrested and punished by fine or by imprisonment." The merchants warned that if left unchecked, assaults might escalate to a race riot. In their minds, there was no doubt that racism infused police work in San Francisco, exacerbating distrust of the Chinese and offering near impunity to white assailants.[46]

It is clear that race influenced arrest patterns, but for many Chinese an arrest was only the beginning of their journey through the criminal justice system. What happened next was determined largely by the nature of the accusation. Misdemeanor arrests often resulted in a swift sentence by the justice of the peace, which typically involved a small fine, between five and ninety days in jail, or a few days' labor on a chain gang.[47] These convictions left behind little or no paper trail for historians to follow. In contrast, felony accusations sent Chinese defendants to court, where they faced additional hurdles and the possibility of severe sentences.

Juries posed particular problems. First was the fact that Chinese could not serve on juries, because membership was limited by race and citizenship.[48] Second, as we will see in Chapter 3, witness testimony laws barred Chinese from bearing witness against white persons in California and Washington until 1870, which meant that juries rarely heard their perspective. And finally, when Chinese people did testify (in their own defense or against their countrymen), juries usually failed to believe them. Juries reflected the sentiment of the day, and by the 1870s the belief that Chinese could not keep an oath had become commonplace. When defense attorneys attempted to root out prospective jurors who held special animus against the Chinese, they had little luck.

In the San Francisco murder case, *People v. Chin Mook Sow* (1876), defense attorney Solomon A. Sharp launched an unusually energetic attempt to select an unbiased jury. First, he challenged the citizenship requirement for jurymen, arguing that a jury consisting of one-half citizens and one-half non-naturalized immigrants would be more likely to provide a fair trial.[49] Judge Samuel H. Dwinelle quickly rejected his request for a "mixed jury," because California state law required jurors to be citizens.

Undeterred, Sharp then proceeded to ask forty-seven prospective jurors if they possessed "any prejudice against the Chinese race."

Their answers were seldom straightforward. At first, prospective juror Hugh Duffy denied his prejudice. "No, sir, nothing biased," he said, "Nothing more than general principles." But when Sharp persisted, asking again if Duffy was "opposed to the Chinese as a race," Duffy answered definitively, "Yes, sir." Another prospective juror, Thomas Cantrell, declared, "I do not like [the Chinese] as a class." This time it was Judge Dwinelle who followed up, asking if Cantrell had "any actual bias against this defendant." "No, sir, nothing more than he is a Chinaman," answered Cantrell. Judge Dwinelle asked if the prospective juror could offer the defendant "a fair, impartial trial notwithstanding your prejudice against the race." Cantrell answered, "Yes, sir. I surely would not hang a man because he was a Chinaman." Against the defense attorney's protests, Judge Dwinelle impaneled Cantrell. Although only three men claimed no bias against the Chinese in the voir dire process, Judge Dwinelle approved the selection of twelve jurors and proceeded to trial.[50] Chin Mook Sow was convicted.

Some judges explicitly instructed the jury to look beyond their prejudices. "The defendant is a Chinaman," began a Jefferson County judge in Washington Territory in 1878, "and amid all the storm and passion of our people against these people it is refreshing to know that in our courts all men are equal before the law. Courts and juries know neither the white, black, or copper colored man as such. We know them all as men who shall receive the protection of the law." Judges frequently professed a belief in equal justice and urged juries to deliberate in good faith.[51]

By the time the court was preparing the jury for deliberation, however, race had already played a prominent role in virtually all proceedings against Chinese. Race determined who could serve on the jury, who could testify against whom, and who could represent the Chinese (since citizenship was also a prerequisite for admission to the bar). Race also acted in more subtle ways, as witnesses offered their accounts of "the Chinaman" in question and attorneys played into racial stereotypes. Language served as an additional barrier. Courts provided Chinese defendants with translators in most cases, but not all, and no doubt the quality of translation varied. Some judges shared the general public's disdain for the Chinese and did not bother to hide it. Others took seriously the promise of equal protection under the law.

THE "CRIMINAL" AND THE FEAR OF A CHINESE UNDERCLASS   87

Even when judges urged juries to exercise impartiality, conviction statistics suggest that judges' pleas may have fallen on deaf ears. While Chinese and white residents had similar rates of arrest in San Francisco, for example, the police chief reported a divergence in conviction rates. In 1876, Chief Ellis reported 1,250 convictions per 10,000 Chinese residents and only 750 convictions per 10,000 white residents.[52] And when researchers surveyed murder conviction rates between 1850 and 1900 across four California counties, they found relative consistency in the rate of guilty verdicts for white defendants, but not for Chinese. On average, juries in Calaveras, Tuolumne, Sacramento, and San Joaquin Counties found 43 percent of white defendants guilty as charged. The gold mining counties show a higher conviction rate for accused Chinese, with a 59 percent conviction rate in Calaveras and an 80 percent rate in Tuolumne. Strikingly, Tuolumne County convicted every Chinese person accused of murder who went to trial.

Conviction statistics look different in the Central Valley counties of San Joaquin (which includes the city of Stockton) and Sacramento (the state capitol). In San Joaquin, Chinese had a 48 percent conviction rate, which was higher than for white defendants, but not egregiously so. Sacramento County was the outlier. There Chinese were convicted at a lower rate than their white counterparts, with only 24 percent found guilty.[53] There are several reasons Sacramento might have differed from surrounding counties. In the city, Chinese residents had greater access to legal representation, which may have significantly improved their trial outcomes. It is also possible that they encountered a more equitable court system in the state capitol. But the most likely driver of this discrepancy is the common practice of mass arrests in Sacramento. Mass arrests of suspects led to a high rate of dismissal (34 percent of charges were eventually dropped) and therefore a lower Chinese conviction rate. Nevertheless, Sacramento County juries showed other signs of anti-Chinese bias. Although there were twenty-three cases brought against white men for killing a Chinese person between 1850 and 1900, and twelve of these led to indictments, not one ultimately resulted in a conviction.[54]

High incarceration rates naturally flowed from this pattern of arrests and convictions. In 1880 the Chinese made up 8.5 percent of California's population but 16.4 percent of state prisoners. The rate

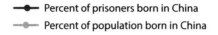
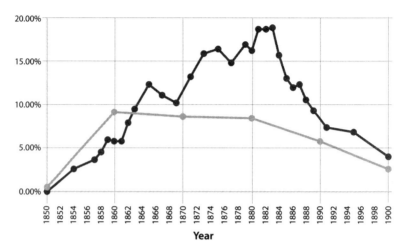

Percent of California's prisoners born in China and percent of total population born in China, 1850–1900. These figures do not include Chinese in local jails or immigration detention. (Data source: Paul Takagi and Tony Platt, "Behind the Gilded Ghetto: An Analysis of Race, Class and Crime in Chinatown," *Crime and Social Justice*, 1978)

of Chinese incarceration in California was so high that it skewed the nationwide figures. According to the 1880 US census, Chinese had the highest rate of incarceration of any racial group in the United States. White people were incarcerated at a rate of 7 per 10,000, "Indians" at a rate of 23 per 10,000, and "Negros" at a rate of 25 per 10,000. For Chinese, the rate of incarceration was 50 inmates per 10,000 Chinese, dramatically higher than any other racial group.[55]

These comparisons come with important caveats, however. The Chinese population in the United States was small at the time: 105,465 in 1880. Although the rate of Chinese incarceration was higher than the rate of Black incarceration, in absolute numbers Chinese were vastly outnumbered in America's prisons by Black people. Of the 16,748 "colored" prisoners in 1880, for example, 526 were Chinese and only 154 were Indian. The remaining 16,068 were Black men and women. And this number still underestimates the effect of policing on the Black community, because African Americans also faced lynch mobs and other forms of extralegal "justice."[56] The vast majority of these incarcerated and persecuted Black people were located outside the Pacific West. California recorded only 8 Black convicts in the state prisons in 1880.[57]

Federal statistics on Indian incarceration are similarly problematic. US census takers counted only part of the total Native population, enumerating those who lived within white society or on reservations. This makes it difficult to interpret the rate of Native incarceration. Moreover, Native incarceration in the West reflected different dynamics than for other groups, because incarceration was used as tool for removal. In Oregon, for example, the US military accused a group of Tukudika men of attacking American settlers and imprisoned them in Vancouver Barracks before placing them in reservations. Incarceration, in other words, could be a weapon of war and part of a larger process of dispossession and confinement.[58]

Incarceration statistics must also be understood within gendered terms. In 1880, when census takers recorded that only 4.5 percent of the Chinese population was female, other racial groups reported relative gender parity in the American West. Given the extremely high proportion of men in the Chinese community, one would expect even higher rates of Chinese incarceration.

The rate of Chinese incarceration remained high when the United States conducted its next census in 1890. Surveying city and county jails as well as state penitentiaries, census takers found significant racial discrepancies. "Mongolians" were imprisoned at a rate of 36 per 10,000 population. In contrast, white people were incarcerated at a rate of 10 per 10,000, "Negros" at a rate of 28 per 10,000, and "Indians" at a rate of 53 per 10,000. Notably, Chinese had the longest average sentences, were more likely to be sentenced to life in prison, and were more likely to be sentenced to death than any other

Table 3 US Census of inmates in jails and prisons by race (1890).

	Total no. of prisoners	Rate per 10,000	Average length of sentence (in years)	Sentenced to life (as percent of those convicted)	Sentenced to death (as percent of those convicted)
Chinese	407	36	6.55	13.8%	0.8%
White	57,310	10	3.46	3.8%	0.2%
Black	24,277	28	4.84	5.0%	0.2%
Indian	322	53	5.42	6.7%	0.3%

Source: US Census Bureau, "Report on Crime, Pauperism, and Benevolence in the United States," 1890.

racial group.⁵⁹ While high rates of incarceration may have emerged from the skewed gender ratio, differences in sentencing suggest that discrimination within the justice system also left a mark.⁶⁰

Moreover, census numbers capture only a portion of incarcerated Chinese. The census did not count those convicted on misdemeanor infractions serving short sentences in jail, and it did not count immigrant detainees. By 1890, customs officials had begun enforcing Chinese exclusion laws and detaining Chinese migrants on immigration infractions. However, those detained for illegal immigration were not included in prisoner statistics, even when they were held in state prisons. In Washington State, for example, the McNeil Island State Penitentiary recorded thirty-seven indefinitely detained Chinese immigrants awaiting deportation in 1890. But during that same year, census takers only recorded seven Chinese inmates in the entire state of Washington. When the New York State Commission on Prisons issued a report in 1901, it found 460 Chinese detained for immigration infractions in four county jails.⁶¹ If immigration detainees had been counted as prison inmates by census takers, the Chinese may well have had the highest national rate of incarceration once again. Although federal statistics offer an incomplete snapshot, it is clear that Chinese residents continued to face high rates of incarceration and severe sentencing in the late nineteenth century.

The rate of Chinese incarceration in US prisons had profound implications for the community. Whether the rate of incarceration was merely a reflection of the gender ratio or was driven by a discriminatory justice system, it meant that Chinese migrants in the United States had a higher likelihood of being incarcerated during their lifetime than other racial groups. They were also more likely to have friends, family, or business partners who were incarcerated. The pervasiveness of Chinese incarceration reaffirmed Americans' perceptions that the Chinese were criminal by nature and fed feelings of social alienation among the Chinese.

※ ※ ※

Numbers can tell us a lot about the policing of the Chinese "criminal." Statistics can describe mass arrests, racial profiling, swift convictions, harsh sentencing, and extended incarceration. They can demonstrate the combined effects of a discriminatory justice system, a disproportionately male community, and an ethnic enclave attempting to regulate itself. While nineteenth-century lawmakers used these numbers to craft a narrative about Chinese criminality, in retrospect the data tell us more about the terms of Chinese inclusion. American lawmakers and the white public tolerated Chinese communities on the condition that they could be controlled and disciplined, often in the name of "health and safety." At times these measures of social control debased Chinese cultural practices and endangered Chinese lives.

Numbers tell powerful stories, but there is still something about faces. Some of the most striking artifacts of Chinese incarceration are the mug books. In the nineteenth century, police regularly segregated the Chinese (and only the Chinese) within their record-keeping systems.[62] In California's cities and towns, including San Francisco, Alameda, Sacramento, Yuba City, and Downieville, the police photographed Chinese "criminals," and produced volume upon volume of Chinese faces.

When created, these mug books were accompanied by a key book that recorded the names, crimes, and descriptions of each man. These keys also capture the racialized gaze of police. In Sacramento, for example, one recorder in 1880 had a simple understanding of Chinese appearance; he recorded that an Ah Kin had "yellow" eyes, "Chinese" hair, and a "China" complexion. Fifty years later, San Francisco police continued this tradition of racialized simplification, recording that each and every Chinese inmate had "black" hair, "maroon" eyes, and a "yellow" complexion.[63] Sometimes photographs do not even include these vague descriptions. In the past century, many key books have been lost, so all that remains is a disturbing visual archive of nameless Chinese.[64]

Among the many faces, some stand out. There are the women, few in number, so their existence alone catches the eye. One is Lin Quay (no. 258) of Sierra City, who the Downieville sheriff later noted was "gone to China, not to return" (see Chapter 4). She had not been accused of a crime, but the sheriff still obtained her immigration number and photograph, added both to his Chinese mug book, and kept track of her whereabouts.[65]

In Sacramento, there are Ah Joe and Ah Lee, pictured together in a single frame and assigned a single prisoner number (434). In 1876 they stood accused of a "crime against nature," in this case, sodomy. The description below notes they were "good looking boys," aged

Ah Joe and Ah Lee, Sacramento Chinese mug book (1876). Police arrested both for a "crime against nature," likely sodomy, and photographed them together. Sex crime accusations against Chinese could arise from same-sex relationships, interracial relationships, and sex work, as well as stereotypes of Chinese deviance. (City of Sacramento Police Department records, CTY0002, Center for Sacramento History)

twenty and fifteen, respectively. The older one was sentenced to three years in state prison; the younger one was discharged.[66]

There are also images of those who were sentenced to death. For Ah Ben, caught in the act of murdering a white man in Marysville in 1878, the only photo that remains of him is at the scaffold. He is standing next to the sheriff and the noose, surrounded by a crowd of witnesses, moments before his hanging.[67]

There are also bruised and bloodied faces. One from a later period is Chin Jong, an alleged member of the Hip Song Tong. In 1924, Chin attempted to escape arrest in San Francisco, but he "was knocked unconscious by a passing truck driver." According to police records, it was that blow, not police interrogation, that left blood streaked across his face.

In the nineteenth century, only Chinese appear in segregated mug books, but this changed in the twentieth century. Starting in the 1920s, San Quintin State Prison in California maintained a "Black and Yellow book" filled with Black, Chinese, Japanese, and South Asian inmates. Much divided the lives of Ah Low, Uriah Black, Dove

THE "CRIMINAL" AND THE FEAR OF A CHINESE UNDERCLASS 93

Hanging of Ah Ben, Yuba City (1879). Convicted of murdering a white man in Marysville, Ah Ben was sentenced to death. A special report by the Census Bureau in 1890 found that Chinese were more likely to be sentenced to death than any other racial group. They also had the longest average sentences and were more likely to be sentenced to life in prison. (From *Looking Back: Images of Yuba-Sutter*, Pediment Publishing, 2003. Reproduction courtesy of the Yuba County Library)

Interrogation of Chin Jong, San Francisco tong wars mug book (1924). Police records claimed that Chin's battered face was due to a blow by a Good Samaritan who aided in his arrest. Although western journalists reported on violent policing of the Chinese, legal records only offer occasional hints of abuse. (San Francisco Police Department Records, San Francisco History Center, San Francisco Public Library)

THE "CRIMINAL" AND THE FEAR OF A CHINESE UNDERCLASS

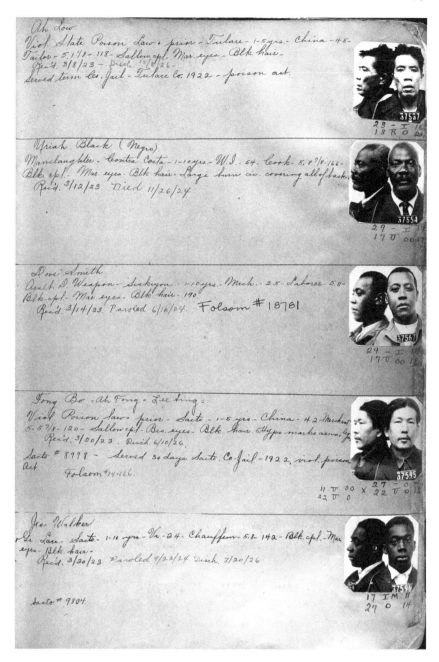

A page from the "Black and Yellow book," San Quentin, 1923. The California State Prison maintained a segregated mug book containing only images of Black and Asian inmates. (San Quentin Inmate Photograph Album, California State Archives, Office of the Secretary of State, Sacramento)

Ah Chewey, Sacramento Chinese mug book (1875). Sacramento police recorded his name and indicated he served two years in state prison. But no man by the name "Ah Chewey" appears in state prison records or the US Census. Like John Doe Chinaman, his true name will be forever unknown. (City of Sacramento Police Department records, CTY0002, Center for Sacramento History)

Smith, Fong Bo, and Jess Walker, but still they found themselves on the same mug book page.[68]

And finally, there are the openly defiant. In 1875, Ah Chewey (No. 327), an accused housebreaker, sat with his arms crossed, queue draped around his neck, glaring into the camera. Surviving records contain Ah Chewey's name, or at least its poor transliteration, as well as his crime and punishment. Police noted that this particular "Chinaman" had been sentenced to two years in Folsom State Prison for stealing a box of tobacco.[69] If he was guilty, it was a harsh sentence. If he was innocent, it was a travesty.

So little can be known about Ah Chewey's life, and about the lives of all Chinese "criminals." But Ah Chewey's stare speaks volumes. His eyes suggest open contempt for the man behind the camera and the justice system he represented.

{3}

The "ALIEN"

and the RECONSTRUCTION *of* CHINESE RIGHTS

IN 1861 SAMUEL CLEMENS headed west. He made his way from the silver mines of Nevada Territory, through the gold rush towns of the California foothills, and on to the San Francisco Bay. While in Nevada, he adopted the pen name "Mark Twain," and while in California, that name became nationally known for his lively and pointed depictions of the American West.

Mark Twain had a lot to say about the Chinese or, more precisely, about their treatment at the hands of white Americans. "I am not fond of Chinamen," Twain explained to his readers, "but I am still less fond of seeing them wronged and abused." And he had seen a lot of abuse.

During his six years in the West, Twain had seen "dogs almost tear helpless Chinamen to pieces in broad daylight in San Francisco" while white men stood around and enjoyed "the sport." Twain had watched "troops of boys assault a Chinaman with stones when he was walking quietly along about his business, and send him bruised and bleeding home." He had seen "Chinamen abused and maltreated in all the mean, cowardly ways possible to the invention of a degraded nature." In all this time, Twain "never saw a policeman interfere in the matter" and he "never saw a Chinaman righted in a court of justice for wrongs thus done him."[1] In the 1860s, Chinese lived in a state of rightlessness that left Twain indignant and unsettled.

National events brought change to the West, although much of it arrived after Twain had departed in 1867. When the Civil War ended in 1865, Congress turned to the project of reconstructing the nation and reimagining Americans' civil rights. Building on a decades-long Black freedom struggle, Radical Republicans primarily focused on the rights of newly emancipated citizens. They drafted constitutional amendments and federal laws to protect the interests of southern freedmen. Among them was the Fourteenth Amendment (1868), a sweeping measure of inclusion that extended citizenship to "all persons born or naturalized in the United States, and subject to the jurisdiction thereof." With this Amendment, Congress defined a single form of national citizenship, granted citizens certain rights and immunities, and pledged federal protection of these civil rights. The promises of Reconstruction would transform US citizenship and the population who laid claim to it, including American-born Chinese.

Reconstruction also raised questions about the rights of "aliens" and the Chinese in particular. As Congress, state legislatures, and the public re-envisioned America's future, most agreed there was no permanent place for the Chinese. In fact, on the very same day that Congress recognized the ratification of the Fourteenth Amendment, it also ratified the Burlingame Treaty with China. No doubt the timing was coincidental, but for the Chinese it would be consequential. The Fourteenth Amendment broadened the ranks of US citizens, but the treaty made it clear that Chinese migrants would not number among them. Western senators had insisted on amending the treaty to clarify that "nothing herein contained shall be held to confer naturalization ... upon subjects of China in the United States." As Congress transformed and expanded US citizenship, it sought to ensure that most Chinese would remain permanent "aliens."[2]

Still, the treaty and amendment did ensure the Chinese some rights, although their precise nature would take some time to work out. The Fourteenth Amendment declared, "No state shall make or enforce any law which shall abridge the privileges or immunities of *citizens* of the United States; nor shall any state deprive any *person* of life, liberty, or property, without due process of law; nor deny to any *person* within its jurisdiction the equal protection of the laws."[3] In a subtle, midsentence shift between the term "citizen" and "person," the Amendment opened the door for Chinese to make civil rights claims despite their alien status.

The Burlingame Treaty also cracked open a nearby window. The agreement guaranteed that "Chinese subjects visiting or residing in the United States shall enjoy the same privileges, immunities and exemptions . . . [as] the citizens or subjects of the most favored nation."[4] In theory, the "most favored nation" clause placed China on a par with Western nations, entitling the Chinese to the equal protection of US law.

When Mark Twain first read the Burlingame Treaty, he saw its potential and penned a lengthy analysis. He believed the treaty could, at last, grant the Chinese some basic rights. If taken literally, the treaty could in "one sweep" undo "all the crippling, intolerant, and unconstitutional laws framed by California against Chinamen." It could lift a "degraded, snubbed, vilified, and hated race of men out of the mud."

Although his assessment glowed with optimism, Twain also recognized there would be backlash. As he explained to his eastern readers, the Burlingame Treaty could protect the Chinese, but it was also certain to create "weeping, and wailing, and gnashing of teeth on the Pacific coast."[5]

※ ※ ※

As the 1870s dawned, Chinese migrants entered the decade newly armed with promises made in the Burlingame Treaty, the Fourteenth Amendment, and related civil rights laws. Based on these pledges of equal protection, Chinese litigants began an assault on the identity-based laws that had proliferated in the previous decades. During the racial reconstruction that ensued, the Chinese fight for civil rights sometimes ran parallel to the better-known Black struggle, but more often it diverged.

Chinese legal challenges forced the courts to reckon with particular, critical questions: What did it mean to be a "person" under the Constitution, "aliens ineligible to citizenship" under the law, and subjects of a "most favored nation" under treaty agreements? What civil rights did the Chinese possess? And what rights could they exert? These were questions about Chinese political inclusion—their civic membership and ability to govern—but the answers would redefine the terms of economic, cultural, and spatial inclusion as well.

Previous scholars have mapped the history of Chinese civil rights primarily in terms of landmark legislation and court cases.[6] But as we have seen, there was a gulf between formal law and legal custom, and this gap mattered for Chinese lives. To probe these differences, in this chapter I push beyond some of the best-known civil rights cases concerning Chinese residents. For example, *People v. Hall* (1854) denied Chinese the right to bear witness against white people, but the historical record shows that despite this ruling, the Chinese found other ways to bear witness. *Yick Wo v. Hopkins* (1886) guaranteed the Chinese equal protection under the law, but in fact these protections had significant limits. *In re Ah Yup* (1878) reaffirmed that the Chinese were racially barred from naturalization, but my research reveals that thousands of Chinese nevertheless naturalized.

What emerges is not a triumphalist story of civil rights progress, but neither is it a relentless story of victimization. Chinese were not silent in the face of their persecution; they bore little resemblance to Mark Twain's depiction of the "helpless Chinamen." Chinese litigants of the 1870s challenged (identity-based) prohibitions of Chinese witness testimony, (behavior-based) regulation of Chinese living arrangements, and (identity-based) prerequisites to naturalization. In these domains and others, Chinese plaintiffs fought for the courts to recognize and delineate their civil rights. In so doing, they rewrote the terms of their inclusion and placed limits on white supremacy.

But Chinese plaintiffs did not win all their legal battles, and their losses foreshadowed what was to come. Lawmakers did more than "weep" and "wail." Rather than abandon the preconditions for Chinese inclusion, western lawmakers noted which laws could withstand judicial scrutiny and worked to rebuild the racial regime on this surviving foundation. Conditional inclusion, lawmakers found, could be achieved in more subtle but durable ways.

WITNESS TESTIMONY AND IDENTITY-BASED LAWS

When it came to the right to give evidence in court, Chinese migrants fell into a trap that was first laid for others. In the early nineteenth century, the eastern states routinely passed laws limiting the ability of Black and Native people to testify in cases in which a white person was party. Generally, northern states restricted testimony from enslaved people, but southern and western states frequently prohibited testimony based on color alone. Following this precedent, the first California legislature passed an Act Concerning Crime and Punishment in 1850, which declared, "No black or mulatto person, or Indian, shall be permitted to give evidence in favor of, or against, any white person." California made no mention of the newly arrived Chinese.[7]

A few years later, a jury in Nevada County, California, convicted a white man, George W. Hall, of murdering a Chinese man, Ling Sing, solely on the testimony of Chinese witnesses. The California Supreme Court overturned this ruling in *People v. Hall* (1854) and extended to the Chinese the state's racial restriction of witnesses. Although the Chinese were not explicitly named in the law, the court deemed the Chinese racially inferior, and therefore more similar to Black and Native people than to white.

In no uncertain terms, the court based its opinion on the purported deficiencies of the Chinese race. Describing "a race of people whom nature has marked as inferior, and who are incapable of progress or intellectual development beyond a certain point," the court declared that Chinese should not have the right "to swear away the life of a citizen." If they had such rights, the justices feared, Americans would "soon see them at the polls, in the jury box, upon the bench, and in our legislative halls."[8] If the Chinese could speak out in court, they might also raise their voices in American politics.

Chinese migrants understood the ramifications of this ruling. Pun Chi, a Chinese merchant, wrote to Congress in protest, "Your Supreme Court has decided that the Chinese shall not bring action or give testimony against white men. Of how [many] great wrongs is this the consummation! To the death of how many of us has it led!" He complained that white men could now "go on in a career of bloodshed without limit, since they find there are none to bear testimony against them."[9] The inability to bear witness against "any white person" threatened to grant impunity to white assailants.

Moreover, by lumping Chinese with Black and Native people, California suggested that they were similarly uncivilized. A Chinese merchant, Lai Chun-chuen, writing on behalf of Chinese merchants in San Francisco, complained that the people of California had "come to the conclusion that we Chinese are the same as Indians and Negroes, and your courts will not allow us to bear witness." He found this conclusion offensive because of his own strongly held prejudices against Black and Native people. He explained, "Indians know nothing about the relations of society; they know no mutual respect; they wear neither clothes nor shoes; they live in wild places and in caves." In comparison, he believed China held an "honorable position" in the world due to the "fame of her civilization."[10]

While Chinese merchants publicly protested the ruling, ironically, it was a short-sighted argument on behalf of a huiguan that extended the bar on Chinese testimony to civil suits. In 1859 the See Yup Company (also known as the Siyi huiguan or Sze Yup Association) issued a promissory note to Jip Wing Kam for $600. Jip Wing Kam promptly sold the note to James F. Speer, a white man. When Speer went to the See Yup Company asking for payment, the huiguan refused. When Speer sued, the See Yup Company denied that it had issued the note or ever raised capital in this way. Clearly, the huiguan wished to keep its business within the Chinese community. To win the case, its lawyers made a rash claim, arguing that no Chinese man could testify in the suit because "an Indian may not testify against a white person; and a Chinaman is an Indian." The See Yup Company won on appeal, but the Chinese community lost the ability to testify in civil actions against white people in California.[11]

Soon state legislatures codified these court rulings. In 1862, Nevada declared that "no black person, or mulatto, or Indian, or Chinese should be permitted to give evidence against or in favor of any white person."[12] Within a few years, Washington Territory (1862), California (1863), Idaho (1864), Arizona Territory (1865), and Montana (1865) amended their criminal codes to explicitly bar Chinese testimony against white persons as well. In Montana the legislature took pains to define the barred witnesses, specifying that "a Chinaman is a person having one-half or more Chinese blood."[13]

Testimony laws were but one example of the identity-based laws of the 1850s and 1860s. During these decades, judges denied that the Chinese community had the legal basis to challenge this targeted discrimination, and in state legislatures, lawmakers refused to hear Chinese protests.[14] Witness testimony laws played a central role in defining the terms of conditional inclusion, distinguishing Chinese witnesses from white, endangering Chinese lives, and constricting Chinese economic and political power. Due to racial restrictions on testimony, Chinese residents had more trouble suing white employers when they were denied pay, fewer protections from violent crime, and less influence in the local application of law.

Racial testimony laws meant that Chinese were free to implicate themselves or their countrymen, but were kept practically mute against white aggressors. It is difficult to tally the full cost of this silence. How are we to count the trials that did not take place because there were no white witnesses? How are we to know which crimes arose because white people assumed they could act with impunity? How are we to enumerate the convictions that did not happen?

Light sentences for white-on-Chinese crime may be one indicator of the damage done by racial testimony laws. In 1860, for example, Charles Birch threw a beef bone at Sam Sing, who retaliated by throwing a footstool. The petty fight became lethal when the white man responded by grabbing his knife and stabbing Sam Sing until he lay at the brink of death. Even after his passing, the dying man's words were disallowed from the trial and the jury returned a guilty verdict only on a lesser charge: assault and battery. Birch was sentenced to thirty days in jail or a $10 fine.[15] Although $10 was a poor price for a Chinese life, the Chinese could be devalued even further. In the Placer County case *People v. Otto Johnson et al.* (1859), Otto Johnson, A. P. K. Safford, Joseph Smith, and several unnamed men were found guilty of assault on "John Doe Chinaman" despite the bar on Chinese testimony. But their sentences revealed the true sentiment of the court: each convicted white man was fined one cent.[16]

The effect of racial testimony laws can also be seen through a comparison with Oregon, where Chinese testimony was permitted. In 1854 the Oregon legislature barred testimony from "Negroes, mulattoes, and Indians, or persons one half or more of Indian blood" when white persons were party, but did not disallow the Chinese. While successful criminal prosecutions for white-on-Chinese crime were rare in California, existing records from Portland, Oregon, tell a different story. In the 1860s the Justice of the Peace in Multnomah County heard cases against white people in which Chinese victims played the role of primary witness. In 1867 the testimony of "Ah Iuam, Ahahie, and Dr. Jin," for example, helped to convict Angeline Roth of breaking a glass window "in a house occupied by Chinese." She faced a $100 fine and thirty days in the county jail. Likewise, the court convicted Patrick McFadden and William

Clarke for assault and battery upon Sing Yuke in 1868, with Sing Yuke as the complainant and primary witness. Each was fined $10 and spent five days in jail.

The difference in Oregon, however, may have resulted more from lax enforcement of racial testimony restrictions than specific allowances for Chinese witnesses. Although Black and Native people were barred from testifying against white persons in Oregon, they did just that in the Multnomah County Police Court. In 1867 a "Kabeau Indian woman" testified against Mary Fallamine for an assault and battery charge; "Indian John and Indian Jim" testified against William Lake on the same charge in 1868; and when Jacob Ripley was found guilty for assault with a deadly weapon against one Mary Petty in 1867, he was found guilty with the help of a witness listed as "negro called Bill."[17] These cases hinged on testimony from Chinese, Black, and Native people, and therefore would likely have been impossible to bring in courts where racial restrictions were more enthusiastically enforced.

The impact of racial testimony laws can be partially gleaned through comparison to other states, but ironically, it is Chinese legal testimony itself that most powerfully conveys the consequences of the prevailing racial gag order. Testimony laws never completely silenced the Chinese in court. Even in states where Chinese testimony against white people was disallowed, Chinese found ways to be heard. These instances were few and far between, and certainly could not counter the prevailing assumption of white impunity. Still, their testimony leaves behind a harrowing record of their persecution and resistance.

Death inquests, for example, provided the Chinese an opportunity to speak on the record. Coroners permitted Chinese witnesses to describe the lethal violence of white men during their inquests, but this searing testimony would never make it into a criminal trial. For example, the death inquest in *In Re Yun Dip* (1868) included the testimony of three Chinese witnesses. After Justice of the Peace J. Slattar convened a jury (likely by pulling a few white men off the street, as was the custom), he brought them to a cabin in the woods to examine the body of Yun Dip. Gathered before the dead man, they heard from his "friends" with the help of an unnamed translator. Ah Gan explained that on the evening of Thursday, June 11, 1868, he and five of his countrymen had been in the cabin when three white men arrived. "Two of the men stood outside of the cabin," he explained, "one went inside, and wanted to get money off the deceased." According to Ah Gan,

> The men tied up all the Chinamen by their queus [sic] two at a time. After the[y] were tied up one of these men asked them (Chinamen) for their money, deceased said he had no money, one of the men drew out a pistol and sai[d] "I want your money or I will kill you." Yun Dip said again he had no money, one of the men then hit deceased with the pistol on the top of his head. The men then commenced hunting in the cabin and found about 30 dollars.

The white men "tied them up by their tails," agreed Ah Chung. "One of the white men struck deceased over the head with a pistol . . . deceased was then stabbed right behind the right ear . . . deceased th[e]n fell down."

He Hoo's testimony revealed that the fatal blow did not have immediate effect. "Deceased died the day following June 12, 1868," he explained, "from the effects of the blows on the head, and the stab in his neck." The justice of the peace didn't seem to notice the man's day of suffering, declaring that "Yun Dip, was a native of the Empire of China, aged about 35 or 40 years [and] came to his death on the eleventh day of June A.D. 1868," due to the "effects of blows upon his head by a pistol and a stab in the neck from a knife in the hands of . . . three white men" who were "unknown" to the jury. With unnamed murderers and only Chinese witnesses, the investigation into the killing ended there. No trial would result, no conviction, and no justice. Yun Dip's friends found a way to bear witness to his death, but testimony laws still deprived them of justice.[18]

In coroner reports, the local legal system acknowledged white violence against Chinese but rarely pursued justice for the victims. Most coroners performed their duties with seeming indifference to Chinese death and a few seemed to revel in the violence. For example, when filing a death inquest on a Chinese miner named Ah Fon, the Nevada County coroner J. J. Rodgers added unnecessary malice: "a dammed Chinaman who was killed by big Boulder Rock." "It is a pity," the clerk noted, that the boulder "had not . . . covered the whole of China town."[19]

In addition to testifying in death inquests, Chinese found another workaround: they turned to private prosecution rather than public. For public prosecution, officials had to recognize a crime as a "public" offense that constituted an injury "against the peace and dignity of the people of the state." For the Chinese, this proved a high bar. Local officials in California, Washington, Arizona, Montana, and Idaho often overlooked crimes against (legally silenced) "Chinamen" and declined to prosecute. But when the legal system refused to recognize their injuries as public offenses, some Chinese responded by turning to private prosecution.

Rather than depend on sheriffs or state prosecutors to recognize when a crime had been committed, Chinese litigants went to court, declared themselves aggrieved parties, and filed complaints. Even though Chinese were not allowed to serve as witnesses against white parties, they could act as complainants and describe their legal injuries. For Chinese migrants, turning to civil law may have felt natural and familiar because the Chinese legal system did not recognize a division between private and public law. Under the Qing judiciary, complainants went to court to accuse each other of crimes, and guilty rulings frequently involved financial remuneration, even in response to assault or murder.[20]

Achunn, for example, filed a civil suit when he was robbed in Yuba County in 1859. One can only guess why Achunn turned to civil rather than criminal law. Perhaps his protests went unheard by the sheriff, perhaps he was turned away by the justice of the peace, or perhaps it was an attorney he sought out for help who pushed him to sue. Whatever it was, Achunn turned to private prosecution to seek damages from an alleged robber: Ackley Lyman.

If the robbery had been tried as a public offense, Achunn would have been barred from testifying, but the private prosecution meant that Achunn could provide a written complaint to initiate the lawsuit. And his account could be entered into the legal record. According to Achunn's complaint, Lyman had "with force and violence seized" him and "struck him, [with] a great many violent blows and strokes" until he relinquished $400 in gold coins. Lyman then tore off Achunn's clothes—breeches, shirt, coat, and all—and after donning them himself, "tied and firmly bound the said Plaintiff's hands and feet and legs with a rope" to a post in the "public highway." Achunn remained tied to the post, without any clothing, for ten hours. He claimed $2,000 in damages, pointing to the "assault, battery, tieing [sic], binding, fastening and imprisonment." According to the suit, "he was then and there not only greatly hurt, bruised and wounded, but also thereby and there greatly exposed and injured in his credit and circumstances."[21] Without ever testifying to the robbery, Achunn had found a way to describe his ordeal and have it heard by a court. Whether Achunn ultimately managed to recover any damages is unclear from the remaining records.

The Chinese may not have been able to testify against white parties, but they could still file suits against them and, on occasion, win. Lawsuits could result in compensation for a Chinese plaintiff, but they also reflected the outsider status of the Chinese. Rather than treat an attack on a Chinese migrant as a crime against the public at large, the judiciary recognized only a private injury.[22] While some Chinese litigants found ways to use the courts in the 1850s and 1860s, they made no progress in challenging the underlying racial restrictions on witness testimony.

But then the political and geopolitical tides turned in 1868. In the Burlingame Treaty with China, America took a friendlier posture, hoping to curry favor with the Qing court and gain access to valuable Chinese commodities. The treaty recognized "the inherent and inalienable right of man to change his home and allegiance, and also the mutual advantage of the free migration and emigration." In addition to validating Chinese migration, the treaty also sought to guarantee Chinese migrants the same privileges as citizens from "the most favored nation."[23]

When the United States and China negotiated a new treaty in 1880, the language became even bolder. The Angell Treaty stated, "If Chinese laborers, or Chinese of any other class, now whether permanently or temporarily residing in the territory of the United States, meet with ill treatment at the hands of any other persons, the Government of the United States will exert all its power to devise measures for their protection and to secure to them the same rights, privileges, immunities, and exemptions as may be enjoyed by the citizens or subjects of the most favored nation, and to which they are entitled by treaty."[24] The treaty acknowledged that Chinese migrants might face "ill-treatment" and promised the same protection granted to subjects of Western nations.

While diplomatic relations gave the Chinese some legal leverage, domestic political events offered another opening. Radical Republicans pushed forward a series of laws and constitutional amendments to protect the civil rights of formerly enslaved people, who faced violence, intimidation, and Black codes immediately following the Civil War. Some of these deliberate attempts to block discrimination based on "race" or "previous condition of servitude" encompassed the Chinese as well. The Civil Rights Act of 1866 focused on granting citizenship to Black people and granted all "citizens" the right "to full and equal benefit of all laws and proceedings for the security of person and property, as is enjoyed by white citizens." To dismantle discriminatory testimony laws in the South, the Civil Rights Act of 1866 also granted "citizens" of "every race and color" the right to "give evidence." The law signaled a dramatic change for Black citizens, but produced uncertainty for the Chinese. The vast majority of Chinese were not US citizens, having been barred from naturalization due to their race. In 1868, the Fourteenth Amendment went a step further, declaring that no state shall deny any "person"—rather than any *citizen*—"equal protection of the laws."[25]

Understanding the newfound power of the equal protection clause, Black litigants immediately sought out the courts to challenge a host of discriminatory state laws. They challenged a provision in the Indiana constitution that restricted Black settlement, a Louisiana law that barred Black people from incorporating churches, a Tennessee law that prohibited Black people from owning billiard saloons, and a Virginia law disallowing Black testimony in court. Black litigation successfully struck down many Black codes and antebellum laws in which states explicitly targeted them based on race.[26]

In California, however, the situation remained murky for the Chinese. The state legislature pointedly declined to ratify the Fourteenth Amendment and not all California courts recognized that equal protection applied to the Chinese. In *People v. Washington* (1869), the California Supreme Court drew distinctions between Black citizens and Chinese aliens. George Washington, who was described as a native-born "mulatto," had been convicted of robbing Ah Wang on the testimony of Chinese witnesses. In a 3–2 opinion, the appellant court overturned the conviction, explaining that Chinese aliens could not testify against Black citizens due to the Civil Rights Act.[27] The California Supreme Court went a step further in *People v. Brady* a year later, finding that even the Fourteenth Amendment did not override state law and grant the Chinese the right to testify.[28]

When Congress sought to strengthen enforcement of the Fourteenth Amendment in 1870, legislators openly discussed the plight of Chinese. Senator William Stewart of Nevada pushed Congress to recognize the rights of "persons" in order to "protect Chinese aliens or any other aliens whom we allow to come here" (although he stopped short of supporting their ability to naturalize). Congress agreed, crafting Section 16 in the 1870 Enforcement Act with Chinese in mind. It declared "that *all persons* within the jurisdiction of the United States" had the "full and equal benefit of all laws and proceedings for the security of person and property as is enjoyed by white citizens" and "no tax or charge shall be imposed or enforced by any State upon *any person immigrating* thereto from a foreign country which is not equally imposed and enforced upon every person immigrating to such State from any other foreign country." This was the clearest statement yet that "persons" were entitled to equal protection under American law, and that the state could not discriminate against some immigrants and not others.[29]

Only after Congress passed the Enforcement Act, granting "all persons" the right to "give evidence," did California lawmakers finally relent. The first identity-based law to fall was the Foreign Miner's Act. As we saw in Chapter 1, the Enforcement Act gave Ah Koo, a Chinese miner, the legal footing to sue his tax collector and render the law unenforceable. After this warning shot, the California legislature understood that racial testimony laws were equally vulnerable. Knowing that the Chinese litigants would likely win in court, California proactively removed all racial qualifications from the state's penal code in 1872.[30]

While formal racial bars on Chinese evidence ended in the early 1870s, the courts continued to question the competence of Chinese witness in the following decades. Lawmakers could no longer formally disallow Chinese witnesses, but in the course of a trial, attorneys and judges could still discount them in more subtle ways.

A burglary case from Colusa County, California, *People v. Ah Ching* (1881), provides a prime example. During jury selection, attorneys and the judge sparred over whether prejudice against Chinese testimony posed a legal problem. As the defense attorney tried to establish the anti-Chinese bias of a prospective juror, the district attorney and the judge argued that racial bias was not grounds for dismissal.

[Defense] Q: . . . other things being equal would you take the word of a Chinaman who is the defendant in this case as soon as you would that of a white man?
[Prospective Juror]: A. I do not hardly think I would.
[Prosecution]: I do not hardly think that is a fair question. We object to that as an improper question. We would be unable to get a jury here in a lifetime.
The Court: I do not think it is a proper question . . .
[Defense]: We challenge the juror.
[Prosecution]: The question asked you by counsel on the other side is to the effect if you have such bias or prejudice against a Chinaman or against the Chinese as a race as would preclude you from giving them a fair and impartial trial?
[Prospective Juror]: A. It does not. I have no prejudice against them as a race whatever.
[Prosecution]: We deny the challenge.
The Court: I think he is a competent juror.
[Defense]: But still you say you wouldn't give the same credit to Chinese testimony as you would to white testimony?
[Prospective Juror]: A. I would not. . . .
The Court: The mere fact that a juror says he would place more reliance generally on white testimony than he would on Chinese testimony is not good ground for challenge. The challenge is disallowed by the court.

Although the prospective juror in this case denied that he held prejudice "against the Chinese as a race," he was more than comfortable declaring his distrust of Chinese testimony. This may seem paradoxical to modern eyes, but for the juror, his distrust was not a matter of bias, it was a matter of common sense (based on the racial knowledge of the day). The jury found Ah Ching guilty as charged.[31]

During the late nineteenth century and early twentieth, Chinese continued to face stereotypes that they belonged to an inherently deceitful and inferior race, and unfortunately, the actions of tongs and huiguan further fueled these beliefs. As discussed in Chapter 2, Chinese litigants sometimes attempted to deploy vernacular law within the US justice system. In other words, some Chinese witnesses lied and did so in calculated ways. They were certainly not alone; witnesses of all backgrounds could speak untruths in court. But the fact that the anti-Chinese stereotype held a grain of truth, no matter how small, made it all the more powerful. Chinese false testimony was uncommon, often unsuccessful, and limited to cases against a Chinese defendant. But rumors of Chinese false testimony were widespread and consequential. Lawyers and judges could use the existence of a few nefarious Chinese men to justify the persecution of an entire race.[32]

The Fourteenth Amendment and the Enforcement Act may have ended the formal restriction of Chinese testimony, but courts still questioned the veracity of Chinese testimony for decades following. In civil and criminal cases, prosecutors routinely challenged Chinese competency, and even when these challenges were unsuccessful, they could evoke racial fears in the jury. Even after the demise of racial testimony laws, racial bias in the judicial system continued in other forms.[33]

LODGING HOUSES, QUEUES, AND BEHAVIOR-BASED LAWS

Still, racial reconstruction was changing the West and lawmakers knew it. Chinese litigants posed a newly potent threat to the legal order, given their right to testify in court and Congress's promises of equal protection. In this shifting legal landscape, lawmakers became wary of singling out the Chinese based on their racial identity.

In anticipation of legal challenges, some policymakers rewrote laws regulating Chinese residents. For example, back in 1860, California had passed a law that declared that "no Chinese or Mongolian shall be allowed to catch or take fish" without paying $4 a month for a license. But in 1880, California used a different approach, banning all "aliens incapable of becoming electors of this state" from "fishing, or taking any fish, lobsters, shrimps, or shellfish of any kind, for the purpose of selling or giving to another person to sell."[34] By shifting their focus from racial classification to alienage status, lawmakers hoped to skirt the doctrine of equal protection. In other domains, like prostitution laws, cities and states simply removed all racial language from statutes and relied on discretionary enforcement to target the Chinese. And lawmakers turned to a new tactic: they crafted behavior-based laws that regulated practices strongly associated with the Chinese.

The Chinese, in turn, fought to expose the discriminatory intent behind these seemingly race-neutral laws. After 1868 they rested many of their challenges on the equal protection clause of the Fourteenth Amendment and the most favored nation clause of the Burlingame Treaty. The ensuing struggle would define Chinese civil rights for decades to come.

Among the earliest points of conflict were the Lodging House Laws (which are also known as the Cubic Air Acts). The first of these laws came into being in 1870, when San Francisco sought to define Chinese living conditions as criminal, and Sacramento swiftly followed. Local officials argued that the tendency of Chinese men to live together in crowded boardinghouses violated both moral and health norms. Based on its police powers—that is, the state's right to enact laws to promote general welfare—San Francisco sought to regulate these threats by mandating that every dwelling include 500 cubic feet of air per resident. Three years later San Francisco doubled down, making any violations of the Lodging House Law a criminal offense. "Though general in its terms," the *San Francisco Chronicle* commented, "it is especially intended against the Chinese who live penned up in dingy and unhealthy rooms and heaped together worse than dumb animals."[35]

Within a week of San Francisco's amended law in 1873, the police had arrested and fined 134 Chinese offenders. Of these, 118 refused to pay a fine and opted to spend ten days in jail instead. It is likely that most of the arrested Chinese could have afforded the modest fine, but by refusing, they filled city jails beyond their capacity and drained city coffers. "There was a good deel [sic] of difficulty in enforcing this ordinance, on account of the number of Chinese who violated it, and their omission to pay the fines imposed," the *San Francisco Bulletin* reported. "They were arrested in great numbers and packed in cells where they had not 100 cubic feet of air to the person." The paper suspected an organized resistance was under way, explaining that "the commandments of the leading men in the Chinese quarter . . . declared, in substance, that they would make the city sick of prosecuting and maintaining Chinamen in prison."[36]

Despite these hiccups in enforcement, other communities began to copy San Francisco's Lodging House Law, including Portland, Oregon, where the law was also only enforced against Chinese residents. In 1876, California instituted a statewide policy requiring 500 cubic feet of air per resident and imposing a $10 to $50 fine or imprisonment for violations.³⁷

In response to the statewide law, Chinese in San Francisco redoubled their efforts to render the act unenforceable. On April 29, 1876, the Chinese-language newspaper *The Oriental (Tang Fan Gongbao,* 唐番公報) urged the people of Chinatown to ignore the law, arguing that city prisons could not handle the large volume of people violating the ordinance. The paper also reported that several men arrested in violation of the law had started passing out fliers arguing that the community should hire a lawyer. A month later, *The Oriental* reported that the campaign had been successful in that the Chinese Six Companies had hired a lawyer to challenge the lodging house law. No trace of this challenge, if it occurred, survives in the legal record.³⁸

Overcrowding the city jail continued to prove an effective form of resistance. At least until Frederick A. Gibbs, San Francisco supervisor and chairman of the hospital committee, devised a solution. "After coming into the board of supervisors, I found our jails were very crowded indeed. I also found that our ordinances were not effective. They were not enforced," he explained to a congressional committee. Gibbs went to the chief of police and the police in Chinatown demanding to know why the department was lackadaisical in its enforcement. "They told me it would be impossible to enforce [the law]; that they would have a thousand Chinamen in the jails if they did; that our jails were overcrowded, and that there was a large number of Chinamen."

After visiting the jails to see for himself, Gibbs found a clever and cruel solution. He drew up a new ordinance providing "for the cutting of the hair on male prisoners' heads to a uniform length," including long braids traditionally worn by Chinese men. Standing before a congressional committee, Gibbs insisted that the behavior-based law was race neutral: "I made it general, applying both to whites and to the Chinese . . ." But he also admitted that the law "had the desired effect." Once Chinese men faced the threat of a haircut against their will, the overcrowding in jail subsided. Gibbs was too proud to be the "author of this ordinance to cut off the tails of the Chinamen" to completely deny its racial intent.³⁹

Now the Chinese faced a pair of seemingly race-neutral sanitary laws: one that targeted overcrowded living conditions and the other

"Out of the frying pan into the fire" (1878) appeared on the cover of *The San Francisco Illustrated Wasp*. It depicts a policeman enforcing the Cubic Air Law (i.e., the Lodging House Law) by grabbing Chinese men out of a boarding house and tossing them into an overcrowded jail. (*The Wasp*, vol. 2, no. 83. Reproduction courtesy of The Bancroft Library, University of California, Berkeley)

that targeted imprisoned men with long hair. Both had discriminatory effect. Under oath, officer James R. Rogers testified about the mass arrests his department had conducted in Chinatown. Reluctantly, he admitted that he did not know the exact size of the rooms the arrestees had occupied in Chinatown or the amount of cubic air they had access to in the overcrowded jail. Asked directly if the city arrested anyone who was not Chinese under the Lodging House Ordinance, Rodgers stated, "I do not know of an instance where it has been required to arrest a white man."[40]

The racial motivations behind cutting male prisoners' hair were similarly clear. The press referred to the law as "the Queue Ordinance" or "the Pigtail Order." It was premised on the idea that the Chinese would do anything to preserve their traditional hairstyle, which was mandated by the Qing Court as a sign of fealty. The results bore out this assumption. During the six months the 1876 law was in effect, 1,012 Chinese were arrested on misdemeanors and paid $9,020 into the city treasury in fines. Only 110 served five days each in jail and lost their queues.[41]

Chinese community leaders reportedly raised $5,000 to challenge the Lodging House Law with a test case. After Chin Ah Win was arrested on February 26, 1878, his lawyer filed a writ of habeas corpus on his behalf in the US circuit court in San Francisco, protesting his unlawful imprisonment by the city. Through his lawyers, Chin complained that "no persons, except Subjects of China, ever have been arrested under this ordinance, though thousands of persons, including citizens of the United States and aliens, daily violate said act." By targeting the Chinese, Chin maintained, the law violated the Enforcement Act and the terms of the Burlingame Treaty. In other words, it denied him equal protection, which he was due based on American law, the Constitution, and diplomatic agreements. The court did not accept his argument, however. The US circuit court found the law to be constitutional, denying that there was sufficient evidence it was discriminatory, and describing it as a neutral public health regulation.[42]

Although Chin failed in his attempt to strike down the Lodging House Law, his case did establish the limits of enforcement. The court ruled that the police could only act on probable cause and did not have the right to raid lodging houses at random. Furthermore, the court openly questioned the related Queue Ordinance. Judge Hoffman stated, "The law requiring jailors to cut off queues, which is equivalent to a mutilation of Chinamen, is undoubtedly discriminatory in its action . . . and if it should come up for consideration, I should say it is unconstitutional."[43]

The Chinese were swift to take up this invitation. Ho Ah Kow, who was arrested, tried, and convicted on April 26, 1878, for violating the Lodging House Law, was sentenced to a $10 fine or five days in jail, and chose the latter. According to his complaint, filed with the US circuit court in San Francisco, on the first day of his imprisonment the sheriff of San Francisco County "wantonly, maliciously and without authority and in violation of the personal rights of the plaintiff cut the plaintiff's hair." The suit explained that "the deprivation of the queue is a mark of disgrace among the Chinese" and "is attended by suffering and misfortune after death."

Ho Ah Kow claimed damages of $10,000 for the mutilation that had "caused great mental anguish and solicitude" and made him "disgraced in his own eyes and in the eyes of his friends and relatives, and ostracized from the association of respectable members of his countrymen."[44] His lawyers argued that the sanitary ordinance was unconstitutional, because it was in excess of the authority of the Board of Supervisors (who could not prescribe additional punishments for the violation of a state law) and it violated the equal protection clause of the Fourteenth Amendment (by targeting Chinese men). Within days, Ho Ah Kow's complaint was followed by three more identical suits, suggesting a coordinated, community-backed effort.

While working on their challenge in the courts, Chinese community leaders protested through diplomatic channels as well. Yung Wing, an envoy of the Chinese emperor, also wrote to the US secretary of state to protest "the humiliation of Chinese people in San Francisco." "Local officials in California established harsh laws," Yung protested, "such as 'the law of cubic meter air' and 'the law of cutting the pigtail' to exclude all Chinese people. How our innocent people are to suffer from this cruelty." Yung complained that these laws amounted to the abrogation of the Burlingame Treaty. "The sixth term of the treaty says that Chinese people who go to or travel across the U.S. and who settle in the U.S. should be treated according to the most-favored-nation treatment, and it is applicable to all [Chinese people]. According to this treaty, the U.S. cannot discriminate [against] our Chinese people."[45]

In his opinion in *Ho Ah Kow v. Nunan* (1878), Judge Stephen Field (a US Supreme Court justice riding circuit in San Francisco) declared queue-cutting to be an example of "cruel and unusual punishment" that violated the equal protection clause, despite the law's race-neutral language. "The reason advanced for its adoption, and now urged for its continuance is, that only the dread of the loss of his queue will induce a Chinaman to pay his fine," Field explained. "That is to say, in order to enforce the payment of a fine imposed upon him it is necessary that torture should be superadded to imprisonment." Field continued, "Probably the bastinado, or the knout, or the thumbscrew, or the rack, would accomplish the same end; and no doubt the Chinaman would prefer either of these modes of torture to that which entails upon him disgrace among his countrymen and carries with it the constant dread of misfortune and suffering after death." Had the law been a true sanitary measure, the court continued, "it would have been limited to such cases and made applicable to females as well as to males."

It was common knowledge, the court recognized, that the so-called Queue Ordinance targeted Chinese. Justice Field argued that the court "cannot shut our eyes" to this common knowledge. Therefore, the court could look beyond the letter of the law to consider its intent and enforcement when determining whether a law discriminated against a particular sector of society. It did not matter that there was "hostility" against Chinese in California, Justice Field asserted, nor that fear of these "vast hordes" was, in his opinion, warranted. The court affirmed that "equality of protection" was "assured to every one whilst within the United States, from whatever country he may have come, or of whatever race or color he may be." Police power gave California the right to regulate health and safety, but it did not give the state the right to discriminate against the Chinese. With his opinion, Justice Field was the first judge to clearly apply equal protection to the Chinese.[46]

On paper, Chinese litigants lost their fight against the Lodging House Law and won their fight against the Queue Ordinance.[47] Neither the loss, nor the win, was complete, however. While lodging house (cubic air) laws proliferated across the US West, police departments only intermittently enforced them due to the crowding of jails. And while the Queue Ordinance in San Francisco no longer applied, state and federal prisons in the United States continued to "torture" the Chinese by forcibly cutting their hair.

The decisions in *Ho Ah Kow v. Nunan* and *In re: Ah Wing* foreshadowed many such wins and losses to come. For example, when local governments sought to indirectly regulate Chinese laundries, they were energetically opposed by Chinese litigants. In 1873 and again in 1876, the San Francisco Board of Supervisors passed laundry ordinances requiring all laundrymen to pay a license fee of $4 for those who owned a horse and $15 for those who did not. Although the supervisors openly discussed their desire to target Chinese laundrymen (who were less likely to own a horse) these behavior-based laws were racially neutral on their face. San Francisco switched tactics in 1880, passing a Laundry Ordinance that made it illegal to run a laundry in a wooden building without a license (since Chinese were less likely to be able to afford a brick building). The city went further in 1882, amending the law to require that laundries in wooden buildings have both a permit and endorsement by a dozen citizens who lived on the same block. The Chinese had started opening laundries in white neighborhoods to save on transportation time, and this ordinance made the Chinese subject to the prejudices of their white neighbors. Similar laundry ordinances were passed in other cities and towns, including Sacramento, Stockton, Alameda, Oakland, Modesto, Chico, Santa Rosa, and Napa in California, and Portland and Salem in Oregon.[48]

Supposedly race-neutral laundry laws faced repeated challenges from Chinese laundrymen. Best known is the US Supreme Court case *Yick Wo v. Hopkins* (1886), in which Justice Field's assertion of the Equal Protection Doctrine, which he first articulated in *Ho Ah Kow*, came into greater clarity. Yick Wo worked in the laundry business in California for twenty-two years before he was arrested in 1885 for operating without a license. At the time, the 1885 San Francisco laundry ordinance required that all operators in wooden buildings pay a fee and obtain permission from the Board of Supervisors before being granted a license. More than 200 Chinese laundrymen had petitioned for a license, but none had secured one. The complaint further alleged that 150 Chinese laundrymen had been arrested for operating without a license, while eighty white proprietors who also lacked licenses operated without any arrests.

Soon after his arrest, Yick Wo was found guilty of a misdemeanor and fined $10. When he refused to pay, he was jailed for ten days in lieu of payment. He petitioned the California Supreme Court for a writ of habeas corpus, and when denied, appealed to the federal courts, naming Sheriff Hopkins in his suit. The city of San Francisco claimed that the ordinance was an exercise of police power designed to protect the health and safety of its citizens.

In a unanimous opinion, the US Supreme Court disagreed. It declared that the law had violated Yick Wo's rights on multiple grounds: his "rights, privileges, immunities" as a subject of a "most favored nation," his right to equal protection as a "person" under the Fourteenth Amendment, and his right to "equal benefit of all laws ... as is enjoyed by white citizens" guaranteed by the Enforcement Act. The justices found that "no reason" existed to deny the petitioner a license, "except hostility to the race and nationality" to which he belonged.[49] The Supreme Court went a step further. It asserted that even though the law was race-neutral on its face, it was unconstitutional because it had been applied in a discriminatory manner.[50]

The win heralded future gains. Based on the precedent set by *Ho Ah Kow v. Nunan* and *Yick Wo v. Hopkins,* the courts struck down a series of anti-Chinese laws in the following decades. Some laws were discriminatory on their face, others primarily in application. For example, the 1879 California Constitution declared, "No corporation ... shall ... employ in any capacity, any Chinese or Mongolian." The California legislature wrote the same provision into the penal code in 1880,[51] but *In re Tiburcio Parrott* (1880) disallowed such racial hiring bars. The Idaho Supreme Court, in *Ex parte Case* (1911),[52] struck down a similar but race neutral law that barred corporations from hiring "any alien who has neither become naturalized or declared his written intention to become a citizen."

Subsequent rulings helped to dismantle other discriminatory laundry laws. *In re Sam Kee* (1887)[53] ruled against an ordinance prohibiting laundries in certain areas of Napa, California, and *Ex parte Sing Lee* (1892)[54] struck down a law that required neighbors to approve any laundries on their block in Chico, California. Following the precedent laid by *Yick Wo,* courts looked skeptically on laws that targeted Chinese by name, or were solely enforced against Chinese, or hindered the ability of the Chinese to carry on a legitimate business.

But the Chinese had a limited ability to contest behavior-based laws, and Chin Ah Win's failed challenge of the Lodging House Law portended more losses ahead. The courts continued to give states and municipalities wide latitude in matters of public health and safety. As a result, lodging house laws spread across California and Oregon. So too did city ordinances that prohibited carrying baskets on shoulders (in the Chinese style) and the exhumation of bones (so they could be sent back to China). And even after the *Yick Wo* decision, cities passed laundry laws regulating work hours (because Chinese often worked at night), requiring health certificates (which Chinese struggled to obtain), and banning laundries from certain sectors of town (to encourage segregation). Although these laws indirectly targeted Chinese, the courts ruled that they were within the state's police power to regulate health, safety, and good order.[55]

Police powers also gave states and cities the right to regulate vice. Although Chinese plaintiffs challenged laws aimed at regulating gambling and recreational opium—alleging that they were discriminatory in their application—these laws withstood judicial scrutiny. Laws regulating prostitution and vagrancy, which also indirectly targeted the Chinese community, operated without legal challenge.[56]

Even some identity-based laws survived racial reconstruction and Chinese litigation. In the name of health and safety, western states barred Chinese from white schools (as we will see in Chapter 5) and prohibited Chinese from marrying white people (as we will see in Chapter 6).[57] The courts allowed such legislation to stand, and in the 1890s, as the number of Japanese migrants in the Pacific West grew, these race laws targeted them as well.

The courts also saw no problems with barring Chinese from public work. By long-standing tradition, cities had only allowed citizens in public service positions (including mayor, judge, and policeman), but in the 1870s cities extended this prohibition to other government work and government contracts. In 1878, for example, Los Angeles prohibited the city from entering into any contract for public works unless the contract specified that "Chinese labor shall not be employed."[58] When California delegates wrote a new constitution in 1879, they included a ban on Chinese labor on public works "except in punishment for crime." These identity-based statutes specifically named the Chinese race, but their justification lay in Chinese alienage. These provisions withstood legal challenges and continued to spread.[59]

California cities such as Pasadena, Eureka, and Sacramento—as well as Portland, Oregon; Tacoma and Olympia, Washington; and even Newark, Ohio—barred Chinese from public employment. Nine states joined in. In 1885, Nevada declared that "no Chinaman or Mongolian shall be employed, directly or indirectly, in any capacity, on any public works, or in or about any buildings or institutions, or grounds, under the control of this state." Montana and Oregon were similarly direct. Other states were more circumspect. Idaho banned persons "not eligible" to become citizens from being "employed upon or in connection with any state, county or municipal works or employment." By broadly targeting non-naturalized aliens, these states could also regulate Japanese residents, and in the twentieth century, Koreans and South Asians as well.[60]

During racial reconstruction, Chinese migrants attacked racial laws in the American West, using the power of lawsuits, diplomacy, and civil disobedience to pursue the promise of equal protection. In response, western courts struck down some discriminatory laws and western policymakers amended or repealed others. But as racial laws fell, new more subtle laws sprang up to replace them.

Local and state governments found many ways to circumvent equal protection. The courts gave them the green light on many behavior-based and general-outcast laws, including those that regulated lodging houses, laundries, schools, marriages, opium, gambling, peddling, and prostitution. The courts disallowed limits on corporate employment, but permitted the prohibition of Chinese labor from public works. And while the courts frowned upon identity-based laws targeting the Chinese race, increasingly they gave a nod to laws that targeted "aliens" or privileged citizens.

NATURALIZATION, ENFRANCHISEMENT, AND ALIENAGE

This posed a problem for the Chinese, because they found their "alien" status particularly difficult to shed. When they first arrived in the United States in the mid-nineteenth century, Chinese migrants found themselves caught in a web of naturalization laws that was originally spun to constrain Black people. The US Constitution, as enacted in 1788, did not specify who would be granted the privileges and duties of citizenship, but the southern states sought to ensure that Black people would not number among them. The Virginia Act of 1779, for example, allowed citizenship for white persons born in Virginia or residing in the state for two years. South Carolina and Georgia passed similar laws granting citizenship and civil rights to resident "free white persons." The southern states feared that Black citizenship could undermine the slave system, but even those in the northern states who opposed slavery questioned the wisdom of granting Black people full membership within the nation. When imagining the future of American democracy, few could conceive of a multiracial citizenry.[61]

State-based racial restrictions on naturalization soon gave way to federal law. To protect the republic from the threat of Black citizenship, Congress passed the Naturalization Act of 1790, which permitted only "free white persons" to become naturalized citizens. Fears of an internal racial threat drove the passage of the law, but with the arrival of tens of thousands of Chinese in the 1850s, it began to have broad consequences for immigrants as well. In effect, the racial prerequisite for naturalization cleaved the stream of arrivals in the United States into two: on one side were the "free white persons" who were imagined to be, in scholar Hiroshi Motomura's words, "Americans in waiting," and on the other were the Chinese who were treated as "forever foreign."[62]

Even as political turmoil in the mid-nineteenth century brought changes to Mexican American, African American, and Native American citizenship, these transformations bypassed the Chinese. At the end of the US-Mexico War, the Treaty of Guadalupe Hidalgo (1848) granted citizenship to former Mexican nationals living within territory ceded to the United States. A US District Court ruling, *In Re Rodriguez* (1898), eventually confirmed Mexican immigrants' eligibility for naturalization. For African Americans, Congress first recognized their right to birthright citizenship with the Civil Rights Act (1866) and the Fourteenth Amendment (1868), and went a step further with the Naturalization Act of 1870, which extended the privilege of naturalization to "aliens of African nativity and persons of African descent." For most Native people, formal citizenship would take even longer, since they were sidelined by the Reconstruction amendments as persons not "under the jurisdiction of" the United States. Eventually, policies designed to dispossess Native people of their land and deny tribal sovereignty, including the Dawes Act (1887) and the Indian Citizenship Act (1924), granted US citizenship in piecemeal fashion. It is important to note, however, that these formal acts of inclusion in the American citizenry for Mexican, Black, and Native Americans were tempered, and at times nearly undone, by dramatic acts of rejection. Discriminatory laws, social practice, and racial violence meant that none of these groups could exercise the same rights as white male citizens.[63]

Throughout this legal transformation of the American citizenry, Chinese immigrants remained "aliens ineligible to citizenship," a status that Congress took pains to reinforce. When the United States and China negotiated the Burlingame Treaty (1868) in hopes of advancing transpacific trade, western senators insisted that the treaty include an amended section clarifying that the agreement did not confer US citizenship to the Chinese.

And when Radical Republicans proposed striking the word "white" from naturalization law, they were met by resistance from western senators. The anti-Chinese faction insisted that the Chinese were racially incapable of assimilation, and if Congress provided them a pathway to citizenship, the result would be disastrous: the Chinese would contaminate the nation, racial violence would roil the US West, and (perhaps most pressingly) Republicans would lose congressional seats. In the end, Congress extended naturalization to people of African ancestry in 1870, but pointedly failed to include those of Chinese ancestry. As if the status of Chinese aliens was not already clear, Congress reaffirmed its position with the Chinese Restriction Act (1882), which included a clause barring naturalization.[64]

A small but growing number of Chinese were born in America, however. The Fourteenth Amendment (1868) granted citizenship to all persons born in the United States and "subject to the jurisdiction thereof." Congress had intended birthright citizenship to include people of Chinese ancestry, but it would take thirty years before the Supreme Court affirmed this right. In the intervening decades, many anti-Chinese westerners denied the possibility of Chinese American citizenship, and Chinese Americans occupied a nebulous legal status.

When the question finally came before the US Supreme Court, the solicitor general opposed the idea of Chinese naturalization. *U.S. v. Wong Kim Ark* (1898) involved an American-born Chinese who sought to reenter the United States after a trip to China. Despite the solicitor general's arguments to the contrary, the Supreme Court found that Chinese born within the territory of the United States were citizens under the Fourteenth Amendment, even if their parents were of "Chinese descent" and "subjects of the emperor of China." The ruling confirmed that Chinese were entitled to citizenship through jus soli or "right of the soil." The landmark case confirmed America's commitment to birthright citizenship.[65]

But the vast majority of Chinese in America were foreign born. These migrants, who were racially prohibited from naturalization, were also presumably debarred from the electorate, but the Pacific states and territories did not want to leave open the possibility that they could gain access to the ballot. Some western states, after all, had opened the franchise to immigrants who had merely declared their intent to naturalize. California's 1849 Constitution limited the vote to "white male citizens of the United States" and any "white male citizen of Mexico, who shall have elected to become a citizen of the United States." In 1854, Washington Territory granted the vote to "white male inhabitants" who were "citizens of the United States, or shall have declared, on oath, their intentions to become such." Oregon's 1858 Constitution granted the vote to "every white male citizen" and "every white male of foreign birth" as long as they had lived in the state for six months. Oregon also declared that "no negro, Chinaman, or mulatto shall have the right of suffrage." Following the Fifteenth Amendment, California emphasized nativity rather than race. The 1879 California Constitution declared that "no native of China . . . shall ever exercise the privileges of an elector."[66] It was a seemingly unnecessary declaration, given that, according to federal law, no "native of China" had a path to US citizenship.[67]

Although the racial bars to naturalization appeared firm, Chinese migrants went in search of loopholes and found some. In 1874 the *Chicago Daily Tribune* ran a headline that asked, "Shall Chinamen Vote?" The newspaper reported that Congress had made an error when codifying the naturalization laws, and the revised statutes had inadvertently omitted the words "being a free white person" from US naturalization laws. (Such a large clerical error raises questions, perhaps unanswerable ones, as to whether Radical Republicans intentionally stripped racial language from the law.) Whatever caused the omission, the result had profound implications. "The law," the *Tribune* noted, "as now standing, breaks down all barriers of race or descent which California has hitherto successfully opposed."⁶⁸

Sensing an opportunity, three Chinese men in San Francisco filed declarations of their intention to become citizens, or "first papers" as they were known at the time. At least two of them were prominent men in the Chinese community: Hong Chung, an officer in the Sam Yup Company, a huiguan of considerable influence, and Chock Wong, the publisher of *The Oriental,* a Chinese-language newspaper. "I like to be citizen," Chock Wong explained later before a state commission. "American man makes no good laws for Chinaman. We make good laws for Chinaman citizens." But Congress, alerted to the mistake, amended the revised statutes in 1875, reinserting the racial prerequisites for naturalization before the three men could complete the naturalization process.⁶⁹

Despite clarification of the law, on April 22, 1878, three more Chinese men declared their intention to be naturalized in the US circuit court in San Francisco. Ah Yup, Li Huang, and Leong Lan were accompanied by two lawyers hired by the Chinese Six Companies. The petitioners argued that the term "white persons" was vague, and within the category "could be found individuals of every hue from the lightest blonde to the most swarthy brunette, some in fact demonstrably darker than the Chinese." In this way, the petitioners attempted to claim whiteness and its privileges. One of the lawyers, Fredrick A. Bee, explained the stakes of the petitions to the press. Bee predicted that there were 3,000 "of the best class of Chinamen" who wished to become citizens. "They have been educated in the English language; have acquired real estate and established themselves in business here," he explained. "The ties which bind them to the country are too strong for them to give up; they wish to live and die here, and, as a natural consequence, to become citizens of the country which they have adopted as their own."⁷⁰

But the court dismissed Chinese claims to whiteness and citizenship in *In Re Ah Yup* (1878). Judge Lorenzo Sawyer rejected the naturalization petitions, noting that "neither in popular language, in literature, nor in scientific nomenclature, do we ordinarily, if ever, find the words 'white person' used in a sense so comprehensive as to include an individual of the Mongolian race," an argument that would later be repeated by the US Supreme Court to deny naturalized citizenship to Japanese and South Asians. Moreover, Judge Sawyer noted that legislative intent in the matter was indisputable. Reviewing the congressional debates over the 1870 Naturalization Act, he found that the Senate retained the word "white" in the law "for the sole purpose of excluding the Chinese from the right of naturalization." In his opinion, Sawyer made it clear that all Chinese immigrants were barred from naturalization based on their race.[71] He also asserted the case was "the first application made by a native Chinaman for naturalization."[72]

Sawyer's last point was patently untrue.[73] Naturalization records reveal that Chinese men naturalized during the nineteenth century in at least nineteen states: Colorado, Connecticut, Illinois, Iowa, Kansas, Louisiana, Maine, Massachusetts, Missouri, Montana, New Jersey, New York, North Carolina, North Dakota, Ohio, Pennsylvania, South Carolina, Texas, and Vermont. Large East Coast cities, like Boston and New York, received the most applications and approved them in significant numbers. There are no indications that courts in the Pacific West permitted Chinese naturalization, but, due to internal migration, census takers recorded naturalized Chinese across the nation.

Between 1900 (when the US census began recording naturalization) and 1940 (the last census before the elimination of the racial prerequisite), naturalized Chinese lived in all forty-eight states as well as the territories of Hawaii and Alaska.[74] In 1900, census takers enumerated 8,415 naturalized Chinese Americans, or 6.7 percent of Chinese-descended people in the United States.[75] Some of these China-born citizens were prominent men with powerful connections, but others were working-class people who encountered friendly local courthouses. When faced with disobedient or ignorant local judges, the federal government lacked the capacity to enforce the racial restriction of naturalization laws.[76]

Harry Lum, for example, arrived in the United States in 1876 at the age of twenty-two. He worked as a miner in Humboldt, California, for several years before moving to Newton, Kansas. There, he married twenty-two-year-old Beckie Swadler, "a lady of color" according to the local paper, and in 1882 opened a "Chinese laundry," which he advertised in the paper three times a week.[77] When Lum declared his intent to seek naturalization and took first papers in

Harvey, Kansas, on February 12, 1889, this was also considered newsworthy. The *Newton Daily Republican* reported, "Our good laundry man on West Fifth street, who was born and reared in the Celestial Empire . . . renounced his allegiance to the Chinese Empire and was by Judge Honk invested with the right of American citizenship." The editor did not see anything amiss with this arrangement, for, he noted, "Lum has always born[e] a good reputation and will not abuse the privilege this day conferred upon him."[78]

When the census taker came around in 1910, he recorded the seemingly contradictory facts of Lum's life: his race was "Chinese," he was born in China, and he was a naturalized US citizen. It appears likely that Lum voted and that he did so even before he began his journey toward naturalization. First registering to vote in 1883, Lum appeared on the rolls of registered voters in Harvey County for the following eighteen years and submitted a change of address six times.[79]

Lum was naturalized after *In Re Ah Yup* (1878) had determined that Chinese were ineligible and the Chinese Restriction Act (1882) had expressly prohibited Chinese naturalization. And he was just one of thousands of naturalized Chinese. How was this possible? Before the naturalization process was federalized in 1906, immigrants could seek citizenship in "any court of record." This meant that naturalization was exercised by more than 5,000 courts, many of which were not part of the federal judiciary.[80] No doubt judges and county clerks did not all agree on who qualified as a "white person" of "good moral character," and no doubt they did not all have the same depth of knowledge in the relevant federal statutes and case law.[81]

Geography also played an important role in determining the possibility of naturalization for the Chinese. In the West, where Chinese were more numerous, state laws and court rulings repeatedly defined the Chinese as nonwhite. In the East, South, and Midwest, where the Chinese were few and scattered, their racial status was never as pressing or obvious. When presented with an assimilated Chinese man, some judges in these regions simply treated him as they would a white man. They signed the paperwork and that was that.

The permissive administration of naturalization law at some local courts by no means guaranteed citizenship as a permanent privilege for the Chinese. Chinese who had been naturalized in the eastern states faced additional scrutiny if they traveled to the West Coast and attempted to exercise their rights of citizenship. For instance, Hong Yen Chang decided to move to California in 1890, after having attended Philips Academy in Andover, Massachusetts, earning an undergraduate degree at Yale, completing a law degree at Columbia, and naturalizing in New York City in 1887. In California, he applied for admittance to the bar. At the time, California law allowed only citizens or intending citizens to practice law. In response to his application, the California Supreme Court not only denied his admission to the bar but also stripped him of citizenship.[82]

Kwang Lee, a veteran of the Union Navy in the Civil War, faced similar treatment when attempting to vote in San Francisco in 1909. Lee had been naturalized in St. Louis, Missouri, in 1874, had held citizenship papers for thirty-five years, and qualified for a war pension, but when he attempted to register in San Francisco, "his appearance denoted his race too plainly to be mistaken and when questioned he admitted he was born in China."[83] His appearance also bore evidence of his Civil War service, for he bore "the scars of wounds received while fighting on a Mississippi gunboat," but these marks of Americanization held little meaning (at least in California). The election officers brought in immigration authorities who promptly canceled his naturalization certificate.

During Reconstruction and the half-century that followed, Chinese litigants made little headway against racial prerequisites for naturalization. In fact, the impact of discriminatory naturalization laws would only widen with the arrival of Japanese, Korean, and South Asian immigrants in the 1890s. For all these groups, restrictions on naturalization meant the inability to vote, serve on a jury, obtain a law license, or engage in many forms of public work.[84] And as other historians have noted, permanent alien status also made Asians uniquely vulnerable to deportation.[85]

Thanks to local and state laws, alienage came with other legal disabilities that went beyond matters of governance or immigration. Western states limited the ability of aliens (who had not declared their intent to naturalize) to own land, hunt or fish, access public records, and become public school teachers. When researchers surveyed the "legal and economic status" of "Orientals" in the 1920s, they found that 50 percent of professional licenses required applicants to be citizens or declarants.[86] Local alienage laws affected all immigrants, but only those who were ineligible to citizenship found them impossible to avoid.

※ ※ ※

Neither the Burlingame Treaty nor the Fourteenth Amendment placed the Chinese on equal footing with white Americans. But together they brought racial reconstruction to the West and gave Chinese the legal foothold to challenge the prevailing racial regime. In the 1870s and 1880s, Chinese litigants made bold strides against identity-based laws, especially those based on race. At the same time, Chinese sought relief through diplomatic channels and they tested the limits of state power through everyday acts of resistance. They filled jails in protest, filed citizenship papers in one county and then another, lined up for the polls despite harassment, and continued to open laundries even as legal obstacles multiplied. They attempted to shift the racial etiquette. They acted as rights-bearing subjects, willing it to be so.[87]

In response, western lawmakers adapted. Local and state governments reacted to Chinese resistance by enacting new racial regulations to ensure that Chinese inclusion would remain conditional. They found new ways to constrain Chinese economic and political power, threaten Chinese life and culture, and separate Chinese communities from white ones. They came to rely on behavior-based and general-outcast laws that regulated Chinese behavior in the name of "health and safety." And lawmakers continued to pass identity-based laws, although they now favored ones based on alien status. Alienage seemed a surefire way to target the Chinese race indirectly, since racial limits on naturalization held firm.

The more the Chinese claimed rights, the more threatening they became. While cities and townships busied themselves passing local ordinances designed to bypass equal protection and regulate Chinese, California state lawmakers also turned to more extreme solutions. They proposed to bar the entry of Chinese "aliens" in the name of health and safety. To do so, they targeted "coolies," "criminals," and in particular, "Chinawomen."

{4}

The "CHINAWOMAN"

and the SEARCH for RUNAWAYS

I N MAY 1884, YUN GEE arrived at a notorious house of prostitution in Los Angeles. This was unexpected. Although she knew that her mother had "sold" her to the merchant Sing Kee for $300, Yun Gee believed she had been purchased as his wife. "He said that he brought [me] here for marrying [me]," she later explained to the court with the help of a translator. "But instead he forced me to be a whore." She insisted, however, that he had not been successful in his effort to prostitute her. "I would not do it so he beat me."[1]

Unwilling to engage in sex work and fearing Sing Kee's reprisal, Yun Gee decided to run away. Within weeks she devised an elaborate escape: she found a willing suitor, hired a policeman for protection, and arranged a horse-drawn buggy ride to the nearest train station. At first everything went according to plan. She boarded a train headed toward San Francisco, watching as Los Angeles disappeared into the distance.

Within hours of Yun Gee's disappearance, however, Sing Kee realized she had gone. Rather than try to track her down on his own, he sought help from the American authorities. He concocted a successful legal ruse to recapture her, which involved going to court, filing a complaint, and using the police to drag her back to Los Angeles.

Although Yung Gee and Sing Kee's conflict began as a physical struggle, it became a legal battle. When Sing Kee failed to beat her into submission, he sought out the courts in an attempt to limit her mobility and enforce his presumed ownership of her body.[2]

Sing Kee did not use the law as American policymakers had intended. At the local level, Los Angeles city officials had outlawed prostitution, ordered the police to raid Chinese brothels, and sought to criminalize both sex traffickers and workers. At the state and federal level, policymakers had recently focused on barring "lewd" Chinese women from entering the country in the first place. These laws made women like Yun Gee subject to arrest, incarceration, detention, and deportation.

For Chinese women, then, Chinese traffickers and American lawmakers represented sources of both constraint and confinement. Traffickers and lawmakers had vastly different objectives and motivations, but they shared a desire to control the lives of Chinese women and restrain their mobility. For Yun Gee, both stood in her way.

✻ ✻ ✻

In the mid-nineteenth-century American West, sexual commerce was common in the Chinese community. Historians believe that, for a time in the 1870s, most Chinese women in the United States worked in the sex trade.[3] This meant that even those Chinese women not engaged in sex work had to contend with the stigma and dangers of trafficking. All at once, Chinese women found themselves restricted by racial stereotypes that assumed their sexual degeneracy, by a political economy that allowed them few other forms of labor, and by a trafficking network that made their bodies into a precious commodity.

They also had to contend with American law. Western lawmakers made Chinese women a constant target of regulation. In the 1860s, California passed identity-based laws that outlawed Chinese prostitution by name. With the arrival of racial reconstruction, state officials had to find new, more subtle ways to enforce the racial regime and skirt promises of equal protection. When it came to prostitution, they turned to two primary strategies: restricting the immigration of Chinese women and selectively enforcing race-neutral prostitution laws. In so doing, they created a blueprint for how to maintain the racial regime in the wake of racial reconstruction.

Historians have primarily viewed the lives of Chinese women from a great distance, relying on the observations of state officials and Protestant missionaries.[4] More often than not, these records anonymized and racialized their subjects, using the label "Chinawoman," the moniker "Mary Chinaman," and, in later decades, the epithet "Chinese slave girl."[5] As difficult as it is piece together the lives of Chinese men in the nineteenth century, historians have found women's experiences even more elusive. In a field bereft of sources, county court records, especially those containing Chinese female testimony, offer a revealing, new glimpse into their lives.

It is clear that for Chinese women constraints came from all directions. Immigration officials, law enforcement, missionaries, husbands, and traffickers all sought to dictate a Chinese woman's movements in order to control access to her body. These diverse projects shared the unspoken assumption that Chinese women were objects—of exploitation, regulation, or potential salvation—and as objects they could be controlled. Whether one wanted to confine a Chinese woman, or to import, trade, deport, cloister, or rescue her, the ability to control her rested on the capacity to regulate her movements. In retrospect, it may be impossible to perceive all terms that governed women's lives, but it is possible to see that confinement and forced movement stood high among them.

In response, Chinese women ran away. They ran from immigration control and policing, and they ran from traffickers, husbands, and missionaries. Fugitive mobility became a central way that Chinese women negotiated the terms of their inclusion in the American West.

Therefore, we can learn a lot by considering Yun Gee's fugitive mobility. Her story raises important questions: What conditions made her want to escape? How did she manage to flee? And where did she seek refuge? For some runaways, like Yun Gee, court cases offered a rare opportunity for the runaways to answer these questions themselves and publicly bear witness to their experiences.[6] The stories they tell are powerful. Despite a legal code and racial etiquette designed to confine her, Yun Gee found a means of escape. And as she ran, she exposed those who sought to restrain her.[7]

Sold

Sing Kee, for his part, denied buying Yun Gee, forcing her into sex work, or running anything more than a boardinghouse. Under oath, he stated that he had lived in Los Angeles for ten years and once owned a slipper shop. Then, he explained, "[I] got no strength to work any so [I] rent a house and so [I] keeps some rooms for rent." He told the court that he ran a small "boarding" house on the street he referred to as "Nigger Alley."[8]

Although Sing Kee likely thought nothing of the street name, the use of the racial slur is worth an aside. Under Spanish rule, the street was originally known as *"Calle de los Negros,"* in reference to the *mulato Californios* who occupied the neighborhood. At the time, many of these *mulato* families were considered respectable *gente de razón*, and the street name did not necessarily hold negative connotations. With the arrival of Americans, however, that changed. The street's name was initially translated into English as "Negro Alley." But when it became associated with vice in the 1860s, locals began to describe it with the more aggressive racial slur—even though no African Americans lived there. Instead, the alley had become the heart of Los Angeles Chinatown, strongly associated with the undesirable Chinese race, and, in 1871, the site of a mass lynching that claimed at least seventeen Chinese lives. By the time Sing Kee lived on the street, the city directory listed it using the more explicitly racist term "Nigger Alley (Chinatown)," as it had by then become customary to use the anti-Black slur to denigrate the Chinese neighborhood.

Sing Kee operated his "boardinghouse" in the heart of Los Angeles Chinatown with the help of his wife, to whom he had been married for fifteen years. In May 1884 they housed four Chinese women in four single rooms. He claimed that he charged the women $5 a month in rent but had yet to collect Yun Gee's first payment. Under cross-examination, he admitted that he did not know how she would be able to pay, nor could he state her profession: "Perhaps she has money of her own. But I don't know." He was definitive in his denial of prostituting her, however. "I didn't whip her at all," Sing Kee told the court. "I never forced her to be a whore."

On that final point, Yun Gee agreed. According to the twenty-three-year-old, she had lived in San Francisco for two years before coming to Los Angeles. In court, she described a nice, albeit improbable, story: she had lived in San Francisco with her mother and father, who made a living "sewing buttonholes or something like that."[9]

If this was an accurate description of her family arrangement, she had a rare experience indeed. This scenario—a grown daughter living with her working-class immigrant parents—was contrary to US immigration law and Chinese migration and marriage patterns. It was an improbability, or perhaps a lie. Instead, she could have been a second wife, concubine, sex worker, or *mui tsai* (female bondservant) before her "mother" sold her. Americans viewed these roles as deviant and degraded, so she would have had many reasons to keep her status hidden from view.

Yun Gee also had every incentive to deny that Sing Kee had successfully forced her into sex work, as a matter of pride and due to fear. What would have happened if she admitted to the crime of prostitution while in court? Certainly she would have been subject to a fine and imprisonment under Los Angeles ordinances, and possibly subject to removal under federal immigration law.[10]

Despite Sing Kee's denials and hers, it is more than possible that Yun Gee did engage in sex work at some point in her life. While American and European sex workers vastly outnumbered Chinese sex workers in California, Chinese sex workers were an outsized proportion of their community. Based on imperfect US census records, scholars have attempted to estimate how many there were. Most estimates combine two figures: the number of Chinese women listed by census takers as "prostitutes" and the number of adult Chinese women living in all-female households. Historians believe that in 1880, a few years before Yun Gee arrived in Los Angeles, the proportion of women engaged in sex work was less than in the previous decade, but still remained dramatically higher than for other ethnic groups.[11]

These figures are, at best, approximations. At worst they prevent us from understanding the work and living arrangements of Chinese women in California. Previous scholars have worried that census takers inflated the number of women listed as "prostitutes" due to racial prejudice and confusion over the status of concubines and domestic servants.[12] It is true that Americans were quick to label all single Chinese women "prostitutes."

Table 4 Estimated number of Chinese women working as prostitutes by region (and percentage of total Chinese female population), in 1870 and 1880. Historians' estimates include both women listed as "prostitutes" in the US Census and women living in all-female households.

	1870	1880
San Francisco	1,565 (63%)	435 (34%)
Northern Mines[1]	472 (82%)	205 (48%)
Southern Mines[2]	348 (79%)	164 (53%)
Sacramento Valley[3]	243 (88%)	71 (32%)

Sources: Chan, *This Bittersweet Soil*, 389, 392; and Tong, *Unsubmissive Women*, 98.
1. Includes Plumas, Butte, Sierra, Yuba, Nevada, and Placer counties.
2. Includes El Dorado, Amador, Calaveras, Tuolumne, and Mariposa counties.
3. Includes Tehama, Colusa, Sutter, Sacramento, Yolo, and Solano counties.

Given the norms of sex work in China, however, it seems more likely that scholars have undercounted the number of women who engaged in sex work at some point in their lives by assuming that only single women participated in the profession. Census figures imply that "prostitute" was a static and all-encompassing identity, rather than a form of work that could be performed temporarily by both single and married women.

Elites in China at the time believed that marriage and prostitution were incompatible, but in practice most sex work among peasants in China was linked to marriage.[13] Impoverished families could turn to a wife's sexual labor to support the family. This social practice flourished within rural peasant communities, where marriage was universal for women, but up to a fifth of men would never marry.[14] The extreme scarcity of marriageable Chinese women in the American West (combined with anti-miscegenation laws) likely reproduced a similar interdependence between marriage and prostitution in the diaspora.

Although it is difficult to estimate the number of Chinese women who engaged in sex work, there is no question that prostitution played a role in the economic development of the US West. Chinese women offering sexual services helped to sustain a Chinese labor force that was predominantly male, sparsely paid, and highly mobile. In the late nineteenth century, Chinese men tunneled through the Sierra Nevada Mountains, drained the swamps of the San Joaquin River Delta, and felled trees in northern Washington State. This strenuous work in remote locations in poor conditions was made possible, in part, by the fact that Chinese laborers lacked local dependents. Prostitution helped sustain the migratory labor that Californian employers had come to expect, and the return migration upon which families in Guangdong depended.[15] In this way, it was an engine for Chinese cultural maintenance.

For some, prostitution also meant profit. Facing a racially constricted marketplace, Chinese entrepreneurs found that trafficking women was a financially sound investment. Women and girls could be purchased in China for as little as $50 and sold in America for more than $1,000. For traffickers and tongs in America, Chinese sex workers brought in a continuous stream of income. In higher-class brothels that catered to Chinese clientele, prostitutes could earn $200 to $300 a month. In lower-class establishments, which served a multiracial clientele, women could earn an average of $70 in the same period.[16] These earnings did not compare favorably to those of white women. Within the racially segregated market for sex, Chinese women regularly made fifty cents for every dollar earned by an American or European woman.

And rarely did Chinese women keep much of the proceeds. While the majority of white sex workers were independent agents or wage workers, most Chinese women in the US West appear to have entered sex work involuntarily through sale, kidnapping, or decoy. Yun Gee, for example, described herself (via a translator) as a "sold" woman.

The selling of a Chinese woman into prostitution was illegal in China, Hong Kong, and, after 1870, in California. By the mid-eighteenth century, the Qing Court prohibited prostitution, defining it as a form of "illicit sexual intercourse." In China, women who chose to "pollute and debase themselves" in this way could be "punished according to law," as could their male customers, owners, and traffickers.[17] These laws reflected the moral standards of the Chinese elite, which increasingly viewed prostitution as exploitative and dishonorable. In Hong Kong, a key node in the transpacific travel of Chinese migrants, British colonial antislavery statutes also debarred the sale of women. Similar mores prevailed among leading members of the Chinese and white communities in California. Acknowledging the growing sex trade, representatives of the Six Companies sent a petition (in Chinese) to the California legislature in 1868 asking for help: "We believe the case of selling women into prostitution is the same as that of selling people into slavery and should also be outlawed by your country."[18]

And yet starting in the 1850s, a sprawling trafficking network linked the province of Guangdong to Hong Kong and on to San Francisco. A flourishing market of sexual commerce, practically unregulated in the British colony, soon fed gold-rush California as well as Canada, Australia, and Singapore. Early San Francisco newspapers reported that Chinese females were openly auctioned on the docks in full view of passersby; entire shipments of women were sold as wives, concubines, prostitutes, and servants. By the 1860s such transactions had moved indoors and into Chinatown.[19]

Being sold across the Pacific, rather than in the next village, had consequences for Chinese women and girls, because they then lacked local familial connections, knowledge of their surroundings, and basic English-language skills. Without these vital social resources, they found it especially difficult to leave the sex trade.[20] It did not help that traffickers were keen to cloister sex workers, control their movements, and keep them out of the public eye. Once sold into prostitution, these women and girls found it difficult to escape.

The simple fact of being sold, however, did not mean inevitable enslavement for Chinese women. Observers in the past, like historians today, have puzzled over the arrangements that underwrote Chinese sexual labor. Likening Chinese prostitution to enslavement, and missionary rescue to liberty, American critics at the time drew a clear line dividing freedom and slavery. Too often scholars have followed suit, imagining Chinese women as either free or enslaved, trying to force complicated lives into the binary notions held by the nineteenth-century white American public. Even in this simplified frame, their status is unclear. Arriving at the end of chattel slavery in the United States, Chinese women were never recognized as enslaved under US law. Nevertheless, both contemporaries and historians have often described Chinese sex workers in the nineteenth century as "slaves" in all but name.[21]

But labeling Chinese women as "slaves" obscures more than it reveals. Late imperial China did not operate on binary conceptions of individual freedom and slavery. Women in Chinese society occupied a spectrum of constrained statuses determined by familial and societal relationships.[22] Rather than trying to slot their experiences into our preconceived notions of freedom, we can learn more by asking how Chinese women and girls narrated their own experiences of unfreedom. For this, legal testimony provides an unparalleled source.[23]

Tellingly, Yun Gee did not protest having been sold. She objected to having been sold as a prostitute rather than a wife. At the time, the Qing government recognized the sale of a daughter to a groom's family as a legitimate and common practice among peasants in rural China. In other words, the selling of women was essential to the Chinese marriage system as well as the sex trade.[24]

For Yun Gee, being sold as a prostitute meant she could expect little compensation if she did "whore" herself, and corporal punishment if she did not. It also meant involuntary movement and confinement: Sing Kee took her from San Francisco to Los Angeles, installed her in his house, and then monitored her movements. The terms of this ownership were unstated, held no expiration date, and did not require her consent. Although the exact circumstances of Yun Gee's captivity are unclear, it is possible to extrapolate based on others' experiences.

For example, while Yun Gee appeared to have no contract, other Chinese sex workers had their terms of work in writing, and a few such contracts survive. By considering one from 1886 for an indentured sex worker named Xin Jin, we can comprehend the conditions endured by Chinese sex workers more broadly.

> The contractee Xin Jin is indebted to her master/mistress for passage from China to San Francisco and will voluntarily work as a prostitute at Tan Fu's place for four and one-half years for an advance of 1,205 yuan (US $524) to pay this debt. There shall be no interest on the money, and Xin Jin shall receive no wages. At the expiration of the contract, Xin Jin shall be free to do as she pleases. Until then, she shall first secure the master/mistress's permission if a customer asks to take her out. If she has the four loathsome diseases, she shall be returned within 100 days; beyond that time the procurer has no responsibility. Menstruation disorder is limited to one month's rest only. If Xin Jin becomes sick at any time for more than fifteen days, she shall work one month extra; if she becomes pregnant, she shall work one year extra. Should Xin Jin run away before her term is out, she shall pay whatever expense is incurred in finding and returning her to the brothel.[25]

Xin Jin signed the contract with a mark, suggesting that she did not know how to write her own name, let alone read the contract that lay before her. In theory, someone read this contract aloud to her. The contract's terms meant an immediate financial boon for her or her family: a lump sum payment up front and free passage across the Pacific. But it also meant four and a half years of prostituting her body without additional compensation, plus the likelihood of additional time due to illness, menstruation, or pregnancy. The final line of the contract is particularly ominous; it threatens to find, return, and fine Xin Jin if she should run away. The contract did not simply promise her labor. It held her captive.[26]

Not only did women like Yun Gee face the possibility of captivity—they also faced the threat of forced movement or "kidnapping." Sensationalist abduction stories, which frequently appeared in the pages of California newspapers, offer an imperfect window into this practice. On December 26, 1875, for example, the *Daily Alta California* reported a "Chinese Kidnapping" in San Francisco. Three "Chinamen" had hired a carriage on Christmas day to drive them to "a vegetable garden beyond the Mission." There they "induced" a fourteen-year-old Chinese girl to enter the carriage and sped away to the wharf. "On the carriage reaching Brannan Street," the paper recounted, "the girl began to cry out, immediately attracting a large crowd, and [she] declared that she was being kidnapped."[27] Such dramatic tales of seemingly random abductions sold newspapers. They also became fodder for nativists and Protestant missionaries, who cited them as evidence of Chinese barbarism. The pervasive threat of trafficking, as well as white prejudice and voyeurism, lay behind these recurrent reports.

Few accounts of kidnapping survive in legal testimony, but what remains offers clues as to what lay beneath the surface of these brief newspaper articles. Consider, for example, the attempted kidnapping of Loui How in 1877. At the time, she was living in the small mining town of Dutch Flat, Placer County, in the house of Ah Quong, a self-described "gambler." In court, Loui How explained that she was alone when a strange man (who, she later learned, was named Yim Gim) came to the house on the night of January 16. This alone did not raise her fears, since it was customary for Chinese men to visit prostitutes after dark. "First Yim Gim came in the House," she recounted. "He asked me to go into the room. We did go into the room and Yim Gim asked me to run away with him. I said I would not go. He said if you will not go, I will kill you[.] he pull'd out his pistol. I got scared and ran away. I did not lock the door when I went out. I made a noise and hollered." Upon hearing her screams, half a dozen men rushed to Ah Quong's house, including two white watchmen employed by the local Chinese community.[28]

In Loui How's description, the attempted abduction was unexpected, and perhaps for her it was, but the watchmen made clear that this was not a random act. In court, they explained that they had been warned to expect a kidnapping in Chinatown. According to watchman G. H. Davidson, the "Chinamen" in Dutch Flat had told him "that they expected some Chinaman from Auburn to steal a Chinawoman. They wanted I should look out so they should not take her off." Davidson and a second watchman, A. A. Ferguson, entered Ah Quong's house after Loui How fled and helped to disarm Yim Gim, who was in possession of a pistol, knife, and bamboo cane. Ferguson scolded Yim Gim for making "a heap of trouble," and asked him, "what he came up here for[?]" "He told me Ah Sing sent him up there for a Chinawoman[.] Ah Sing wanted to marry her," testified Ferguson, "He said he had a warrant from the judge for that woman."[29]

The conflicting accounts raise questions: What kind of kidnapping was this? Was it a suitor attempting to rescue his beloved from a brothel? Or a pimp trying to recapture a runaway? Or a trafficker raiding another man's wares? For that matter, were the watchmen there to protect her or to prevent her escape? For Loui How, the answers to these questions were consequential. A stark line divided kidnapping and rescue, and that line was her consent. But determining her consent was difficult for observers at the time, and even more so for historians now.[30] And yet reconciling these accounts is not necessary for seeing what underlies them: a contest over female Chinese mobility. Sex trafficking and acts to undermine it relied on the ability to control the movement of Chinese women.

Legal testimony also makes it clear that sex work could be a violent business. Yun Gee accused Sing Kee of trying to beat her into submission, and no doubt the threat of violence helped to confine her and other women. Rarely did sex workers' accusations of beatings by their owners make it into court. An adjacent threat—robbery and assault by customers—was more likely to be adjudicated. Robbery cases exposed Chinese prostitutes' vulnerability to violence, but also how they found ways to seek recourse.

For example, Ah Chow may have been a sex worker when she was attacked in the small mining community of Big Oak Flat, Tuolumne County, California, in 1867. That would help to explain why she, the wife of a domestic servant, would have been in possession of $140 in gold coins and why she allegedly "sassed" two men who were in her bedroom. According to her affidavit, Cum-Chow and Ah-pe-o entered her house while she was "yet in bed." Seizing her, they "stuffed a cloth into her mouth to prevent her making noise and put a rope around her neck & chocked [sic] her and struck her over the head with a hatchet and otherwise beat and injured her." Armed with a knife, pistol, and hatchet, they "cut off a belt from her waist" and removed the gold coins, along with a ring and earrings. Ah Chow's husband, Ah Li, learned of the attack only after it had ended. Hearing the news that "two Chinamen had been beating my woman," he rushed home to find her "bruised and bloody about the face." Ah Chow filed a complaint under oath with the justice of the peace.

One of the two men, Cum-Chow, stood accused of robbery. He had been arrested by a white citizen, Andrew Rocca, who accepted money from Ah Chow's husband in return for tracking them down. In police court, Cum-Chow did not deny the attack, only the extent of it. "Ah-Choy 'sassed' me, and I fought her," he testified, "Then she said I robbed her." He denied stealing from Ah Choy or tying a rope around her neck. "I did not hit her with a hatchet but only with my fists." After gathering initial statements, the justice of the peace ordered Cum-Chow to be held to answer for the crime of robbery. But there would be no justice; the defendant escaped from the constable before he could be tried. Court records from this case expose the physical and financial vulnerability that Chinese women faced, as well as the sources of power that remained available to them. With the help of her husband, a white man for hire, and the American legal system, Ah Chow brought about the arrest of the men who had attacked her.[31]

Chinese women's legal testimony reveals a shared experience of forced movement, involuntary confinement, and threatened violence. But the routes Chinese sex workers took into the profession varied, as did their resulting status. Some worked under fixed-term contracts; others were sold in perpetuity. Some lived under the thumb of a trafficker, others were married and contributed to their household income, and some operated alone or with other women. These differences make it problematic to generalize about their state of freedom.

This did not stop American politicians and police officers from doing just that. "I look upon them as slaves, sold for such and such an amount of money, to be worked out as prostitutes," testified San Francisco police officer James R. Rogers in 1876.[32] The San Francisco Board of Supervisors agreed. In a special municipal report on Chinese immigration in 1885, they declared Chinese prostitution in San Francisco to be "the most abject and satanic conception of human slavery."[33]

Policed

Sing Kee's role in the Los Angeles network of sex trafficking was well known to the local police. In court a constable testified that he knew Sing Kee operated a "whore house," because "half a dozen Chinamen" had told him so; another police officer claimed he operated three houses of "ill-fame."

Even police captain Louis Froklick had firsthand experience with Sing Kee's establishment, having "pulled a woman out of there one night." According to Captain Froklick, he was walking through the alley with another officer when the woman "called us in . . . as we passed along." The officer went into the establishment, "made an arrangement with her and brought her down" for arrest. The woman quickly pled guilty to solicitation and "paid her fine," but before she could be released, Kee showed up at the jail and "wanted to bail her out."

That was five months before Yun Gee arrived. Under cross-examination, Captain Froklick was asked: "Why did not you arrest Sing Kee long ago, if you knew that he kept a house of prostitution?" The captain explained: "We did whenever we got a chance."[34] But how often did California officials actually "get the chance" to police Chinese women and girls? To what extent did the state enact and enforce measures of social control?

San Francisco was the first American city to target Chinese sex workers. As early as 1854, when there were no more than a few hundred Chinese women in the city, the Board of Aldermen barred all brothels within city limits.[35] The trade grew, despite the law, and in subsequent decades the city took a more moderate and perhaps pragmatic approach to houses of prostitution. Instead of outlawing prostitution entirely, San Francisco sought to regulate sex workers it deemed particularly repugnant and spaces deemed central to the white community. The city carefully crafted an identity-based ordinance to target Chinese "prostitutes"—as enslaved, immoral, diseased, and a source of racial contamination—and the Chinese brothels most visible to the white public.[36] On October 9, 1865, the Board of Supervisors passed an "Order to Remove Chinese Women of Ill Fame from Certain Limits in the City," specifying the neighborhoods where Chinese prostitution establishments were banned.[37]

The law, as originally written, stayed on the books for only eight days. Under the counsel of the city attorney, the ordinance was quickly amended to remove the term "Chinese," transforming the identity-based law to a general-outcast law, which lessened the chance it would be deemed discriminatory. The change in wording, however, did not reflect any change of intent. According to a municipal report the following year, the police quickly alerted Chinese brothel owners "of the necessity and cause of their removal," and then granted them "ample time" to "obtain possession of some other locality removed from public view." Those who did not comply within a few months faced criminal prosecution. Between December 1865 and June 1866, city police arrested 137 Chinese women for prostitution and secured 124 convictions. According to the municipal report, another 300 Chinese women departed the city, leaving 200 working in the sex trade, presumably outside the barred zones.[38]

In 1866 the California legislature followed suit with "An Act for the Suppression of Chinese Houses of Ill Fame." The identity-based law declared "all houses of ill fame, kept, managed, inhabited or used by Chinese women for the purposes of common prostitution" to be "public nuisances." It set penalties for owning or renting such properties and granted sheriffs the power to take possession for noncompliance. But they must have lacked the will or capacity. Within a few months, the *Alta California* reported that California officials and leaders of the Chinese community had reached "an amical settlement." State officials were more invested in confining prostitution geographically than eliminating it. In return for a slowing of prosecutions, Chinese brothel owners agreed to move their establishments to locations deemed acceptable. Fearing a constitutional challenge amid racial reconstruction, in 1874 the California legislature also amended its law to (again) strike the word "Chinese." They relied on discretionary policing—that is, legal custom rather than formal law—to ensure that the general-outcast law would continue to regulate the Chinese in particular.[39]

The California legislature also turned to a new form of policing: identity-based immigration restriction. The 1870 "Act to Prevent the Kidnapping and Importation of Mongolian, Chinese and Japanese Females, for Criminal or Demoralizing Purposes" declared that the importation of Asian females "without their consent" had been "carried on extensively during the past year, to the scandal and injury of the people of this State." To end trafficking, the law deemed Asian females to be inadmissible unless they could provide proof of voluntary migration and good character. Aware of the law's shaky constitutional grounds, California legislators affirmatively declared their state's right to bar involuntary female migration based on "the police power appertaining to every State in the Union."

The importation law was amended twice, and then in 1874 it was enfolded into California's general immigration law in newly race-neutral terms. Instead of explicitly targeting "Mongolian, Chinese and Japanese females," the immigration law barred any "lewd or debauched woman" as well as other undesirable passengers, including aliens who were "lunatic, idiotic, deaf, dumb, blind, crippled," or "likely to become a permanent public charge." The legislature once again hoped to rest the law firmly on the state's police powers to protect public health and safety.[40] The amended immigration law faced a judicial challenge nonetheless.

In August 1874 the steamer *Japan* arrived in San Francisco from Hong Kong with eighty-nine Chinese women aboard. Under the direction of the immigration commissioner, state officials detained the women and questioned them, hoping to discern the difference between wives and "prostitutes." All of the women claimed to be married, but only some could produce their husband and children. In the end the commissioner found twenty-two of the women's testimonies to be unsatisfactory, declared the women to be lewd, debauched, or abandoned, and informed the master of the vessel that he would have to pay a $500 bond in gold for each of the twenty-two women before they would be allowed to land. The ludicrous sum meant their inevitable deportation.

Before they could be deported, one of their number, Ah Fong, filed a habeas corpus petition alleging that she was being illegally held by the city and county of San Francisco. So began a series of legal challenges that would end at the US Supreme Court. At issue was the ability of Chinese women to control their own movement, and the right of the State of California to immobilize them. Ironically, these legal challenges were likely funded by traffickers.[41] Without the aid of Chinese elites and white attorneys, these twenty-two newcomers would not have had the resources or legal know-how to mount such an extensive challenge.[42]

As the San Francisco District Court heard *In re Ah Fong,* the California papers took interest in the spectacle of twenty-two anguished and angry Chinese women. The *Alta California* described a particularly contentious moment in court when "one of the women jumped to her feet and let out a most unearthly yell. Immediately the whole lot were jabbering and screaming at the top of [their] voices, and it was found impossible to quiet them until they were hustled from the court-room." The Chinese interpreter later told the *San Francisco Chronicle* that the women had been protesting the legitimacy of their confinement. They were "expostulating against being kept in prison, saying that they had not killed anybody, stolen anything, or set fire to anything." The trial may have been dramatic, but the conclusion was not. The state court ruled against the women without a written opinion, apparently accepting that their exclusion had been within the police power granted to the states.[43]

The fight was not over. Another woman in the group filed a complaint in the California Supreme Court. The named party, Ah Fook, had been outspoken in her district court testimony and was declared "very obstinate and saucy" by the local paper. During cross-examination she had lashed out. "She says now you are foolish," reported the translator. "She said if you were doing right, you would not ask her so many questions; that she went home with a good intention, and that she brought her sister here with a good intention." Her writ of habeas corpus alleged that her exclusion violated the due process clause of the Fourteenth Amendment and the most favored nation clause of the Burlingame Treaty. Within a week, however, the state court also found that the immigration law fell well within the state's police power.⁴⁴

Undeterred, the women appealed *In re Ah Fong* (1874) to the US circuit court at San Francisco, where they received their first affirmative ruling from the federal court. In a decision written by Supreme Court justice Stephen Field (who was riding circuit at San Francisco), the federal court found that the immigration act violated the US Constitution, federal law, and treaty stipulations with China. According to Field's decision, the California statute went far beyond the police power granted to states by the Constitution, contravened the principles of equal protection in the 1870 Civil Rights Act, and breached the Burlingame Treaty.⁴⁵ Justice Field sympathized with the "feeling prevailing in this state against the Chinese" and used his decision to suggest two alternative ways to regulate Chinese prostitution. First, state and local governments should use race-neutral laws and "a vigorous police" to combat "lewd conduct." Second, anti-Chinese advocates should turn to Congress, "where the whole power of this subject lies."⁴⁶

The twenty-two women were released following the US circuit court decision, but one of their number, Chy Lung, brought a writ of error to the US Supreme Court, hoping to firmly establish that the law was unconstitutional. Basing their argument on the Fourteenth Amendment, attorneys for the plaintiff argued that "every person, whether native or foreign is entitled to equal protection of our laws." In the end, the court sidestepped the issue of equal protection, invalidating the law under foreign commerce power. In *Chy Lung v. Freeman* (1875), the Supreme Court reaffirmed that Congress, rather than the states, held the power to pass "laws which concern the admission of citizens and subjects of foreign nations to our shores." This ruling, and others handed down the same day, affirmed that the federal government held jurisdiction over immigration.⁴⁷

For the plaintiffs, however, there was little to celebrate. Even before Chy Lung's writ of error could be heard by the US Supreme Court, Congress anticipated she would prevail and decided to step in with a federal solution. The Page Act, signed into law on March 3, 1875, mirrored California's earlier efforts to regulate the involuntary migration of Asian women. The law criminalized the immigration of all felons and sex workers regardless of country of origin, but also contained specific regulations on "the subjects of China, Japan, or any Oriental country." For the latter, the law barred the importation of "cooly" workers under contract and immigrants entering for "lewd and immoral purposes," requiring those from "Oriental" nations to obtain certificates proving that they did not fall under these categories.[48]

This shift from state law to federal law had profound consequences for the legal regulation of Chinese migrants. With the help of the Fourteenth Amendment, the Burlingame Treaty, and the Civil Rights Act of 1870, Chinese litigants in the US West had been waging a surprisingly successful battle against the proliferation of discriminatory state and local laws in the 1870s, when state legislatures found their attempts to directly regulate Chinese work and behavior curtailed by Reconstruction laws and amendments. At the time, however, the US Supreme Court interpreted equal protection narrowly, applying its promise of nondiscrimination solely to state actions. The federal government remained free to target immigrants by race and nation. Therefore, federal law became a popular way to bypass guarantees of equal protection.[49]

Federal immigration law against Chinese women proved more severe than any previous local or state legislation. Whereas city ordinances and state laws had sought to circumscribe the neighborhoods in which Chinese sex workers were permitted (increasingly on race-neutral terms), the Page Act banned them from the country entirely. Moreover, not only did the Page Act prohibit the entry of "lewd and immoral" women; it also deterred Chinese women and girls in general. When Chinese women learned that migrating to America meant an elaborate, invasive, and expensive investigation of their moral status by the US consul in Hong Kong, many chose not to even make the attempt.[50] American lawmakers claimed that the Page Act was designed to combat sex trafficking, which it did, but it also curtailed the already limited options available to Chinese women and girls. The law made it difficult for Chinese women to migrate to the United States, led to the separation of families and the stunting of generations, and solidified the sexualized image of the Chinese woman.

Although the Page Act named Japanese women as well, officials focused their enforcement on Chinese migrants. In fact, scholars believe that the combination of the Page Act and the Chinese Restriction Act led to an increase in Japanese female migration, and with it, Japanese prostitution. Japanese sex workers began to appear in historical records of the Pacific West in the 1880s and reached significant numbers in the 1890s. A Japanese Consul Survey conducted in 1898 found 150 Japanese prostitutes in California, 69 in Washington State, and 75 in Oregon. Like Chinese sex workers, many Japanese women found themselves indebted to their procurers, who paid for their transpacific passage in return for a term of service.[51]

Even after federal law barred many Chinese women, local and state governments in the Pacific West continued to police Chinese sex work, and increasingly Japanese as well. Los Angeles, where Sing Kee operated his brothel, passed its first ordinance regulating prostitution in 1874. Like San Francisco, Los Angeles initially sought to confine prostitution to sections of the city. The Board of Supervisors amended the section of the city they wished to protect in 1877 and 1878. Then, in 1882, the board banned prostitution within the city limits.[52]

But how often were these local anti-prostitution laws enforced? The unevenness of the historical record makes the answer difficult to ascertain. There are few extant cases regarding Chinese prostitution in Los Angeles. Despite Captain Froklick's claim that the police arrested Sing Kee "whenever we got a chance," no records remain to substantiate this claim. If the police did previously arrest Sing Kee for running a house of prostitution, they left no apparent trace. The lack of records may simply indicate that most prostitution-related prosecutions were straightforward and swift.[53] Following an arrest for solicitation, many women simply paid a fine and gained release without a trial or so much as a note in the court register of actions.

Only when defendants contested the charges were courts likely to produce and retain records. There are surviving documents, for example, from another case in Los Angeles, *People v. Ah Hoy et al.* (1876), that bears striking similarity to Captain Froklick's descriptions of policing Sing Kee. In contrast to the arrest records for Sing Kee, this earlier case offers a snapshot of what routine policing of Chinese sex workers may have looked like in nineteenth-century Los Angeles.

It was past one o'clock in the morning on May 5, 1876, when officer John Fronk walked down Sanchez Street and ran into Ah Hoo. The encounter was not a coincidence. Fronk and his partner, officer John McFadden, had headed to that street at that hour with

THE "CHINAWOMAN" AND THE SEARCH FOR RUNAWAYS 149

the hope of entrapping Chinese sex workers, "knowing that these women were in the habit of calling people in their House." Officer Fronk disguised himself by taking off his overcoat and covering his badge before he entered Chinatown. McFadden stayed within earshot but out of sight.

In court, Fronk described what happened next: "Ah Hoo called me and pulled me by my coat through a hole in the fence and asked me how I liked it[.] I asked her what she ment [sic]. She said you fuck me for two bits[.]" Once they had come to an agreement, Ah Hoo unlocked the gate, took Fronk by his clothes, and pulled him inside the courtyard. Opening his jacket to flash his star, Fronk took hold of the woman and called out to McFadden for assistance. They struggled to remove Ah Hoo and two other women when the apparent owner of the establishment, Ah Hoy, rushed over. According to the officers, he attempted to stop the arrest by pushing his way between them and the women, perhaps to offer a bribe.

The result was criminal charges against him for resisting arrest and against the three women for soliciting prostitution. The justice court held one combined trial for Ah Hoy, Ah Hoo, Ah Choy, and Ah Lee. The women did not testify, were found guilty, and each paid a $25 fine. Ah Hoy was allowed to testify and vigorously denied having resisted the officers but was initially found guilty. His conviction was then reversed in an appeal to the county court.[54] Ah Hoy's appeal is likely the only reason that records survive from what appears to be an otherwise routine example of regulating prostitution.

The routine, it is worth noting, was an act of racial policing. The officers targeted Chinatown, worked to entrap a sex worker, and then rounded up all the Chinese women present, assuming they too were guilty. In this way, a general-outcast law could be put to racialized effect. But the punitive fine, although costly for the women, fell short of the sort of punishment that would threaten the brothel's existence or the women's livelihoods. It is far below the maximum sentence described by the ordinance: ninety days' jail time, a $90 fine, and hard labor. The enforcement of the law appears to have been both more and less than statute would suggest—more racial targeting and less stringent punishment.[55]

Another case from Los Angeles, *People v. Ah Son et al.* (1873), shows how law enforcement could be a source of both unwanted regulation and protection for Chinese women. In this robbery case, two young women, Si Choy and Ah Choy, accused three Chinese men of attacking them and stealing their jewelry. Although no one in court explicitly labeled the women as "prostitutes" living in a woman-owned brothel, clues to their circumstances abound. The young women described themselves as "sisters" and seamstresses (a common euphemism for sex worker), who were living with their "mother" on Sanchez Street and in possession of jewelry worth $2,000. The trouble began because the Los Angeles police had just arrested their mother, Gook Nai, on unstated charges. Sensing the young women's vulnerability without their mother to protect them, Chris Low, Ah Son, and Wah Hing entered their house and attacked them.

With the help of a translator, Si Choy described the scene, "Chris Low took hold of my arm[s] and pulled and jerked me & Ah Son took my [hair] pin out . . . I was afraid he would take me away and sell me." Ah Choy agreed. "Wah Hing came in and took hold of me and wanted to take me away and I cried and hollered and did not want to go." Si Choy and Ah Choy, it seems, preferred their existing arrangement to the threat of being stolen and sold. Perhaps their brothel was operated by a woman, and they took some comfort in the fact.[56] The three men dragged the women out of the house and into the street but ran into police there. Ah Choy recalled, "A Police man took him off and put me back in the house." They told their mother when she "came back from the jail" that evening and filed a robbery complaint against the men.[57]

In this incident, the police assumed multiple roles. They actively policed the household, having arrested the mother in the morning and, in so doing, put the daughters in danger of abduction. But the police also prevented the assailants from robbing and kidnapping Si Choy and Ah Choy, protecting them from men who were likely traffickers. And when the women sought retribution, they helped the women file a complaint in court.

Another data point comes from Portland, Oregon, where arrest records between 1871 and 1887 survive. At the time, Chinese females were arrested for prostitution at a rate of 49 per 10,000, whereas all other females were arrested at a rate of 6 per 10,000. Rather than consistently police sex workers, officers launched periodic raids followed by long stretches of inactivity. When the police showed complacency, private individuals sometimes took it upon themselves to demand action, and their complaints could spur new raids.[58] Even so, Chinese women in Portland reportedly regarded American policemen as a potential source of protection. According to the *Daily Oregonian* in 1865, Chinese sex workers in Portland carried whistles to call the police and found that they would "faithfully" respond.[59] Law enforcement and the courts policed Chinese sex workers, but that is not all they did.

Fled

When Yun Gee finally understood that she was to become Sing Kee's "whore," she knew one route of escape. "He forced me to be a whore but I would not do it," she explained in court. "So [I] thought I must have somebody marry me."

Within a week, she found the ideal suitor. Ah Sing was a store clerk who worked just down the block and responded to her tears. Under oath, Ah Sing testified that he had known Yun Gee back in China, and after meeting again in Los Angeles, they had decided to wed within days. A resident in the city for more than four years, Ah Sing had the proper connections to arrange the wedding quickly and quietly. On May 7, 1884, they stood before Justice of the Peace Robert A. Ling exchanging vows. The bride was dressed in simple attire, save for two gold bracelets holding tight to her wrists. Both Chinese and white witnesses were in attendance, including a lawman, Constable John W. Griffin.

Yun Gee had pursued a common path out of sex work. Contemporary observers noted that Chinese sex workers often sought out husbands as a means to exit a brothel, and census data document this trend. The majority of Chinese girls and women in the US West were single, not wives or family members, when they arrived. A small subset of these single female arrivals married quickly, but most lived in the United States for years or decades before marrying. Given the lack of economic opportunities for Chinese women in the US West, it is probable that many of these single migrant women worked in the sex trade before marriage (and some continued even after being wed).[60] Chinese sex workers found it possible to make the transition to esteemed wife and mother because it was considered an act of filial piety, as opposed to a sign of moral debasement, to accept being sold into prostitution by one's family.

Demographic realities may have eased the transition as well. The scarcity of Chinese migrant women and the passage of antimiscegenation laws meant that Chinese men who wished to marry in the United States faced limited prospects.[61]

By finding a husband, Yun Gee believed she had saved herself. In a few short days, she acquired two forms of protection: a marriage contract recognized by the American legal system and a partner with social and financial resources. It is likely, however, that the white officials at Yun Gee's wedding believed they were the ones rescuing her. Later in court, Ah Sing described how he had taken pity on Yun Gee and sought to save her from the violence of a notorious whorehouse. Likewise, Judge Ling and Constable Griffin knew of Sing Kee's dealings, having spent years enforcing laws against prostitution in Los Angeles. In their eyes, this "prostitute" was a newly "fallen woman," and marriage represented an ideal form of rescue and reform.[62]

A marriage certificate could be a powerful legal instrument. Some Chinese women paired proof of marriage with habeas corpus petitions to fight their involuntary detention. Even before Chinese women began using habeas petitions to challenge immigration detention, they used them to challenge other forms of confinement. As early as 1855, for example, Aye-Ying petitioned a Tuolumne County court on behalf of his wife, Ah-hoi, asking for her release from a brothel. The petitioner claimed he had "entered into the bonds of matrimony with the said Ah-hoi," and that she was now "illegally restrained of her liberty against the will of this Petitioner in a certain ill-fame house situated in the City of Sonora." Aye-Ying begged the court to release her from her involuntary "detention." The court granted his petition and, one can only hope, helped to release his wife.[63]

But marriage alone was not enough to save Yun Gee. Following the ceremony, Yun Gee returned to Sing Kee's house and the abuse there. It took the newlyweds five days to put together an elaborate escape plan and the necessary funds to free her from the brothel. On Monday, May 12, 1884, Ah Sing headed to Griffin's office with $600 in his pocket and the knowledge that the constable was headed to San Francisco by rail the next day. They hatched a plan. The constable would pick up Yun Gee near her residence, together they would board a train en route to San Francisco, and then Ah Sing would join them at Newhall Station, forty miles outside of Los

Angeles. Once the couple made it to San Francisco, Yun Gee believed, they would continue on to China.[64]

At first, everything went to plan. When Griffin pulled up in front of Sing Kee's house the next day in a horse-drawn hack, the woman hurried inside. Ah Sing did not accompany them on the first leg of the journey because, according to Griffin, "he was afraid Chinamen here would kill him." To keep Yun Gee safe aboard the train, Griffin hid her in a baggage car.[65] "I didn't want to have any trouble with Chinamen and I put her there for safe keeping," Griffin explained. "I didn't want to kill anybody on the road or hurt anybody." His defensive testimony suggests he may have feared retribution from Chinese traffickers.

Finally, three or four hours on the other side of Mojave, Griffin took her out of baggage and placed her in his car along with another member of law enforcement, Sheriff F. W. Tyler, who was conveying prisoners to San Francisco. Yun Gee emerged from the baggage car in some distress; her arms had swollen, and her solid gold bracelets had begun to cut off circulation. Once reunited with her husband, Yun Gee spent considerable time trying to get the jewelry off, eventually succeeding with the help of soap and water.

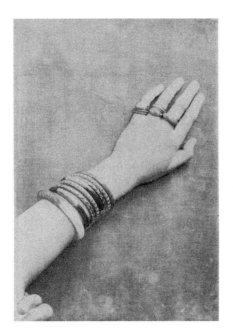

This undated photograph, taken in San Francisco Chinatown, shows a woman's forearm with bracelets and rings. There is a hint of force in this picture, because a hand appears to hold the woman's arm down. (Alice Iola Hare Photograph Collection, BANC PIC 1905.04663-05242:04688, The Bancroft Library, University of California, Berkeley)

Unlike Yun Gee, who sought a husband, other runaways turned to missionaries for help. Lilac Chen, who spoke to researchers in 1971, explained how she had been "rescued" by the Presbyterian Chinese Mission Home in San Francisco. Born in China in 1887, Chen was six years old when her father told her they were going "to see grandma," and instead brought her aboard a steamer and sold her to "a strange woman." A few months later, she was working as a domestic servant in a large brothel run by "Mrs. Lee" in San Francisco. She remembered Mrs. Lee as kind but often short on money. Soon Mrs. Lee's mistress began to lend Chen out to other women, one of whom beat her. Black and blue bruises covered her back when missionaries and police officers found her during a raid of a Chinese brothel. "And they took me, a fat police man carried me all the way... to the mission," remembered Chen. "So I got my freedom there."[66]

Not all Chinese women were happy to be "rescued." Although some women reached out to the missionaries for help, raids often rounded up all Chinese females present in a brothel, regardless of their preference. In 1897 the Presbyterian Chinese Mission Home took in sixty women from a government raid, but Chen recalled that the women "shrieked and wailed beating the floor with their shoes" and "denounc[ed] the Home in no unmeasured terms." Even after the matron removed the most outspoken women to another room, she reported that the others still rejected her "protection" "with scorn and derision."[67] For Chen, the Mission Home had been a site of liberation, but for these women it represented discipline, confinement, and loss of income. They had arrived at the missionary home through the same means, but Chen had been rescued and they had been kidnapped.[68]

Legal testimony from Tin Sing offers a rare example of a woman who ran away without the help of a missionary or a man, but unfortunately her story comes to us as a dying declaration. Lying in the county infirmary at San Jose in March 1877, she said that she dictated her statement "under the full belief that I am about to die." Before she passed, she wanted it known that she had escaped from Fong Ah Tuck because he had cut her with a small hatchet and beat her with a "long china pipe." "He said why he was beating me," stated Tin Sing, "he wanted me to pay him the money I owed him which was a little over two hundred dollars." But she "could not earn the money." Although Tin Sing never explained the reason for her debt, this appears to be another story of involuntary prostitution and the violence that accompanied it.⁶⁹

Tin Sing had been living with Fong Ah Tuck and his wife, On Chou, in Sacramento for the preceding four months. The *Sacramento Daily Union* described Tin Sing as Fong Ah Tuck's "slave," but the relationship between Tin Sing and On Chou was a matter of some debate at trial. What bound the women together? Friendship? Polygamy? Or whatever one calls the relationship between a brothel owner's wife and a resident sex worker? Some sort of bond did exist between the two women, because when On Chou returned from a trip to San Francisco to find Tin Sing beaten to the edge of death, On Chou decided they both needed to flee. The women absconded together to San Jose's Chinatown.

"When I first saw her[,] she was lying on a mattress on the floor apparently in a very deplorable condition. The stench from her was almost unbearable," remembered Dr. A. McMahon. "I removed her to the hospital and I then examined her. I found a wound on her shoulder and on one of her hands." The doctor faulted On Chou for failing to bring Tin Sing in sooner. "Nothing apparently had been done for her," he observed. On Chou had taken Tin Sing 120 miles from her abuser, but the doctor only saw her lack of medical care. After examining the patient, Dr. McMahon told her in English, "Maybe you die." Tin Sing simply looked at him and made no reply.⁷⁰

Within days, San Jose sheriff N. R. Harris and Sacramento chief of police E. N. Stevens were at Tin Sing's bedside, together with On Chou, a notary, and Gaston Strauss as translator. "She looked very sick and weak, she could not raise herself," remembered Strauss. After making her dying declaration, Tin Sing then explained that "her friend" On Chou "took her away from Sacramento to get her away from Fong Ah Tuck." But when Tin Sing passed away several days later, the policemen arrested On Chou as well as her husband and charged them both with murder.

Facing a combined trial in Sacramento, the two entered pleas of "not guilty" with the help of separate attorneys. According to their testimony, Tin Sing had been a "whore" with "the pox," and no man had ever beaten her. For On Chou, this defense meant recanting her multiple statements to the San Jose and Sacramento police, as well as to the doctor and interpreter. Despite her inconsistent story, the jury found On Chou not guilty. In contrast, it found Fong Ah Tuck guilty of murder in the second degree and sentenced him to thirteen years in state prison. Tin Sing had managed to escape her abuser and accuse him, but she did not live to see justice.[71]

The stories of Tin Sing, Lilac Chen, Aye-hoi, and Yun Gee defy images of the powerless "Chinawoman," subject to the will of traffickers and American authorities alike. None of these women were completely cut off from American society, ignorant of its ways, or victim to its laws. In her bid for fugitive mobility, Yun Gee turned to a fellow countryman, a judge, and a constable. In the process, she sought out the American justice system as a source of refuge. This was made possible by a legal system that did not presuppose the guilt of all Chinese. Unfortunately, Chinese women were not the only ones to discover the flexibility of American law.[72] Chinese traffickers did as well.

Captured

Yun Gee's escape had been observed. Ah How, the brothel keeper's wife, watched as Yun Gee climbed aboard a passenger wagon with Constable Griffin and took off. "A policeman came and took her away," she testified later, "she run away." In court, Ah How explained what happened next: "Then my husband send telegraph to take her back."

It took more than a telegram to bring back Yun Gee. The brothel keeper Sing Kee headed to court and found himself standing before Justice of the Peace Robert A. Ling, who (unbeknownst to Sing Kee) had presided over Yun Gee's wedding a week earlier. According to the judge, Sing Kee explained that he wanted to swear out a complaint against Yun Gee and have her arrested. He claimed he had sold jewelry to her—a ring, hair pins, and two gold bracelets—and she had left without paying in full. "Well I told him because it was a civil debt he could not arrest her for it on his statement of the case," testified Judge Ling. Sing Kee demanded that the court "fetch her back anyway and we will pay all the expenses." The judge explained, "You can't catch [her] back on that." According to the judge, Sing Kee persisted. "He says, 'You no give [com]plaint in the case? Me pay all expenses to get her back. Me want to get her back.'"[73]

The next judge Sing Kee approached was more amenable. Later that day he filed a complaint against Yun Gee with Justice John C. Morgan. His story changed slightly: rather than having *sold* her the jewelry, he had *loaned* it to her for a few hours, and she had run off with it. With this modification, she could be charged with embezzlement. Since she had run away with a police officer, it was a fairly simple matter to have her arrested and returned. Justice Morgan sent an urgent telegram that intercepted Constable Griffin while he was still en route to San Francisco. Under the judge's orders, Griffin placed Yun Gee and her husband under arrest. A week after she fled, Yun Gee sat in a Los Angeles courtroom while Justice Morgan heard testimony on whether she should be "held to answer" on the charge of embezzlement.

Ordering the arrest of Yun Gee and her return to Los Angeles, there is little doubt that Justice Morgan facilitated trafficking. Did he do so knowingly? Yun Gee's attorney, John F. Godfrey, believed so. He alleged that Justice Morgan had been bribed, introducing evidence that the judge was promised winnings from gambling halls in Chinatown if he agreed "to hold said woman to answer even though there was no evidence at all against her." Morgan admitted to having visited Chinatown after the first day of the trial but stated that the allegations were "wholly and maliciously false." He had visited "that part of Los Angeles City called China Town" for the "sole purpose of employing a servant, as is his custom."[74]

This was not the first allegation against Los Angeles officials for accepting Chinese bribes and it would not be the last.[75] In the 1876 investigation of Chinese immigration, the California legislature made a point of inquiring into abuses of the justice system. "Is it not very common, when these women try to get away, for the people who own them to have them arrested for larceny, and things of that kind?" the committee asked repeatedly. Officer O. C. Jackson agreed, "Yes sir; in a great many cases to my knowledge. They will swear out a warrant for her arrest for grand larceny or some felony. Sometimes it is sworn out against the man who has her, sometimes against both. As soon as they get possession of the woman, they trifle with the cases until they fall through. It is almost impossible for a woman to escape."[76]

The legislative committee implicated tong members, often described as "highbinders" or "hatchet men," for exploiting the police to increase their control over Chinese women. American officials, as a rule, denied that they played a role in these criminal schemes. But in fact, bribery may have accompanied some of these false accusations. The case *People v. Ah Fook* offers an example of this shady business. In 1880, Ah Fook stood accused in Sonoma County of "offering a bribe to a deputy constable," namely Deputy W. H. Mead. In the course of the trial, Deputy Mead described, with startling candor, the arrangement he had formed with Ah Fook.[77] The trouble began when two Chinese men, Charley John and Ah Fook, allegedly had "a contest for the possession of a Chinese woman." The woman, Me Fook, had apparently fled from Santa Rosa to San Francisco. Charley John first turned to law enforcement in his effort to recover Me Fook, swearing out a complaint of grand larceny against her. Deputy Mead entered the story when he was ordered to serve a warrant for her arrest, apprehended her in San Francisco, and returned her to Santa Rosa. At that point, Ah Fook came to Mead with his own request for the woman. According to Mead and two other officers present, Ah Fook's attempted bribe was unmistakable. "You catchee Chinawoman so as I can get her in a buggy," said Ah Fook, "and I give you $200."

Mead refused (he had already handed the woman over to the sheriff) and swore out a complaint against Ah Fook for offering him a bribe. But only a few weeks later, Mead entertained another offer, this time more favorably. Me Fook had been released, hastily married, and had "run off" with Charley John to the small town of Greenville. Hoping to regain possession of her, Ah Fook returned to Deputy Mead for help. This time around, according to his own admission, Mead accepted $5 to simply "keep track of her," but demanded the "regular fees" of "over a hundred dollars" to "arrest her." Ah Fook agreed, "If you . . . catch her and arrest her and bring her to Sacramento, I will give you one hundred and ten dollars."

According to Mead, this conversation took place in the presence of a local judge, a Sacramento police officer, and a lawyer named Mr. Starr. The other men, it appears, were active participants in the discussion. When Ah Fook suggested that Mead "arrest the Chinawoman and turn her over to them and not bring her in Court," Mr. Starr intervened. "No you cannot do that," Starr explained to Mead, "you have got to take her before the Police Judge and then we can give bail and get [her] out." The lawyer's message was clear: problems would arise if an officer of the law captured runaway women and directly handed them over to the highest bidder. Instead, the woman should be arrested, arraigned, and released on bail, before being delivered to the men who had paid for her capture.[78]

The casual nature of Mead's testimony, the presence of others in the room, and the guidance from a lawyer all suggest that Mead's actions did not violate his understanding of the norms of the time. Numerous contemporaneous news reports of Chinese traffickers using trumped-up charges to capture Chinese women bolster this supposition. According to the *Daily Alta California:* "The kidnapping of Chinese women through sham prosecutions for offences never committed is a matter of almost everyday occurrence in California."[79]

But if this sort of arrangement was a common occurrence, one wonders why Ah Fook ended up accused of bribery at all. Perhaps the problem was that Ah Fook ultimately reneged on the deal. "If I found the Chinawoman I was to take her [to Sacramento] and was to get my money," testified Mead, but Ah Fook "went back on his agreement." This may have been his undoing. A few weeks later, Ah Fook was convicted of bribery and sentenced to a year-long prison term. In an appeal to the California Supreme Court, Ah Fook's lawyer noted "the frequent abuses of judicial process by Mongolians," but argued that in this case, the officer of the law bore more responsibility than the "Chinaman."[80]

Chinese sex traffickers also depended on internal community networks to capture runaways. These networks were shrouded in secrecy and have been mostly lost to history. However, a rare collection of 120 telegrams from 1874 offers a unique, if incomplete, window into these dark dealings. The telegrams were sent and received by Chinese men in the small, forested mountain town of Downieville, California. When sending a telegram, the author paid by the word, so messages were often brief and cryptic. The men sent each other notes about lawsuits, debts, and the price of opium, much of which holds little meaning out of context.

But one topic is clear—because the men returned to it again and again—the problem of Gan Que, a Chinese woman who ran away at least seven times. Fook Sing, a Downieville merchant, claimed her as his wife and, it appears, his property. Over the course of six months, he sent more than a dozen telegrams attempting to locate her and invested hundreds of dollars in her capture. To Fook Sing, her body was a highly valuable commodity. Although the woman herself is silent in the historical record, her choices speak volumes.[81]

Only the outlines of Gan Que's ordeal survive. Her first recorded escape occurred in July 1874. Fook Sing learned Gan Que had run away when an associate telegraphed him with the news: "Your woman she go Colusa. You want her go there [?]" Fook Sing did not want Gan Que in Colusa; he wanted her with him Downieville. But he could not immediately find her. Thirteen days later, she was still running and had crossed the state line. Fook Sing telegraphed a friend in Wadsworth, Nevada: "Don't you let her go. I will come over tomorrow and see her." The message appeared to have no effect. From Wadsworth, she headed to Virginia Town, California, reportedly in the company of a man.

Perhaps Fook Sing filed a trumped-up legal complaint, because what finally stopped Gan Que's flight was an arrest. Fook Sing received word from both a Chinese man and a white man when she was arrested and held in Auburn. Fook Sing hurried to meet her, and after writing to his business partner asking for $200 for "expenses"—perhaps he meant legal expenses or a bribe—Fook Sing successfully returned Gan Que to his home in Downieville. So ended her first attempt to run away.

Her second escape began days later. A Chinese informant telegraphed Fook Sing on August 12 to tell him she was bound for Marysville. In an attempt to head her off, Fook Sing wrote to an associate in Marysville, Sing Lung, promising $300 for her safe return. "Watch woman close. I come tomorrow," Fook Sing instructed. In fact, it took him three days to arrive in town and catch up with Gan Que. But before he could leave with the woman, he had to prove his claim to her. By telegram, Fook Sing instructed his partner back in Downieville to "Send marriage certificate." His partner promised to send the valuable certificate on the next stage.[82] Apparently Fook Sing hoped the legal document would prove his claim on Gan Que, and in fact it did. Fook Sing brought Gan Que back to Downieville once more.

October marked Gan Que's third flight. Arrested by police in Colusa, California, by October 5 she was in jail in Marysville.

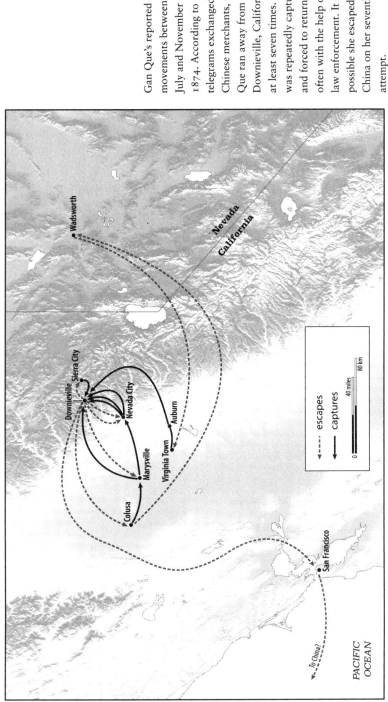

Gan Que's reported movements between July and November 1874. According to telegrams exchanged by Chinese merchants, Gan Que ran away from Downieville, California, at least seven times. She was repeatedly captured and forced to return, often with the help of law enforcement. It is possible she escaped to China on her seventh attempt.

Fook's Marysville associate, Sing Lung, who had helped capture Gan Que two months before, wrote to Fook Sing promising to deliver her again in return for $100 in expenses. Sing Lung delivered on his part of the bargain, transporting the woman to Nevada City and from there to Downieville. But a week later, Fook Sing had yet to pay him. Sing Lung and his associates began to send threatening messages via collect telegrams, demanding payment. "If you don't settle immediately," they wrote on October 15, "will bring sheriff up." The Chinese merchants wrote again on October 24 to explain that the "Colusa policeman" demanded payment for the arrest: "Money no come he go to Downieville to collect." Having enlisted the police to help capture Gan Que, the Chinese merchants needed to pay the constable promptly or they could be the ones in trouble.

Gan Que's fourth escape quickly landed her in jail. Her fifth attempt ended when Fook Sing's associates in Nevada City promised to "send officer up today to stop Gan Que." On her sixth flight, she only made it as far as neighboring Sierra City. Perhaps the problem was weather; in late fall, the mountain passes become frigid and often blanketed with snow.

On her seventh attempt—and one can only hope her last—Gan Que headed west, down the Sierra Mountains across the central valley to the San Francisco Bay. On November 25, 1874, an associate of Fook Sing sent an urgent message saying, "Your woman go to San Francisco tonight with Lee Hung[.] Sing Hoe go back to China[.] you want to let her go[?] answer quick." This urgent question is the last remaining trace of Gan Que. Fook Sing's reply, if there was one, did not survive.

These terse telegrams tell the story of a woman trapped within a web of traffickers, police officers, jailhouses, courtrooms, and money. No government records survived from this contest over Gan Que's movements, but the private messages bear witness to the centrality of law enforcement in the trafficking of one Chinese woman.[83] Rather than fear anti-prostitution and anti-kidnapping laws, Fook Sing relied on law enforcement to constrict a woman's mobility. Although the American legal system and Chinese trafficking network seemed entirely at odds, they occasionally worked in tandem to confine Chinese women.

Sierra County Chinese mug book (1890–1930). When a photographer came to Downieville in 1894, Gan Que was not present. Pictured is another Chinese woman, Lin Quay, of Sierra City, who has "gone to China not to return." This mug book is unusual in that it also includes pictures of people who were not considered criminals. Instead, the local sheriff compiled a book of all resident Chinese, using photographs obtained by federal immigration officials. (VAULT 184, California Historical Society)

A decade later, when Sing Kee turned to American law enforcement in his attempt to recapture Yun Gee, he was following an established playbook.

✻ ✻ ✻

Following her arrest and return, Yun Gee found herself sitting in a crumbling adobe cell in the Los Angeles jail. She needed to escape once more, this time from the city sheriff and charges of embezzlement.[84] With the help of lawyers, she filed a writ of habeas corpus, alleging that Justice Morgan had "acted in excess of his jurisdiction, wholly without authority and contrary to laws" by committing her to the sheriff. In the Los Angeles Superior Court, her lawyers filed a transcript of her hearing together with two sworn affidavits attesting to Justice Morgan's corruption.

How did she know to find a lawyer and file a writ of habeas corpus? Perhaps it was at the direction of someone else, or perhaps she herself knew the law. Speaking a few decades later, Los Angeles attorney T. J. K. McGowen observed, "[The Chinese] know more about our law than the average American. They know. They know what their rights are under the law and how to get their rights. . . . An ignorant uneducated Chinese woman down here in Chinatown will know more about the law than you do, and you may be a college graduate. Don't ask me how they learn it, I don't know, they just do."[85] Traffickers could use habeas petitions to entrap Chinese women, but Yun Gee used one to set herself free. Without fanfare or even a written opinion, Judge V. E. J. How granted Yun Gee freedom from jail and dismissed the embezzlement case against her.

She had won her battle against Sing Kee in court, but what happened next remains unknown. When she stepped out of the overcrowded jail, where did she go? Perhaps she departed Los Angeles with her new husband and, as she had hoped, boarded a steamer across the Pacific. Or perhaps Sing Kee compelled her to return to his house in Chinatown. We cannot know. What we do know is that where she went next determined the course of her life. In the late nineteenth century, Chinese women retained only limited control of their bodies and what control they had depended on their ability to govern their own mobility.

Local racial laws and federal immigration laws sought to immobilize and regulate Chinese women and girls based on accusations of lewdness. But conditional inclusion and Chinese exclusion were not the only constraints in their lives. Within a political economy that offered Chinese women few choices beyond sexual and reproductive labor, the threat of trafficking held more sway over their daily lives than the threat of state regulation. Sexual commerce, its deep stigma in America, and its power to commodify female bodies, proved the greatest force limiting the agency of Chinese women in the nineteenth-century West.

While Chinese men's unequal access to resources resulted from the discriminatory practices of lawmakers and white employers, for Chinese women it was their male counterparts who often set bounds on their labor and claimed their profit. To protect the market in sex,

Chinese traffickers fought to cloister Chinese women, distance them from the white community, and deny them access to the American legal system. Trafficking fundamentally constricted Chinese women's lives, and efforts to regulate trafficking only further restricted them. As they ran away from brothel owners and traffickers, husbands and missionaries, immigration officials and the police, Chinese women exposed these many sources of constraint.

But what, if anything, were Chinese women running toward? Never legally recognized as enslaved, Chinese women were not running toward a formal status of freedom. Nor were they running toward an abstract notion of individual autonomy. Instead, most seemed to be in search of a place to belong. Where they sought belonging differed widely. Some ran toward marriage, hoping to gain a more respectable and secure status within the Chinese American community. Others ran toward white missionaries and the salvation they offered. Some looked for homosocial communities, which could be found in female-operated brothels or Protestant mission homes. Still others sought to return to China and the lives they had left behind.

{5}

The "INVADER"

and the ENTRENCHMENT

of CHINESE SEGREGATION

THE FIRE BEGAN AT 3 P.M. and by midnight it was all over. Where once there was Chinatown, only one building remained among the embers. The twenty wooden tenement houses lining Ah Toy Alley were gone, as were the grocery stores, restaurants, pharmacies, brothels, barbers, butchers, employment offices, and storefront factories. Despite the Chinese fire brigade's best efforts, even the temple had fallen. On May 4, 1887, San Jose's Chinatown, home to more than a thousand residents, was no more.[1]

The San Jose fire was one of the final acts in an unprecedented wave of anti-Chinese expulsions. Repeated recessions and a growing white workforce in the West had pushed economic and racial anxieties to new levels in the Pacific states. Federal attempts to calm white residents through promises of border control only seemed to enflame them. Starting in the fall of 1885, at least 168 communities across the US West attempted to drive out their Chinese residents through a dizzying array of harassment, intimidation, arson, and assault. The expulsions killed scores of Chinese migrants and dislocated tens of thousands.[2]

In the spring of 1886, as the movement peaked, San Jose hosted a mass meeting to coordinate expulsion campaigns across California and send a clear message to Congress: "The Chinese must go." White workingmen did not want Chinese in their neighborhoods, their schools, or their theaters. In fact, they did not want Chinese in the country at all. They demanded that the city council contain Chinese residents and that Congress bar all future Chinese immigration.

The movement to drive the Chinese out of downtown San Jose did not begin with the 1887 fire and it did not end once the embers had cooled. The next day, the editor of the *San Jose Evening Herald* declared that Chinatown had been "removed by the hand of Providence," and urged that it "stay removed by the hand of man."[3] As they awaited federal relief from Chinese immigration, white residents in San Jose turned to a local solution: segregation. If the vigilantes could not drive Chinese from the country altogether, they could separate these "invaders" and contain them in designated neighborhoods. Or at least they could try.

※ ※ ※

The anti-Chinese expulsions that swept the West from 1885 to 1887 ushered in a new period of racial retrenchment. Although the violent movement would gradually abate, the beliefs and emotions that drove it endured. Describing the Chinese as "alien invaders," anti-Chinese groups warned that they would contaminate America.[4]

In both rhetoric and tactics, the anti-Chinese movement bore some resemblance to the white counter-revolution gripping the South in the 1880s. Black and Chinese legal gains in the previous decades helped to provoke a violent white backlash. Reactionary forces in both regions sought to end racial reconstruction before it could threaten white supremacy. Both South and West were willing to go to extreme lengths.

In the West, anti-Chinese forces pushed for change at the local and national scale. The national history is better known. Frustrated with the Chinese Restriction Act (1882), which was underfunded and full of loopholes, anti-Chinese advocates demanded that Congress enact total exclusion. While constitutional guarantees of equal protection could partially shield Chinese from local and state identity-based laws, they did not restrain the federal government. In response to western unrest, Congress passed the Chinese Exclusion Act (1888), which barred all Chinese laborers from entering the United States, and then the Geary Act (1892), which also required registration of all Chinese aliens residing in the country. These Chinese exclusion laws significantly slowed Chinese migration, especially that of the working class.

Historians have paid less attention to local forms of racial retrenchment during this period. While federal lawmakers sought to exclude new arrivals, local officials understood that Chinese residents would continue to live in their communities and focused their attention on social control. City officials, for example, attempted to delineate white spaces from Chinese spaces and reinforce the social distance between them. In other words, they attempted to segregate the Chinese. Segregation was yet another form of conditional inclusion—it allowed Chinese migrants access to society in carefully controlled ways—but Chinese experienced segregation as anything but inclusionary, especially when it came in the form of arson.

Enforcing Chinese segregation was not simple. Segregationists faced a legal landscape that was hostile to direct racial management, and therefore they were forced to experiment with indirect forms of social control in neighborhoods, schools, and public accommodations. To enforce residential segregation in San Jose, for example, the white community combined seemingly race-neutral public policies with private acts of discrimination, arson, and violence. This private-public collaboration proved a powerful way to segregate the Chinese.

When it came to public education, California took a more direct approach. When Chinese children attempted to enroll in San Francisco's public schools, for example, the California legislature passed a law to establish separate Chinese schoolhouses. Such policies would later be affirmed by the Supreme Court through the "separate but equal" doctrine, which allowed for separate facilities as long as they were deemed "equal" in quality.

As racial management tools, both public-private collaboration and "separate but equal" schemes had the advantage of being nominally legal. But white residents did not work entirely within the law. For example, although many western states had laws against discrimination in public accommodations, this did not stop theaters, pools, restaurants, hotels, and barber shops from separating Chinese customers or refusing them service.

New forms of racial management emerged in the West as Jim Crow laws took hold in the South, and these projects were deeply connected. Western segregationists borrowed strategies from southern white supremacists, and vice versa. But there were also fundamental differences between these racial projects. For example, southern white supremacists codified racial segregation in public spaces and enforced racial etiquette with unparalleled levels of violence. They also targeted a different racial group. In the South, Black people formed the largest racialized minority and racial segregation schemes were built to contain them.[5] In this context, where the predominant racial divide was between Black and white, historians have found that Chinese occupied a nebulous and shifting position. At times Chinese were treated as Black in the South, but more often they could access the privileges of whiteness.[6]

Conditions were different in the West. In the 1880s in California and Washington Territory, the Chinese population was approximately ten times the size of the Black population. In Oregon, the Chinese population was close to twenty times larger than the Black population.[7] According to the 1880 census, there were 75,132 Chinese and 6,018 African Americans in California; 9,472 Chinese and 487 African Americans in Oregon; and 3,186 Chinese and 325 African Americans in Washington Territory. As a result, the sites associated with America's history of racial segregation—residential neighborhoods, public schools, and public accommodations—operated differently in the West.

With a larger density of Chinese residents and a longer history of anti-Chinese laws, many western towns and cities guarded white spaces more carefully against the Chinese "invader" than all other races. Western segregationists used anti-Chinese stereotypes to justify and guide this project of racial management. But their tactics did not only impact Chinese residents. As segregationists fought to contain the Chinese, the West became a racial laboratory, a site of experimentation and innovation. Even though western segregationists may have had their sights originally trained on the Chinese, they developed strategies that would ultimately affect all communities of color.[8]

SAN JOSE AND RESIDENTIAL SEGREGATION

Chinese segregation in the West started long before the 1887 fire in San Jose. In fact, the history of Chinese segregation is as long as the history of "Chinatowns" in America, which means it begins with San

Francisco's Chinatown in the 1850s. Upon arrival in the West, Chinese migrants formed ethnic enclaves, white people labeled these neighborhoods as racially distinct spaces, and local officials viewed these spaces with suspicion. As Chinese migration increased, these ethnic enclaves grew and spread. San Jose's first Chinatown emerged in the 1860s.

My collaborator, Hannah Postel, has found that the 1870 and 1880 US censuses show a strong pattern of Chinese residential segregation in California. She used classic statistical measures of segregation, including the index of dissimilarity, to quantify the degree of Chinese segregation in various economic regions of California. The index of dissimilarity measures the percentage of Chinese who would need to relocate to a different building or residential block to achieve complete racial integration. In San Jose in 1870, for example, Postel found the dissimilarity index to be .97 at the level of the building and .82 at the level of the census page (which serves as an approximation of a city block). In other words, 97 percent of Chinese in San Jose would have had to relocate to a different building to achieve complete integration and 82 percent of Chinese would have had to relocate to a different block. A decade later, the extreme level of Chinese segregation in San Jose had lessened only slightly; building-level dissimilarity measured .94 and page-level measured .78.[9]

According to the 1870 and 1880 censuses, Postel found that Chinese experienced segregation in areas far beyond San Jose. At the level of the building, statistical measures indicate that Chinese residents in California's urban centers, mining districts, and economically diverse regions faced levels of segregation comparable to those of Black residents in major southern cities (including Atlanta, Baltimore, Charleston, New Orleans, and Memphis) during the same period.[10] California's agricultural regions, albeit still segregated, showed the least residential isolation. Although California showed regional variation in Chinese segregation, the statewide patterns are still striking. In 1880, Postel found, 79 percent of Chinese lived in Chinese-only group housing.

At the time, white residents blamed the Chinese for their own segregation, describing the problem as "clannishness." The prevailing view was that Chinese were reluctant to mingle with other communities and racially incapable of assimilating to American ways. It is true that many Chinese migrants maintained strong transpacific ties,

A back alley in San Francisco's Chinatown (1880). The photographer, Treu Ergeben Hecht, captured two men in the frame: a man looking down from a window (top right) and a blurred man in motion (bottom left). Chinese called buildings like this home, but officials described them as a nuisance. (San Francisco Historical Photograph Collection, San Francisco History Room, San Francisco Public Library)

enjoyed their ethnic enclaves, found comfort in the Cantonese-speaking community, and wished to return to China one day. The extreme sex imbalance also may have exacerbated segregation, because single Chinese men were more likely to live in segregated group quarters.[11]

However, Chinese migrants' choices of where to live cannot be separated from the hostile environment they encountered in the American West. It is impossible to understand the emergence of Chinatowns without considering white communities' repeated attempts to enforce spatial boundaries and deprive Chinese residents of equal access to healthy neighborhoods and public services.[12]

To enforce the spatial terms of conditional inclusion, segregationists turned to three primary strategies: First, they experimented with identity-based laws, which directly targeted the Chinese race. Second, they engaged in private-public collaboration, often combining the power of discretionary policing and extralegal vigilantism. Third, they practiced housing discrimination, in part through the invention of racial restrictive covenants.

As segregationists worked to remove Chinese from downtown San Jose, they employed all these strategies. The history of San Jose reveals how a local anti-Chinese movement coordinated with city officials, why they encountered legal obstacles, and what creative (and devastating) solutions they developed. The history of San Jose does not, however, offer a clear window into the experience of Chinese residents. Approximately a thousand Chinese residents were in Chinatown the day of the fire, and newspapers reported that all survived, but the displaced Chinese at the center of this story still remain "John Does." Scholars know only a handful of names of the displaced, and I have yet to locate any Chinese accounts of the expulsion. But the fire that destroyed San Jose's first Chinatown did leave behind remnants of the neighborhood buried beneath a layer of ash. Archeologists have uncovered personal objects—including rice bowls, bracelets, medicine bottles, dolls, dice, combs, toothbrushes, and shoes—that hint at the vibrant community that once existed in the center of San Jose.[13]

Chinese first settled on San Jose's Market Street in 1866, when three Chinese leased land in an area designated "Block 1" by a city survey. The land had once been a public plaza in the Pueblo de San José, and before that it was part of the traditional territory of the

Tamien Ohlone tribe. By 1869 several hundred Chinese lived within the block. When an accidental fire destroyed the neighborhood in 1870, the Chinese tenants immediately rebuilt. To protect against future fires, Li Po Tai and Ah Fook (also known as Ung Fook) constructed four brick buildings known as "Brick Chinatown." This construction was soon followed by the adjacent "Wood Chinatown" in 1875. The buildings of Market Street Chinatown were closely packed together and oriented toward the interior of the block rather than toward the surrounding white community. Although census takers only counted 294 men, forty-eight women, and eight children on the block in 1880, historians believe this was a severe undercount.[14]

The trouble in San Jose was inspired by events elsewhere. When a violent anti-Chinese movement roiled across the West in 1885, the San Jose branch of the Anti-Chinese League called for the end of Market Street Chinatown. The League asked city officials to spearhead the effort. W. H. Holms, representing the League, turned up at a Common Council meeting in November 1885 and petitioned publicly "for the removal of Chinatown outside the city limits." In response to the bold request, the council agreed to hold a special meeting on the subject.

Three days later Holmes spoke again at the special meeting, deriding the disgraceful condition of San Jose's Chinatown and pointing to the successful expulsion of Chinese elsewhere. On behalf of the Anti-Chinese League, he asked permission to introduce "certain ordinances looking to the removal of the evil in question." According to the *San Jose Herald*, he asserted that "the higher courts have given evidence that they are ready to support the validity of such measures as the League asks the Council to take."

In fact, the courts had done no such thing. During the previous two decades, anti-Chinese lawmakers experimented with identity-based "removal" measures, but none appear to have survived legal challenge.[15] In Portland, for example, the Common Council initiated several abortive experiments in racial zoning. In 1865 the council considered "An Ordinance to Prevent Chinese Using Any Building or Dwelling for Habitation Within Certain Limits." The proposed law barred not only residence but also "carrying on any business, trade or occupation in part of the city of Portland . . . unless upon express permission of the Common Council." If found in violation,

Chinese would "be deemed guilty of committing a nuisance. . . . punished by a fine not exceeding one hundred dollars, or by imprisonment in the city jail not exceeding fifty days." But the city attorney objected before the proposal could go to a vote. He explained, "I am clearly of the opinion that the City of Portland has no power to provide that only one class of people should not reside within any part of the City."[16] Portland's bid to pass a racial zoning law failed, but even abortive attempts at legal segregation could discourage Chinese settlement.

The State of California also worked to inscribe Chinese segregation in law. The 1879 California constitution directly addressed Chinese residing in the state and included provisions for their removal (see Appendix). In the late nineteenth century, southern states used constitutional conventions to enact the terms of Jim Crow, and California took a similar approach. California's Article 19 promised, "The Legislature shall delegate all necessary power to the incorporated cities and towns of this State for the removal of Chinese without the limits of such cities and towns, or for their location within prescribed portions of those limits."[17] Given the Fourteenth Amendment, however, the constitutionality of this section was in question from the moment it was adopted. In 1880, Nevada City, California, passed an ordinance to implement Article 19, but quickly abandoned the plan when the Chinese Consulate vowed to challenge the ordinance in court.[18]

The violent anti-Chinese expulsions in 1885 and 1886 revived interest in ordinances to remove the Chinese from local communities. For example, the *San Jose Herald* reported favorably on an ordinance proposed in Sacramento. In January 1886 the capital city's board of trustees considered an ordinance announcing that "the presence of Chinese within the limits of the city of Sacramento is dangerous to the morals and prosperity of the city," and cited the state constitution as a remedy. The proposed ordinance made it "the duty of each and every Chinese within the limits of the city of Sacramento . . . to remove without the limits of the city of Sacramento on or before the 1st day of March, 1886." Any Chinese remaining in the city after March 1 would be subject to a misdemeanor violation punishable by "a fine not less than $50 nor more than $500, or by the imprisonment in the County Jail for not less than fifty days or more than six months, or by both such fine and imprisonment."[19]

San Jose and other towns watched the proposal in Sacramento "with great interest."[20] But even supporters recognized that the measure might inspire lawsuits. Sacramento city officials called on a local attorney, Amos Catlin, for an opinion on the constitutionality of the proposal. Catlin found the answer clear: he said that the ordinance was "a self-manifest and palpable violation of the Federal Constitution" and a contravention of diplomatic agreements with China. Fearing the bill could not withstand legal challenge, Sacramento did not move forward with the ordinance, and similar proposals in San Jose, Chico, Willits, and Santa Cruz failed as well.[21]

Four years later—after San Jose had removed Market Street Chinatown by other means—the unconstitutionality of racial zoning was confirmed in court. When San Francisco passed the Bingham Ordinance, which sought to remove "any Chinese" from the desirable real estate of Chinatown to a segregated neighborhood full of slaughterhouses, Chinese plaintiffs challenged the city in federal court with *In re Lee Sing* (1890). In his opinion for the circuit court, Judge Sawyer allowed his exasperation to show:

> The obvious purpose of this order, is, to forcibly drive out a whole community of twenty-odd thousand people, old and young, male and female, citizens of the United States, born on the soil, and foreigners of the Chinese race, moral and immoral, good, bad, and indifferent, and without respect to circumstances or conditions, from a whole section of the city which they have inhabited, and in which they have carried on all kinds of business appropriate to a city, mercantile, manufacturing, and otherwise, for more than 40 years.

The judge declared it was "so obvious" that this racial zoning ordinance was "a direct violation" of the Constitution, treaties with China, and US statutes that any "reasonably intelligent" mind would find explanation "superfluous." Therefore, he would "not waste more time, or words in discussing the matter."[22]

Although the matter appeared closed when it came to Chinese segregation in the West, two decades later eastern cities resurrected the idea of racial zoning laws in their effort to regulate Black communities. Baltimore (1911), Richmond (1911), Winston-Salem (1912), Atlanta (1913), and Louisville (1914) passed ordinances to separate white and Black residents. These identity-based laws, like their anti-Chinese forerunners, were struck down as unconstitutional. In 1917 and again in 1927, the US Supreme Court found them to be a violation of individual property rights. (As in the Chinese case, this did not stop cities from finding other ways to segregate Black people.)[23]

Within this hostile legal landscape, the San Jose city attorney, D. W. Herrington, dismissed calls for a Chinese removal law in 1885. Herrington explained at a Common Council meeting that the "laws guarantee equal rights and protection to all the inhabitants" and this made direct action difficult. Instead, Herrington suggested selective "enforcement of existing laws" that prohibited opium dens, regulated sanitation, and established "cubic air" minimums in lodging houses. In other words, San Jose could aggressively enforce the many behavior-based laws already in place.

San Jose's Anti-Chinese League agreed that the city should enforce "such ordinances as are now in existence" and, in the interest of speeding the process, petitioned the city with specific suggestions. The petitioners explained that the vague provisions of "An Ordinance to Preserve the Peace and Good Order of the City of San Jose" and "An Ordinance Prohibiting Offensive Trades and Occupations and for the Prevention and Removal of Nuisances" might be used to mitigate "the evils of an alien race dwelling in our midst."[24] In other words, San Jose could enforce general-outcast laws against Chinese residents.

City police, at the urging of private petitioners and the newspapers, targeted Market Street Chinatown and redoubled their efforts to sweep up gamblers, prostitutes, vagrants, and any Chinese migrant who could be mistaken for one of these undesirables. And in March 1887, Mayor Charles Breyfogle ordered an investigation of Chinatown, which (not surprisingly) affirmed his own assessment: Chinatown was a cesspool of crime and filth. Based on these findings, the mayor directed the city attorney to "take such proceedings, legal or otherwise, in conjunction with the Chief of Police and Street Commissioner, as may be requisite to forthwith abate and remove" the nuisance.[25]

The city attorney readily took up the charge. Herrington sued the white men who owned property in Chinatown, attempting to treat the entire neighborhood as he would a derelict building. The suit proposed to condemn the neighborhood as a nuisance, evict current tenants, and disinfect the premises.[26] Speaking at a council meeting, Herrington promised, "If no system can be devised to abate these

Fearing the spread of bubonic plague, San Francisco's Health Department systematically destroyed 160 buildings in Chinatown in 1903. Western cities often cited health and safety concerns when removing or restricting Chinese neighborhoods. (J. M. Williamson, M.D., Board of Health Photograph Album of Chinatown, San Francisco, San Francisco History Center, San Francisco Public Library)

nuisances without the removal of these buildings, the whole of them may be removed."[27]

At the same time, Herrington also began researching a second lawsuit to quiet property titles in Chinatown, deploying a legal strategy used to reclaim previously public land. During Mexican rule, the area of Block 1 had included a public plaza, and the city attorney sought to explore the possibility of challenging private claims to the land. Observers found it easy to decipher the city's intent. "If those who own the Chinatown property had ejected their Chinese tenants in accordance with the wishes of the whole people," commented the *Morning Times*, "there can be no doubt that their titles would never have been attacked."[28]

Herrington's first suit to condemn the neighborhood as a nuisance never came to fruition. Perhaps it would have if the fire had not consumed Chinatown on May 4. Although Herrington privately reported to the Common Council that the second suit had little legal basis, he continued to pursue quieting titles late into the spring of 1887. The Common Council and mayor also acted boldly. They called for a referendum on a public improvement bond measure, which proposed to raise funds to build a new city hall "on the ground now occupied by Chinatown."[29] They scheduled a special election for May 5. City officials had done a lot in a short period of time—initiated two lawsuits, ramped up policing, and scheduled a special election—but they could not directly remove Chinatown, at least not legally.

In April 1887, local newspapers in San Jose acknowledged that city officials needed the public's support. On April 12 the *Morning Times*, under the banner "Help to Remove It," urged the people of San Jose to offer "every assistance" to the city attorney "in the endeavor now being made to remove the shanties in Chinatown." The next day the paper made a veiled suggestion. "The Chinese were expelled from Eureka within thirty-six hours," its editors reminded readers, and "the Eureka Chinatown like our Chinatown, was situated just on the edge of the business part of the town." Now free of Chinese, Eureka's business center was reportedly booming, but the paper believed that Eureka had made one mistake in its expulsion: "the omission to burn the remains."[30]

When San Jose's Chinatown burned on May 4, 1887, the city fire brigade did not come to the rescue. The city had carefully omitted Block 1 from the city's fire limits, which meant the Chinese had to fend for themselves. The Chinese community was prepared to fight fires, for Chinatown had long maintained a private fire engine, but on the afternoon of May 4 they found the water tank had been drained. Someone did not want them to put out this fire.

Local papers conceded that the fire was likely arson, but pointed their fingers at the Chinese, alleging that Chinese merchants had set the fire themselves to claim the insurance money. This conspiracy theory only partially concealed what everyone knew. White vigilantes had set Chinatown ablaze. They had done so the day before the special election, with the hope of ensuring that the public improvement bond measure would succeed, which it did.[31]

Now the city had the money and space to build a new city hall, as long as the former Chinatown remained vacant. "The Boom is here, Chinatown is in ashes and the bonds carried more than ten to one. That is nearly joy enough for twenty-four hours," declared the *Morning Times*. But the city could not rest, the editor cautioned. San

Aftermath of the San Jose Chinatown Fire (1887). White spectators walk among the smoldering ruins of Market Street Chinatown. Chinese residents appear to have all fled. (Reproduction courtesy of History San Jose)

Aftermath of the Point Alones fire (1906). When arson was used to remove Chinese settlements, the results could be devastating. Here Chinese residents pick through the rubble looking for their belongings after the burning of a fishing village near Monterey. (California History Room Archives, Monterey Public Library)

Jose must "do all possible to prevent Chinatown from again disgracing that section of the city."[32]

"It is a thousand pities that the laws should be so construed by coolie-loving judges that we cannot drive them altogether out of the city," commented the *Evening Herald*. Instead, the paper supported a plan to set up a Chinese "reservation." Drawing inspiration from the removal and confinement of Native Californians, the paper proposed that the city forcibly relocate Chinatown outside the city center. "There may be no strictly legal method of carrying out such a suggestion," the paper admitted, "but we think it can be done nevertheless, if the authorities will act promptly and resolutely, and the people generally will second their efforts." According to the newspaper editors, the city could remove the Chinese from downtown through a combination of urban planning (to create a reservation), aggressive policing (of city ordinances), and public support (of an unspoken nature).[33]

It was true that the city leaders had to be creative if they wanted to prevent the Chinese from rebuilding. At the mayor's urging, the city attorney pressed ahead with a suit to quiet titles near Market

Street (despite his own assessment that the suit was baseless), naming thirty white landowners and nineteen Chinese. The suit listed all but two of the white landowners by name, but used nonsense fictitious names to stand in for the unknown Chinese. These nineteen "John Doe Chinamen"—listed as "Ah Hick, Ah Heck, Ah Hock, Ah Huck, Ah Lick, Ah Leek, Ah Lock, Ah Luck, Ah Tie, Ah Toi, Ah Too, Ah Turn, Ah Moh, Ah Moo, Ah Muh, Ah Mum, Ah My, Ah Meh, Ah Mo"[34]—were "in possession of portions of the lands" that the city claimed as its own. Arguing that Chinatown sat on land that was once a public plaza, the city claimed the defendants had "wrongfully and unlawfully entered into and took possession of said plaza." The city wished to repossess Block 1 and demanded $40,000 in damages.

Newspaper reports suggest that the city paired the lawsuit with a deal. In July 1887 the San Jose mayor and Common Council took up a resolution that instructed the city attorney to drop the suit against any defendants who would ensure "that said property and each portion thereof will not be leased or subleased, rented or subrented or occupied in any manner by the Chinese race for a period of ten years."[35] It is unclear whether the landowners took this deal, since all relevant legal records have been lost.

Either way, it is noteworthy that the city was suggesting that property owners begin to write racial restrictions into their deeds and leases, promoting a practice that came to be known as racial restrictive covenants. The earliest known racial restrictive covenants in property deeds date to the anti-Chinese expulsions of the mid-1880s.[36] As western towns and cities turned away from removal laws because of the likelihood of lawsuits, some turned toward private acts of discrimination. If landlords refused to rent or sell to the Chinese, or better yet, wrote these prohibitions into their property deeds, then the Chinese could be permanently removed from desirable neighborhoods.

Even before the fire in San Jose, property owners occasionally wrote racial restrictions into their leases. In 1884, when Ralph Lowe agreed to lease property to Wy Kee in Market Street Chinatown for the following ten years, he added an unusual clause: "In the event all the Chinamen shall be compelled to move from the present locality occupied by those in the vicinity of Market Square including foregoing described premises by municipal command or other competent authority that then this lease and the term thereof shall cease."[37] Lowe wished to protect his interests against the possibility that the city or some other "authority" would expel the Chinese from downtown San Jose.

What had been an occasional practice became better known and widespread during the anti-Chinese expulsions of 1885 and 1886. For example, when vigilantes in Eureka, California, drove the Chinese out of town by force, they followed up with a warning to landlords. Newspapers reported that the ringleaders had issued a notice "to all property owners . . . requesting them not to lease or rent property to Chinese."[38] Similarly, in Willow Creek, the Anti-Chinese League condemned "the action of all parties who will attempt to sell or lease land to the Chinese, rent them houses or in any manner seek to shelter or afford them aid or comfort."[39]

But when landowners sought to enforce racial restrictive covenants in court, they ran into legal problems, as was the case in *Gandolfo v. Hartman, Fong Yet, and Sam Choy* (1890). In the spring of 1886, Marvin Stewart decided to sell two adjoining properties facing East Main Street in South Buena Ventura, California, and he wrote into the property deeds the stipulation that no "Chinamen" may take possession in the future. The racial restrictive covenant read: "The party of the first part shall never, without the consent of the party of the second part, his heirs or assigns, rent any of the buildings or ground owned by said party of the first part, and fronting on said East Main Street, to a Chinaman or Chinamen." Both buyers, Alexander Gandolfo and Fredolin Hartman, agreed to the purchase terms.

But a few years later, in 1890, Gandolfo took his neighbor, Hartman, to federal court. Gandolfo alleged that Hartman had leased his property to Fong Yet and Sam Choy, violating the terms of the deed. Moreover, by allowing "Chinamen" to live in the neighborhood, he had caused his neighbor $10,000 in damages. The attorneys representing Gandolfo in his complaint made an impassioned case that the covenant should be enforced. It was a matter of private property, not a matter of trade (which might be governed by treaty) or public policy (subject to equal protection under the Fourteenth Amendment). But at the close of their brief, the attorneys admitted some uncertainty: "In conclusion it may be well to frankly confess to the Court that the most careful examination of all the books within our reach has failed to disclose a single case even analogous to the instant one."[40]

The US Circuit Court ruled against the plaintiff, finding that the racial restrictive covenant could not be enforced. The court held the covenant to be in violation of the Fourteenth Amendment and treaty agreements with China. If "state and municipal legislatures are forbidden to discriminate against the Chinese in their legislation," then it made no sense to the judge that "a citizen of the state may lawfully do so by contract, which the courts may enforce." Gandolfo lost his case, and presumably had to tolerate his new Chinese neighbors.[41]

But rather than sound the death knell for this new segregationist tool, the ruling helped to popularize it. The judge's opinion immediately drew criticism from the legal profession, and the controversy helped spread news of this novel tactic. Racial restrictive covenants targeting African Americans began appearing in the South around 1904, in border states in 1905, and in northern states in 1922.[42] And when these anti-Black deeds faced legal challenges, the courts often upheld them. The most powerful endorsement came in 1926 when the US Supreme Court reviewed a case from the District of Columbia. *Corrigan v. Buckley* involved an agreement among thirty white neighbors who maintained that "no part of [their] properties should ever be used or occupied by, or sold, leased or given to, any person of the negro race or blood."[43] The lower court enforced the covenant, and the Supreme Court let the ruling stand, asserting that it lacked jurisdiction over the private transaction. Following the ruling, racial restrictive covenants continued to spread and became a critical element of Black segregation. On the West Coast, some racial restrictive covenants included restrictions against "Chinese," "Mongolians," "Orientals," or "Asiatics" in addition to Black residents.[44]

In San Jose, it is unclear whether racially restrictive leases, or just the threat of them, prevented Chinese from rebuilding on Market Street. But what is clear is that racially restrictive leases allowed the Chinese to rebuild elsewhere. A private property owner, John Heinlen, offered to build a "new Chinatown" on his property in the Second Ward, and applied to the city for a permit expressly for this purpose. He sought to designate a permissible neighborhood for the

Chinese to occupy and personally profit from the result. At the same time, L. M. Hoeffler offered a second site for a Chinese district north of the Woolen Mills.[45]

White residents in these two neighborhoods did not approve of this solution, however. They wanted the city center to be rid of Chinese, but they also did not want the Chinese in their own backyard. Concerned citizens gathered to oppose the proposition. "It is not a question of race prejudice," one citizen declared at a mass meeting. Instead, he believed it was just a fact that one should not build "a town of slaves within a town of free men."[46]

Second Ward residents held rallies to draw attention to their cause. The largest of these gatherings featured a giant bonfire, fireworks, and a band. At one rally, more than 150 concerned mothers signed a petition against the planned Chinatown and the "social and moral destruction" that would ensue. "We plead that our children may not be exposed to such contact, that our streets may not be made the thoroughfares to the haunts of vice," they begged, for "the safety, honor, and virtue of our children." To organize ongoing advocacy, they also formed the San Jose Home Protection Association, which had the express purpose of fighting the "threatened invasion." They declared, "John Chinaman will never obtain a foothold on the Heinlen tract."[47]

Despite the outcry and a lawsuit, Heinlen signed a lease with eleven Chinese merchants to construct and lease twenty buildings. The lease contained affirmative racial language, guaranteeing that the merchants had the right to let the buildings "for the use and occupation of any Chinese whatsoever."[48] The result was what came to be known as Heinlenville Chinatown, a new ethnic enclave, located two miles from its predecessor, that would thrive for the next three decades. It had been a winding road, but San Jose had removed the Chinese from the city center and segregated them in a designated neighborhood. It had taken an anti-Chinese movement, willing city leaders, complicit private property owners, bogus lawsuits, discretionary policing, and arson.

The particularities of San Jose's path toward removal and segregation may be unique, but many other western cities found ways to segregate Chinese. One bird's-eye view of segregation practices comes from the 1920s, when the California Real Estate Association queried local realty boards about their practices (with the hope of encouraging more segregation in the future). The survey offers a statewide assessment of Chinese segregation several decades after the Market Street fire.

Every realty board in California received a one-page form. It began with the question: "Are there segregated sections in your locality based on the color line? If so, what races are affected?" The Bakersfield Realty Board answered in the affirmative, reporting that "Negroes, Chinese, Japanese, Mexicans & any others not of white or caucasian race" lived in segregated sections. Yolo County responded that there were "fairly well defined sections for Chinese and for Negroes." In contrast, Redlands only segregated "Mexicans" and "Negroes." In Fresno, a segregated "Russian" section was reported alongside "Negro, Chinese and Japanese." The Burlingame and San Mateo board reported they had "None" but there "should be." "We have no colored population in our city," bragged the Orland board. "We discourage settlement of the colored population."[49]

The second survey question asked whether the town used "local ordinances" to advance segregation. In general, the repeated legal rulings against racial zoning laws seem to have had the intended effect, because the boards reported that California towns no longer tried to segregate through local ordinances. One board did allude to alien land laws. These laws (which will be addressed in Chapter 6) restricted noncitizens' ability to own land and, to a lesser extent, real estate. If racial zoning ordinances were not behind residential segregation, then what was? The survey offered some options: Was a "special understanding between local residents" in place? Or did minorities engage in self segregation due to "preference of lessee or buyer"? How about "community custom" or a particular "real estate practice"? Most towns and cities reported that segregation was primarily achieved through special understandings, community customs, and real estate practices.

The final question asked realty boards to elaborate on current and best practices to address this "important problem." In El Centro, the board reported that it primarily relied on a "custom of real estate men not to sell a foreigner a lot in any location that would be the means of causing criticism by the adjoining property owner." Santa Barbara attributed its successful segregation of nonwhites to a "high code of ethics" that realtors "rigidly adhered to." "We have a Gentleman's agreement not to place any of the above in white districts and we believe this is the best way to handle it," explained the Bell Realty Board in Southern California.

In total, forty-six California realty boards returned the segregation survey, and thirty of them reported restrictions on Chinese residency in particular. Less formal queries to Seattle and Portland yielded similar results. The Seattle board reported, "The question of the segregation of these people is one that has largely taken care of its self [sic]." According to the Seattle Realty Board, the city had previously weighed the possibility of racial zoning, but understood it to be unconstitutional and therefore had turned to deed restrictions.

The Portland Realty Board sent a copy of its bylaws, which declared that a broker should "not under any circumstances directly or indirectly sell or be a party to the sale of Portland residence property to persons of the Negro or Oriental races in districts now in-

Tanner Creek Gulch, Portland, Oregon (circa 1880s). Chinese homes and vegetable gardens lie in the foreground; a wealthy white neighborhood lies in the background. Chinese and white residents lived in tight proximity, but in carefully separated spaces. (Oregon Historical Society)

habited almost exclusively by white persons." The board explained, "This rule is not on account of any prejudice against people of these races, for it has none, but because it is common knowledge that the residence of Negros or Orientals in any district greatly depreciates, in the public mind, surrounding property values." It was simply a matter of profit.[50]

In San Jose, the survey arrived forty years after the burning of Market Street Chinatown. James B. Clayton, vice president of the local realty board, reported "no color line" in the city. What he meant was that "Jap Town" and "China Town" were "not zoned" and, therefore, "the Japs are spreading." He thought segregation "should be zoned by law," and wrote that "the State Association would do a wonderful work if they could appoint a commissioner to work with the State of California to place the various nationalities and people of African decent [sic], even though citizens of the United States, in segregated areas."[51] Whether he knew it or not, Clayton's suggestion was in keeping with San Jose's history. The city had long relied on public-private collaboration to bolster segregation.

SAN FRANCISCO AND SCHOOL SEGREGATION

The white residents who did not want Chinese as neighbors also balked at the idea of Chinese students in their children's classrooms. And in the 1880s there was a small but growing population of Chinese American children, especially within urban enclaves. In San Francisco there were nowhere near "2700 boy babies" in Chinatown, but in 1884 the city government reported that 722 children "of Chinese parentage" lived in the city.

This rang alarm bells for San Francisco's city supervisors. The children had been born in the United States, but city officials warned that "in every attribute of juvenile life they are Mongolian." The supervisors believed Chinese children's lack of Americanization posed a growing threat to white society. A city report claimed, "Mongolian children, born and nurtured in such conditions of immorality and degradation, become indeed a more serious problem than any which the American people have ever yet been called upon to solve."

Although city leaders believed the problem was a lack of Americanization, school officials insisted that the solution was not education. In fact, the superintendent of education told city leaders that it was imperative to "guard well the doors of our public schools" and stand firm against "this invasion of Mongolian barbarism."[52]

The "invasion" of San Francisco schools was not hypothetical; in 1884 a so-called barbarian stood at the door of a San Francisco public school. Mamie Tape, an eight-year-old Chinese American child, arrived for the first day of school at Spring Valley Primary School. Mamie was the daughter of Mary and Joseph Tape, Chinese immigrants who had distanced themselves from Chinatown as they attempted a steep upward climb toward social inclusion in America.

Although the couple had been educated privately by missionaries, they wished for their American-born daughter to attend public school in the middle-class neighborhood of Cow Hollow. But when they arrived at Spring Valley Primary with their daughter, Principal Jennie Hurly stood at the front door and would not allow the family to enter. Rather than send Mamie to a private Chinese mission school in San Francisco Chinatown, Joseph Tape sued Principal Hurley and the San Francisco School District.

The result was *Tape v. Hurley* (1885), a case that has garnered a fair amount of scholarly attention.[53] It has become emblematic of the Chinese fight for civil rights and the lengths to which local and state officials would go to deny them. Some have compared the Tape family's appeal for access to public education to Homer Plessy's appeal for access to the white-only train car in *Plessy v. Ferguson* (1896), the case that established the doctrine of "separate but equal." But any similarities are primarily visible in retrospect. The logics of racial segregation operated differently in the West.

Initially San Francisco and the State of California treated all nonwhite students in similar ways, but this approach did not hold. From 1859 to 1871, San Francisco allowed all children in the city to attend public schools, but it maintained separate facilities by race, dividing white, "colored," and Chinese children. This system was a form of inclusion—after all it provided a public education to all children—but one conditioned on racial segregation. The California legislature endorsed this complicated system in 1863, passing a law that barred "Negroes, Mongolians and Indians" from attending regular public schools. The law allowed (but did not require) districts to establish "separate," publicly funded schools for these pupils. In 1866 they provided an exception for districts with fewer than ten "children of African or Mongolian descent, and Indian children not living under the care of white persons." If there was no other way to provide them education, and if the local board of education and white parents did not object, these "colored" children could attend school with white children.[54]

This system continued until 1870, when state lawmakers amended the law and left out any mention of "Mongolians." This omission could have resulted in permissiveness with respect to Chinese enrollment. Under the revised statutes, San Francisco could have maintained a separate "colored" school for Native and Black students, while integrating white and Chinese. But the San Francisco school board took the opposite approach. The board argued it was under no obligation to continue to educate Chinese students at all and shuttered its small Chinese schoolhouse the following year. San Francisco continued to include Black and Native students in segregated schools, but now rejected Chinese students entirely from the public education system.[55]

This arrangement first came under fire from the Black community. The parents of Mary Frances Ward challenged the segregation of Black pupils in San Francisco in 1872. Their attorney applied for a writ of mandate from the California Supreme Court that would order Ward's neighborhood school to admit her, but the court refused in 1874. Under the pressure of school boycotts by the Black community, the San Francisco school board nevertheless decided to abolish its two "colored" schools a year later. "These schools have never been successful or popular among the colored people," the school superintendent noted. "They would not be satisfied with anything but the admission of their children to the schools for white children." Years of Black protest and the financial burden of maintaining a "colored" school had made San Francisco's system untenable.[56] After closing the "colored" school, the district transferred its pupils to other schools in the city, integrating the small number of Black and Native children into San Francisco's public schools.[57]

San Francisco, however, continued to deny the Chinese a public education. Private missionary schools provided the only education available to Chinese and Chinese American children. But missionary schools were only available in a few western cities, and most only offered basic language instruction alongside Bible study. The Chinese community found this arrangement unacceptable. Chinese residents communicated their dissatisfaction through repeated petitions to the San Francisco school board and, after receiving no relief there, the state legislature.

In 1878, Chinese residents sent a petition to the California state legislature with 13,000 signatures, demanding access to the public school system.[58] The petition asserted that "Chinese merchants and laborers, being here under the protection of your Constitution and laws, are entitled to the same rights and privileges accorded to foreigners generally." The petitioners described themselves as "law-abiding people" who added to the "prosperity of this State," and added that they were taxpayers who directly supported public schools. In San Francisco alone, the Chinese community had paid more than $42,000 in school taxes the previous year. The petitioners estimated that there were 3,000 Chinese children in the state, all of whom were "anxious to learn the English language," and asked for their admission to public schools. The petitioners did not ask for integration; instead they stated a preference for separate (that is, segregated) schools for Chinese children.[59] They received no response.

But in 1880 the California legislature decided to strike all racial language from the school code and terminate all "colored" schools. It was a win for Black parents, who had fought for integration for decades, and a win for cash-strapped school districts, which had found segregation to be expensive. In law, if not always in fact, California had desegregated its schools. And the western state had done so even as southern states rushed to codify the segregation of Black students within elementary schools.[60]

Chinese children, however, continued to be routinely rejected by public schools. But the revised statute left a legal opening that the Tape family seized. When Mamie Tape attempted to enroll in 1884, there were no longer any racial prohibitions written into California's school laws and there was no longer a "colored" public school for Mamie Tape to attend. Either the courts would allow her to attend Spring Valley Primary School, or she would be denied a public education entirely.

The Tapes sued in state court to establish Mamie's right to public education and the rights of the other 700 Chinese American children in the city. The lower court swiftly ordered the primary school to admit Mamie based on California's 1880 school law, but the school board appealed to the California Supreme Court. The school board's appeal rested on race-neutral language in the law, which granted it "the power to exclude children of filthy or vicious habits, or children suffering from contagious or infectious diseases."[61] In other words, they sought to use legal language targeting general outcasts against Chinese children.

Joseph Tape's attorneys filed a brief with the California Supreme Court that made an impassioned case for admitting Mamie to school.

The Tape Family (1884). They pose in the westernized dress of a middle-class American family with Mamie in the center. Joseph sits to the left with an arm around little Emily seated on his knee; Mamie and Frank stand tall holding hands; and Mary sits on the right. (Smith Collection/Gado/Archive Photos/, Getty Images)

To persuade the court, his attorneys worked to establish Joseph Tape's bona fides as well-educated, Americanized, and Christian, noting that he had "cut off his queue" fifteen years earlier. Then the respondent's brief explained that Mamie was born in America, had grown up in an assimilated family, and had none of the "filthy" habits associated with the Chinese race.[62]

Joseph Tape's response highlighted the unique qualifications of his own family, but his lawyers also implicitly made a larger case for providing public education for Chinese and Chinese American children. Denying Mamie a public education, the brief claimed, would violate her right to equal protection under the Fourteenth Amendment. (Mamie was a citizen, but even if she were an alien, the lawyers pointed out, she would be entitled to protection under treaty agreements.) Moreover, Joseph Tape paid city taxes "regularly and willingly," including school taxes. Rejecting his child was equivalent to "taxation without representation," a violation the brief tied to the American Revolution.[63]

Finally, Joseph's lawyers raised the issue of Japanese children. According to Tape and his lawyers: "The public schools of San Francisco have on their rolls quite a large number of Japanese, who belong to one branch of the Mongolian race." These Japanese children were not denied a public education and they were not even American born. They were "subjects of the Emperor of Japan," but even so "no thought of excluding them is raised." If Japanese children were recognized as "bright scholars," why not the Chinese?[64]

The appellant brief filed on behalf of Principal Hurley responded to the Tapes with a straightforward argument: "Mamie Tape is a person of the Mongolian or Chinese kind, ineligible to become a citizen of the United States," and the "parents and children of said race have filthy and vicious habits" that endangered the community. The city had the right to protect the health and safety of its white children.[65]

In a terse opinion, the California Supreme Court rejected the principal's reasoning, upheld the lower court, and ordered the school to admit Mamie. The court stayed silent on the issue of equal protection or treaty rights, focusing instead on statute: existing California law provided no legal basis to prohibit Mamie from attending Spring Valley. While previous school laws protected the rights of "white children," the 1880 law had no mention of race at all.[66]

California lawmakers rushed to correct the situation and offer San Francisco an alternate solution. The opinion in *Tape v. Hurley* was published on March 3, 1885, and nine days later the legislature amended the school law to establish "separate schools for the children of Mongolian or Chinese descent" and mandated that "when such schools were established, no Chinese child was to be admitted to any other school."[67] The law went into immediate effect, and San Francisco raced to open a separate Chinese public school as quickly as possible. To maintain segregation in the meantime, Principal Hurley insisted that Spring Valley was overenrolled and placed Mamie on a waiting list.

Mary Tape did not remain silent as California lawmakers, the San Francisco school board, and Principal Hurley conspired to keep her daughter out of Spring Valley. Instead, she wrote to the school board a searing public letter that was published in the *Daily Alta California*. "What right have you to bar my children out of the school because she is [of] Chinese descent[?]" she demanded to know. Mary took pains to explain that Mamie had grown up in a white neighborhood. After her painstaking work to raise an Americanized family, Mary experienced this blatant racism as a hard blow. "It seems no matter how a Chinese may live and dress so long as you know they are Chinese, then they are hated as one. There is not any right or justice for them."

Mary declared she would not back down. "Mamie Tape will never attend any of the Chinese schools of your making! Never!!!"[68] But quickly Mary found it untenable to follow through on her threat and deprive her children of a public education. Five days after Mary sent the letter, on April 13, Mamie arrived at the brand-new Chinese public school together with her younger brother and four other children. The Tapes' courtroom victory had been a Pyrrhic one. Rather than forcing integration in one San Francisco primary school, their suit inspired lawmakers to institute Chinese educational segregation throughout the state.

In 1902 a Chinese parent again challenged the school segregation law, this time in federal court. The suit alleged that Chinese school segregation "is arbitrary, and the result of hatred for the Chinese race" and a violation of the Fourteenth Amendment. But by then the doctrine of separate-but-equal was well established in the South. The US circuit court at San Francisco declared it "well settled that the state has the right to provide separate schools for the children of different races."[69] Even so, in San Francisco in 1905 the Chinese made some headway in secondary school education. After Chinese parents threatened to boycott Chinese schools and thereby cause a withdrawal of state funds, the board of education agreed to allow some Chinese students to enroll in regular high schools. But San Francisco's Chinese primary school remained.[70]

In 1906, San Francisco proposed to extend segregated education to Japanese students, relocating ninety-three Japanese students out of neighborhood schools and placing them in the "Chinese School," which was renamed the "Oriental School." But the proposal sparked outcry from Japan, a menacing imperial power. The San Francisco school board eventually relented and allowed Japanese to remain in neighborhood schools, but only after President Theodore Roosevelt brokered a deal to slow Japanese migration (known as the Gentleman's Agreement). As a result, San Francisco's Oriental School continued to educate solely Chinese children.[71]

Although California law mandated Chinese segregation, oral histories conducted by researchers in 1924, 1970, and 1979 suggest that Chinese education varied widely by location and that Chinese response varied as well. For example, John Jeong arrived in San Francisco in 1900 and several years later attempted to enroll in "the American school on Geary Street." Jeong attended the school for a week before "someone told me it was not for Chinese. We was only supposed to go to the Oriental School." For Jeong, this expulsion meant the end of his formal education. "After that I just studied at home and worked in my brother's store," he explained. Jeong's family chose a path different from the Tapes'; they avoided sending him to a segregated school by withdrawing him from school entirely.

Leland Chin, in contrast, found San Francisco public schools to be more accommodating than schools elsewhere in the state. Chin's family left San Francisco following the 1906 earthquake and moved to agricultural communities along the Sacramento River, including Isleton, Walnut Grove, and Locke. When the local high schools would not allow "Orientals," Chin's parents sent him back to San Francisco. There he gained admission to integrated Lowell High School in 1910.[72]

The Los Angeles school board did not implement formal segregation, but Chinese residents remembered feeling unwelcome in the public schools. Nellie Chung recalled to a researcher in 1979 that her father hired a white woman to teach her at home in the 1910s. When the researcher inquired, "Did you ever ask your father why he didn't send you to study in a white school?," Chung explained: "At the time no Chinese children went, no Chinese students. . . . Only 3 or 4 went to study in Los Angeles schools." She did not know the reason. "Whether [schools] did not allow Chinese students to go to their school or whether the Chinese parents did not want their children to go . . . I don't really understand why." Instead, Chinese in Los Angeles remembered children attending private missionary schools or receiving tutoring at home. Even in an integrated school district, Chinese pupils could be deprived of a public education.[73]

Chinese students had a range of experiences in California, and it is clear that San Francisco's strictly segregated elementary education was not the norm. Few California communities had the capacity, resources, or will to establish separate Chinese schools. (It is notable that the South took a different and more extreme approach to Black education.) While San Francisco and three towns in Sacramento County had created segregated schools for Chinese families, other communities found it too expensive to maintain separate schools.[74] Some schools systems practiced de facto segregation, as Chinese, Japanese, Mexican, and Black children living in segregated neighborhoods were funneled into particular schools. Other schools, like Lincoln Elementary in Oakland, established special Chinese classrooms under the pretense of providing rudimentary language instruction. And some schools quietly dissuaded Chinese children from attending entirely (in violation of the mandatory education laws). This haphazard system continued until 1947, when the California Supreme Court found school segregation to be unconstitutional and California repealed the Chinese school segregation laws.[75]

RENO, SEATTLE, FRESNO, AND SEGREGATED THEATERS

On August 15, 1916, Ruby Tsang and her two friends, Flora Woo and Yum Lee, headed out to the new Rialto Theatre in Reno, Nevada, for a night of moving pictures, vaudeville, and music. They bought tickets, passed through the lobby, and started to settle into seats on the ground floor when an usher confronted them. In a "loud, boisterous, and offensive manner," the usher ordered Tsang and her friends to vacate the seats. According to Tsang's lawsuit, he told her to "go upstairs" to the balcony or "leave the theater" because people of her "nationality were not allowed in that part of the house."[76] Ruby Tsang walked out and then filed suit against the theater company.

This was not Ruby's first experience with segregation. Born in 1897, Ruby spent her early years living with her family in the heart of San Francisco Chinatown in a rented apartment at the corner of Washington and Stockton streets. Her mother, Tsang Wong Kiew, was raised by Methodist missionaries who taught her to read and write in English and blessed her marriage to a cook named Tsang Won in 1895. Literate and converted, the couple gave Americanized names to all of their children. Ruby had an elder brother, Benjamin, born in 1895, and two younger siblings, Pearl and Ernest.[77] Perhaps the young family wished to live in the segregated urban enclave, but perhaps not. By then, covenants, etiquette, and profit had built invisible barriers between Chinatown and the white spaces beyond.

When Ruby was eight, her father abandoned the family. Tsang Wong Kiew was left with four children and her meager salary as a seamstress. She sought out the Methodist Chinese Mission Home, which had raised her, and which now agreed to take charge of her daughters. Ruby weathered one dislocation only to face another within a year. The 1906 San Francisco earthquake and fire destroyed 500 city blocks, including the one in which the Methodist Mission Home stood. The Methodist Church found temporary housing across the bay in Berkeley as it worked to rebuild. That is where census takers found Ruby Tsang several years later, along with thirty-two other Chinese, ranging in age from two to thirty-five, whom they listed as "inmates" of the home.[78]

Under the care of white missionaries, Ruby and her sister's assimilation accelerated. They spent their days speaking English, studying the Bible, learning to sing, and consuming American food and ideas. To raise funds for a new permanent home, the missionaries selected eight children, including Ruby and Pearl, dressed them in traditional Chinese style, taught them religious and patriotic songs, and embarked on a grand musical tour of the United States. In 1908 and 1909 they visited Buffalo, Scranton, and forty other eastern cities, often performing several times a day in churches, theaters, and private homes. In Philadelphia they sang in front of Independence Hall. In Washington, DC, they visited the Chinese Legation to sing for Minister Wu Tingfang and the White House to sing for President Theodore Roosevelt.[79]

Ruby Tsang was welcomed into the president's home, but once the Methodist Church had used her earnings to rebuild the mission, she found herself back in segregated San Francisco. She lived in Chinatown, a few blocks from her mother's new apartment, and attended the city's Oriental School. Even within these segregated spaces, Tsang continued to learn lessons in American ways, including the US legal system. In 1909 her mother sued for divorce and made national headlines. Under the banner "Becoming Americanized; Second Chinese woman in America to get Divorce," the *Topeka State Journal* explained that Tsang Wong Kiew alleged desertion, asked for custody of her four children, and made a plea for alimony. The court granted her divorce and request for child support but could not locate her ex-husband. Ruby Tsang would remain in the Mission Home until she graduated (with a top prize) from the Oriental School in 1912.[80]

Then Ruby Tsang and another "inmate" from the home, Flora Woo, moved to Reno, Nevada, to study music. Perhaps Tsang hoped her youthful days spent singing across the Eastern Seaboard signaled the start of a career. She met a local young man, Yum Lee, who was born in neighboring Wadsworth and was known about town in Reno. Together, the trio entered the Rialto Theatre one August night in 1916 and attempted to take their seats. But despite their assigned seats in the orchestra section, the usher told them to move to the balcony. He referred to their "nationality" to justify the change of seats, but since all three were American-born citizens, the term was a euphemism for "race."

Editors at the *Sacramento Daily Union* had no trouble reading the subtext. Under the banner "Race Question Raised in Reno," the paper announced that Tsang had sued the theater company, and others threatened to follow. The suit sought $10,000 in damages, explaining that "the plaintiff is a woman of education and refinement and at all times in said theater and elsewhere has conducted herself in a ladylike quiet manner." The expulsion from her seat had caused "humiliation" and "disgrace" in front of "a large number of people then and there assembled."[81] Tsang had grown up in a segregated neighborhood and attended a segregated school, but something about her experience in the theater pushed her to act. Perhaps she took offense because she was trying to break into show business. Perhaps she had expected her assimilation to protect her, as it had in the past. Or perhaps the indignity of being publicly ejected from a seat as an adult compounded the indignities of her childhood.

The Reno Amusement Company, which owned the theater, and Turner & Dahnken Enterprises, which ran it, argued for dismissal. Among their lawyers' many arguments, one stands out: "that the defendant had the right to segregate people of different nationalities." In other words, it was within the theater's right to discriminate based on nationality or (in Tsang's case) race.

It was true that no Nevada law prevented segregation in public accommodations, and there was no longer a federal law. During racial reconstruction, Radical Republicans understood the importance of racial equality in public accommodations, including places of amusement. Congress had passed the Civil Rights Act of 1875, which guaranteed that "all persons . . . shall be entitled to the full and equal enjoyment of the accommodations, advantages, facilities, and privileges of inns, public conveyances on land or water, theaters, and other places of public amusement." But shortly after, the Supreme Court invalidated the law in the *Civil Rights Cases* (1883) and narrowed the scope of the Fourteenth Amendment's promise of equal protection by applying it only to state action. The court declared public accommodations a private matter and affirmed the right of private individuals to discriminate. The *Civil Rights Cases* would pave the way for "white only" and "colored only" policies that became typical in the public spaces of the Jim Crow South.[82]

In Nevada, there was no law that explicitly permitted segregation in theaters, but there was also no law to prevent it. In addition to their motion to dismiss, the theater company threatened to follow the path laid by the southern states. The *Reno Gazette-Journal* reported, "As a result of the affair, local moving picture house properties may ask the next state legislature to pass a segregation law." Whether due to the weak legal basis for her claim or the threat of a segregation law, Tsang dropped her lawsuit and the case ended there.[83]

If Tsang had been in her home state, however, she would have had a stronger case. When the Supreme Court invalidated the Civil Rights Act of 1875, eighteen states took it upon themselves to mandate equal protection in public accommodations, including the western states of California, Colorado, and Washington.[84] Washington's law, "An Act to Protect All Citizens in Their Civil and Legal Rights" (1890), is emblematic. It stated, "All persons within the jurisdiction of the State of Washington shall be entitled to the full and equal enjoyment of the public accommodations, advantages, facilities and privileges of inns, public conveyances on land or water, theaters and other places of public amusement and restaurants, subject only to the conditions and limitations established by law and applicable alike to all citizens of whatever race, color or nationality."[85] Washington's law (along with provisions in the state constitution barring school segregation) outlawed the "separate-but-equal" system that soon proliferated in the South.

But Washington's law did not stamp out de facto segregation in theaters. In 1924 a white researcher sat down with Charlie Lui, a Seattle-based merchant, and asked, "Have you had any trouble with people refusing to wait on you in stores, barber shops, etc.?" At first, Charlie denied having any trouble. "Not yet," he began. "I usually find out where they treat Chinese good before I go." For example, Lui explained that he knew about Pantages Theatre in downtown Seattle. "I heard Chinese could not sit downstairs," he said; "I have only gone there once. I don't think that is right. I understand a few moving pictures houses will not allow Chinese to buy loge seats."

S. C. Eng had a similar experience at another Seattle theater, the Orpheum. "When we were seated," he told researchers, "I noticed that the entire row in which we were was filled with yellow and colored people." Eng reacted in anger. He "began to hate this theatre" and warned his friends to "keep away from it." He complained to researchers that Americans were "narrow-minded, strong in race prejudice and money mad." Whereas Lui had downplayed the affront of segregation in theaters, telling white researchers, "I don't care for movies," Eng was livid.[86]

While Lui and Eng avoided Seattle theaters due to segregation, a Black man by the name of Clarence R. Anderson pursued a different approach in 1920. According to the Black-edited *Cayton's Weekly*, Anderson was "one of Seattle's very successful attorneys and a heavy investor in her realty." As one of the city's few Black lawyers, Anderson was a well-known figure in Seattle's Black community. In 1917 he offered a public lecture on "Necessity of Negroes Entering Commercial Enterprises," in which he admitted to "the weak points in his race" but made a strong case that Black people were "quite capable of developing into just as strong minded men and women as are to be found among the white [race]." Anderson, for his part, seemed confident in his success. When the paper ran a Thanksgiving feature asking locals to explain "why they are thankful," Anderson answered, "[I am grateful] that I have the world by the tail with a down-hill pull."[87]

On the evening of July 7, 1919, Clarence Anderson walked into the Pantages Theatre in Seattle with two "colored" friends to see the vaudeville show. The Pantages Theatre on Third Street, which showed vaudeville acts and short moving pictures, opened in Seattle in 1915. The well-appointed theater was touted as refined and family-friendly, at least in comparison to its bawdier predecessors, which is perhaps why the theater chain insisted on segregating patrons.[88]

Anderson had dressed up for the occasion—"immaculate, neat, and dapper" were the words used at trial—and had his tickets in hand for nice box seats, because an unnamed third party had previously purchased them. But Anderson and his friends didn't make it past the lobby. First, the usher told them that all the box seats were filled, then told them they could not sit in a box in any event, and finally offered to exchange the tickets for balcony seats. When Anderson protested, the attendant "became gruff and insulting in his language, saying to the respondent that he was not admitted because he was a colored man, and that 'none of his kind of people could sit in any box seat or on the ground floor of that theater.'" With that, the attendant shoved Anderson through the crowded lobby and out onto the street.

For Anderson, this turn of events was probably not that surprising. Ten days earlier, a jury had ruled in favor of another Black man, Samuel Simon Moore, who was denied the seat of his choice at another Pantages Theatre in Spokane, Washington.[89] Moore accused the theater of discrimination and sought $5,000 in damages. The jury awarded him $200. Following the ruling, *The Spokane Chronicle* ran the headline: "Must Let Colored Men Sit Beside White Men."

The paper reported that the Spokane theater had been in the practice of putting "Negroes" in the second balcony. In Seattle the court found it was "the policy and practice of the management of the theater to refuse admission to box seats, seats in the loges, and seats on the ground floor of the theater to all colored people, and to all orientals [sic], and to all persons whose dress or physical appearance might render them obnoxious to other patrons of the theater." Perhaps Anderson headed to the Seattle theater that night to test whether the ruling had done anything to change the larger Pantages chain. If so, he quickly had his answer.

Anderson sued the Seattle theater, representing himself. He alleged wrongful discrimination and sought damages for the "indignity and humiliation to which he was subjected" and "injury to his standing in the community as a professional man." In so doing, he joined a long line of Black plaintiffs challenging segregated public accommodations.[90] Based on the Washington state law barring discrimination, the King County Superior Court awarded Anderson $300 in damages, but the Pantages Theatre appealed the decision to the Washington Supreme Court. Again, Anderson prevailed and his win forced the Pantages Theatre to stop segregating Black and Asian patrons.[91]

A similar case in California, *Errol Jones v. Kehrlein et al.* (1920), also resulted in a win for a Black plaintiff. Errol Jones, a young man just shy of his eighteenth birthday, had taken a "young woman friend" to the movies in Fresno. When he was barred from sitting in "the center section of the house," he asked why. "You know the reason why," the attendant responded, "Because you people can't sit there.... Because it is the orders of the management." Jones's father returned to the theater to question the manager, Oliver Kehrlein. Based on the father's testimony, the Fresno County Superior Court found that "the management put all of the dark races (with whom he included colored persons, Japanese, Chinese, and Mexicans) on the left side." Kehrlein claimed his motive was not owing to his own prejudice, but because "doing otherwise would hurt his business."[92]

The county court found in favor of Jones and awarded him $100. When the theater appealed, the California Court of Appeals affirmed the lower court's ruling. In doing so it rejected the theater management's argument that the US Supreme Court's decision in *Plessy v. Ferguson* (1896) endorsing the doctrine of separate but equal applied.

The state court noted that *Plessy* validated a Louisiana state law mandating discrimination, whereas in California there was no such law and, in fact, the state prohibited such discrimination. In 1893, California prohibited places of public amusement from refusing admission to any person over the age of twenty-one. In 1897, the state passed "An Act to protect all citizens in their civil and legal rights," which banned discrimination "on account of color or race" in "public accommodations" and "inns, restaurants and hotels."[93] But notably, California's civil rights law only applied to citizens.

These cases reveal the important role that civil rights laws in Washington and California played in protecting not only African Americans, but also Chinese Americans, Japanese Americans, and Mexican Americans. These laws assured Black Californians that they would not encounter large signs marked "white only" and "colored only" when riding on trains, visiting a beach, or seeking a restroom. And it gave men like Anderson and Jones the grounds upon which to sue when they encountered unwritten segregation.[94]

But their suits also suggest that racial discrimination against Black people persisted in public accommodations in violation of state law. And as aliens, the Chinese in the West had to navigate an even more complicated maze of segregation and discrimination when deciding whether to visit public accommodations like a theater, inn, restaurant, or barber. Oral history interviews reveal that the theaters in Reno, Seattle, and Fresno were not alone in segregating Chinese patrons. Nai-Ming Ginn, who lived in Los Angeles in the early twentieth century, remembered "the theater divided up into sections, some sections for the white people only, some for the color, such as Chinese, Filipino, Japanese and others from Asia."[95] Lansing Lee had the same experience in Los Angeles when he bought a "first-class seat" and was still led to the balcony. When he protested, he remembered the usher answering, "'That's how it is. Stay if you want to watch and get out if you don't.'"[96]

Sometimes theaters made exceptions. Lew Kay, a well-educated American-born Chinese resident of Seattle, recounted in 1924 how he talked his way into better seats. "I speak English better than some others," he explained to his interviewer, "and make myself known and sometimes get results." According to Lew, when theaters refused to sell him loge seats, "I then threaten the manager with the information that I am acquainted with the president of the Company owning the theater (as I sometimes am) and they generally give me what I want." But most of the time Lew did not try to talk his way out of discrimination. Instead, he avoided it. "I generally know the places where discrimination is shown, and I make no attempt to go. That has been my policy after high school and University, and since I have been in the business world, I find that there are plenty of other places where I can go and enjoy myself."[97] Lew had created a mental map of white-only spaces.

Theaters were not the only problem. "My countrymen sometimes feel uneasy on account of some people having racial prejudice toward them," reported Hung Kei Lui of Los Angeles. He explained, "Some of barber shops, theatres and cafes do not allow Chinese to go in." He complained that his neighbor, a Baptist missionary, "never allows Oriental people to stay in her hotel." In San Diego, Look Ting Tom remembered encountering "for whites only" signs at restaurants. "They stop for the race," he told an interviewer three decades later. "They don't let you in entirely, they only for the white people. Isn't that a shame?" Kit Quan remembered "a period in Fresno when we went to eat and they wouldn't let Chinese eat there." "Once when I went to get my hair cut," James W. Fing of Los Angeles remembered, "I'd gone in and sat down." The barber "didn't chase you out, but no one paid you any attention." When he told his family about it afterward, they said, "You shouldn't have gone to that one, they don't welcome Chinese there."[98]

Some Chinese residents learned to carefully mind this racial etiquette and meet the conditions of their inclusion. "No, I never have trouble to get my hair cut in the barber shop or have trouble to go in restaurant and not have them serve me," Chin Cheung told researchers in 1924. Chin attempted to avoid discrimination by carefully noting where he was wanted and where he was not. "I know where they treat Chinese all right, then I go," explained Chin. "I stay away from other places."[99]

※ ※ ※

For Chinese in the West, the racial etiquette was uneven: one restaurant would welcome them in, the next would usher them out. Generally there were no signs on the door to demarcate white spaces; state law barred such blatancy. Segregation projects, like the establishment of Chinese schools, proved too expensive in all but the largest urban areas. And white residents might not like their Chinese neighbors, but they still turned to the Chinese for domestic labor, laundry service, and fresh vegetables. Whether they liked it or not, both lawmakers and the public had come to rely on Chinese workers, traders, consumers, manufacturers, businesses, and taxpayers. Removal of the Chinese altogether could threaten state revenue, city budgets, and white income.

The spatial terms of inclusion held that Chinese should be separated from white communities whenever possible, but in the course of daily life, segregation was often deemed to be impossible. As Black segregation spread and solidified in the South, in the West there were no hard-and-fast rules for the Chinese to follow. Rather, it mattered who you were, how you were dressed, and where you were located. Still, Chinese who wished to avoid "trouble" could observe, learn, and internalize the racial etiquette.

But not everyone found it possible or preferable to obey racial rules. The Chinese community in San Jose in 1887 knew city leaders wished to remove Market Street Chinatown and replace it with a city hall, but they continued to build their lives on Ah Toy Alley anyway—until the fire. The Tapes knew that no Chinese children attended San Francisco public schools, but still brought Mamie to Spring Valley Elementary. Ruby Tsang did not expect the rough treatment she received in the Rialto Theatre in Reno, but when faced with it, she fought back. These individuals all refused to acquiesce when confronted with spaces that white people claimed as theirs alone. Segregation, they understood, did not merely mean separation. Segregation also meant limited access to education, public safety, and healthy living conditions. It meant poorer quality of life and less opportunity for social mobility. Above all, segregation meant a conditional existence in the West.

{6}

The "PREDATOR"

and the PROBLEM of INTERRACIAL INTIMACY

MAY AND HATTIE LUCAS began life far from California. Their father, James Lucas, was a farmer from Wisconsin, and their mother, Elizabeth Flynn, was a farmer's daughter. Elizabeth was James's second wife, and she cared for his older children in addition to her own three girls, who were born in Nebraska in 1888, 1890, and 1891.

An economic panic struck the nation in 1893 and the next year drought struck Nebraska, ruining crops and sending the Lucas family westward, via the Union and Central Pacific Railroad, to the small community of Loomis, California. Blessed with both fertile soil and a railroad station, Loomis was beginning to transform from a goldfield ghost town into a growing agricultural community. There, thirty miles from Sacramento in the foothills of the Sierra Nevada Mountains, farmers grew peaches, pears, persimmons, grapes, oranges, and olives for local and interstate markets. It was a good place for a farming family to start anew. James Lucas bought a thirty-acre fruit ranch, and all might have been well had he not died a couple of years later in 1898.[1]

When James died, he left Elizabeth with five children aged five to fifteen, a small house, and the fruit ranch. With the death of her husband and the loss of the economic stability he had provided, Elizabeth decided to reconfigure the family farm. At first Elizabeth's stepson, thirteen-year-old Charley, ran the ranch; but by the end of the year, Elizabeth had leased half the orchard to a Chinese tenant farmer, Ah Dick. Taking an advance of $100 to pay for supplies, Ah Dick promised to repay the loan plus 8 percent interest within the year, using the fruit crop as collateral. This arrangement appears to have been profitable for all. In 1902, feeling encouraged, Elizabeth leased the entire orchard, all thirty acres, to a new tenant farmer, Ah Lung.[2]

Though Elizabeth had a roof over her head and a tenant to work the farm, she struggled to keep her three youngest daughters fed and clothed. Facing profound economic distress, she made a conventional decision to use child labor and an unconventional choice to invert the racial hierarchy of the farm. In the summer of 1902, Ah Lung hired fourteen-year-old May, twelve-year-old Grace, and eleven-year-old Hattie to work on his leased land watering the trees and horses for 50 cents per day, making cherry boxes for 40 cents per hundred, and packing fruit for 2 cents per box. As startling as this arrangement may seem, it was part of a wider practice in Placer County and, at times, elsewhere. White poverty, it seems, could break down the usual racial etiquette.

For two years of harvests in full view of the neighbors, Ah Lung and his three white female employees worked dawn to dusk in the orchards. But even after all this labor, the Lucas girls were hungry and their clothes were falling off their backs. Then, sometime in the winter of 1904, the middle daughter, Grace, died. Ah Lung showed pity on Hattie after her sister's death.

"He bought me a new pair of shoes because I really had none fit to wear," Hattie later recalled, "and he bought me the new dress because I was pretty near naked."[3]

※ ※ ※

Chinese segregation in the Pacific West could not prevent moments of interracial intimacy. Despite segregationists' best efforts, white Americans continued to encounter Chinese in neighborhoods, restaurants, schools, and workplaces. The Chinese could not be completely confined, especially in rural agricultural areas and poor communities. Chinese and white residents lived near each other and worked with each other, and this could breed familiarity, intimacy, and, at times, intimate crimes.

For the most intimate interracial encounters, law could only dictate so much. Local and state laws could, and did, bar prostitution, rape, and interracial marriage. But they did not offer guidance on how Ah Lung was to treat Elizabeth Lucas (his white female landlord) and her daughters (his white female laborers). Instead, the terms of inclusion came in the form of an unwritten racial etiquette and the possibility of its legal or extralegal enforcement.

Historians of the Jim Crow South have found that racial etiquette, or cultural codes of conduct that regulated routine face-to-face interracial encounters, allowed white southerners to navigate the physical proximity and economic codependency of daily life while maintaining a racial hierarchy. This was the case, historian Neil McMillen argues, in contemporaneous Mississippi, where "there was little cause legally to separate black from white" because whites were "confident" in their domination and "popular convention and white sensibilities governed virtually every phase of interracial contact."[4] If racial etiquette was central to upholding race relations in the Jim Crow South, then what about the West? For the Chinese, what was the racial etiquette of intimate life?

Part of the answer lies in the small community of Loomis, California, and the events that unfolded on the Lucas farm. In December 1904 the State of California charged two Chinese men, Ah Lung and Ah Woon, with the statutory rape of the Lucas sisters. A month later, all-white juries swiftly convicted Ah Lung of assaulting thirteen-year-old Hattie Lucas and Ah Woon of raping fifteen-year-old May Lucas. As a result, the men spent the next seven years in San Quentin State Prison and the sisters spent the remainder of their youth at St. Catherine's Home and Training School for "delinquent" girls.[5]

In these bare facts there lies little intrigue. It was the turn of the twentieth century, deep into the period of racial retrenchment, as western states and cities worked diligently to widen the distance between white residents and Chinese. In the previous decades, anti-Chinese lawmakers had criminalized the Chinese in the eyes of the white public, portrayed Chinese women as prostitutes, and fought for school and residential segregation. In so doing, they instituted a system of legal codes and cultural norms that constricted Chinese movement, conduct, and power. Within this system, men like Ah Lung and Ah Woon were not supposed to know girls like May and Hattie, let alone know them intimately. The conviction and imprisonment of Ah Lung and Ah Woon seem utterly familiar in this context: state officials, alerted to extreme infractions, successfully restored the racial regime.[6]

But this predictable conclusion was preceded by seemingly inexplicable events. Hattie and May were not assaulted by alien strangers but by men whom they knew intimately as neighbors, employers, benefactors, and friends. Their story may culminate in racial transgression and punishment, but it began with years of interracial toleration and intimacy.[7] In part, these incidents reflected relations of power forged elsewhere, but it is important to note that intimate acts could also help to generate the terms of inclusion.[8]

Though the individual actions of Ah Lung, Ah Woon, May Lucas, and Hattie Lucas might not represent normative behavior, their choices still illustrate what forms of social intimacy were possible within the constraints of conditional inclusion. We may not be able to see the web of social conventions in which these individuals were caught, but their movements offer clues as to its form. There is ample evidence, for example, that maintaining Chinese segregation involved policing the racial, gender, and sexual behavior of both Chinese males and white females. There are also indications that these forms of social control were less pervasive in rural areas, lending credence to past indications that Progressive Era reforms disproportionately regulated urban and industrialized spaces. Reformers, who associated sexual delinquency and racial transgression with urbanism, may have ignored the interracial intimacy occasioned by farm life.[9]

In addition, events in Loomis reveal how the terms of conditional inclusion could diverge from the terms of exclusion. While federal exclusion imagined a nation without the Chinese, local inclusion dealt with the social reality of Chinese presence. These dual impulses produced a tangle of anti-Chinese stereotypes, especially concerning the sexuality of Chinese men. Starting in the nineteenth century, the image of the Chinese man as sexual "predator" gained traction in the context of the anti-Chinese movement and became a strong argument in favor of continually renewing Chinese exclusion. While fears of Chinese sexuality became central to the case for exclusion, their power over inclusion remains less clear. In Loomis, the racial stereotype did little to circumscribe interracial encounters in real time, only helping to establish the legal fiction of racial hierarchy after the fact.[10]

THE "PREDATOR" AND INTERRACIAL INTIMACY   209

Rape cases are an uncomfortable place to search for the history of exclusion and inclusion. The courtroom pitted Chinese defendants against white accusers, producing multiple conflicting narratives brimming with racism and misogyny. It is tempting to search for the "truth" behind these accusations of sexual assault, but I caution against this. There are too many silences in these sources, too many biases, and too many potential problems with the witness testimony of minors. Unfortunately, the legal documents offer no easy answers about the alleged crimes, but they do enable us to peer inside the daily mechanics of race and see unspoken racial etiquette in operation.[11]

AH LUNG

Like the Lucas sisters, Ah Lung was the child of a farmer and, like them, he traveled far from his birthplace in search of opportunity. His given name, no doubt, was not "Ah Lung." "Ah" was a diminutive prefix (rather than a proper name), and "Lung" was a poor (but common) transliteration of two different surnames.[12] (The 1900 US Census recorded 137 Chinese with the name "Ah Lung" and another 106 with the surname "Lung.")

Upon entry into San Quentin some years later, Ah Lung briefly recounted his life history, probably with the help of a translator. He was born in 1853 in the bustling, cosmopolitan port city of Guangzhou (Canton), which sent tens of thousands of Chinese migrants to the United States in the nineteenth century. In 1870, Ah Lung left his family and joined the stream of young, male Chinese workers who crossed the Pacific before the United States began to restrict their entry in 1882. Over the next three decades, Ah Lung bounced from job to job, showing an uneven pattern of economic mobility: from cigar roller in San Francisco, to hydraulic miner in Montana, to store owner in China, to vegetable gardener in Wheatland, California, to store owner in Penryn, California, to Elizabeth's tenant farmer in Loomis.

Ah Lung had spent the better part of three decades in California; his longest sojourn in China had been during 1878–1882. While he probably married and had two children during that time in China, he did not stay to see his children grow. In 1882, as rumors spread that the United States would soon close its gates to the Chinese, he returned to California and spent most, if not all, of the remainder of his life far from his family. He continued, however, to wear his hair in a queue, in loyalty to the Qing Court. Keeping the braid meant he could return to the place of his birth someday.[13]

As Ah Lung began his lease of the Lucas Ranch in the spring of 1902, initially nothing appeared amiss. Elizabeth Lucas sold her share of the property to her stepson, Charley, shifting her from the unusual role of business partner to the traditional role of female dependent. The Lucas family and their Chinese tenant farmer lived in close proximity, but in neatly segregated spaces: Elizabeth and her three youngest daughters continued to live with Charley at the main house, while Ah Lung lived in a nearby "China cabin."

Some of the most frequently cited historical records seem to suggest that this level of residential proximity was rare: the local newspaper reported on a distinct "Chinatown" within the small town of Loomis, suggesting that the Chinese community was residentially segregated, a view apparently backed by the 1900 census, which lists all but a handful of Chinese in one section of the town.

But in rural California the sight of a Chinese man living and working on a ranch was nothing out of the ordinary. Farming widows in rural California had made a practice of turning to Chinese tenants.

Farming in the California foothills (circa 1900). Here, an unknown farming family in El Dorado County (a few miles from Loomis) was photographed with their Chinese farmworker in the background. This family was clearly better off than the Lucas family, but still worked closely with Chinese labor. (El Dorado County Historical Museum)

In Santa Clara County, historian Cecilia Tsu has found that only 6 percent of agricultural landowners were women, but those women signed nearly 31 percent of all leases between white employers and Asians tenants.[14] This arrangement had advantages for both parties. Owning land was financially advantageous, but Chinese could still make money through leasing. Sharecropping could mean a lifetime of struggle reminiscent of slavery for Black farmers in the Jim Crow South, but sharecropping was sometimes lucrative for Chinese in California. This was likely the case for Ah Lung, who signed at least three leases in 1903 and 1904.

In California at the time, Ah Lung could have theoretically bought land himself instead of collecting leases. No law stood in his way, but there may have been unspoken barriers to Chinese landownership. White Californians frowned on Chinese landowners, and lawmakers in other western states went further. In Oregon and Washington, lawmakers prohibited Chinese migrants from owning agricultural land using identity-based alien land laws.

Alien land laws were not new. In the eighteenth century, the American colonies had routinely restricted alien access to land, and into the nineteenth century, eastern states continued to deny foreigners equal property rights. But in the nineteenth-century West, alien land laws took on a new racial meaning, as western states adapted an old legal tradition to target Chinese migrants.[15] Western states used alien land laws to limit Chinese access to mining claims, agricultural land, and real estate. These laws reinforced the economic terms of Chinese inclusion—forcing the Chinese to lease rather than own—and became an instrument of segregation as well.

For example, Washington turned to alien land laws when anti-Chinese violence swept through the territory in 1885 and 1886. The territorial government passed a law that prohibited all aliens incapable of becoming citizens from owning real estate. Upon statehood in 1889, the new state constitution repeated this restriction, stating that "the ownership of lands by aliens, other than those who in good faith have declared their intention to become citizens of the United States, is prohibited in this state." Chinese migrants, racially barred from naturalization, could not own real property in the fledgling state.[16]

Eventually Californian lawmakers passed alien land laws as well, but not until the twentieth century and with the primary intent of regulating Japanese farmers. Passed a decade after Ah Lung leased from the Lucas family, California's 1913 Alien Land Law targeted all "aliens ineligible to citizenship," and impacted Japanese, Chinese, and South Asians. The law and its successor in 1920 directly curtailed Asian ownership of agricultural land, but its vague reference to "real property" meant it could also be used to discourage homeownership as well.[17] Eventually fifteen states restricted the ability of aliens ineligible to citizenship to acquire land, including the nine western states of Arizona, California, Idaho, Montana, New Mexico, Oregon, Utah, Washington, and Wyoming.[18]

Even before California enacted alien land laws, Chinese found it difficult to buy farmland and instead turned to wage work or tenancy arrangements. In the area surrounding Loomis, for example, Chinese made up more than a quarter of all farmworkers and Chinese tenant farmers held half of all farm leases. Contemporaries estimated that Chinese leased over 500 acres, or 15 percent of the total acreage of fruit, in Placer County.[19]

Farmwork meant that Chinese migrants were far from being segregated in Loomis; local oral histories recall that these scattered Chinese farmers made only weekly treks to Loomis's "Chinatown" to purchase supplies. This arrangement was common in other agricultural areas, especially in the Sacramento Valley, the San Joaquin Valley, and the coastal valleys of central California. While urban Chinatowns allowed for a Chinese-centric economy, the social relations of production in rural areas necessitated interracial contact.[20]

But Ah Lung's interactions with the youngest sister, Hattie, went beyond the necessities of farm labor. Everyone who watched fifty-one-year-old Ah Lung and thirteen-year-old Hattie work together in the summer of 1904 saw a special relationship between them. Hattie's stepbrother, Charley, described only light-heartedness. "I have seen them playing together," Charley testified, "[Ah Lung] would grab her by the arm and she would hit him back and the like of that." But the neighboring Keely family described a more disturbing scene. During an initial trial in the justice court, Frank Keely remembered one occasion when he had spied Ah Lung hugging Hattie. And, by the time he was in front of the county court, Frank had remembered "one particular occasion [when] I saw him kiss her." Frank's mother, Ida Keely, "saw them walking with his arm around her neck and hers around his waist." None of Hattie's neighbors or family members saw fit to intervene.[21]

At first glance, it is surprising that this interracial proximity did not immediately raise suspicion. Though the image of the Chinese predator has largely been erased from American memory, it was a common stereotype at the turn of the twentieth century. As early as the 1870s, Chinese men were seen as lecherous perverts known for luring or tricking unsuspecting children and women into unsavory activities.

One representative example of this pervasive racial stereotype is a propaganda pamphlet that circulated in San Francisco, titled "Chinese Servants. Full Particulars of What a Chinese Servant Did to Pretty Lillie Leslie and How He Was Caught." The pamphlet, which is likely fictionalized, tells the story of Mr. and Mrs. Leslie, white migrants from Boston, who settle in San Francisco where they become ardent pro-Chinese advocates. Not only do they employ a Chinese man, Charley Lee, as a servant, but they also favor open migration, naturalization, and Christianization of Chinese. When the story opens, the Leslies' only child, Lillie, is seventeen years old and the personification of white female purity, with "skin perfectly white which shone like white polished marble."[22]

At first the Leslie family sings the praises of their Chinese servant. They believe they have made him into an ideal worker and a "good Christian." But one day a neighbor, Mr. Palmer, hears voices in the Leslies' basement and, upon investigating, he finds "Lillie Leslie and her Chinese servant . . . locked in each other's arms." Mr. Palmer reportedly rushes up to the "Chinaman and grabbed him by his cue [sic] and smashed him right square in the face." Mr. Palmer turns to Lillie, who is sobbing about her disgrace in the corner of the room. She eventually admits that Charley "began to do it a little while after he came here, I was only a little girl then, and I did not know what I was doing."

Turning back to the Chinese servant, Mr. Palmer declares, "You low, vulgar, two faced villain! You were treated with the greatest kindness by the Leslies, who taught you how to read and write and speak our language and you went to Sunday school, and made believe that you were a Christian, so that you would be all the more able to ruin this poor girl." The anti-Chinese pamphlet declares the Chinese servant to be an internal threat to the moral sanctity of the white home. Charley Lee had been converted and domesticated, yet his innate perversion and physical proximity still threatens the Leslie family.[23]

This pamphlet epitomizes a pervasive fear of Chinese male sexuality. Stories of Chinese sexual perversion crossed the Pacific before the Chinese themselves arrived in California. American missionaries living in China depicted the Chinese as hypersexual, and wrote voyeuristic reports of Chinese polygamy, sodomy, and child brides. When Chinese started to arrive in large numbers after 1850, Californians observed their skewed sex ratio and assumed that homosocial Chinese communities were further evidence of sexual deviance. Scholar Robert Lee argues that Chinese men were understood as a "third sex" that was "ambiguous, inscrutable, and hermaphroditic," at times effeminate and at times hypersexual. According to scholar Nayan Shah, Chinese were understood to exhibit "deviant sexuality" that was incompatible with American society.[24]

Like all racial stereotypes, the image of the Chinese sexual predator gained currency in a particular time and place, in this case during the movement for Chinese exclusion in the US West. When agitators spread news of the downfall of Lillie Leslie and others, they provided fodder for the fight against Chinese immigration. Like many representations of the Chinese, the sexual predator image was often deployed to reinforce the terms of exclusion. It proved that Mr. and Mrs. Leslie were hopelessly naive when they believed they could reform and integrate the Chinese. If Chinese perversion was innate, then the only remedy was excluding Chinese men altogether. The stereotype of the Chinese sexual predator made a compelling case for total exclusion.[25]

The menacing image of the Chinese sexual predator did not, however, seem to have much sway over the spatial terms of inclusion in Loomis, California. Ah Lung and Hattie were permitted their special relationship. "While they were together they were playing pretty near all the time," recalled fifteen-year-old May, "kissing one another and fooling around." This continued until September 1904, when Ah Lung found a new tenancy at the Jansen Ranch and moved down the road. Hattie had just lost her sister Grace, and she proved unwilling to let Ah Lung go.

A week after Ah Lung moved, Hattie left her house one morning, hurried down the dirt road, and found her way to Ah Lung's small cabin on the Jansen Ranch. That evening, her mother came after her to bring her home. But Hattie ran away again the next week, and the week after that. She sat in Ah Lung's kitchen, watching him cook breakfast for his Chinese and Japanese friends. She followed him as he worked, and when he wanted to go to town, she hitched up his horses to the buggy and they went together.

"She would go every day she could if we would let her go," Hattie's mother recalled, "she would stay there a long while if I didn't go after her and take her home." One night, or maybe several, Elizabeth failed to come and fetch Hattie home. So Hattie slept overnight in Ah Lung's bedroom, him in the wooden bed, she testified, and her in a cot nearby. "It started to rain about 5 o'clock. . . . I had staid there too long and it was too dark to go home," Hattie remembered, "so I staid all night."[26]

Hattie's sister, May, saw nothing amiss. "She went over to fix up the house for him," she recalled when prompted at trial. "Me and my mother knew she was going over for that purpose. We did not object." May recognized this as gender-normative behavior, even if it appears racially anomalous to us today. Hattie's brother, Charley, also knew about her frequent visits and occasional overnights, but did not see them as cause for alarm. "I have seen her in his house," he told the jury, "and I didn't see anything out of the way at all."

Family members were not the only ones aware of Hattie's visits. One day in October the son of Ah Lung's landlord arrived unannounced to renegotiate the lease. F. H. Jansen saw "the Lucas girl" sitting around the kitchen with three "Chinamen" and a "Jap," and that afternoon he met Ah Lung and Hattie again on the road to Loomis. If he found anything unscrupulous about the sight of a young girl trailing around a Chinese man, Jansen did not give voice to these thoughts at the time or at trial.[27]

Hungry, living in poverty, and struggling with the recent death of her sister, Hattie was desperately searching for friendship and perhaps even courtship. The racial divide made her source of comfort (a Chinese man) suspect to some at the time. The age divide (thirteen versus fifty-one) and their imbalance of power (employee versus employer) would make the relationship suspect to most people today. Hattie was vulnerable to abuse and may have been abused. At trial she described, with the help of the prosecutor's coaxing, one incident of assault. Once, when they were in the barn together watering horses, Ah Lung grabbed hold of Hattie's skirts, removed her drawers, and "got on top of" her. This assault, if it occurred, was said to be an isolated incident.[28]

In contrast to her description of this assault, Hattie repeatedly insisted that her relationship with Ah Lung was innocent. She was, in her words, "friendly with Ah Lung" and she liked him "just a little." "We [played] in the packing house," she remembered, "throwing clods and peaches at each other." "He never put his arm around me," she said, "he always treated me nicely and kindly." Whether or not this was an abusive relationship, it is noteworthy that a young white girl in rural, turn-of-the-century California found it conceivable that she could befriend a Chinese man.

Hattie was not the only white child visiting older Chinese men in rural California. Decades later, several white Loomis residents remembered having interacted with Chinese men as children in the early 1900s. According to a local historian, groups of children would stop at the "old Perry place" to visit a "tall, thin Chinese man" who handed out Chinese candy and "liche nuts." Perhaps local racial etiquette made allowances based on youth and poverty. Then again, Progressive Era reformers did not tend to offer class- or age-based exceptions. On the contrary, they focused particular attention on regulating urban working-class adolescent females. So perhaps local racial etiquette in this rural space simply allowed such familiarity.[29]

As for Ah Lung, he may have been looking for a friend, a surrogate daughter, a second wife, or, perhaps, a victim. America's laws had denied him most forms of female companionship. The Page Act and strict gender taboos in China made it difficult for Chinese women to migrate to the United States. The sex ratio in the Chinese community was still extremely lopsided; in 1900 the US census counted nineteen Chinese males for every one Chinese female. For this reason Ah Lung, and many other Chinese men, married during a return visit to China and lived an ocean away from their families. The 1888 Chinese Exclusion Act made cyclical migration to and from China increasingly hazardous, further distancing Ah Lung from his family. At some point during these years apart, Ah Lung's wife died.

Living in Loomis, Ah Lung had little hope of remarrying. While federal immigration statutes dashed Ah Lung's chances of courting a Chinese woman, an 1880 California statute prohibited his marriage to a white woman. Anti-miscegenation laws like this one had a long history in America. In 1661, Virginia legislators prohibited marriage and bastardy between an "English or other white man or woman" and any "negroe, mulatto, or Indian man or woman bond or free." The British colonies of Massachusetts, North Carolina, Pennsylvania, and Georgia adopted similar laws. Between the American Revolution and the Civil War, laws against interracial marriage were in effect in twenty-eight of the thirty-three American states. The Civil War and the anticipated emancipation of slaves heightened fears about racial mixing, spurring the invention of the term "miscegenation" and new efforts to prevent it.[30]

Many western states and territories instituted anti-miscegenation laws that named the "Chinese" or "Mongolians" specifically. Laws were in effect in Nevada (1861–1959), Idaho (1864–1959), Arizona (1865–1962), Oregon (1866–1951), Wyoming (1869–1882, 1913–1965), California (1880–1948), Utah (1888–1963), and Montana (1909-1953). In the late nineteenth and early twentieth centuries, states in the Midwest and South also wrote the Chinese into existing miscegenation laws: Mississippi (1892–1967), Missouri (1909–1967), Nebraska (1913–1963), South Dakota (1913–1957), Virginia (1924–1967), and Georgia (1927–1967).[31]

How then did Ah Lung forge a relationship with a white adolescent? How did he overcome their racial, cultural, and linguistic differences, which were granted such significance in western life? Somehow Ah Lung, using uncommon amounts of charity and humorous food fights, found a connection with Hattie. Transcripts from the justice court reveal that Ah Lung's English was far from perfect. Knowing his own limitations, Ah Lung told the judge, "I like interpreter," but the justice court denied his request because "he understands English enough." In truth, Ah Lung could form simple and straightforward statements in English; for example, he told the justice court: "You no see me do nothing." Though his English skills were not strong enough to mount a sophisticated defense on his own behalf, Ah Lung had the language skills to communicate with Hattie.

And he was not the only Chinese worker in Loomis who was bilingual; the 1900 census recorded that 92 percent of the Chinese in this rural town could speak enough English to converse. (This was higher than for the United States as a whole, in which an estimated

68 percent of Chinese could speak English.) The alleged English skills of the Loomis Chinese were not terribly surprising given the migrants' lengthy stays in the United States and their relative isolation in the rural countryside; on average, the Loomis Chinese reported they had first disembarked twenty years before. In turn-of-the-century Loomis, the white and Chinese communities could communicate with each other, and with communication came moments of interracial intimacy.[32]

As the fall of 1904 grew colder, things were getting worse for Hattie at home. The thirteen-year-old only understood the bare facts. "My half brother lived in the house with us, and he told us, if we were ready to move we could move, so mama went away," Hattie testified. "He did not want us there." Hattie, her mother, and her sister were being kicked out of the house. Her half brother, who could have maintained a white patriarchal household in her father's stead, failed to comport with this normative ideal.

It was the beginning of December, the wet winter had begun, and Elizabeth and her daughters were homeless. The widow must have had few connections to the Loomis community, because she ultimately turned to an unlikely source for support: Ah Woon, another Chinese tenant farmer for whom she had worked the previous summer.[33]

AH WOON

At thirty-five years old, Ah Woon was not an old-timer like Ah Lung. The sixteen years that separated them likely meant the difference between lawful and unlawful status in America. Like many Chinese workers who sought admission to the United States after the Chinese Restriction Act of 1882, Ah Woon claimed to be a US citizen by birth.

Upon intake at San Quentin, Ah Woon told an elaborate story about his birth in Walnut Grove, California, in 1870, the death of both his (unnamed) parents, his migration to China as a ten-year-old with an (unnamed) uncle, and his return to Walnut Grove around 1884. It is most likely that the only factual part of this story was his arrival in America as an adolescent.

During his slow ascent of the economic ladder, his proximity to white employers and employees was a constant. First he worked as a cook in Walnut Grove, then as a farmhand in nearby Cosumnes, and then as a tenant farmer of two orchards in Loomis, where he employed several white workers, including the Lucas family. Though Ah Woon was probably not American-born, he identified strongly with his adopted country. By 1905 he had cut his queue, spoke near-fluent English, and professed that he was "among the Chinese very little."

At trial, Ah Woon vividly recalled when Elizabeth, suddenly homeless, came to him in desperation. Without the help of a translator, Ah Woon testified:

> Mrs. Lucas ask me, 'Woon, I got boy kick me out; I got no place to live; I got no price to rent a house.' She say, 'You can help me about one month, two month, with a house[?]' I say I go to Sacramento, ask the boss man first. [The boss man] Mr. Henshaw say he want to rent one month. I said, 'Mrs. Lucas, my boss man rent house to you one week or two week, you go away.' She say, 'Yes, [in] two week I move away.'

Ah Woon was probably aware that Elizabeth's request transgressed the racial etiquette of the community, so he sought the approval of his landlord. It appears his landlord, Mr. Henshaw, was also apprehensive about the arrangement, but still permitted the interracial household on a short-term basis.[34]

For thirty-five-year-old Ah Woon and fifteen-year-old May, living in the same house quickly turned into romance, or sexual exploitation, or a little of both. May described Ah Woon as a "friendly" man who gave her "a bicycle and a couple of dresses and a pair of shoes." According to May, Ah Woon quickly proposed to marry her, "asked my mama if he could," and promised they would move to San Francisco. May could apparently imagine being the wife of a Chinese man and found this offer appealing. Like Hattie, she had suffered from her impoverished upbringing and here was a wealthier man who could provide regular meals, a roof over her head, and companionship.

After a quick courtship, May testified, Ah Woon "asked if he could do it to me" and on five separate occasions she agreed to have sex.

May was under the age of consent, which California lawmakers had raised from fourteen to sixteen in 1897, so this sex (assuming it occurred) constituted statutory rape. When Elizabeth testified, she largely agreed with May's version of events. She only contested their order, saying that she only approved the marriage because May had already had sex with Ah Woon. Like her daughter, Elizabeth could imagine that a white girl and a Chinese man could have a future together in turn-of-the-century California.[35]

It appears Ah Woon had sought companionship and found a proximal, willing, and vulnerable adolescent. In court he flatly denied having sex with May—stating simply "I no fuck the girl"—and declared he never intended to marry her despite her mother's urging. But when pressed, Ah Woon revealed that they had discussed marriage. "I tell her I dead broke this year, I lost thousand dollars and I can't marry her," he testified. "If I make money I marry her." Ah Woon believed he could marry a white female and live openly with her in San Francisco. No one in this rural household seems to have known that marriage between a "Mongolian" and a white person was illegal in California at the time.

Perhaps the existence of Chinese-white marriages was more conspicuous than their illegality. By 1900 the *San Francisco Chronicle* estimated that there had been twenty such marriages in the city alone. Some of these partnerships must have existed without legal blessing, others must have occurred out of state, and a few must have somehow acquired licenses from sympathetic local judges. The *San Francisco Call* found it newsworthy, in January 1905, when a marriage license was denied to a Japanese man and white woman. "The woman became quite indignant," the paper reported, "saying 'There are lots of Japanese and Chinese married to white women.' 'I cannot help that,' said [the judge]. 'They must have gone somewhere else to get married.'"[36]

It was Ah Woon and the Lucas family's unconventional living arrangement that finally crossed an invisible line and drew the attention of the Loomis community. One day, Ah Woon was walking down a street in Loomis when a few white men fell into step with him. They told Ah Woon "you different Chinaman," and demanded that he stop living with the Lucas family. Ah Woon started to hear the same message from "all around Loomis." He remembered, "I

[']fraid somebody"—"some white people" he later clarified—"give me trouble." These white men continued to hold violent or legal tactics in reserve as they attempted racial policing through subtler means. Even after these warnings, Ah Woon took the time to seek guidance from a wealthy white couple in Sacramento and, surprisingly, the Loomis constable, J. M. Pockman, whom he seemed to know personally. In the end, it was probably Ah Woon's naive search for advice that landed him, Ah Lung, Elizabeth, Hattie, and May behind bars.[37]

Constable Pockman may have been unsure what action to take, because no law prohibited cohabitation between Chinese and whites in California, so he turned to an out-of-town expert, Daniel Healy, an agent of the Sacramento Society for the Prevention of Cruelty to Children. While some in Loomis seemed to prefer to police the terms of inclusion through warnings and extralegal harassment, Healy was practiced at using the law to protect and police the chastity of white girls. According to the *Sacramento Daily Record-Union*, the progressive reformer traveled throughout California to save young white girls from prostitution, seduction, and rape at the hands of "debased white men and Mongolian beasts." Healy took particular interest in protecting "runaways" and "wayward girls" by returning sexually rebellious urban youth to their parents or consigning them to institutions. While the locals of rural Loomis may have been unsure of the racial etiquette, Healy knew immediately that Ah Lung and Ah Woon had violated it.[38]

Healy raced to Loomis, bringing with him the norms of urban progressivism. In San Francisco at the time, progressive reformers relied on strategies of containment for unruly Chinese. (It would be another two decades before they turned to strategies of assimilation and reform.) With the help of the constable, Healy apprehended the Chinese males and white females. Prompted by Healy, local officials immediately filed charges of statutory rape against Ah Lung and Ah Woon in the justice court. Two days later the constable successfully petitioned the court to remove the sisters from their mother's care, declaring their home an "unfit place" "by reason of the depravity on the part of their parent." The court found the interracial household to be evidence of maternal failure, stripping Elizabeth of her parental rights based on racial and gendered grounds.[39]

Healy was a private citizen with no official jurisdiction, yet he was allowed private meetings with the sisters, Elizabeth, and the men. It appears he approached the situation with two preconceived, culturally viable explanations for interracial cohabitation: either Ah Lung and Ah Woon were predators or Elizabeth and her daughters were prostitutes.[40] Behind closed doors, without the aid of counsel, Ah Woon and May allegedly admitted to having sexual intercourse and Hattie alleged that Ah Lung had raped her once the previous summer. Ah Lung denied any misconduct. He later testified (with the aid of a translator), "I was taken down to Rocklin and see Mr. Healy there. Me and Ah Woon had a talk with [Healy]. He told me to admit that I had been with her mother—that I slept with Hattie's mother. He told me to admit that I slept with Hattie too, so they will have her mother arrested instead of me. Wanted me to admit that I had sexual intercourse with Hattie, and I can't do it; I haven't done it." After swift indictments by the justice court, Ah Lung and Ah Woon's cases went to the Placer County Superior Court in January 1905, where they faced separate juries.[41]

In Loomis, cohabitation proved to be the breaking point, the moment when toleration gave way to persecution and prosecution. Although the Lucas sisters had worked and played alongside the Chinese men for several years in full view, they went too far when they moved their relationships behind the closed doors of a shared home. A case from later decades offers another example of cohabitation leading to arrest. In 1928 the *Madera Tribune* reported that Ah Sing and Mrs. Hazel Morris (a "pretty divorcee") had been "prevented by the law from marrying" and now were "prosecuted by the law because they are not married." Arrested in their San Francisco apartment, they were each fined $100 for an unspecified crime.[42] Charged with statutory rape, Ah Woon and Ah Lung faced the possibility of a graver fate.

Before turning to their trial, it is worth pausing to consider the significance of their prolonged interracial intimacy, as precarious as it turned out to be. Sexual accusations aside, theirs was clearly an intimate relationship born of shared work, space, and circumstance. The white people of Loomis did not treat Ah Lung and Ah Woon as segregated strangers or as probable predators. The two men had found inclusion in this rural community—at least until they violated its unspoken conditions.[43]

IN COURT

Ah Lung and Ah Woon may have experienced a permissive racial etiquette in the orchards of Loomis, California, but in the courtroom they quickly faced harsher norms. Dragged to the larger town of Auburn, the two men found themselves in the public arena, subject to the will of state officials resolved to maintain social order, jurors charged with enforcing the law, and a reformer determined to uphold urban, middle-class, Protestant mores. Together, these white men held the power to rewrite the terms of inclusion and they did so by generating a legal fiction of a rigid racial regime after the fact.

The cases against Ah Woon and Ah Lung show, once again, the systemic discrimination against the Chinese in California's legal system at the time. Though Ah Lung and Ah Woon were accused of sexual crimes, the cases against them were based primarily on assumptions of Chinese perversity and won primarily on evidence of racial transgressions. Given the initial titles of the cases—"*People v. Ah Lung, a Chinaman*" and "*People v. Ah Woon, a Chinaman*"—perhaps it is not surprising that race was central to the state's prosecutions.[44]

It is impossible to assess the veracity of the charges a century later, but recorded testimony quickly reveals problems with the state's legal case. The cases against both men suffered from reluctant (perhaps traumatized) witnesses. In *People v. Ah Lung*, Hattie gave detailed and clear descriptions of working with Ah Lung, but became painfully confused when asked to describe when he raped her. She testified that Ah Lung "didn't do anything to me, and he did not attempt to do anything to me or to take any familiarities with me." But prosecutors pushed for details of the rape she had allegedly described when alone with Healy.

With the aid of leading questions and a pause to consult privately with Healy, Hattie eventually described a single incident of rape. Her responses were contradictory. He was standing; she was lying on the ground. "Yes, sir" he put something in her; "No, sir" she felt nothing inside of her. Under cross-examination, Hattie recanted the entire incident. Unfortunately, it is impossible to discern the cause of Hattie's confused testimony, but what is clear is that her statements made for a thin case against Ah Lung. Without a confession by the accused or a corroborating witness, prosecutors should have found it nearly impossible to prove Ah Lung's guilt beyond a reasonable doubt.[45]

By the standards of the day, the case against Ah Woon was stronger, but not by much. May readily admitted that she and Ah Woon had sexual intercourse, but she asserted that they planned to marry and had the blessing of her mother, and that the sex was consensual. Legally, the admission of consent was irrelevant to the case because California law protected all females below the age of sixteen regardless of their consent, morality, or sexual history.

But historian Mary E. Odem, in her study of statutory rape cases in California in the years 1885–1920, discovered that in practice judges and juries often treated victims' consent as exculpatory. When the accused was a white man, female witnesses routinely faced long interrogations about their sexual past and whether they had resisted the defendant. The implication was that white men could fall victims to "loose girls" and their immoral sexuality. Conviction rates also reflected the court's reluctance to enforce statutory rape law. For example, from 1910 to 1920, Alameda County Superior Court juries convicted 43 percent of defendants who were accused of forcible rape, but convicted only 5 percent of defendants who were accused of nonforcible rape. If Ah Woon had been a white man, May would have had to defend her own behavior and prosecutors may have found it difficult to secure a conviction.[46]

Occasionally attorneys acknowledged the power of racial stereotypes upon the jury. In *People v. Ah Yek* (1865), a case concerning a Chinese domestic servant accused of raping a nineteen-month-old child, the defense attorney closed his case with a plea for the court to be above the racist fears of the day: "The defendant is a chinaman. We cannot disguise the fact that a deepseated prejudice exists against Mongolians as a class in California. . . . [W]e venture the assertion that in all professions engaged in the criminal branch of the law that a chinaman can be convicted here with less evidence than a native of any other country. While it is humiliating to make the confession, it is yet within the range of truth."[47] The defense made similar allegations of prejudice in the case of Ah Woon. In a letter to his parole board years later, defense attorney John Fulweiler maintained that racial prejudice helped to condemn Ah Woon. "Public sentiment in the neighborhood was aroused by reason of the girl being white," he explained, "and had much to do with his conviction." Fulweiler continued, "[Ah Woon] did not know the girl was under age, or of any law prohibiting such intercourse and would have married the girl at any time she and her mother desired." So perhaps if Ah Woon were white, there never would have been a trial at all. But Ah Woon and Ah Lung were Chinese, a fact that was constantly reinforced by their bodily presence in the courtroom and the repeated use of the term "Chinaman" in place of the defendants' names by the judge, both attorneys, and all white witnesses.[48]

The weaknesses of the cases against Ah Lung and Ah Woon put into stark relief the power of racial stereotypes in the courtroom. In the absence of conclusive evidence, the prosecutor A. K. Robinson invoked the fearful image of the Chinese sexual predator. In the justice court, for example, Robinson asked Hattie's neighbors leading questions about Ah Lung, inquiring if he had "taken a couple little girls and exposed them, raised their clothes and painted them with ink or something?" Though their answers were in the negative, the question alone fed popular assumptions about Chinese men's exotic perversion.

For Ah Lung and Ah Woon, mere evidence of proximity, viewed alongside assumptions of Chinese perversity, became evidence of wrongdoing at trial. Robinson spent extensive time measuring Ah Lung and Hattie's physical proximity. It was not enough for Robinson to establish that Ah Lung and Hattie had previously lived on the same ranch in houses "close" to each other. He pressed Elizabeth to name an exact distance—"200 yards?" or "100 yards?"—but she could not. Other witnesses were also asked to estimate the distance. "The house where the Chinaman lived was built right close," testified neighbor Frank Keely. "I don't think over 20 feet from the door where the family lived." Not only did Hattie and Ah Lung live near each other, they also worked uncomfortably close to each other. Keely reported, "I have often seen them, many, many days together, out in the orchard. I have seen them around the packing house together." Prosecutor Robinson's obsession with proximity suggests a dubious logic: that the closer Ah Lung lived to Hattie and the longer he spent in her presence, the more likely it was that he raped her.[49]

Robinson's cases against Ah Lung and Ah Woon also depended on depicting Chinese spaces, in this case the men's residences, as inherently threatening. Witnesses proved ready to support this view.

A neighbor, Ida Keely, described Ah Lung's residence as a "China cabin," a racially marked space, and commented that she "thought it strange that [Hattie] should go [there]." Witnesses who had visited Ah Lung's residence could describe little more than Hattie and Ah Lung sitting in the kitchen together, but the setting alone made such innocuous interactions suspicious.

Fear of Chinese spaces is a common thread in many cases against Chinese men for sexual crimes. *People v. Sing (A Chinaman)* (1905), for example, was prompted when Alexander McHardy, a stonecutter who lived near the defendant, spotted twelve-year-old Clara Nager entering a Chinese man's house and, based on this fact alone, called the authorities. Chinese businesses were also suspect. In urban areas, rape cases often revolved around events that took place in a stereotypically dangerous Chinese space: the laundry. For example, a Milwaukee paper set off a race riot in 1887 when it claimed that two Chinese men had molested twenty-two children who visited their laundry. When social critic Jacob Riis published *How the Other Half Lives* in 1890, he added fuel to the fire by reporting "the arrest of a Chinaman for 'inveigling little girls into his laundry'" in New York City. Riis made sure readers understood that all Chinese laundries, as "outposts of Chinatown," posed a similar threat. They were the "outer threads of the spider's web that holds its prey fast." Like the cases against Ah Woon and Ah Lung, the circumstances surrounding these alleged crimes suggest that Chinese in America had many moments of casual contact with white Americans. But in the courtroom, these quotidian interracial encounters could become evidence of treacherous interracial proximity.[50]

Many Chinese targets of rape accusations were men who possessed more financial and social capital than the imagined Chinese "John Doe."[51] Ah Lung and Ah Woon were English-speaking tenant farmers who were wealthy enough to hire white females and socially skilled enough to befriend them. Robinson clearly saw Ah Lung and Ah Woon's ability to employ white children as inherently threatening. Writing years later to a parole board, he explained, "I have been District Attorney of this County, all told six years, and during that time, I had much trouble about young children employed by Chinese tenants of fruit ranches. It seems to be the rule with but few exceptions, that young girls so employed are subjected to many temptations, to my mind it is a horrible thing to allow a young child, either girl or boy to be so employed." At trial, Robinson assumed the jury would share similar reservations about Chinese employers. He emphasized the financial power Ah Lung and Ah Woon held over the sisters, pushing the men to admit that they had aided the girls financially, buying them clothes when theirs were tattered, feeding them when they were hungry, and providing shelter when they had none. The defense attorney argued this was simply evidence of charity and good will: "In fact the mother . . . and the two girls would have been homeless and without any support if it had not been for Ah Woon and the other Chinaman." But the prosecutor used racial assumptions to transform these seeming acts of kindness into signs of low Chinese trickery. "The testimony shows to my mind clearly," Robinson argued, "that Ah Lung sought by cunning wilyness by presents to seduce the child."[52]

Far beyond Loomis, financial and social capital marked Chinese men as sexually dangerous. In 1895, for example, the *Los Angeles Times* reported that a wealthy Chinese man, Ah Sam, was accused of raping a twelve-year-old girl. The reporter underscored that Ah Sam "is the boss of the Chinese celery ranch. . . . He has plenty of money and is one of the most influential of his race in this vicinity." Ah Sam allegedly used money to quiet his victim, "readily supplied" his $400 bail, and disappeared from the county. In *People v. Sing (A Chinaman)* in 1905, charity was again a sign of guilt. The accused was wealthier than the family of the alleged victim and had "been in the habit of giving them food," which the prosecutor suggested was a form of bribery.

Social capital also enabled Leon Ling, an accused murderer in New York City, to seduce a white missionary and evade police in 1909, according to historian Mary Ting Yi Lui. New York newspapers described Ling as a "Chinese sport" who "talks good English" and wears patent leather shoes, "tight-fitting" trousers, and cropped hair. In Los Angeles, a "sporty American Chinaman" named Jim Wong Fook, who was "completely dropped into American ways and boots and high collars," allegedly used his cultural knowledge to court a white woman, sixteen-year-old Julietta Roberts. When they applied for a marriage license, the judge not only refused to grant it, he had Fook arrested for "assault upon the girl" despite the fact that she was above the age of consent. The Chinese predator stereotype labeled Chinese assimilation as mere deception and undermined Chinese bids for integration and belonging.[53]

Ah Lung and Ah Woon's relative proximity, power, and assimilation had long been tolerated by the Loomis community, but a series of judges and juries found their violation of racial stereotypes to be damning proof that they had also violated the young Lucas sisters. In his closing argument, the prosecutor told the juries it was their patriarchal duty to convict the men of rape. Dismissing the sisters' reluctant testimony, he argued, "We have to protect the young if the parents are dead or gone or the mothers are too ignorant or stupid to do it. I have got to do my share, you have got to do your share." The progressive state would act *in loco parentis,* imposing on May a narrative of victimhood that she resisted to no avail. And yet the assumption of Chinese guilt did not absolve the Lucas family of all culpability, and they too faced punishment: the state denied Elizabeth her daughters and institutionalized the "delinquent girls" in urban San Francisco.[54]

The juries complied with the prosecutor's urging, convicting Ah Woon of "the crime of rape" and Ah Lung of "assault with intent to commit rape." The difference in language had little effect. Judge J. E. Prewett sentenced both men to eleven years at San Quentin State Prison. Through these convictions, the county court became a vehicle for urban progressivism to reach rural Loomis. Ah Lung quickly appealed his case to the district court of appeals, but the court found that Hattie's "testimony was ample to prove" his guilt. Upholding Ah Lung's conviction, the court concluded that "though a chinaman, he must have known that the course pursued would inevitably subject him to suspicion and bring disgrace and shame on the girl."[55]

When Ah Lung and Ah Woon arrived at San Quentin, they traded in their western-style jackets and hats for black-and-white striped uniforms. As a matter of routine, prison officials shaved all prisoners bald, but this seemingly race-neutral policy had unequal effect on Chinese migrants. By cutting his braided queue, the guards effectively cut Ah Lung off from his homeland, marking him as an outcast in his native land. Both men were denied early parole in 1909, but they were granted it in 1912 with the help of two different white businessmen who wrote letters pledging to employ them.

These mug shots of Ah Lung (left) and Ah Woon (right) were taken when they arrived at San Quentin State Prison in 1905. The sequential images of Lung vividly capture the severing of his queue, an act that would have marked him as an outcast in his homeland. Though Lung is listed as thirty-six years old here, this appears to be an error since elsewhere he claimed to have been born in 1853. (San Quentin Inmate Photographs no. 21440, no. 21094, California State Archives, Office of the Secretary of State, Sacramento)

In the end, they spent nearly seven years behind bars, then stepped out into the world and—with the help of their nearly anonymous names—disappeared from the historical record.[56]

※ ※ ※

No doubt this story would have ended differently if it were about Black men in the South. In the nineteenth and early twentieth centuries, American popular culture depicted both Chinese and Black men as sexual threats, but these representations had strikingly different results. In the Jim Crow South, white vigilantes used accusations of Black-on-white rape to justify the lynching of thousands of Black men. Rape allegations, and the spectacular violence that frequently followed, became a powerful way to deny Black social and political ascendancy in the years after emancipation. The South's racial etiquette was rigid: Black men could not employ white females, as Ah Lung and Ah Woon did, and Black men accused of rape faced the threat of death rather than an eleven-year prison sentence.[57]

Compared to the hysteria over the imagined Black rapist, the local response to the Chinese predator was less severe. Even widely publicized accusations did not lead to inevitable violence or convictions. For example, in 1894 the *Los Angeles Times* published an incendiary article under the headline "Assaulted a Child." The paper alleged that Wing, a Chinese washerman, had visited the Mandich household to pick up laundry and afterward exited through the backyard. When Mrs. Mandich went looking for her three-year-old daughter a few minutes later, she found "the heathen was just in the act of outraging the child." Officials charged Wing with rape, but a few weeks later the charges were dismissed after "the evidence appeared to be very weak and of a decidedly improbable nature." Similarly, the next year the *Los Angeles Times* reported that a "little girl" had been assaulted in a barn and suspicion had immediately fallen on a Chinese cook. The cook faced immediate arrest, but later he was released ("the evidence being insufficient to hold him") and a white "tramp" was charged in his place. A year later, the paper reported on "revolting" evidence that a man named Charlie Sui had assaulted a five-year-old white girl, but a month later the accused was released after the prosecutor admitted he had "no prospect of winning."[58]

In short, a rape accusation against a Chinese man did not mean inevitable persecution, prosecution, or conviction. At times, sexual anxieties became a compelling rationale for white Americans to police Chinese men at the local level, but such incidents were relatively rare. Popular culture may have cast Chinese men as dangerous sexual predators, but the state and local communities did not necessarily act on these beliefs. That said, the Chinese predator stereotype was not simply a muted version of the staggeringly lethal image of the Black rapist. The two representations descended from different genealogies of thought and were distinct in their particulars: while Chinese men were imagined to be inscrutable sexual predators who attempted to lure their prey, Black men were imagined to be aggressive sexual animals who could only be controlled through violence.

Moreover, the two images were put to different societal work. The stereotype of the Black rapist was used to deny Black men the full privileges of citizenship and segregate them from white society. By the 1890s, white southerners largely defined rape as a "Negro crime" and described lynching as the only "remedy." Vigilantes used accusations of rape and other crimes to justify lynching more than 3,000 Black people between 1882 and 1929.[59] The Chinese stereotype never commanded this level of vitriol and violence. This does not mean that the racial stereotype was impotent, but it does suggest that its strength lay elsewhere.

Fear of the Chinese predator conveyed only limited power to police daily encounters in rural Loomis, but wielded more influence in the public courtroom, and still more in the national debate over Chinese exclusion. While the representation of the Black rapist regulated local norms, it seems that of the Chinese predator held more sway in federal immigration policy.[60] In other words, the same anti-Chinese stereotype could operate differently at the border and within the interior—at the scale of the nation and the scale of the community.[61]

At the border, the federal government attempted to codify, standardize, and record the terms of exclusion, but within local communities the etiquette of daily life was more informal, irregular, and often unspoken until violated. As a result, conditional inclusion took many forms as it cut across labor and living arrangements, laws and legal practices, public and intimate acts. The terms of inclusion differed by class, status, and gender. They shifted and evolved, as progressive norms radiated out from urban areas and rural crises made news in the city. In these disparate spaces and spheres, there were moments when the logics of conditional inclusion aligned with those of exclusion and moments when they parted ways.

{7}

The "IMMIGRANT"
and the MEANING of CHINESE EXCLUSION

RUMORS INSPIRED THE RAID on 747 Clay Street. A tip led missionary Donaldina Cameron to believe it to be the home of an adolescent girl who was in desperate need of rescue. Cameron first headed to the San Francisco Juvenile Court to secure a bench warrant and then assembled an eclectic group to raid the house. One of her recruits was an interpreter, Lonnie Lee, who worked with Cameron at the Presbyterian Chinese Mission Home. She also enlisted the help of San Francisco policemen, including Sargent John Manion and his Moral Squad, to act as muscle. Finally, she persuaded Inspector John A. Robinson from the Immigration Service to join them, although his role was less clear.

In the evening hours of February 17, 1917, they stood in front of 747 Clay Street. The apartment building lay at the center of San Francisco's Chinatown with windows overlooking Portsmouth Square. No one recorded how the raiding party entered the building, although entering the room they had targeted required that the police "smash the panel of the door with its many bolts and fastenings."[1] At first they found only a man, Hom Wah Bow, in bed. Then they caught a second man, Chon Tong, leaving the scene.

Finally, in the next room, they found the person they were searching for—an adolescent known by two names, "Yick Yok Lan" and "Suey Ching"—in bed with an older woman, Low Shu. At first the wanted adolescent "baffled" the "would-be rescuers" by refusing to give her name or admit that she was in any distress. Only once they produced the Juvenile Court bench warrant did she consent to leaving her "barred room."[2]

The policemen swiftly arrested all three adults and brought them to the city jail under charges of "contributing to the delinquency of a minor." They also took the youth with a double name, but did not send her with the others. Instead the missionaries offered to detain her themselves. Under court order, Cameron held her at the Presbyterian Chinese Mission Home while she awaited a hearing at the Juvenile Court.

As the policemen and missionaries busied themselves with arresting the adults and rescuing the adolescent, the immigration inspector appears to have watched and taken notes. Why was he present in the first place? The bench warrant questioned the youth's guardianship but said nothing about her immigration status. According to the Immigration Service's own records, she was a native of California, not China.

But for Inspector Robinson, raids like this had become a common part of his workday. As Chinese Inspector for the service, Robinson treated any Chinese person he encountered as an immigrant, unwanted and possibly illegal.[3]

※ ※ ※

By the early twentieth century, the machinery of immigration enforcement in San Francisco had become intertwined with the criminal justice system. Federal immigration agents had begun to coordinate with local police, sometimes making it difficult to tell where policing ended and border control began.

For example, Inspector Robinson may have been only an observer in the raid of 747 Clay Street, but his presence is telling. Robinson, an agent of federal exclusion, stood side by side with the police, agents of local regulation, as if they shared a common legal role. Increasingly, they did. As the Immigration Service constructed the infrastructure for Chinese exclusion in the early twentieth century, it built upon an existing apparatus of police work, charitable services, criminal courts, and jails. The workforce that had long sustained conditional inclusion helped launch the new regime of Chinese exclusion. Robinson worked with these local agents because he could not hope to ferret out criminal or unauthorized immigrants on his own. He relied on his collaboration with more established arms of state power.

If lawmakers had designed policing and border control as separate systems, and the courts had affirmed that ideal, then how had they become so entangled? By tracing the lives of Cameron's raiding party and their target, it is possible to see the threads that connected local racial regulation to federal immigration control. Inspector Robinson's presence shows the expansion of federal immigration services into the interior; Donaldina Cameron's rescue work exposes the depth of missionary involvement, as does the presence of her translator, Lonnie Lee; and Sergeant Manion's police work reveals how local police enforcement benefited from the Immigration Service. Finally, we will consider Suey Ching, also known as Yick Yok Lan, whose double name shielded her identity. Her experience shows the cumulative weight of Chinese exclusion and conditional inclusion, as well as the particular perils faced by women and girls.

Although San Francisco police had been raiding Chinatown for decades, Inspector Robinson's presence at this raid, and others like it, signaled a substantive change. As an agent of federal exclusion Robinson held certain powers. While state statutes criminalized certain behaviors associated with the Chinese, exclusion laws criminalized a Chinese person's mere presence. Immigration inspectors needed only suspicion of unlawful residence to detain a Chinese person, and administrators could deport them without judicial review. Moreover, while local and state laws had to conform to the tenets of equal protection, federal immigration law could explicitly target the Chinese race. In short, exclusion laws gave federal officials broad authority over Chinese migrants, power that local and state officials lacked.

At the time, federal officials focused their attention on the process of exclusion—that is, how the government would keep Chinese immigrants from entering the United States—and historians have mostly followed suit. But the Immigration Service also held indirect power over the process of conditional inclusion; that is, how the government would regulate the behavior of Chinese residents already within the country. By making the lives of Chinese in America uniquely precarious, Chinese exclusion laws provided new tools for local social control. The looming threat of deportation could be used to enforce the terms of Chinese inclusion.

THE TARGET: YICK YOK LAN

In the spring of 1901, a child named Yick Yok Lan lost her mother. It is unclear whether the death had been expected, or came as a shock to her father, Yick Ki Wing. Either way, he acted swiftly. Only a few days later, Wing took Lan to a studio in San Jose, California, to be photographed.[4] At two and a half, she was old enough to sit on a chair and look directly at the camera, but too young to have any defining features beyond round cheeks, stern lips, and dark eyes.

Those eyes had likely just witnessed the rites of mourning and burial; now they would look on as her father performed the rituals of departure. After he obtained a photograph, Wing found and paid two white officials, the president and secretary of the San Jose Board of Health, to attest to Lan's name and parentage. They swore that "Yet Yook Lan" was born in San Jose in 1898 to Yick Ki Wing, a merchant working for the firm of Quan Tai and Company, and his

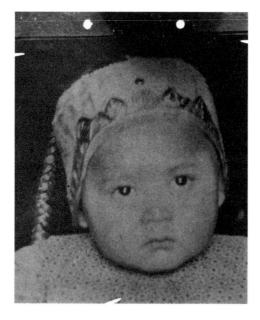

Yick Yok Lan as an infant (1901). Before departing for China, Lan's father filed an affidavit and attached this photograph. He hoped to facilitate his daughter's return to the United States in the future. (Chinese Immigration File no. 15597/19–26, National Archives at San Francisco)

wife, Yick Lai Shee. More precisely, Lan was born in San Jose's Heinlenville Chinatown, one of two "reservations" where the Chinese community rebuilt after the burning of Market Street Chinatown.[5]

According to the affidavit, the local health officials understood that "said father desires to take said child upon a visit to China and this certificate is made for the purpose of identifying said child, and facilitating the landing of said child upon their return to the United States." After signing, the local officials affixed the glossy golden seal of the Board of Health to add another marker of authenticity.[6]

For longtime Chinese residents in the United States such as Yick Ki Wing, a series of exclusion laws made a temporary visit to China with his daughter difficult, expensive, and risky. The Chinese Restriction Act (1882), the Chinese Exclusion Act (1888), and the Geary Act (1892) required that Chinese migrants provide documentary evidence that they had the right to enter or reenter the United States. But documentation often proved difficult to obtain, especially after years of public disregard for Chinese names. Federal officials often lacked records of Chinese births, marriages, deaths, and businesses in the United States or China, and what records they did have were filled with monikers like "John Chinaman" and "Mary Chinaman," and vague transliterations like "Ah Sing" or "Shee Wong." Local and state governments had rendered the Chinese nearly indistinguishable, which made it difficult, if not impossible, for federal immigration officials to differentiate between an alien and a citizen. It also made it difficult, if not impossible, for men like Wing to prove their right to reentry.

As a result, Chinese exclusion created a feverish business in record production, as the federal government produced reams of paperwork and the Chinese responded in kind. Wing secured a photograph and an affidavit; other Chinese migrants collected marriage certificates, birth certificates, and testimonial letters. When documents were lacking, the government turned to extensive interrogations of Chinese migrants. Officials worked relentlessly to produce, collect, and preserve testimony of Chinese lives in the vain hope that such documentation would slow migration.[7]

But instead the system opened the door to widespread fraud. Chinese migrants found ways to style themselves as legal immigrants and produce the required documentation. US officials and Chinese migrants understood themselves to be engaged in a game of cat and mouse with broad consequences. Officials zealously investigated birthplaces and family relationships, and Chinese migrants (whether authorized or not) worked to document their claim on America. The exclusion laws had disallowed most Chinese migrants but allowed a few key exceptions. Therefore, unauthorized Chinese could assemble the correct records to impersonate a merchant, a minor child of a merchant, a US citizen, or an unmarried child of a US citizen.[8] Lan was, at least allegedly, both a minor child of a merchant and a US citizen by birth.

For Wing, his first step was to have his daughter photographed and an affidavit signed. With the right paperwork, a Chinese merchant should be able to take his American-born daughter to visit China and then return to the United States. Wing appeared to have the legal know-how, funds, and connections to procure that paperwork. Having armed himself against Chinese exclusion to the best of his ability, Wing departed on the SS *Siberia* in 1903 to deliver his daughter to the arms of his family in China. When he returned to San Jose two years later, he left his daughter behind in Guangzhou (Canton) with an aunt who would care for her through childhood and adolescence.[9]

A decade passed. Lan grew up. And then, in September 1916, a young woman bearing the name "Yick Yok Lan" arrived in San Francisco after a month's journey on the SS *China* from Hong Kong. The ship's manifest indicated that she was nineteen years old, single, and a dressmaker by trade. Her passage had been paid by her father, and with his help she had retained an attorney. Based on the affidavit collected thirteen years prior, she was born in San Jose, and therefore returning to America as "a native" and a merchant's daughter. Either status should have been enough to admit Lan, but both depended on proving her relationship to her father.[10]

As soon as the steamer pulled into port, immigration inspectors boarded the ship to begin inspections. Passengers in the first- and second-class cabins could expect to be swiftly approved and landed in San Francisco, along with some returning Chinese merchants who were known to the inspectors. Chinese passengers in steerage, such as Lan, had more to prove. She was transferred from the SS *China* to a small ferry, which shuttled migrants to the Angel Island Immigration Station for further processing. There, inspectors searched her bags, issued her an ID number (15597/19–25), and sent her to the hospital building for a medical examination. Doctors and nurses poked and prodded, hoping to determine her approximate age and identify any diseases or defects. Officials then issued Lan a bunk in the women's detention barracks to await interrogation.[11]

Five days later, father and daughter appeared separately before the immigration board. Officially, Lan applied for admission to the United States based on her native status, but in practice her case rested on three related suppositions. Because the status of all Chinese women derived from that of their male relatives, she first needed to establish that she was indeed the daughter of Yick Ki Wing, and second, that he was a Chinese merchant lawfully conducting business in San Jose. Third, thanks to the Page Act, she needed to prove she was a respectable woman, without any tie to prostitution.

Inspectors' fears of fraud meant that the 1901 affidavit obtained by her alleged father was not enough to prove her native status. Instead, US officials depended on separate interrogations of Lan and Wing to determine the legitimacy of their claims. Officials asked a series of basic questions—Where were you born? What is your mother's name? Who has been taking care of you in China? In what part of Canton did you live? How many rooms had that house?—and then compared the answers of father and daughter.[12] Officials viewed this process as a model of modern efficiency, but Chinese arrivals often found the questioning to be intimidating and humiliating.

After listening to her testimony and reviewing the transcripts, Inspector William Thiess declared that he was "reasonably satisfied that the person who applicant purports to be was born in the United States." He was not convinced, however, that the adolescent who stood before him was the same person. He pointed out numerous discrepancies: The father identified photographs of his brother, but the daughter could not recognize her uncle. The father stated that he smoked a water pipe, but the daughter claimed he smoked cigarettes. He claimed they washed themselves in the river, but she claimed there was a water well in the house. He explained he now ran a business in the city of Stockton, she stated that he ran a business on Stockton Street in San Francisco. "Considering every feature of this case," Thiess concluded, "I am of the opinion that the testimony offered is adverse to the applicant's claims." The Immigration Service denied her application, implying that she had arrived under a false name.[13]

With the help of her lawyer, Lan appealed the decision, which entailed another round of interrogations and three additional weeks of detention while awaiting her fate. Angel Island Immigration Center segregated detainees by race and sex. Officials confined "Orientals" to detention barracks, where each large room had four rows of metal bunks and an attached lavatory. When filled, the space felt small and stifling. Chinese women enjoyed an occasional respite from the barracks in the form of a weekly walk of the island while under guard; Chinese men were only permitted time in the small "Oriental" recreation yard.

Detainees also ate their meals in segregated dining rooms. The European dining room included tablecloths, but the Chinese dining room had none. Some Chinese men passed the time by reading newspapers and carving poems into the barrack walls, but Chinese women were mostly illiterate. "There was nowhere to go," a woman detainee remembered. "There was no mah jongg, no recreational activities for the women. I read or knitted, made some clothes, or slept. When you got up, it was time to eat again. Day in and day out, eat and sleep. Many people cried. I must have cried a bowlful of tears at Angel Island. It was so pitiful!"[14]

Few new facts emerged in Lan's case during those weeks of detention and appeal, but a new inspector assigned to the case, Charles W. Pierce, arrived at a different conclusion than his predecessor. Reviewing the details of the case and the second round of interrogations, Pierce excused Lan's failure to identify photographs of her kin. The pictures were old, and the forgotten uncle had died long before. In one way or another, Pierce brushed aside the list of discrepancies. Instead, he seemed to take particular interest in two photographs of Lan—one from her infancy and one from her recent arrival—both of which the department had blown up to four times their original size. "It is extremely difficult to state whether the photograph appearing upon the departure papers, which was taken at an early age, represents the applicant," Inspector Pierce acknowledged, but he still believed that "there is sufficient resemblance in the features to say that it may be the same person." Perhaps she had arrived under her true name. He recommended her admission.[15]

This was by far the most frequent outcome. Between the passage of the Chinese Restriction Act in 1882 and the repeal of Chinese exclusion in 1943, historian Erika Lee estimated that 303,000 Chinese arrivals gained admittance to the United States. Many of these arrivals were Chinese migrants making repeated trips across the Pacific, but still this was a significantly higher number of Chinese arrivals than the estimated 258,000 who entered the United States before exclusion laws were in place.[16]

The Chinese who landed at Angel Island faced higher hurdles than the Europeans who arrived at Ellis Island Immigration Station on the East Coast. During the period 1910–1930, officials rejected 7 percent of Chinese immigrants at Angel Island but only 2 percent of Chinese immigrants at Ellis Island. The rejection rate of Chinese reeks of racial discrimination, but it also shows that the Chinese exclusion laws failed to fully exclude. Officials may have regarded "every Chinese applicant for admission as a cheat, a liar, a rogue and a criminal," but they did not prevent every Chinese from landing.[17]

Government officials, it seems, lacked the power, capacity, and will to end Chinese migration. Even though federal officials were granted broad discretionary power by Chinese exclusion laws and subsequent US Supreme Court rulings, they faced a barrage of legal challenges from Chinese migrants. Chinese resistance taxed the Immigration Service's limited capacity. Each new habeas corpus case required manpower, funding, and extensive record-keeping—all of which were limited resources for government officials.

But the primary impediment appears to have been lack of will. The United States could have excluded the Chinese through arbitrary force, but instead it prioritized the ideals of modern bureaucratic efficiency. Federal officials could have turned away almost all Chinese arrivals, but instead they faithfully processed them. Immigration officials believed in following the law, and lawmakers did not want to risk endangering diplomatic relations with China.[18]

Chinese exclusion dissuaded many Chinese from attempting to enter the United States—and in this way dramatically slowed Chinese migration—but for those who braved the ordeal at Angel Island, the vast majority ultimately gained admittance. Even so, the detention center left scars. The ordeal of segregated detention and extensive interrogation taught Chinese migrants that they were unwanted in America, that they were considered inferior and illegitimate. The degrading ritual of exclusion, in the words of historian Adam

McKeown, left Chinese migrants with only "a skeleton of a social identity" in the United States.[19] Whether their border crossing took a few days or many months, Chinese migrants carried the experience of racialized humiliation with them into the interior.

Lan made it through this ritual of exclusion. She entered the United States on October 24, 1916, twenty-four days after she had arrived and four months before she would be arrested.[20]

THE IMMIGRATION INSPECTOR: JOHN ANDREW ROBINSON

John Andrew Robinson was born in 1870 in the mining town of Jackson, California. In childhood he moved to the more urban Bay Area, attending grammar school in Oakland and high school in Livermore. But he did not earn a high school diploma and instead set to work. His first job was as a "helper" at the Oakland Electric Light and Motor Company, followed by a period as a streetcar conductor. He then entered law enforcement, working as a deputy constable and then a special police officer in East Oakland.

But his ambitions, it seems, lay elsewhere. In 1904 he took the civil service exam and the "Chinese watchman exam," demonstrating a modest level of aptitude in both. But his scores proved good enough for the Immigration Service. Sworn in as a "watchman at large" in 1904, Robinson pledged "to defend the constitution," "prevent and detect frauds," forbid "the importation of aliens under contract to labor," and enforce "the exclusion of Chinese persons." Four years later he received a raise and a promotion to the role of "Chinese Inspector."

In his performance reviews, his superiors described Robinson as a bit slow, but relatively effective. "While Inspector Robinson is not so clever in examining cases of arriving Chinese as he might be," one superior noted, "he is nevertheless a very useful man." Another explained, "What he lacks in mentality he makes up for in his earnest probing efforts and his success in locating violators of the immigration law." He worked hard, showed up with surprising punctuality, and rarely called in sick. He used his steady job to support his mother and two sisters.[21]

In 1909 Robinson began a new journal, which survives to this day. After adorning the inside cover with his name and title, "U.S. Immigration Inspector," he penned his first entry: "Monday April 5th 1909 Received appointment from Washington D.C. to go on Special Duty. White slave work."[22] For the next three decades, Robinson made daily notes in his journals, recording the cases he was working, addresses he visited, and the cost of ferry rides as he circled the San Francisco Bay.

As a special inspector, he was not moored to the docks like other Immigration Service officers. He did not regularly board transpacific steamers to stand before Chinese arrivals and demand their papers. Neither was he one of the officials at the Angel Island Immigration Station who processed, interrogated, and investigated Lan and other migrants. Those immigration officials primarily focused on exclusion, preventing "illegal aliens" from entering America's gates. Robinson, in contrast, worked primarily on expulsion, deporting "aliens" already in residence.

When Robinson began his "white slave" assignment, Congress was still debating the White-Slave Traffic bill, which was signed into law as the Mann Act in 1910. The law criminalized the movement of "debauched" women and gave federal agents broad powers to police women's mobility, morality, work, and choice of sexual partner. But Robinson soon found that "white slave work" was a niche business. The international trafficking of white "slaves" into prostitution loomed larger in lawmakers' minds than in reality.[23] As his journal entries show, even when on special assignment, he retained his particular focus on Chinese immigrants and Chinese women in particular.

After all, even before the Page Act of 1875, Chinese women had been closely associated with prostitution in the American imagination, especially in San Francisco. Robinson began by collecting tips on Chinese "prostitutes" and "procurers," but eventually began to investigate Chinese for "illegal residence" as well. When an immigrant named Lim Mon escaped from detention, for example, Robinson worked with the Oakland Police Department to track him down. Another time, Robinson used "decoy letters" to lure a man named Chan Chun to an Oakland post office, so he could arrest him for illegal residence and deliver him to the US marshal.

One day he accompanied San Francisco police officers on an opium raid and nabbed Tue Ying, a Chinese woman, on charges of "illegal residence."[24]

While he did not often record the content of his conversations, Robinson dutifully reported on his travels (and the resulting ferry costs). His route included sites closely associated with border control: the docks in San Francisco and the dilapidated Detention Shed, where federal officials held Chinese immigrants until 1910. After Angel Island Immigration Station opened, he traveled by ferry to the offices, hospital, and detention barracks there.

His circuit also included key outposts of the criminal justice system. In San Francisco, he made the rounds between the city prison, Juvenile Court, US district attorney's office, and police department offices on Bush Street, Kearny Street, and Eddy Street. In the East Bay, he visited the Alameda County Jail, Oakland Courthouse, and Oakland Hall of Records. In the North Bay, he journeyed up to San Quentin State Prison. In addition to his tour of courts and police stations, Robinson circulated through the religious institutions of the Bay Area: the Presbyterian Mission, the YWCA, and the Methodist Mission in San Francisco, as well as the Presbyterian Mission in Berkeley.[25]

There was nothing natural about this circuit, which combined sites of immigration detention, criminal justice, and missionary work. In fact, lawmakers had gone to great lengths to separate border control from policing, as well as church from state. The Supreme Court had determined that the federal government held plenary (or absolute) power over matters of immigration, and that states should have no direct role in related legislation or enforcement.[26] Therefore, federal agents, rather than local police, were tasked with building America's border control. In previous decades Congress had placed immigration control within the Treasury Department and deployed federal customs officers to enforce immigration measures. Beginning in 1891, federal funds fed a growing bureaucracy in the Department of Customs led by a superintendent of immigration and staffed by immigration commissioners, inspectors, and interpreters.

In *Fong Yue Ting v. United States* (1893), the Supreme Court attempted to further separate criminal proceedings from immigration matters. The case established that federal officials had the right to expel Chinese immigrants even if they had established longtime residence in the United States. To bolster federal discretionary power and reduce immigrant rights, the court held that immigration proceedings were "in no proper sense a trial" and "deportation is not a punishment for crime." In immigration matters, the court found that "the provisions of the Constitution securing the right of trial by jury and prohibiting unreasonable searches and seizures and cruel and unusual punishments have no application."[27]

In other words, for criminal offenses, police officers required probable cause and a warrant to search and arrest, but for immigration infractions, federal inspectors could act without these safeguards. In a criminal trial, defendants had the right to a lawyer, a jury, and due process, but immigration proceedings were merely administrative hearings and carried none of these guarantees. Criminal courts relied on jails and prisons to punish the guilty, but the courts did not recognize detention or deportation as punishment at all.[28] By granting Chinese migrants different rights under criminal and immigration law, the Supreme Court operated as if immigration control existed in a realm separate from criminal justice.

But there are signs that these regulatory structures were intertwined from the beginning. When twenty-two "lewd" Chinese women were detained in San Francisco harbor in 1874, for example, they were placed in a county jail to await their fate.[29] But starting in 1876, the Page Act entirely prohibited immoral women from *landing* in the United States, which prompted an awkward system of detention aboard ships. This was not a practical solution, because processing a Chinese arrival could take weeks, so the Customs Department experimented with ad hoc solutions. They tried transferring detained Chinese from ship to ship, sending Chinese women to the Chinese Mission Home, transferring long-term detainees to the San Francisco county jail, or releasing them on bond.[30]

During these early years of exclusion, city jails and state prisons began to house detained immigrants as a matter of necessity. When Congress charged the Customs Service with implementation of immigration law, the department did not have adequate resources or infrastructure for immigrant detention and therefore applied the law haphazardly. For example, although the Restriction Act dictated that unlawful Chinese immigrants should be deported rather than imprisoned, courts in Washington Territory did not initially listen. There, Chinese found guilty of "being in U.S. unlawfully" found themselves incarcerated at the McNeil Federal Prison, serving sentences of six to nine months. Starting in 1890, federal officials in Washington State worked harder to follow the law, ordering deportations of any immigrant found in violation of Chinese exclusion. Even so, several hundred Chinese were incarcerated in the federal prison while they awaited deportation, a process that could take months, and sometimes years.[31]

In 1892 the Pacific Steamship Company erected on the docks of San Francisco Bay a "shed" that would serve as a federal detention site until the construction of Angel Island in 1910. But local jails continued to serve as sites of incarceration. Starting in 1892, for example, booking records from the Alameda county jail list Chinese who were detained on immigration charges. Ching, Ah Yeun, Ah Chon, and Ah Lee arrived on March 10, 1892, for "deportation," and were released to the US inspector four days later. When the warden recorded Lun Hing Pong, Fong Jow Gum, Yeap Ngun, Leung Choy, Chun Yow, and Fong Toy Jun on July 9, 1892, he noted the reason as "on H.C." It appears the six men had been allowed to enter the country following habeas corpus petitions, but had been imprisoned again, perhaps due to parole violations. Their stay at the Alameda county jail lasted more than a month. Altogether, ninety Chinese accused of immigration infractions passed through the Alameda county jail in 1892 alone. Only scattered Alameda jail registers from other years survive, but from what remains, it is clear that this practice persisted for more than a decade. In January 1907, Leung Foo, Ng Gum, and Lum Poo, all "illegally in U.S.," were held in jail for six weeks and then deported.[32]

Historian Briana Nofil has found that, starting in the early twentieth century, county jails began detaining Chinese for immigration infractions on the East Coast as well. Fueled by federal funds, four counties in upstate New York opened dedicated "Chinese jails." Nofil also documented individual cases of Chinese detained in county jails across the United States, including Brownsville, Texas; Luna County, New Mexico; and Montgomery, Alabama.[33] Federal officials, it seems, were making a practice of relying on county jails to administer Chinese detention.

Therefore, Inspector Robinson was not acting alone when he built his corner of immigration control on top of local structures of policing and incarceration. Robinson traveled around the bay to visit the men and women who had decades of experience policing and rescuing Chinese prostitutes and (to a lesser extent) Japanese prostitutes. He relied on their aid. The task of regulating Chinese immigration was too large for a few Chinese inspectors to accomplish on their own.

It was in this context that Inspector Robinson accompanied Sargent Manion and the Moral Squad, as well as Donaldina Cameron and Lonnie Lee on the raid at 747 Clay Street to apprehend Yick Yok Lan. Robinson's diary only offers the barest sketch of what happened:

Feb 17–1917
Went with Miss Cameron [and] Miss Lon Lee, her interpreter, to serve Juvenile Court Warrant at 747—Clay St. S.F. Was arrested by Lieutenant Char Goff of S.F. Police Dept., Detective Mannion [sic] and Officer—Yick Yuk Lon—female—was arrested on Juvenile Court Warrant and Han Wah Bow—who had been in bed with Yick Yuk Lon—was arrested for contributing Also Chan Tong—who was found with Low She—alleged Keeper, were locked up and charged with contributing.

These arrests concerned civil and criminal matters—guardianship, prostitution, and contributing to the delinquency of a minor—but Robinson also saw the possible application of immigration law. He returned to his office to pull immigration files and found that "Yick Yok Lan" (15597/12-26) claimed to be a native, "Chan Tong" claimed to be a bone fide merchant, and "Low She" claimed she was a merchant's wife (although her husband was away in China).[34] As the police gathered evidence that a crime had been committed, Inspector Robinson investigated whether the Chinese men and women had the right to remain in the country.

This arrangement was ripe for abuse. If the police could not prove criminal guilt, then the inspector could initiate immigration proceedings, in which he could avoid the hurdles of due process. All of the hard-won guarantees of equal protection—built upon the Reconstruction Amendments and a steady stream of Chinese legal challenges—could not save the Chinese from the despotic authority of immigration law.

However, Robinson did not choose to wield that power in Lan's case. He suspected Lan was unauthorized, but the documentation provided by her father was extensive. He questioned her place of birth and her name, and he noted that she had allegedly confessed to Presbyterian Mission women, but she would not confess to him. Although he could have initiated deportation proceedings, in the end he did not. Perhaps he was not quite sure who she was.

If he had, few traces of Lan's story would remain today. Robinson carefully labeled all his deportation cases with the classification "No. 12020" and filed them at Angel Island Immigration Station. But when a fire burned the station to the ground in 1940, it destroyed all No. 12020 deportation files and left a gaping hole in the historical record.[35] Historians have ample evidence of Chinese arrivals and interrogations at San Francisco Bay, but for deportations of residents from the interior, often No. 12020 is all that remains.

For example, on February 1, 1915, Robinson logged a case in his diary that bore some resemblance to Lan's. It involved a Chinese juvenile female who was held at the Presbyterian Mission and an alleged smuggler, S. K. Lee. In that case, however, their numbers, 12020/1193 and 12020/240–11, suggest that the authorities took another path and worked to deport both the trafficker and his alleged victim. But due to the fire, no records remain. Similarly, on January 24, 1917, a raid that involved the same interested parties— Robinson, Donaldina Cameron, Lon Lee, John Manion, and members of the Chinatown Squad—resulted in the apprehension of an alleged prostitute, Sue Gim Ying. Her number, 12020/1227, scrawled across Robinson's journal is the only remaining trace of what happened next.

On the one hand, Robinson's presence at these raids represents the extension of border control into the interior and the resulting loss of rights for Chinese migrants. His work shows how an agent of exclusion could reinforce the terms of conditional inclusion. He used immigration law to police a Chinese female's work, living arrangements, and sexuality, thereby drawing bounds on Chinese economic and cultural rights.

But on the other hand, Robinson's ultimate inaction is also telling. Robinson's circuit, although large for navigation by ferry on a daily basis, was only a small extension of federal authority. The Bay Area cities of Oakland, San Francisco, and Berkeley were not far into the domestic interior, geographically. And his coordination with the police, although extensive, remained an ad hoc affair, far from the systematic collaboration that would emerge later in the twentieth century. In theory, immigration control spanned the nation; but in reality, federal authorities had limited capacity to enforce exclusion outside of the port cities and border towns.[36]

During the early twentieth century, immigration officials dedicated more resources and manpower to rejecting Chinese arrivals than to arresting and deporting long-term Chinese residents. What resources they did invest in deportations appear to have disproportionately gone to suspected "criminal aliens." Still, US officials maintained that deportations played an important role in the general policy of Chinese exclusion.

A 1906 federal report, for example, explained that deportations from the interior, even if few and far between, could help to keep Chinese migrants in a state of fear. Officials worried that the migrants would "in ever increasing numbers, find the means of evading the officers on our borders and effecting surreptitious entry into the United States." These evasions would continue to multiply if migrants believed they could live in the country without being "disturbed." Therefore, the "aggressive" application of "the provision of law relating to the expulsion" was recommended. The Immigration Service believed the looming threat of deportation would help to deter illegal immigration and encourage voluntary exit.[37]

When the raiding party arrived at 747 Clay Street, there was no practical need for Inspector Robinson. He did not help break down the door, arrest the men and women, or arrange for their incarceration. The police could do all those things without him. But Robinson carried with him one potentially valuable power no one else held: the authority to deport. It was a mighty weapon, even when held in reserve.

THE MISSIONARY: DONALDINA CAMERON

Donaldina Cameron joined the Presbyterian Chinese Mission Home in 1895 as a twenty-five-year-old fresh from a broken engagement. Soon the Mission Home became her job, her calling, and her identity. Cameron began by assisting Head Matron Margaret Culbertson, the home's ailing leader. A few years later, Cameron informally guided the Mission Home through the difficult period after Culbertson's death and then, from 1900 until 1934, formally held the title of superintendent.[38]

Presbyterian women had established the Mission Home decades earlier, in 1874, to provide a refuge for Chinese prostitutes. Missionaries believed that most Chinese migrant women and girls in America were powerless victims of a Chinese trafficking network. While lawmakers worked to ban or exclude Chinese sex workers, the missionaries did what they could to protect them, whether this meant joining a police raid, housing a runaway, or educating and raising a child. At a time when the American public viewed Chinese as unwanted and irredeemable, the missionary women welcomed Chinese migrants into the home and worked to save their souls. Cameron believed missionary women could act as mothers to wayward Chinese daughters, with all the care and duty that entailed.[39]

To hold these beliefs and do this work, the mission women ignored some inconvenient facts. They refused to recognize that some of the Chinese women they encountered had become sex workers of their own volition while seeking to build a better life in America. Sex work could provide financial security, money to send home, and a possible path to marriage. Many of the women who ran away from brothels to the Chinese Mission Home did so not because of their trade, but because they found themselves in particularly poor circumstances. An abusive brothel owner or a poor share of profits could send Chinese women in search of the Mission. The mission women also elided distinctions between sex workers, concubines, second wives, and *mui tsai* (bonded servants), lumping them all under the label "Chinese slave girl." Chinese migrants, in contrast, understood these to be distinct roles in the community and chafed at the infantilizing and dehumanizing term. The mission women believed they knew best who needed rescue.[40]

In 1924, researchers interviewed "Miss Cameron" and marveled at her unusual approach with Chinese migrants. "To Miss Cameron they are real human beings, and they represent a great nation," a researcher observed. Cameron believed that "these people come here to absorb western civilization. If they are segregated and only absorb our vices they become a menace instead of an asset as they might be." Cameron trusted that, given exposure to American society, the Chinese could change and improve—or at least the women and girls could. Cameron despaired over the "evil" ways of Chinese men and sometimes lapsed into racial determinism in her descriptions. "The Chinese themselves will never abolish the hateful practice of buying and selling their women like so much merchandise," she wrote. "It is born in their blood, bred in their bone and sanctioned by the government of their native land."[41]

The Presbyterian Mission Home's work with local police and immigration officers predated Cameron's arrival in 1895. While some Chinese women and girls came to the home by choice, many found themselves held at the home involuntarily. After conducting a raid in Chinatown, San Francisco police made a practice of incarcerating Chinese sex workers in the Mission Home rather than the local jail. Mission women reported that individuals who arrived after a raid proved to be the most difficult residents.

Following a particularly large raid in 1897, for example, the police brought sixty women to the home for detention. After immigration officials inspected the women, forty-seven were given their liberty and, despite the entreaties of the mission women, swiftly departed the home. The rest remained confined at the Mission as the Immigration Service conducted further investigations into their immigration status. A missionary took note in their "Register of Inmates" that "The 13 who ... were compelled to remain acted like demons, some had to be carried upstairs refusing to walk." These inmates remained in the home, under police guard, for several days more. Following police and immigration investigations, all but one were ultimately granted their liberty. The last was "convicted and remanded to China."[42] In cases such as this—involving arrest, detention, and the threat of deportation—"rescue" hardly seems a fitting term.

Starting in 1890 the home also housed immigrant detainees: women and girls who had recently arrived and had been placed on "parole" while they faced investigation. Parole at the home, everyone agreed, was preferable to incarceration at the "unsanitary" Detention Shed. In 1890 Superintendent Culbertson reported that the home had cared for seventy-one women, thirty-seven of whom were "supposed to be entering the State unlawfully, and to prevent this, the United States court officers [conceived] the idea of sending them to the 'home,' with [the hope of] getting confessions from them and thereby thwarting [the] schemes of their importers."[43]

The mission women seemed to welcome these new immigrant "inmates." In an 1896 annual report, Cameron explained that the home had again served as "a temporary refuge and protection to a number of poor slave girls who were bought in China and brought over to this country to be resold into the worst kind of bondage. These girls [are] entrusted to our keeping until the Custom House officers have time to investigate their cases and decide whether they have the right to land or not." The missionaries were pleased that customs officials provided federal funds for the women's upkeep. Like county jailers, they welcomed the federal funds that immigrant detention could provide. They also declared themselves "truly thankful to be given the privilege of caring for them and giving them at least a glimpse of something better and purer than they have ever known in all their sad sin darkened lives."[44]

Missionaries had no apparent qualms about the home acting as a site of detention, because it gave them a chance to convert their temporary guests. The missionaries did, however, feel conflicted about their role in deportation. In 1895, for instance, the missionaries housed eight "United States boarders; four of whom were deported by our government to China." In her annual report, Culbertson bemoaned the "particularly sad" case of "Little Leong Dong."

> She was brought into the country illegally, and after coming to the Home to await being landed, confessed that she had no right here, but dreaded to return, fearing the fate that awaited her, namely, being sold away to Singapore, where the life is terrible, without hope of escape from its suffering. We made heroic efforts to save her, but without avail. The Government was obdurate and turned a deaf ear to our plea. Heartbroken, she was born[e] away by the officers of the law, and all that we could do was look tearfully on and commend her to the care of our kind Heavenly Father, praying that he would shield her from all evil.[45]

Culbertson saw herself as Leong Dong's advocate, pleading with immigration officials to grant her leniency and the right to remain in the United States. While deportation might rid the United States of another Chinese "prostitute," Culbertson understood it did nothing to safeguard trafficked women. But while the missionaries advocated on behalf of their residents, the hard truth was that the home aided the government in deportation. Missionaries facilitated these expulsions by detaining immigrant parolees, encouraging them to confess, and reporting their confessions to the federal government.

THE "IMMIGRANT" AND THE MEANING OF CHINESE EXCLUSION 253

After 1910 the Immigration Service began detaining Chinese arrivals on Angel Island, but this did not end immigrant detention and deportation at the Mission Home. Cameron reported on the case of Fun Dai, a young girl who was paroled from Angel Island to the Mission Home "in return" for confessing to her "true story." Fun Dai proved a "helpful" witness for the government against her traffickers, but despite her assistance, she faced expulsion. "The gentle, wistful face of this young girl haunts us," Cameron wrote. "Always her eyes hold the anxious question: 'What will become of me when parole days in this safe home are ended?' and our own hearts ask the question 'Whither then?'" Cameron did her best to protect Fun Dai from traffickers by arranging female escorts for her journey back to Hong Kong. Cameron also raised the prospect of building a Mission Home in southern China to receive the deportees. But in the meantime, they relied on prayer.⁴⁶

Donaldina Cameron and police from the Chinatown Squad remove a Chinese girl from a gambling club (circa 1920). In the second photo, Cameron holds the "rescued" girl limp in her arms, possibly with the help of a translator. (Reproduced from Mildred Crowl Martin, *Chinatown's Angry Angel*, Pacific Books, 1977)

It was Cameron who, based on a tip, initiated the raid on 747 Clay Street in February of 1917. She was not looking for "Yick Yok Lan," the girl born in San Jose's Heinlenville Chinatown in 1898. Instead she was searching for "Suey Ching,"[47] a Chinese adolescent she believed had been trafficked under Lan's name. When the police broke down the door and arrested the adults, Cameron took charge of Suey Ching, although she would not answer to the name, and brought her to the Presbyterian Chinese Mission Home, even though she did not wish to go.

Once she had possession of the adolescent, Cameron and another matron, Ethel V. Higgins, went to the Juvenile Court to request legal guardianship. The Act for the Protection of Children (1878) allowed benevolent associations in California to sue for guardianship of children found destitute, begging, or in the company of thieves or prostitutes.[48] Records showed that Yick Yok Lan was nineteen years old, but Cameron alleged that Suey Ching was only sixteen or seventeen. She had to be underage if the Mission Home had any chance of winning legal guardianship. And if the Mission Home could win guardianship, then Suey Ching's putative father could not reclaim her. She could be free of the man who they believed trafficked her.

Cameron and Higgins did not only want guardianship of Suey Ching, however; they also wanted to prosecute the traffickers who brought her to the United States. If they could prove Suey Ching was an alien brought into the country against her will for lewd purposes, they could aid the prosecution of her "father."

Therefore, while they held Suey Ching and awaited trial, the mission women attempted to gain her confidence and obtain her "confession." Not only was this an important step on the path to salvation; it was central to the government's legal case.

THE TRANSLATOR: LONNIE LEE

It was Yoke Lon Lee, also known as Lonnie, who finally won Suey Ching's confidence and took her confession.

Lonnie Lee herself was a Chinese woman who first entered the Presbyterian Mission Home when she was only one year old. According to newspaper accounts, Lee's mother had "escaped from degrading slavery" into the open arms of Margaret Culbertson in

1891. When the head matron heard that the infant daughter remained in a house of ill fame, Culbertson teamed up with the Society for the Prevention of Cruelty to Children and the San Francisco police. Together they raided the "disorderly house in Fish Alley" where they located little Lonnie Lee, hidden away in the attic. "The proprietor of the place was loath to give her up, as all the inmates made a great pet of the child," the *Philadelphia Times* reported. But Culbertson persisted, knowing "there was no other legal claimant than the mother." Based on the mother's claim, Culbertson took the child, and even once her mother left the Mission Home, kept the infant and raised her. A year later, the paper reported that Lonnie had "grown finely. As a pet she is quite as available, quite as responsive as a white baby."[49] In the eyes of American reporters and the missionary women, Lonnie Lee had been rescued before she could be abused. And it appears, according to the newspapers, that her mother agreed with this assessment and consented to her placement in the home.[50]

But even when they did not have parental consent, missionaries "rescued" Chinese children and raised them in the Mission Home. And when Chinese family members went to court to protest the

Missionary Margaret Culbertson with "Lonnie" Lee (circa 1891). Lee entered the Presbyterian Chinese Mission Home as an infant and, once grown, worked as a missionary and translator. (Reproduced from Carol Green Wilson, *Chinatown Quest: The Life Adventures of Donaldina Cameron*, Stanford University Press, 1931)

taking of a child, they were often dismissed as traffickers. This made it difficult to assess parental consent in any Chinese guardianship case. Although no guardianship cases survive from San Francisco County, a case in Oregon reveals a level of complexity beyond simple narratives of "rescue." In 1889 Ah Wah (age ten) and Ah Tie (age eight) found themselves adrift, having recently lost their mother, and living with a "stepmother." The Boys & Girls Aid Society, in coordination with the North Pacific Presbyterian Mission, "rescued" the children from the stepmother and proposed to raise them. But their father, Wong Chin Way, fought the arrangement in court, pleading to be allowed to send the girls to China so they could be raised by their grandmother.

In the hope of reassuring the court, Wong had arranged for his daughters to be accompanied on the long transpacific journey by a Chinese Christian minister and his white American wife. Wong also produced several witnesses, including Frank Wong Woon, who begged the court to keep the family together. Upon cross-examination, Woon was asked, "Do you know whether the [father] wants the children or not?" His response was unequivocal: "Of course [like] most all Chinamen he like his own children; he don't like to lose his own children . . . You don't like to lose your own children." After a protracted legal battle that ended in the Oregon Supreme Court, the North Pacific Presbyterian Mission was granted custody of Ah Wah and Ah Tie. From the perspective of the mission, two more Chinese children had been "saved."[51]

Although no account of Lonnie Lee's childhood survives, there is every indication that she was as deeply invested in the mission as Donaldina Cameron. Another woman, Lilac Chen, who was also rescued as a young child and became a translator for the mission, expressed no regrets when interviewed decades later. "I'm so glad I heard about Jesus and know about HIM, and HE took care of me," Chen recounted. "Just think of the narrow chance!"[52]

Donaldina Cameron saw Lilac Chen and Lonnie Lee as two members of a new generation of "native workers." Cameron reported in a missionary magazine in 1912 that these Chinese American "native teachers" had begun to fill positions previously occupied by "foreign workers." This was the product of "nearly forty years sowing, and watchful tending watered by God's loving care." Cameron explained, "Year by year from among the Chinese girls in our home have come forward helpers sufficiently capable and faithful to occupy positions of trust and blessing to others."[53] In order to be "helpful" and complete their studies, both Chen and Lee went east in search of further education. Chen remembered, "I need more schooling, because I have to go to court to interpret. Because I didn't understand all the English, and you know, the American attorneys like to use technical terms. Especially when they see a helpless, inexperienced girl, they choose harder words, you know."[54]

Lonnie Lee not only wished to learn more English, but she also pursued a trade. She journeyed to the East Coast to attend a nursing program at the Presbyterian Hospital in Philadelphia and then a postgraduate course in New York City. When she passed the state board exam in Pennsylvania, she became the first certified American nurse of Chinese descent. Her rare achievement made the papers in both the United States and China.[55] Although journalists reported that she intended to practice her trade in China, in fact she returned to the Mission Home in San Francisco in 1914. She settled in the Bay Area, and in 1916 she registered to vote as a Republican. Lee continued to work for the Presbyterian Church the rest of her life, as a nurse, teacher, translator, phone operator, and bookkeeper.[56]

That is how Lonnie Lee came to be present at the raid of 747 Clay Street, and how she came to hear the double-named youth's confession. Once detained in the Mission Home, the woman they believed to be Suey Ching admitted that she had "occupied a room" with "the Chinaman known as Hom Wah Bow, and that she was a prostitute before she came to the United States." Lee passed this revelation on to Cameron, who dutifully passed it along to Inspector Robinson. Cameron and Lee, no doubt, hoped the information could aid in the prosecution of Lan's traffickers.

The missionaries also arranged for a medical examination of the youth, which "showed she had had no less than three abortions performed upon her." (How they could tell this was not explained.) Finally, Cameron and Lee produced and translated two letters found with her, which allegedly described her "importation." The first letter, from a "god-mother" in Hong Kong, informed the recipient that "the $1,000 you sent has been received, and I am sending someone over to the United States on S. S. China for you as requested." The second letter referred to "Yoke Lan," and explained that a "friend" had been ordered to "look after" Lan on board. Lee and Cameron believed the letters confirmed their suspicions that the youth had been trafficked.[57]

Still, it was not an open-and-shut case. The young woman's alleged father, Yick Ki Wing, reemerged to contest the Mission's guardianship case. Wing claimed Yick Yok Lan had been living with him in Stockton the prior few months, but had recently taken a trip to San Francisco to visit her friends. He disclaimed any knowledge of the character of the apartment in which Lan was found and promised to take her safely back to Stockton. Further complicating the Mission's case, the young woman refused to testify in court, although a translator had been provided. Perhaps she did not wish to openly defy her "father" or perhaps she did not wish to openly confess to illegal entry.

Despite the youth's refusal to testify, Cameron had reason to hope that Judge Frank Murasky would rule in the Mission's favor. Cameron had often worked with the Juvenile Court judge and believed they shared a common cause. When speaking to a biographer some years later, Cameron spoke fondly of the "long, serious hours we often spent together. Lunch hours, recesses after court, all were given with unstinted interest to better understanding of each little bruised body we brought him for protection." Judge Murasky was, in her remembrance, an "unfailing friend."[58]

Murasky, however, took an absence from the court in March 1917 and his replacement, Judge Parker, called in sick the day of the guardianship hearing. Yet another judge stepped in to sub for the substitute. Someone saw an opening in this turn of events, and the ruse they concocted is perhaps why Cameron, Manion, and Robinson would recall this particular case for years afterward. An unknown individual (perhaps bribed by traffickers) called the courthouse pretending to be Judge Parker, explained that the Mission's case was going nowhere, and ordered Suey Ching set free. Before the police, court, or missionaries could discover that this was the work of an impersonator, Suey Ching was released and promptly disappeared.[59]

Upon learning of the subterfuge, Judge Parker raged against the clever kidnapping and promised to provide every assistance in his power. He granted Suey Ching's guardianship to the Mission Home—provided they could find her—and issued a new bench warrant. The police department and Immigration Service spread word of her disappearance. Missionary Ethel Higgins traveled to Stockton in search of Suey Ching, to no avail. Higgins did, however, speak with local police officers to gather evidence that the alleged father, Yick Ki Wing, was a disreputable man.

Mere happenstance led to Suey Ching's eventual recapture. In April, Higgins and another matron, Miss Banks, traveled to Oroville, California, in a futile attempt to rescue another "slave girl," and on their way home, stopped over in Sacramento. The capital city was teeming with people; 30,000 spectators had come to view a fraternal parade that boasted twenty-five electric floats.[60] Amid this gargantuan crowd, at this improbable moment, the missionaries rounded a corner and spotted Suey Ching. She sat on the sidewalk, holding a red balloon, viewing the spectacle.

Higgins grabbed Suey Ching by the arm, but the adolescent refused to move. Even without the presence of a translator, she must have understood what the missionaries wanted. But when Suey Ching failed to come with the missionaries, Banks ran for a police officer. At first the officer did not believe the excited missionaries, but eventually they persuaded him to escort the unmoving youth to the police court, where Miss Higgins could contact officials in San Francisco. All the while, Suey Ching hung onto the balloon and kept silent.[61]

When at last the telegraph brought confirmation of the outstanding warrant, the Sacramento police agreed to hold Suey Ching overnight to await transport. Ethel Higgins, fearful another ruse would steal Suey Ching away, insisted on staying with her at the jail that night. The men who had spirited her away did make one more attempt to reclaim her, filing a habeas corpus petition in an attempt to force her release from jail. But Higgins stood her ground and successfully fought the action in court. According to records of the Sacramento jail, "Yick Yoke Long" was held for one night while "Enroute to San Francisco" and then released on April 20, 1917.[62] In the company of Higgins, Banks, a San Francisco police officer, and a translator—perhaps Lonnie Lee—Suey Ching then headed "home" to the Presbyterian Mission.

At least according to Cameron's biographer, the story ended happily. "The girl had been so completely won by the cheerful life in the home that she chose voluntarily to remain and repudiated all of her former associations. And it was her special joy in later years to help her rescuers in many another raid to free girls in similar plights." There are no records, however, of a "Suey Ching" or "Yick Yok Lan" living in the home during subsequent years. If she did stay and join the rescue mission, perhaps she changed her name once again.[63]

THE POLICEMAN: JACK MANION

John J. Manion (Jack to his friends) first joined the San Francisco police force in 1907 as a patrolman. Known for his patience, Sergeant Manion soon found himself assigned to "vagrancy detail," a predecessor of the Moral Squad which monitored petty criminals. He built his experience with the Chinese residents of the city slowly, pursuing a string of accused pickpockets, gamblers, and prostitutes. In 1921 he put his experience to work when he became Inspector Manion at the helm of the Chinatown Squad, a position he held for two decades.

No other officer managed to hold leadership of the Chinatown Squad for that long. Since 1878, when San Francisco formed the specialized detail, there had been several leaders, none of whom proved popular. Sergeant Jesse Brown Cook, who led the Squad in 1895, for example, lasted only a few months before his ouster. Cook enforced city ordinances with aggressive tactics, and in his enthusiasm deeply angered the Chinese community. Within months the Six Companies sued him for "brutally" assaulting and maiming Chinese residents.[64]

The next man in charge of the Squad, Sergeant George M. Gano, had the opposite problem. He became too friendly with the Chinese community and his service ended with bribery charges.[65] These alternating problems of harassment and corruption continued for years. In 1902 Sergeant Cook returned to head the Squad once again and his aggressive tactics earned him the nickname "the white devil." After Cook left the position (this time for a promotion that would set him on a path to police chief), the Squad was led by a series of men who never lasted long before accusations of corruption surfaced.[66]

Sergeant Manion's twenty-year reign at the Chinatown Squad (1921–1941), then, showed considerable skill. In a retrospective on

THE "IMMIGRANT" AND THE MEANING OF CHINESE EXCLUSION 261

Jack Manion and a child with firecrackers. Manion led the Chinatown Squad from 1921 to 1941 and became a well-known figure in the community. (Reproduced from Carol Green Wilson, *Chinatown Quest: The Life Adventures of Donaldina Cameron*, Stanford University Press, 1931)

his career, a police journal declared that he was "internationally famous for his great work in cleaning up Chinatown." After all, he was "absolute ruler of the largest Chinese kingdom . . . outside of China."[67] Local papers claimed that he also commanded respect within the Chinatown community. Reportedly, when it became known that he might be transferred away from the district, Chinese merchants circulated a petition to keep Manion, the "mayor of Chinatown."[68]

Still, Manion bore some resemblance to the men who had preceded him in the Squad. They all believed that their experience policing Chinatown gave them unique insight into the Chinese race. Sergeant Cook, for example, had published an article describing this "peculiar class of people" and collected photographs of Chinese for his many scrapbooks. In addition to the prodigious collage of "2700 Chinese Boy Babies of San Francisco China Town in 1889" he kept carefully labeled photos of Chinese opium smokers, vagrants, and murderers. Similarly, Sergeant Manion wrote articles on the Chinese, gave speeches and interviews, and denounced local tour companies for peddling lies. His writings describe "John Chinaman's" cuisine (fried ducks, salted eggs, green ginger, soy, and pickles); the violent threat of "Highbinder Tongs" ("they always try to do [their] killings when no white witnesses are present"); and the plight of "slave women." Manion pitied these women—"so ignorant, so stupid, so destitute of any consciousness of their own personal and individual rights . . . that they really consider themselves bound to do service as common prostitutes for the benefit of the man or woman who has paid money for their purchase."[69]

Not only did Manion write about the Chinese community, he also recounted his work with Cameron. He was a Catholic and she a Protestant, but he admired her grit. "It is part of our everyday work for me and my men of the police Chinatown squad to make raids," he told the readers of *Women and Missions* in 1931, "but Miss Cameron willingly has gone with us into the most dangerous and notorious of Chinese places, often helping us to chop through heavy paneled oaken doors in the work of rescuing 'slave girls.'"[70]

When recalling the raid of 747 Clay Street in 1917, Manion remembered the name of the trafficker, not that of the rescued young woman. "We went into a place in Clay Street, almost in the center of the Old Chinatown, run by the On Yick Tong," he wrote. "A young Chinese girl was rescued and taken to the mission. A notorious drug and slave girl dealer, Hom Wah Bow, alias Tom Wah, was arrested in the place, and tried in Juvenile Court; but the poor little girl was so frightened that she was afraid to testify and his case was dismissed." In the end, Cameron rescued her "slave girl," but Manion did not successfully nab his "slave dealer."[71]

In his ode to Cameron, Manion recounted one triumphant raid that suggests what could have happened to Suey Ching had she been found to be an alien. In the early hours of Saint Patrick's Day in 1924, Miss Cameron waited on the street with Inspector Robinson while Manion and two members of his squad climbed to the roof of 654 Jackson Street. As they had hoped, they found the skylights unlocked, and with the help of timbers and rope they quietly descended into the house. Inside they found the alleged keeper along with five of her "slave girls." That day Manion, Cameron, and Robinson all won. Manion arrested Mrs. China Bow, her daughter, and "half a dozen" men; a few months later, they were convicted for their crimes. Cameron rescued a girl named Yum Gee, a California native, who became a ward of the Mission Home. And Robinson deported the remaining four girls back to China.[72]

By the 1920s Manion had come to view deportation as another important tool in the fight against crime in Chinatown. While the raid on 747 Clay Street in 1917 was prompted specifically by accusations of prostitution, Manion concerned himself with a wider array of crime. When queried by reporters, Manion offered a simple "recipe" for ending the "tong wars" in America: "It consists of two ingredients: stop gambling among Chinese and deport those illegally in the country."[73] His essay on the subject admitted it was not quite that simple. "The solution to these tong wars is a problem," he explained. "Deportation to China would be a means of stopping them," but unless they clearly violated federal immigration law, the government would be "unable to act." Therefore local policing still remained essential.[74]

Under Manion's lengthy leadership of the Chinatown Squad, San Francisco police began to methodically check the immigration status of known Chinese criminals. San Francisco police had maintained a segregated mug book for Chinese criminals since the 1870s, but the 1930s brought a new level of record keeping: each criminal received an entire page devoted to his or her physical description, addresses, arrests, convictions, prison terms, and citizenship status. Officials dutifully compared records with the Immigration Service, recording immigration numbers and, when applicable, deportations.[75] For example, Manion arrested Lum Gong in 1935 and charged him as a "$1000 Vag[rant]." This nebulous charge was commonly deployed as a low-evidence, high-penalty catchall, which could be used to arrest undesirables of all sorts and hold them under $1,000 bond.[76] Lum Gong served his time, but soon the police arrested him again,

San Francisco police compiled Chinese mug books from 1870 to 1949. This page from a "tong war" mug book features personal photographs that were likely obtained in police raids. Subjects are labeled with both inmate numbers and immigration numbers, indicative of the coordination between policing and immigration control. (San Francisco Police Department Records, San Francisco History Center, San Francisco Public Library)

this time on charges of forgery. After his second brush with the law, the police looked up his immigration record and found him to be an alien. A judge sentenced him to only one year probation for his crimes, but before he could be released, records indicate he was "sent to China."[77]

Through proactive coordination with the Immigration Service, Manion could wield an additional weapon in his battle against crime in Chinatown. And as he leaned on his federal counterparts, he helped knit together the enforcement of criminal and immigration law.

THE IMMIGRANT: YICK YOK LAN, ALSO KNOWN AS SUEY CHING

What can be known about the young woman apprehended at 747 Clay Street? If she was not Yick Yok Lan, then who was she? According to the policemen, immigration officers, missionaries, and judges, she was a girl (maybe sixteen or seventeen years old) who went by the name "Suey Ching." They believed that Yick Yok Lan had been an American citizen born in San Jose, but they suspected that Suey Ching was a Chinese migrant who had assumed her identity.

There is very little we can know of Suey Ching with certainty. Any truths that might be found in the words she uttered on the record lie beneath layers of fraud, coaching, and translation. She tried very hard to hide from the officials who witnessed and dutifully recorded her existence. And yet some things are clear: she was four feet eleven inches tall; she had black hair and dark eyes; she could not sign her own name, in English or Chinese.

Most of all, we know that she did not wish her life story to be known. Reportedly, during her first weeks at the Mission Home, she let slip that she was born in China and was not the true daughter of Yick Ki Wing. But apparently that was the first and last time she spoke about her past. She refused to testify at her first guardianship hearing in March 1917, and when the missionaries brought her second guardianship hearing in April, she remained silent once again.

Cameron, Manion, Lee, and Robinson sought her confession primarily to implicate her alleged father. To charge Wing with trafficking under the Page Act, the Immigration Service had to "prove" that "the girl is an alien." Immigration records indicate this would have

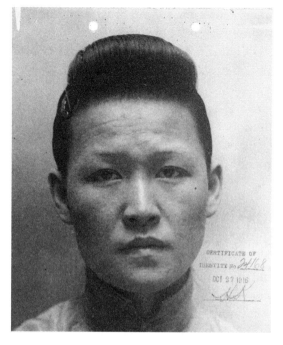

This woman claimed to be Yick Yok Lan in 1917, but may have been Suey Ching. In order to obtain legal guardianship, Donaldina Cameron claimed this woman was underage. (Chinese Immigration File no. 15597/19-26, National Archives at San Francisco)

been an uphill battle because she had landed as a US citizen only months earlier. Her alleged confession to Lonnie Lee did nothing to change that. It would have taken a confession under oath to override the department's previous ruling. An immigration official noted, "If the girl will make a formal statement agreeing to testify upon the witness stand that she was born in China, and that she was imported into this country by the alleged father for the purpose of prostitution or for some other immoral purpose, I will take the matter up with the U.S. Attorney's office."[78] But Suey Ching remained silent.

After two years of her silence, once the world war was over and the terrible wave of flu had receded, Robinson followed up and attempted once again to close the case. He found "Yick Yook Lan, who is known as Sue Ching" to be still residing at the Mission Home and inquired about getting her testimony. He reported resistance from Cameron, who "would not want her to make a statement as regards her alleged father unless the government insisted, that two years having elapsed she did not think anything could be gained through opening up this case at this time." Cameron suggested that he instead reach out to the Juvenile Court to procure her previous testimony. Of course, there was no such testimony, which Robinson verified a few months later. In October 1919, Robinson believed he had reached a dead end and stopped pursuing the case. After that, the written record of Suey Ching's existence ceases.[79]

If Suey Ching was impersonating Yick Yok Lan, then she had made three false claims: first, that she was a natural-born US citizen; second, that Yick Ki Wing was her father; and third, that her name was Lan. If she did engage in this extensive fraud, then she was not alone. The most conservative estimates of historians are that at least 25 percent of the 303,000 Chinese arrivals during 1882–1943 were unauthorized. But many contemporaries believed the rate of subterfuge to be significantly higher. Immigration inspectors at Angel Island put the figure as high as 90 percent, and Chinese Americans who lived through this period cited a similar number. In short, there were tens of thousands of unauthorized Chinese residing in the United States during the exclusion era, and even more who faced assumptions of illegality based on their race. Not only did Chinese exclusion help to build American border control, but it also created an unauthorized underclass.[80]

The "child of a citizen" category became the dominant means of fraudulent entry at the turn of the twentieth century, due to the confluence of two unrelated events. First, in 1898 the Supreme Court case *U.S. v. Wong Kim Ark* clarified that a child of Chinese ancestry who was born in the United States held US citizenship based on the Fourteenth Amendment. Then, in 1906, the San Francisco earthquake and fire destroyed the city's birth records. As a result, a male Chinese migrant could claim to have been born in the United States and, once his US citizenship was a matter of record, travel to China and bring back children who claimed derivative US citizenship. Fraud could happen at either stage of this process: the father's original claim to citizenship or the relation between father and son or occasionally daughter. These invented kinships fed a stream of unauthorized immigrants, whom Chinese migrants and US officials called "paper sons" and "paper daughters."[81]

By using false documentation and adopting multiple names, paper sons and daughters were taking advantage of the anonymity of being Chinese in America. For decades American officials had disregarded the individuality of Chinese migrants and only haphazardly recorded their names. Ironically, this erasure allowed so-called John

Doe and Mary Chinaman to reinvent themselves and claim multiple identities.[82]

The exclusion laws appeared to draw a clear boundary dividing authorized immigrants from unauthorized ones; the lives of Chinese migrants, though, blurred this line. In their attempts to navigate and circumvent the law, Chinese migrants forged an in-between space, which afforded them some of the privileges of documentation, but not all. Using false citizenship papers under the name Yick Yok Lan, Suey Ching could claim the right to remain in the United States, exit the country, and return as she pleased. But she also had to live with the possibility that government bureaucrats would change their minds, either by deporting her from the interior or refusing her re-entry at the border.

She straddled the world of the documented and the undocumented, holding many of the privileges of the former while living with the anxieties of the latter.[83] Such insecurity inevitably affected her decision making, as she chose who to befriend, where to work, and whether to speak. Perhaps she would not testify against her "father" because she feared him. Or perhaps it was the government she feared most. If she had testified against her alleged traffickers, she would have incriminated herself.

Her silence could not guarantee protection, however. Exclusion cast a shadow over all people of Chinese descent in the United States. While the local racial laws had criminalized particular behaviors, the exclusion laws criminalized mere presence. The federal government demonstrated neither the intent nor the capacity to implement mass deportations, but the possibility alone had the power to condition Chinese lives. By rendering the Chinese perpetually precarious, Chinese exclusion restricted Chinese economic mobility, restrained Chinese political power, devalued Chinese lives and culture, and separated Chinese from white communities. Exclusion, in short, added further conditions and disappointments to the terms of inclusion.

EPILOGUE

EXCLUSION NEVER HALTED Chinese migration, but eventually it stemmed the flow of new Chinese immigrants to a trickle. By 1920 the census counted only 61,639 Chinese in the states, down from a high of 107,488 in 1890. Only 55 percent of these Chinese lived in California, Oregon, and Washington, where they were now outnumbered by both African Americans and Japanese. As the overall population of the West Coast expanded rapidly, the Chinese population dwindled and scattered. Urban Chinatowns in the West began to shrink, and rural Chinatowns lay abandoned. Exclusion would stunt the Chinese American community for generations to come.[1]

And once lawmakers had slowed the stream of Chinese, they turned their attention to other Asian immigrants. First diplomatic agreements restricted Japanese and Korean immigrants in 1907, and then Congress targeted South Asian immigrants in 1917, followed by all Asian immigrants in 1924. In 1934, Congress even barred Filipinos despite their status as US nationals. What had been a targeted policy of Chinese exclusion became a broad policy of Asian exclusion.

As exclusion tightened its grip, what happened to the terms of conditional inclusion for Chinese in the Pacific West? What happened to the laws, norms, and racial etiquette that governed their lives?

In the 1920s, lawmakers continued to heavily regulate the economic terms of Chinese inclusion. Chinese migrants found it impossible to acquire agricultural land and difficult to buy a house or a storefront. They could not fish in public waters or receive contracts from city governments. In Oregon a 1923 law prohibited "aliens" from operating a pawnshop, billiard hall, dance hall, or soft drink establishment. The same law allowed noncitizens to operate a grocery store, meat market, fruit stand, hotel, or lodging house, but only if they prominently displayed a card stating their nationality.[2] And the government was not the only problem. Unions continued to oppose Chinese workers and employers continued to discriminate. Fifty percent of state-licensed professions would not grant Chinese a license.

The terms of political inclusion remained largely unchanged. The federal government continued to bar Chinese from naturalizing, and the Pacific states continued to deny Chinese noncitizens the ability to vote, serve on juries, practice law, or hold public office. California defined public office broadly, denying Chinese the opportunity to become firefighters, policemen, public school teachers, or other kinds of civil servants. The vast majority of Chinese residents could not directly participate in American democracy. Only those with US citizenship, by birth or by fraud, could hope to overcome these barriers.[3]

A shift had begun in the terms of cultural inclusion, as city governments spent less time outlawing Chinese cultural norms and more time promoting middle-class white norms. Local governments continued to regulate firecrackers, fan tan, and recreational opium. They continued to enforce lodging house laws against "overcrowded" living conditions in Chinese neighborhoods. And in San Francisco, the specialized Chinatown Squad continued to police the streets for vice crimes. But increasingly, enforcing the terms of cultural inclusion was the prerogative of health departments, social workers, and progressive reformers. These groups relied on softer forms of social control. In San Francisco, the Public Health Department partnered with the Baby Hygiene Committee and the Presbyterian Mission Home to spread American standards of health, education, and family. The Chinese community joined this drive for reform. Chinese doctors opened a westernized Chinese hospital, Chinese social workers guided mothers in American infant care practices, and the Chinese YMCA and YWCA helped to instill "modern" values in Chinese American youth.[4]

EPILOGUE

When it came to the spatial terms of inclusion, rarely did local laws govern Chinese access to white spaces; instead, the unwritten rules of racial etiquette prevailed. The school segregation law remained on the books in California, but rather than establish separate Chinese schools, education officials more often quietly placed Chinese in separate classrooms. Restrictive covenants prevented Chinese from buying in certain neighborhoods, but realtors refused to consider Chinese buyers even when no restrictions were in place. Anti-miscegenation laws barred marriage between Chinese and white people, but social norms prevented them from even pairing up at a YMCA dance. Although no laws prevented Chinese from joining a chamber of commerce, Elks Lodge, or Kiwanis Club, these groups and others routinely refused them membership.[5] In response to these social restrictions, Chinese often sought out segregated spaces. In his 1928 study of "the American Chinatown," Ching Chao Wu observed that "it is the only place where the Chinese immigrants may expect to have a taste of social life that is at once intimate and human."[6]

In short, Chinese continued to live under specific economic, political, cultural, and spatial constraints. From the perspective of lawmakers, this state of affairs represented success. Exclusion had reduced the Chinese population. Bars on naturalization had closed off paths to political power. Social control measures, racial norms, and the ever-present threat of deportation regulated Chinese behavior.

By 1920 the Chinese community had low immigration numbers, low birth rates, and a short life expectancy. Meanwhile, the Black population in California had increased by 45 percent and the Japanese population had increased by 110 percent. From the perspective of many white Americans, these "outsiders" represented the new racial threat. The Chinese were no longer their primary concern.

As our story comes to an end, the Pacific states continued to impose conditions on Chinese inclusion, but they did so with less urgency and less violence.

✹ ✹ ✹

The Chinese, however, still felt the conditional nature of their day-to-day existence. Theirs was a world of shrinking Chinatowns, rampant prejudice, and few job prospects.

Chinese youth, especially the American-born, had high hopes and deep disappointments in the 1920s. Like others their age, they believed their generation heralded the arrival of modernity. Modern life meant urbanization, automobiles, mass media, electricity, and jazz, and all these changes led them to question the ongoing constraints on their lives.

When researchers approached one young Chinese American woman in 1924 and asked to record her life history, she told them she could write it herself. She decided to remain anonymous, using only the initials "MLL," but to write down her story and the lessons it held.

MLL was born in Southern California, attended public schools, and then enrolled in a college not far from home. She reported that elementary school had been tolerable. *I was very seldom called chink and then only by bad boys whose opinion I did not care for in any case. The good treatment I received from the other kids more than offset the momentary humiliations. Of course I resented it, but not enough to fight back or to be embittered.*

She found that the racial divide between white and Chinese became starker as she grew up. *High school made my sense of race consciousness keener. I received a few snubs from former friends, which really shocked and amazed me.* The unexpected rejections made her wary and detached. *Then and there I resolved to make no advances to American students; I was very glad to make friendships, but did not care to run the risk of being snubbed.*

By the time she reached college and recorded her story, MLL did not expect to belong. *Being American born, my adjustment to college life was very simple; I knew what to expect, and received no disappointments.* But she noticed that not all Chinese students were as accepting, especially the newcomers. *Many of our Chinese students, however, come from China to study in the states. They bring with them the highest expectations of goodwill and fellowship. They are buoyant and hopeful at first, but this optimism does not last long. Rebuffs, snubs, and rudeness soon change their feelings to great bitterness against the Americans.* The terms of inclusion felt especially arbitrary and unfair to the uninitiated.

MLL agreed that these newcomers had reason to be upset. *I know of many instances where these boys really have good cause to believe that they are unwanted and disliked.* Humiliations arrived without warning. *One of our boys had registered in a swimming class which met in the YMCA in town. What was his surprise and indignation to learn from the secretary of the Y that Orientals were not allowed to use the pool!*

Housing remained a common problem. *I know personally of many cases where boys have looked in vain for rooms in the university district! They're told that "we don't take Orientals" or "the room is already taken."* Being denied housing could produce a particularly sharp pain. *Many of them have come to the country without friends or connections of any kind; the people, the language, the customs are all strange and bewildering; what, then, could be more disheartening than to be refused shelter?* Although MLL had learned to tolerate conditional inclusion, she understood why newly arrived Chinese students would chafe under the same restrictions.[7]

One of those newcomers, Fred Chew Wong, also wrote up his life history for researchers in 1924. Educated first in China and Canada, Wong spent four years in Seattle attending the University of Washington and working toward a degree in chemistry. In that time, he had grown bitter about his treatment in America. *During my four years at the university I have never had the opportunity to taste the so-called college life which all American students enjoy.* He tried very hard to join that life but found that he did not belong. *I was a member of a varsity hockey team for three years. I received fairly good treatment from my teammates, although there were still some small prejudices existing which caused me to feel that I was out of place amongst them. During the games I could hear the spectators razzing me [with] phrases which they would not [have] dared to say to a white man. They called me yellow belly chinky chong, kill that chink, etc. while the opposing players were trying their best to hurt me and put me out of the game.*

Wong also tried to join the college social scene but found it impenetrable. *No Oriental students ever went to the university mixers. Whenever they went, they would surely come back with shame and embarrassment. Nobody knew that they were there and nobody cared to have them there. It is not an unusual sight to see beautiful and proud coeds making faces at them and turning them down in dances. It was better to stay away.*

Some of the rejections held bitter irony. Wong remembered when a landlady kicked two female Chinese students out of "the Mandarin

Apartment." *Mind you the name of the place.* Then there was the time that a fraternity held a mixer called "the Oriental Night." *I remember that several members of the Chinese student club had to work every evening for a week in order to get the lanterns and other decorating materials ready.* But it turned out that Oriental Night was only for the enjoyment of white students. *Many Orientals went to the mixer and were only to find that they were made to be wallflowers watching the Americans having a good time.*

Still, the social ostracism in college could not compare to what came next. *There is no color line drawn against Oriental students to attend school but there is a line drawn against employing our students after they have graduated from the institution of higher learning. Business firms on the Pacific Coast offer us no opportunity to practice what we learn at school.*

Wong managed to find a job, but some of his classmates were not so lucky. *Recently two friends of mine wrote to no less than fifty engineering firms thruout the country to apply for a position where they could get some experience along their own line and all they have got were negative answers.* In their desperation, these college graduates widened their job search to include manual labor. *Recently they went to the Oriental Admiral line to apply for a job as common labor on the boat. The Superintendent at first told them that it was not the policy of the firm to hire people other than Americans. The boys told him that they were American born and did not come into the excluding list.* They hoped that their citizenship might be the ticket to a job. *They talked with the Superintendent for a while and finally he said "I am sorry boys, I cannot employ you people."*

Like the previous generation, MLL and Wong faced name-calling, rejection, and discrimination. Being born in the new century and educated in the American system had not saved them from these humiliations. But they were young, clear-eyed, and determined that modern notions should take hold.

Change, Wong believed, would only come if white Americans opened their minds. *They must change their hearts; they must bear in mind that all men under the sun are worthy in the measure of their intelligence and moral excellence and not according to their grade of life or the hue of their skin.*[8]

The problem, MLL believed, was a profound level of ignorance. *I have met several college students who say that I am the first Chi-*

nese girl they have ever known personally. They sometimes seem quite surprised to find me as human as they.

※ ※ ※

Although MLL and Wong did not know it, profound changes were on the horizon. They recorded their "life histories" during a period of stagnation and frustration, but they would live to witness a new age.

With World War II would come the end of Chinese exclusion. Congress repealed the law as a gesture to China, America's wartime ally. In 1943 the United States began admitting 105 Chinese immigrants annually—a trivial number that represented a symbolic concession—but it also allowed all Chinese immigrants, past and future, to naturalize. In 1946 lawmakers extended a small quota and naturalization rights to South Asians and Filipinos, and then in 1952 to other Asian immigrants as well. By 1965, Congress had stripped all remaining vestiges of Asian exclusion from its immigration laws. With this policy reversal came a demographic transformation as large numbers immigrated from China and India. As of 2025 there are more than 24 million Asian Americans in the United States. Asian Americans constitute the nation's fastest growing racial group.[9]

It is tempting to assume that the end of exclusion brought an end to conditional inclusion as well. It is easy to imagine that, once Chinese and all other Asians could enter the United States and become US citizens, the barriers to unconditional inclusion naturally fell away. But it was not that simple. Exclusion's repeal may have offered Asians newfound paths to citizenship and set in motion a demographic shift, but it did not dismantle local racial laws nor replace local racial norms. The end of the exclusion regime did not stop the segregation of Chinese neighborhoods nor prevent the underemployment of Chinese workers.

This meant that in the battle for rights and belonging, Chinese had to fight on multiple fronts. It was fortunate for them that the mid-twentieth century was a period of change both in the United States and around the world. Domestically, the Black movement for civil rights would prove transformative. It brought legal gains for all people of color and fueled Asian American activism. At the same time, the global movement for decolonization forever altered the political terrain. As nations in Africa and Asia gained independence from European colonial powers, global attention shifted to focus on human rights. The United States, keen to present itself as a champion of democracy and freedom, faced mounting international pressure to address its own racial inequalities. If America wished to win "the hearts and minds" of the decolonizing world, it would first have to solve its domestic race problems.

American lawmakers adopted a new approach to racial management, one scholars have called "racial liberalism." Racial liberalism was a series of policy proposals designed to tame racial unrest in America and cultivate US power overseas. Racial liberalism held that racial differences could be managed through assimilation (wherein people of color adopt white norms) and integration (wherein people of color are incorporated into white institutions). Racial liberals proposed to fix existing legal structures by eliminating discriminatory laws. They believed that equal protection of the law would mean equal opportunity to compete in the free market. They expected equal opportunity, in turn, to end racial disparities.[10]

Many scholars have argued that Asian Americans had an important role to play in this national project of racial liberalism. They were called upon to prove its premises: first, that racial difference did not preclude integration and, second, that equal opportunity could lead to racial equality. Asian Americans could do this by acting white (while remaining racially distinct from white people) and climbing the socioeconomic ladder (without the need for government support, affirmative action, or economic redistribution). If they could do these two things, Asian Americans could become the poster children for racial liberalism. Asian American achievement would prove that people of color could live the American dream. Asian American success would model the benefits of American democracy at home and abroad.[11]

But this was conditional inclusion again, under a new guise. Racial liberalism granted Asians probationary membership in America as long as they adhered to certain ideals. Asians should be hardworking, self-sufficient, and uncomplaining. They should be family-first and all-American, a model minority for others to emulate. They should not ponder the cost of their inclusion. They should simply internalize these unspoken rules, ignore the consequences, and mind their racial manners.[12]

Chinese exclusion may have ended, but Chinese inclusion remained conditional.

❊ ❊ ❊

A century after MLL recorded her history, I continue to worry over her words: "They sometimes seem quite surprised to find me as human as they." What happens if we still cannot see her humanity, let alone the humanity of all the John Does? MLL may have purposefully withheld her name to avoid backlash, but others had no choice in the matter: their names were lost to history, regardless of their wishes.

As western states and towns attempted to control Chinese migrants in the nineteenth century, they also stripped them of their individuality. No one cared enough to record Chinese names with any accuracy, let alone document their lives. As a result, Chinese have become ghostly historical figures, mere shadows of their living selves, appearing in one record only to disappear in another.

The gravity of this loss struck me one day as I was paging through the account book of a gravedigger in Nevada City, California.

William Groves had dutifully recorded the name of each person he buried, the date, and the price for his services. Therefore, we know that Susan Jacobs, Richard Bell, and Fredrick Kooler all met their end in the foothills of the Sierra Nevada mountains. But looking at the years 1861 to 1868, all I could see were the anonymous Chinese.

Burial of John Chinaman .... Paid 35^{00}
Burial of John Chinaman .... Paid 25^{00}
Burial of A Chinaman .... 25^{00}
Burial of John Chinaman .... Paid 35^{00}
Burial of John Chinaman .... Paid 20^{00}
Burial of A Chinaman .... Paid 25^{00}
Mr. John Chinaman .... Paid 25^{00}
Coffin for Chinaman .... Paid 20^{00}
Burial of John Chinaman .... Paid 25^{00}
Burial of John Chinaman .... Paid 25^{00}
Burial of John Chinaman .... Paid 25^{00}
Burial of John Chinaman .... Paid 25^{00}
Burial of John Chinaman .... Paid 31^{00}

Burial of John Chinaman .... Paid 25^{00}
Burial of John Chinaman .... Paid 25^{00}
Burial of Mary Chinaman .... Paid 25^{00}
Burial of Mary Chinaman .... Paid 30^{00}

Who were these men and women whom William Groves laid into the ground? What can we know of their lives? It bothers me that we can see their erasure more clearly than their existence. And it frustrates me that we can see the legal restraints that confined Chinese more clearly than the moments they broke free.[13]

The scale of what we do not know can be overwhelming, but my hope is that a few basics are now clear. When the Chinese arrived in the US West, they encountered a racial regime defined by white dominance. The racial regime regulated Chinese life in two interlocking ways: formal law and racial norms.

The leaders of this regime passed more than five thousand laws that marginalized and controlled Chinese people. These laws had pattern and purpose, continuously and persistently regulating Chinese access to economic, political, cultural, and spatial rights. Describing this local racial regime as the road to exclusion does not do it justice. Local racial laws existed before the passage of the Chinese Exclusion Act, but they also continued for decades after. Moreover, most local racial laws were not devised to exclude and expel. They were designed to control. Federalism allowed the American government to pursue exclusion and inclusion simultaneously at different scales. At the national level, Congress centralized enforcement of Chinese exclusion through a single federal agency. At the local level, western lawmakers enforced conditional inclusion through a sprawling web of laws, which targeted the Chinese in different ways, regulated multiple domains of life, developed in fits and starts, and were enforced by an eclectic group of sheriffs, policemen, tax collectors, judges, missionaries, teachers, realtors, and public health officials. As a result, the history of exclusion has been consolidated in federal archives, but the history of inclusion is dispersed across state and county archives, historical societies, public libraries, and operating courthouses.

Racial laws were not the only way that white society controlled Chinese residents. The force of law, custom, and violence merged, producing an unwritten but pervasive racial etiquette. Codes of conduct operated beyond formal law to constrain Chinese life. Documenting these racial rules is difficult, because most found their expression in fleeting interactions or invisible barriers. Although more elusive in the archive than formal law, racial etiquette has proven to be more enduring. It is true that much has changed since the Chinese first arrived in the American West. No longer do they encounter racial violence on a daily basis, and no longer are their racial disadvantages inscribed in law. But scholars have argued that Asian Americans are still called upon to adhere to racial norms as they strive for inclusion. Spurred on by the dream of belonging, many Asian Americans have internalized these unspoken racial rules and begun to discreetly regulate themselves.[14]

The racial regime Chinese encountered in the nineteenth-century West was not the same as the anti-Black regime known as Jim Crow. Nor was it akin to the violent removal of Native peoples known as expansion. To be sure, there were many connections, but the anti-Chinese regime was not a mere derivative of other racist systems. For a moment in the late nineteenth century, the Pacific states feared the Chinese above all others, and they carefully tailored their response to meet this "alien" threat. In the interest of accurate and ethical history, we must distinguish the resulting racial regime from other histories of white supremacy.

The fact that we have all but forgotten the anti-Chinese regime does not mean it was peripheral to US history. Recovering the history of Chinese inclusion is essential to understanding the history of race, racial reconstruction, and immigration in the United States. Simply put, the history of Chinese inclusion *is* the history of how race became embedded in US law. The history of Chinese litigation *is* the history of how racial reconstruction remade the West. And the history of coordination between policing and exclusion *is* the history of how border control penetrated the interior. Chinese American history *is* American history, and it deserves a place in our collective memory.

When the Nevada City gravedigger buried John and Mary Chinaman, it is possible that the deceased had not yet found their final resting place. Chinese believed that the dead must be returned to their native place where proper rituals could transform them into a spiritual ancestor. Without these rites, the dead would become wandering ghosts, unfed, unclothed, and unable to bring good fortune to their descendants. To avoid this fate, Chinese migrants in the American West prepared for the possibility of death far from home. They bought shares of mutual aid organizations that promised to exhume their bones and repatriate them for reburial. Even after western cities passed laws to restrict this practice, or at least tax it, Chinese continued to reclaim their dead.[15]

It is possible, therefore, that someone returned for John and Mary Chinaman years or decades later. Perhaps someone knew their real names, knew where they had come from, and knew where they lay buried. Perhaps someone reclaimed their bones.

But just in case no one ever remembered them, perhaps we can.

Appendix

Abbreviations

Notes

Acknowledgments

Index

Appendix

SELECTED SECTIONS OF STATUTES REGULATING CHINESE RESIDENTS

Starting in the 1850s, western lawmakers passed hundreds of laws that regulated Chinese economic, political, cultural, and spatial behavior. This appendix includes relevant sections from a small subset of those laws. Some examples have been selected based on their singular historical significance; others have been included because they were replicated repeatedly and became pervasive. In the excerpts below, note the use of identity-based laws (regulating Chinese based on their racial identity or alien status), behavior-based laws (regulating Chinese-associated work and cultural practices), and general-outcast laws (regulating Chinese alongside other undesirables).

MINING LAWS

In an effort to regulate Chinese miners, California, Oregon, and Washington Territory passed identity-based mining laws that required licensure for foreigners. One example is California's Foreign Miner's Act (1852), which applied to all foreigners. Subsequent amendments narrowed the law to target foreigners who had not declared their intent to naturalize. Several California mining districts also passed local bylaws that explicitly prohibited Chinese. These localities included Dutch Flat (Placer County), Centreville and Helltown (Butte County), and Columbia (Tuolumne County).[1]

Foreign Miner's Act (California, 1852)[2]

AN ACT to provide for the protection of foreigners, and to define their liabilities and privileges: Whereas, great prejudices exist in the mining districts in relation to the propriety of foreigners being permitted to work placer and quartz diggings, inasmuch as they are not liable to the same duties as American citizens whilst they enjoy the same privileges . . .

SEC. 1. That from and after the 1st day of June next, and until the Congress of the United States shall by law assume control of the mining lands of California (passage of this act), no person not being a citizen of the United States (California Indians excepted) shall be allowed to take gold from any of the mines of this State, unless he shall have a license therefor as hereinafter provided . . .

SEC. 6. The amount to be paid for each license shall be at the rate of $4 per month, and said license shall in no case be transferable . . .

Columbia Mining Laws (Columbia, California, 1853)[3]

Art. 10. None but Americans and Europeans who have or shall declare their intentions of becoming citizens shall hold claims in this district. But foreigners shall have until the first of November next, to declare their intentions.

Art. 11. Neither Asiatics nor South Sea Islanders shall be allowed to mine in this district, either for themselves or for others.

Art. 12. Any person who shall sell a claim to an Asiatic or South Sea Islander, shall not be allowed to hold another claim in this district, for the space of six months . . .

POLL TAXES

California, Oregon, and Washington Territory all experimented with per capita taxes (or "poll" taxes) on Chinese residents in the 1860s via identity-based laws. In Oregon the 1862 poll tax applied broadly to "every negro, chinaman, kanaka and mulatto." ("Kanaka" referred to Pacific Islanders.) In California and Washington Territory, similar "police taxes" targeted only "Chinese" residents.

Poll Tax (Oregon, 1862)[4]

Sec 1. That each and every negro, chinaman, kanaka and mulatto, residing within the limits of this state, shall pay an annual poll-tax of five dollars, for the use of the county in which such negro, chinaman, kananka or mulatto may reside. . . .

Sect 4. Should such negro, chinaman, kanaka or mulatto, fail to pay the tax required by section 2 of this act, and should the sheriff be unable to collect the same, or make the same out of property belonging to such tax-payers, then it is made the duty of the sheriff to arrest such negro, chinaman, kanaka or mulatto, and put him at work on the public highways. . . .

Chinese Police Tax (Washington Territory, 1864)[5]

An Act to protect free white labor against competition with Chinese coolie labor, and to discourage the immigration of the Chinese into this Territory.

Section 1. Be it enacted by the Legislative Assembly of the Territory of Washington, That there is hereby levied on each person, male and female, of the Mongolian race, of the age of eighteen years and upwards, residing in this territory, a quarterly capitation tax of six dollars, which tax shall be known as the Chinese police tax.

Sec. 4 The sheriff shall collect the Chinese police tax provided for in this act, for all persons liable to pay the same, and may seize the personal property of any such person refusing to pay such tax, and sell the same at public auction . . .

Sec. 7 Any person or company who shall hire persons liable to pay the Chinese police tax, shall be held responsible for the payment of the tax due from each person so hired . . .

STATE CONSTITUTIONS

The Oregon Constitution (1857) and the amended California Constitution (1879) included provisions relating to the Chinese. Oregon prohibited Chinese suffrage, barred Chinese ownership of real estate or mining claims, and claimed the power to regulate immigrants "not qualified to become citizens of the United States." Additional sections of the Oregon Constitution took an even more strident approach to Black people, barring the entry of "free negroes or mulattos," providing for their forcible removal, and prohibiting Black suffrage.

In contrast, California amended its constitution during the Reconstruction Era to protect the property rights of all citizens and "foreigners of the white race or of African descent." But the California Constitution devoted an entire article to the Chinese, singling them out for distinct treatment. Article XIX "Chinese" asserted the state's right to regulate aliens "who are or may become" vagrants, criminals, or diseased; prohibited corporations and local governments from employing Chinese; declared "Asiatic

Coolieism" a form of human slavery; and endorsed the removal of Chinese by cities and townships.

Constitution of the State of Oregon (1857)[6]

Article I Section No. 31. White foreigners who are, or may hereafter become residents of this State shall enjoy the same rights in respect to the possession, enjoyment, and descent of property as native born citizens. And the Legislative Assembly shall have power to restrain, and regulate the immigration to this State of persons not qualified to become Citizens of the United States. . . .

Article 1 Section No. 35. No free negro or mulatto not residing in this state at the time of the adoption of this constitution, shall come, reside or be within this state or hold any real estate, or make any contracts, or maintain any suit therein; and the legislative assembly shall provide by penal laws for the removal by public officers of all such negroes and mulattoes, and for their effectual exclusion from the state, and for the punishment of persons who shall bring them into the state, or employ or harbor them. . . .

Article II Section No.6

No Negro, Chinaman, or Mulatto shall have the right of suffrage. . . .

Article XV Section No. 8

No Chinaman, not a resident of the state at the adoption of this constitution, shall ever hold any real estate, or mining claim, or work any mining claim therein. The Legislative Assembly shall provide by law in the most effectual manner for carrying out the above provisions. . . .

Constitution of the State of California (1879)[7]

Article I SECTION 17. Foreigners of the white race or of African descent, eligible to become citizens of the United States under the naturalization laws thereof, while bona fide residents of this State, shall have the same rights in respect to the acquisition, possession, enjoyment, transmission, and inheritance of property as native-born citizens.

Article II SECTION 1. . . . [N]o native of China, no idiot, insane person, or person convicted of any infamous crime, and no person hereafter convicted of the embezzlement or misappropriation of public money, shall ever exercise the privileges of an elector in this State. . . .

ARTICLE XIX. CHINESE.

SECTION 1. The Legislature shall prescribe all necessary regulations for the protection of the State, and the counties, cities, and towns thereof, from the burdens and evils arising from the presence of aliens who are or may become vagrants, paupers, mendicants, criminals, or invalids afflicted with contagious or infectious diseases, and from aliens otherwise dangerous or detrimental to the well-being or peace of the State, and to impose conditions upon which persons may reside in the State, and to provide the means and mode of their removal from the State, upon failure or refusal to comply with such conditions; *provided,* that nothing contained in this section shall be construed to impair or limit the power of the Legislature to pass such police laws or other regulations as it may deem necessary.

SEC. 2. No corporation now existing or hereafter formed under the laws of this State, shall, after the adoption of this Constitution, employ directly or indirectly, in any capacity, any Chinese or Mongolian. The Legislature shall pass such laws as may be necessary to enforce this provision.

SEC. 3. No Chinese shall be employed on any State, county, municipal, or other public work, except in punishment for crime.

SEC. 4. The presence of foreigners ineligible to become citizens of the United States is declared to be dangerous to the well-being of the State, and the Legislature shall discourage their immigration by all the means within its power. Asiatic coolieism is a form of human slavery, and is forever prohibited in this State, and all contracts for coolie labor shall be void. All companies or corporations, whether formed in this country or any foreign country, for the importation of such labor, shall be subject to such penalties as the Legislature may prescribe. The Legislature shall delegate all necessary power to the incorporated cities and towns of this State for the removal of Chinese without the limits of such cities and towns, or for their location within prescribed portions of those limits, and it shall also provide the necessary legislation to prohibit the introduction into this State of Chinese after the adoption of this Constitution. This section shall be enforced by appropriate legislation.

SCHOOL LAWS

California shifted its approach to school segregation over time. The original Consolidated School Act (1866) mandated exclusion or segregation for children of "African," "Indian," and "Mongolian" descent. In 1870 the amended law continued to mandate Black and Native segregation, but no longer provided any public education for Chinese children. In 1880 California removed all racial language from the school code and terminated segregated schools. A behavior-based stipulation remained, however: schools could expel "children of filthy or vicious habits." But in 1885 the state reintroduced identity-based school segregation, when it provided for separate schools for "Mongolian or Chinese" children.

Consolidated School Act (California, 1866)[8]

Sec. 57. Children of African or Mongolian descent, and Indian children not living under the care of white persons, shall not be admitted into public schools, except as provided in this act; provided, that upon the written application of the parents or guardians of at least ten such children to any Board of Trustees or Board of Education, a separate school shall be established for the education of such children; and the education of a less number may be provided for by the Trustees in any other manner.

When there shall be in any district any number of children, other than white children, whose education can be provided for in no other way, the Trustees, by a majority vote, may permit such children to attend schools for white children; provided, that a majority of the parents of the children attending such school make no objection, in writing, to be filed with the Board of Trustees.

Amended Consolidated School Act (California, 1870)[9]

Sec. 7545. The education of children of African descent, and Indian children, shall be provided for in separate schools upon the written application of the parents or guardians of at least ten such children to any Board of Trustees or Board of Education, a separate school shall be established for the education of such children; and the education of a less number may be provided for by the trustees, in separate schools, in any other manner.

Amended Consolidated School Act (California, 1880)[10]

Sec. 1662. Every school, unless otherwise provided by law, must be open for the admission of all children between six and twenty-one years of age residing in the district. . . . Trustees shall have the power to exclude children of filthy or vicious habits, or children suffering from contagious or infectious diseases.

Chinese School Law (California, 1885)[11]

Every school, unless otherwise provided by law, must be open for the admission of all children between six and twenty-one years of age residing in the district, and the Board of Trustees, or City Board of Education, have the power to admit adults and children not residing in the district whenever good reason exists therefore. Trustee shall have the power to exclude children of filthy or vicious habits, or children suffering from contagious or infectious diseases, and also to establish separate schools for children of

Mongolian or Chinese descent. When such separate schools are established, Chinese or Mongolian children must not be admitted to any other schools.

MARRIAGE LAWS

Identity-based laws that prohibited marriage between white persons and nonwhite persons became widespread in the late nineteenth century. Anti-miscegenation laws that listed the "Chinese" or "Mongolians," among other racial undesirables, were instituted by many western states and territories, including Nevada (1861), Idaho (1864), Arizona (1865), Oregon (1866), Wyoming (1869), California (1880), and Utah (1888). Eventually, states in the Midwest and South also wrote the Chinese into existing anti-miscegenation laws: Mississippi (1892), Missouri (1909), Montana (1909), Nebraska (1913), South Dakota (1913), Virginia (1924), and Georgia (1927).[12]

Anti-Miscegenation Law (Oregon, 1866)[13]

Hereafter it shall not be lawful within this state for any white person, male or female, to intermarry with any Negro, Chinese, or any person having one fourth or more Negro, Chinese or Kanaka blood, or any person having more than one half Indian blood; and all such marriages or attempted marriages, shall be absolutely null and void.

EMPLOYMENT

State and local governments experimented with ways to curtail Chinese employment through identity-based laws. Western public employment laws often explicitly prohibited Chinese from working directly for the government or on government contracts. Some public employment laws regulated aliens ineligible to citizenship (including the Chinese) by allowing only citizens and declarants to work. In 1880, California attempted a private employment law that barred corporations from hiring Chinese, but the courts quickly struck that down.[14]

Cities also routinely limited public offices to citizens and electors, barring all aliens from serving as city council members, police officers, health officers, and school directors. Although they were not the specific target of these restrictions, Chinese faced the effects due to their inability to naturalize and vote.

Chinese Private Employment Law (California, 1880)[15]

Any officer, director, manager, member, stockholder, clerk, agent, servant, attorney, employe[e], assignee, or contractor of any corporation now existing, or hereafter formed under the laws of this State, who shall employ, in any manner or capacity, upon any work or business of such corporation, any Chinese or Mongolian, is guilty of a misdemeanor, and is punishable by a fine of not less than one hundred nor more than one thousand dollars, or by imprisonment in County Jail of not less than fifty nor more than five hundred days, or by both such fine and imprisonment . . .

Chinese Public Employment Law (Nevada, 1885)[16]

No Chinaman or Mongolian shall be employed, directly or indirectly, in any capacity, on any public works, or in or about any buildings or institutions, or grounds, under the control of this state.

Public Office Statute (Oakland Charter, 1888)[17]

The mayor, members of the council, auditor, treasurer, city attorney, police judge, commissioners of public works, school directors, members of board of health and health officer must each, at the time of their election or appointment, have been a citizen of the United States and a resident and qualified elector of the city for three years next preceding their election or appointment.

Public Employment Law (Idaho, 1891)[18]

No person not a citizen of the United States, or who has not declared his intention to become such, or who is not eligible to become such, shall be employed upon any state or municipal works; nor shall any such person be employed by any contractor to work on any public works of the state or any municipality. *Provided,* That any State prisoner may be employed within the State prison grounds. . . .

LAUNDRY LAWS

Chinese laundrymen were a frequent target of state and local laws. Some early examples, like the one below from Sacramento, were identity-based, but more often cities used behavior-based laws. In 1880, for example, San Francisco required public laundries to secure approval from the Health Officer, prohibiting laundry work during nights and Sundays, barring diseased persons from lodging nearby, and making violations an offense punishable by imprisonment and heavy fines.

Chinese Washhouses (Sacramento, 1879)[19]

Section 1. The existence of Chinese washhouses on Sutter Lake or slough, and all that portion of the city lying north of 1 street and west of sixth street, is hereby declared to be a public nuisance, and no person shall conduct, carry on, or maintain, either as owner, agent, tenant, or employee, any Chinese washhouse, or place where clothing is washed by the Chinese method of washing, in that portion of the city above set forth.

Sec. 2. The occupancy, living in, or doing or conducting any kind of business excepting storage of grain, merchandise, etc., in any wooden building, shed, or platform erected over the waters of Sutter lake or slough is hereby declared to be a public nuisance ...

Sec. 3. Every person convicted of violating any of the provisions of this ordinance shall be punished by a fine of not more than five hundred dollars, and may be imprisoned until the fine is satisfied, in the proportion of one day's imprisonment for every dollar of the fine.

Public Laundries and Public Wash-Houses (San Francisco, 1887)[20]

Whereas, the indiscriminate establishment of public grounds and public washhouses, where clothes and other articles are cleansed for hire, is injurious and dangerous to public health and public safety and prejudicial to the well-being and comfort of the community, and depreciates the value of property in those neighborhoods where such public laundries and such public wash houses are situate[d]; Now, therefore,

Section 2. It shall be unlawful for any person or persons to conduct or maintain a public laundry or wash-house within the City and County of San Francisco without having first obtained a certificate, signed by the Health Officer ... also a certificate, signed by the Board of Fire Wardens. ...

Section 4. No person or persons owning or employed in the public laundries or public wash-houses ... shall wash or iron clothes between the hours of 10 o'clock P.M. and 6 o'clock A.M., nor upon any portion of that day known as Sunday.

Section 5. No person or persons engaged in the laundry business within the limits of the City and County of San Francisco shall permit any person suffering from any infections or contagious disease to lodge, sleep or remain within or upon the premises used by him, her or them for the purposes of a public laundry. . . .

Section 6. Any person or persons establishing, maintaining or carrying on the business of a public laundry . . . without first having complied with the provisions of Section 2 of this order, shall be guilty of a misdemeanor and upon conviction thereof shall be punished by a fine of not more than one thousand dollars, or by imprisonment of not more than six months, or by both . . .

CITY HEALTH AND SAFETY REGULATIONS

Western cities passed a range of health and safety regulations. Often these were behavior-based or general-outcast ordinances, but they still directly impacted the Chinese community. This ordinance from Portland in 1878, for example, detailed a long list of misdemeanor infractions, including the standard crimes of assault and disorderly conduct. But the ordinance also included sections regulating behaviors specifically associated with the Chinese, including fan tan, opium smoking, prostitution, firecrackers, and carrying baskets on poles. Similarly, a firearms and fireworks ordinance from Oakland in 1891 applied alike to all residents but included a specific ban on Chinese firecrackers and an exception for the Fourth of July. The vague language in city health and safety regulations granted police broad discretion over what constituted "disorderly conduct," "roaming about the streets at night," or "necessary self-defense."

An Ordinance Concerning Offenses and Disorderly Conduct (Portland, 1878)[21]

Section 1. That any person or persons who shall be guilty of any violent, riotous or disorderly conduct . . . or who shall be guilty of any indecent or immoral act or practice in said city upon conviction thereof in the Police Court, pay a fine of not less than ten dollars or more than two hundred dollars, or be imprisoned in the City Jail not less than five days nor more than (90) ninety days, or both, at the discretion of the Court. . . .

Sec. 4. That any person or persons who shall be guilty of any assault, or assault and battery, within the limits of the City of Portland, shall be deemed guilty of a misdemeanor. . . .

Sec. 14. It is hereby forbidden and declared unlawful for any person, either as owner, proprietor, manager, employer or lessee, or otherwise to play, deal, set up, open or cause to be carried on, . . . or engage in any game of faro, monte, roulette, rouge et noir, rondo, twenty-one, poker, draw poker, bluff, brag, tan, tan tan, or fan fan, for or with anything of value. . . .

Sec. 21. If any person or persons shall be found roaming about the streets at night, after the hours of 12 o'clock, without having any lawful business upon the streets at that time, they shall be deemed guilty of a misdemeanor . . .

Sec. 25. That any person or persons who shall set up, open, cause to be opened, or keep any house as a resort for the purpose of smoking opium, . . . or who shall sell or furnish opium for the purpose of being smoked upon the premises, shall be guilty of a misdemeanor . . .

Sec. 27. That any person or persons who shall smoke opium in any house not occupied by them as a residence . . . or who shall be found in any house or place kept as a resort for the purpose of smoking opium, without any lawful business, shall be deemed guilty of a misdemeanor . . .

Sec. 30. Any person or persons who shall solicit any person to visit or enter any house of ill fame, or bawdy house, or any house or place for purposes of lewdness or prostitution . . . shall upon conviction therefore before the Police Court be fined not less than five dollars nor more than twenty dollars . . .

Sec. 34. If any person or persons shall carry any basket or baskets, bucket or buckets, bag or bags, or any other thing, suspended from or attached to poles across or upon the shoulders, or shall carry any rubbish, garbage, swill or filth so as to be offensive to pedestrians upon any sidewalk they shall be deemed guilty of a misdemeanor, . . .

Firearms and Fireworks (Oakland, 1891)[22]

Section 1. No person shall fire or discharge, or cause to be fired or discharged within the limits of the city of Oakland, any cannon, anvil, gun, pistol or other firearms, Chinese or other firecracker, bomb, fireworks or explosive preparation of a similar nature . . .

Section 2. The foregoing provisions as to the use of firearms shall not apply to peace officers in the discharge of their official duties and using reasonable care nor to persons using firearms in necessary self defense or in a careful manner for the purpose of destroying noxious animals upon land owned or occupied by them nor to persons firing firecrackers, bombs, fireworks or similar preparations or pistols with blank cartridges on the 3d, 4th and 5th days of July.

Section 3. Cannons, anvils, or fireworks may be discharged upon occasions of public parade, procession, or rejoicing, after permission in writing first obtained therefor from the mayor, specifying time and place. . . .

ABBREVIATIONS

Archives and Collections

ACC	Alameda County Court Records, Wiley W. Manuel Courthouse (Oakland, CA)
ACS	Alameda County Sheriff's Office Archive (Dublin, CA)
ANC	Ancestry.com [database on-line] (Lehi, UT, USA: Ancestry.com Operations Inc.)
BL	The Bancroft Library, University of California, Berkeley (Berkeley, CA)
CCC	Contra Costa County Court Records, Contra Costa County Historical Society (Martinez, CA)
CCS	Colusa County Superior Court (Colusa, CA)
CFA	Carlo di Ferrari Archive (Sonora, CA)
CFA/TCR	Tuolumne County Court Records, Carlo di Ferrari Archive (Sonora, CA)
CHS	California Historical Society (San Francisco, CA)
CMM	City of Monterey Museums (Monterey, CA)
CPA	City of Portland Archives and Records Center (Portland, OR)
CSA	California State Archive (Sacramento, CA)
CSA/CSC	California Supreme Court, California State Archive (Sacramento, CA)
CSH	Center for Sacramento History (Sacramento, CA)
CSL	California State Library (Sacramento, CA)
HI/SRR	Survey of Race Relations Records, Hoover Institution Library & Archives (Stanford, CA)

ABBREVIATIONS

HL/LACC   Los Angeles Criminal Combined Files, The Huntington Library (San Marino, CA)
HSJ   History San Jose (San Jose, CA)
MC   Multnomah County Courthouse (Portland, OR)
NARA/R   National Archives and Records Administration (Riverside, CA)
NARA/S   National Archives and Records Administration (Seattle, WA)
NARA/SB   National Archives and Records Administration (San Bruno, CA)
OSA/OSC   Oregon Supreme Court, Oregon State Archives (Salem, OR)
PCC   Placer County Court Records, Placer County Archives (Auburn, CA)
SCCA   Santa Clara County Archives (San Jose, CA)
SCS   Sierra County Superior Court (Downieville, CA)
SCSU   Special Collections, Stanford University (Stanford, CA)
SCSU/MM   Mildred Martin Papers, Special Collections, Stanford University (Stanford, CA)
SFHC   San Francisco History Center, San Francisco Public Library (San Francisco, CA)
SHL   Searls Historical Library (Nevada City, CA)
SHL/NCC   Nevada County Court Records, Searls Historical Library (Nevada City, CA)
UCLA/SC   Southern California Chinese American Oral History Project, Collection 1688, UCLA Library Special Collections, Charles E. Young Research Library, University of California (Los Angeles, CA)
WA/NW   Washington State Archives, Northwest Regional Branch (Bellingham, WA)
WA/PS   Washington State Archives, Puget Sound Regional Branch (Bellevue, WA)
WCS   Washoe County Second Judicial District Court (Reno, NV)

NOTES

Introduction

1. "2700 Chinese Boy Babies of San Francisco China Town in 1889," Jesse Brown Cook Scrapbooks Documenting San Francisco History and Law Enforcement, ca. 1895–1936, BANC PIC 1996.003: vol. 21, p. 033—fALB, BL.
2. "Collection Summary," BANC PIC 1996.003—fALB, BL.
3. Police reserved photography for mug shots; immigration officials had yet to insist on photographic evidence. Chinese San Francisco Key no. 3 (#875–1474), 1875–1878, vol. 6, San Francisco Police Department Records, 1870–1983, SFH 61, SFHC; Beth Lew-Williams, *The Chinese Must Go: Violence, Exclusion, and the Making of the Alien in America* (Harvard University Press, 2018), 57.
4. I base this conjecture on the work of Charles R. Savage, who compiled photo composites of Mormon children in the 1870s and sold them as novelties. "Utah's Best Crop, Gathered by C. R. Savage" and [Collage of Children's Faces] (ca. 1870), Charles R. Savage Photograph Collection, L. Tom Perry Special Collections, Harold B. Lee Library, Brigham Young University; Bradley W. Richards, *The Savage View: Charles Savage, Pioneer Mormon Photographer* (Carl Mautz, 1995); Amy K. De Falco Lippert, *Consuming Identities: Visual Culture in Nineteenth-Century San Francisco* (Oxford University Press, 2018), 148, 152–155.
5. In 1880 there were 949 male Chinese in San Francisco who were age sixteen or younger; in 1900 the number dropped to 765. Wendy Rouse Jorae, *The Children of Chinatown: Growing Up Chinese American in San Francisco, 1850–1920* (University of North Carolina Press, 2009), 48.
6. Emma Woo Louie, *Chinese American Names: Tradition and Transition* (McFarland, 1998), 95–105.

7. "John Doe Chinaman," Coroner's Inquest no. 128 (1858), TCR; Warren Courtney Wood, "City Fathers: Social Change, Economic Transformation, and the Lives of Fathers in San Francisco, 1849–1920" (PhD diss., University of California, Santa Barbara, 2011), 419; Sacramento Jail Register, 1867–1872, CSH; People v. Ah Lim, case file no. 991, box 7 (1870) HL/LACC; People v. John Doe (a Chinese), no. 333, Register of Actions, SCS. For assault upon John Doe Chinaman, see People v. Otto Johnson et al., case no. 238 (1859), Court of Sessions, PC; Warren C. Wood, "Fraud and the California State Census of 1852: Power and Demographic Distortion in Gold Rush California," *Southern California Quarterly* 100, no. 1 (2018): 5–43.
8. People v. Charley Jones, case file no. 2637, Tuolumne County (1909), TCR.
9. W. E. B. Du Bois, *Black Reconstruction in America, 1860–1880* (Free Press, 1935, 1998); Crystal Feimster, *Southern Horrors: Women and the Politics of Rape and Lynching* (Harvard University Press, 2019).
10. For connections between the regulation of slavery and immigration, see Kevin Kenny, *The Problem of Immigration in a Slaveholding Republic: Policing Mobility in the Nineteenth-Century United States* (Oxford University Press, 2023); Moon-Ho Jung, *Coolies and Cane: Race, Labor, and Sugar in the Age of Emancipation* (Johns Hopkins University Press, 2008); Kunal M. Parker, *Making Foreigners: Immigration and Citizenship Law in America* (Cambridge University Press, 2015); Stacy L. Smith, *Freedom's Frontier: California and the Struggle over Unfree Labor, Emancipation, and Reconstruction* (University of North Carolina Press, 2013).
11. "Sergeant Cook's Case," *San Francisco Call*, July 27, 1895; "A Change in Chinatown," *San Francisco Call*, June 14, 1895.
12. Erika Lee, *At America's Gates: Chinese Immigration During the Exclusion Era, 1882–1943* (University of North Carolina Press, 2003); Adam M. McKeown, *Melancholy Order: Asian Migration and the Globalization of Borders* (Columbia University Press, 2008); Lucy Salyer, *Laws Harsh as Tigers: Chinese Immigrants and the Shaping of Modern Immigration Law* (University of North Carolina Press, 1995).
13. Key works include Gabriel J. Chin and Sam Chew Chin, "The War Against Asian Sailors and Fishers," *UCLA Law Review* 69, no. 2 (2022): 572–622; Gabriel J. Chin and John Ormonde, "The War Against Chinese Restaurants," *Duke Law Journal* 67, no. 4 (2018): 681–741; Hudson N. Janisch, "The Chinese, the Courts, and the Constitution: A Study of the Legal Issues Raised by Chinese Immigration to the United States, 1850–1902" (PhD diss., University of Chicago, 1971); Charles J. McClain, *In Search of Equality: The Chinese Struggle Against Discrimination in Nineteenth-Century America* (University of California Press, 1994).
14. Hannah Postel and Beth Lew-Williams, "Beyond Exclusion: The Anti-Chinese Legal Regime in the American West," unpublished manuscript, doi: https://osf.io/uhgf4/?view_only=b7ed844175fb4a488471a6bd071c83b7. Additional laws can be found in other western states; see Appendix.
15. For example, Angelo N. Ancheta, *Race, Rights, and the Asian American Experience*, 2nd ed. (Rutgers University Press, 2006), 5. On the South, see James W. Loewen, *The Mississippi Chinese: Between Black and White*, 2nd ed.

(Waveland Press, 1988); Leslie Bow, *Partly Colored: Asian Americans and Racial Anomaly in the Segregated South* (NYU Press, 2010).

16. Claire Jean Kim has argued that Asian Americans are "pushed down by white supremacy and lifted up by anti-Blackness." Others have also recognized the "middling" space Asians occupy on the racial ladder. Such abstractions, although based in fact, only describe race relations in the most general terms. I believe the history of Chinese racialization must account for geographic variation, change over time, and historical contingency. Claire Jean Kim, *Asian Americans in an Anti-Black World* (Cambridge University Press, 2023), 10–11; Mari J. Matsuda, "We Will Not Be Used: Are Asian-Americans the Racial Bourgeoisie?," in *Where Is Your Body? And Other Essays on Race, Gender, and the Law* (Beacon Press, 1996); Colleen Lye, "The Afro-Asian Analogy," *PMLA* 123, no. 5 (2008): 1732–1736.

17. For identity-based laws targeting Black people, see Pauli Murray, compiler and ed., *States' Laws on Race and Color* (1951; University of Georgia Press, 1995).

18. Risa Lauren Goluboff, *Vagrant Nation: Police Power, Constitutional Change, and the Making of the 1960s* (Oxford University Press, 2016), 2; Neil R. McMillen, *Dark Journey: Black Mississippians in the Age of Jim Crow* (University of Illinois Press, 1990), 8–9, 31, 140–142; David M. Oshinsky, *"Worse than Slavery": Parchman Farm and the Ordeal of Jim Crow Justice* (Free Press, 1996), 33, 74–77.

19. Rather than focus on legislative intent, I center the impact on people's lives, taking inspiration from critical race studies. For example, see Allan David Freeman, "Legitimizing Racial Discrimination Through Antidiscrimination Law: A Critical Review of Supreme Court Doctrine," *Minnesota Law Review* 62, no. 6 (1978): 1049–1120.

20. On "conditional inclusion" in the twentieth century, see Madeline Y. Hsu and Ellen D. Wu, "'Smoke and Mirrors': Conditional Inclusion, Model Minorities, and the Pre-1965 Dismantling of Asian Exclusion," *Journal of American Ethnic History* 34, no. 4 (2015): 43–65; Ellen D. Wu, *The Color of Success: Asian Americans and the Origins of the Model Minority* (Princeton University Press, 2013), 29; Andreas Hackl, "Good Immigrants, Permitted Outsiders: Conditional Inclusion and Citizenship in Comparison," *Ethnic and Racial Studies* 45, no. 6 (2022): 989–1010.

21. Mae M. Ngai, "History as Law and Life: Tape v. Hurley and the Origins of the Chinese American Middle Class," in *Chinese Americans and the Politics of Race and Culture*, ed. Sucheng Chan and Madeline Y. Hsu (Temple University Press, 2008), 62–90.

22. For Black inclusion without equality, see Devon W. Carbado, "Racial Naturalization," *American Quarterly* 57, no. 3 (2005): 633–658; Kim, *Asian Americans in an Anti-Black World*, 5–6.

23. For "predatory inclusion" in the twentieth-century housing market, see Keeanga-Yamahtta Taylor, *Race for Profit: How Banks and the Real Estate Industry Undermined Black Homeownership* (University of North Carolina Press, 2019), 17–19.

24. Barbara J. Fields, "Slavery, Race and Ideology in the United States of America," *New Left Review*, no. 181 (1990): 95–118, at 113–114; J. Williams

Harris, "Etiquette, Lynching, and Racial Boundaries in Southern History: A Mississippi Example," *American Historical Review* 100, no. 2 (1995): 387–410, at 390–392; Neil R. McMillen, *Dark Journey: Black Mississippians in the Age of Jim Crow* (University of Illinois Press, 1990), 24–28.

25. Madeline Y. Hsu, *Dreaming of Gold, Dreaming of Home: Transnationalism and Migration Between the United States and South China, 1882–1943* (Stanford University Press, 2000).

26. On Reconstruction and the white counterrevolution often called "redemption," see Eric Foner, *Reconstruction: America's Unfinished Revolution, 1863–1877* (Harper, 2011), 228–260, 564–601.

27. This term has been used previously; for example, see Edlie L. Wong, *Racial Reconstruction: Black Inclusion, Chinese Exclusion, and the Fictions of Citizenship* (NYU Press, 2015). While the modifier "racial" is meant to narrow our attention to one aspect of Reconstruction, I pair this with a broadening of geographic and temporal scale. I am interested in the "the Greater Reconstruction" occurring in both the South and the West, which extends beyond 1877. Elliott West, "Reconstructing Race," *Western Historical Quarterly* 34, no. 1 (2003): 6–26; Richard White, *The Republic for Which It Stands: The United States During Reconstruction and the Gilded Age, 1865–1896* (Oxford University Press, 2017), 103–135.

28. Department of Commerce and Labor, Bureau of the Census, "Negros in the United States," Bulletin 8, 1900 U.S. Census (Government Printing Office, 1904), 19; Rodger Daniels, *Asian America: Chinese and Japanese in the United States Since 1850* (University of Washington Press, 1988), 115.

29. On the Chinese use of white lawyers, see Todd Stevens, "Brokers Between Worlds: Chinese Merchants and Legal Culture in the Pacific Northwest, 1852–1925" (PhD diss., Princeton University, 2003); Tian Atlas Xu, "Immigration Attorneys and Chinese Exclusion Law Enforcement: The Case of San Francisco, 1882–1930," *Journal of American Ethnic History* 41, no. 1 (2021): 50–76. On court translators, see Mae M. Ngai, "'A Slight Knowledge of the Barbarian Language': Chinese Interpreters in Late-Nineteenth and Early-Twentieth-Century America," *Journal of American Ethnic History* 30, no. 2 (2011): 5–32.

30. Louie, *Chinese American Names*, 95–105. For new approaches to this problem, see Hannah M. Postel, "Record Linkage for Character-Based Surnames: Evidence from Chinese Exclusion," *Explorations in Economic History* 87 (2023): 101493.

31. Hendrik Hartog, "Pigs and Positivism," *Wisconsin Law Review* 1985, no. 4 (1985): 899–936; Laura Edwards, *The People and Their Peace: Legal Culture and the Transformation of Inequity in the Post-Revolutionary South* (University of North Carolina Press, 2009); Dylan C. Penningroth, "Everyday Use: A History of Civil Rights in Black Churches," *Journal of American History* 107, no. 4 (2021): 871–898; Ariela Gross, *What Blood Won't Tell: A History of Race on Trial in America* (Harvard University Press, 2008).

32. Ariela J. Gross, "Beyond Black and White: Cultural Approaches to Race and Slavery," *Columbia Law Review* 101, no. 4 (2001): 640–690, at 640–650; Barbara Young Welke, *Law and the Borders of Belonging in the Long Nineteenth Century United States* (Cambridge University Press, 2010).

33. Patricia Ewick and Susan S. Silbey, *The Common Place of Law: Stories from Everyday Life* (University of Chicago Press, 1998), 15–23.
34. "Social Document of Pany Lowe," interviewed by C. H. Burnet, July 5, 1924, Major Documents 28–242, HI/SRR; "Pan Low," *World War I Draft Registration Cards, 1917–1918*, ANC.

Chapter 1. The "Coolie" and the Threat of Chinese Labor

1. Diaries of C. E. DeLong, March 24, 1855, Charles E. DeLong Collection, CSL. "DeLong" is sometimes recorded as "De Long."
2. Diaries of C. E. DeLong, March 24, 1855. Portions of DeLong's diaries were transcribed, annotated, and serialized; see Carl I. Wheat and Charles E. De Long, "'California's Bantam Cock': The Journals of Charles E. De Long, 1854–1863," *California Historical Society Quarterly*, vols. 8–11 (1929–1932).
3. "Doctor Jim," *Oregonian* (Portland), October 16, 1868.
4. Beth Lew-Williams, *The Chinese Must Go: Violence, Exclusion, and the Making of the Alien in America* (Harvard University Press, 2018), 23.
5. Mark Kanazawa, "Immigration, Exclusion, and Taxation: Anti-Chinese Legislation in Gold Rush California," *Journal of Economic History* 65, no. 3 (2005): 779–805; "State Controller's Reports," in Mary Roberts Coolidge, *Chinese Immigration* (Henry Holt, 1909), 37.
6. On "coolie," see Moon-ho Jung, *Coolies and Cane: Race, Labor, and Sugar in the Age of Emancipation* (Johns Hopkins University Press, 2006); Kornel Chang, "Coolie," in *Keywords for Asian American Studies*, ed. Cathy J. Schlund-Vials, Linda Trinh Vo, and K. Scott Wong (NYU Press, 2015), 37–38.
7. Gabriel J. Chin and Sam Chew Chin, "The War Against Asian Sailors and Fishers," *UCLA Law Review* 69, no. 2 (2022): 572–622; Gabriel J. Chin and John Ormonde, "The War Against Chinese Restaurants," *Duke Law Journal* 67, no. 4 (2018): 681–741.
8. For a recent example, see Mae Ngai, *The Chinese Question: The Gold Rushes and Global Politics* (W. W. Norton, 2021), 95. One notable exception is Kanazawa, "Immigration, Exclusion, and Taxation."
9. Coolidge, *Chinese Immigration*, 498.
10. "Governor's Special Message," *Daily Alta California* (San Francisco), April 27, 1852.
11. Sue Fawn Chung, *In Pursuit of Gold: Chinese American Miners and Merchants in the American West* (University of Illinois Press, 2014), 30; US Census Bureau, *Population of the United States in 1860* (Government Printing Office, 1864).
12. State attempts to regulate immigration in New York and Massachusetts had been found to be unconstitutional in Passenger Cases, 48 U.S. 283 (1849).
13. *Journal of the Assembly . . . 3rd Session . . . State of California* (1852): appendix, p. 668, https://hdl.handle.net/2027/uc1.c109112228?urlappend=%3Bseq=672.
14. Michael F. Magliari, "Masters, Apprentices, and Kidnappers: Indian Servitude and Slave Trafficking in Humboldt County, California, 1860–1863," *California History* 97, no. 2 (2020): 2–26.

15. *Journal of the Assembly . . . 3rd Session . . . State of California* (1852): appendix, pp. 669–675. Three years later the California legislature would debate another Chinese indenture law, S.B. 1855. "The Chinese," *Daily Alta California* (San Francisco), February 21, 1855.
16. *Journal of the Assembly . . . 3rd Session . . . State of California* (1852): appendix, pp. 668, 731.
17. J. W. Thompson, *California Mining Statutes Annotated* (Government Printing Office, 1918), 36–37, https://hdl.handle.net/2027/hvd.hl39bx?urlappend=%3Bseq=55.
18. Susan Lee Johnson, *Roaring Camp: The Social World of the California Gold Rush* (W. W. Norton, 2000), 214.
19. "An Act to Provide for the Protection of Foreigners, and to Define Their Liabilities and Privileges," chap. 37, *The Statutes of California* (G. K. Fitch & Co., and V. E. Geiger & Co., State Printers, 1852), 84.
20. *Journal of the Assembly . . . 3rd Session . . . State of California* (1852): appendix, p. 673.
21. "The Cooleys," *Sacramento Daily Union*, April 27, 1852.
22. Estimating the financial impact on a Chinese miner is difficult. Sue Fawn Chung found that such workers in Sacramento County earned $40 to $50 a month in the 1860s; Mae Ngai found that, in Tuolumne County, small-claim partnerships earned an average of $75 per month in the same decade. Mae Ngai, "Chinese Gold Miners and the 'Chinese Question' in Nineteenth-Century California and Victoria," *Journal of American History* 101, no. 4 (2015): 1082–1105; Chung, *In Pursuit of Gold*, 28.
23. Brian Sawers, "The Poll Tax Before Jim Crow," *American Journal of Legal History* 57, no. 2 (2017): 166–259, at 182; Christopher Bryant, "Without Representation, No Taxation: Free Blacks, Taxes, and Tax Exemptions Between the Revolutionary and Civil Wars," *Michigan Journal of Race & Law* 21, no. 1 (2015): 91–123, at 103.
24. "Correspondence of the Union," *Sacramento Daily Union*, May 5, 1852.
25. "Miner's Meeting at Centerville, El Dorado Co.," *Sacramento Daily Union*, May 14, 1852.
26. *San Joaquin Republican* (Stockton, CA), August 21, 1852.
27. "Difficulties with Chinese," *Daily Alta California* (San Francisco), May 15, 1852.
28. "The Chinese," *Daily Alta California* (San Francisco), June 17, 1852.
29. "Columbia Mining Laws," *The Columbia Gazette*, November 12, 1853, CFA.
30. The 1855 revision targeted all aliens, but aliens who were ineligible for citizenship were taxed at a higher rate. The 1857 revision returned to targeting only those aliens ineligible for citizenship. Kanazawa, "Immigration, Exclusion, and Taxation," 779–805.
31. Oregon Constitution, art. 15, sec. 8 (1857); Todd Stevens, "Brokers Between Worlds: Chinese Merchants and Legal Culture in the Pacific Northwest, 1852–1925" (PhD diss., Princeton University, 2003), 165–168.
32. As quoted by Wheat and De Long, "California's Bantam Cock," *California Historical Society Quarterly* 11, no. 1 (1932): appendix, 59.
33. Although bounties have their origins in the Middle Ages, in the United States bounties for tax collection did not become common until the 1870s. Nicho-

las R. Parrillo, *Against the Profit Motive: The Salary Revolution in American Government, 1780–1940* (Yale University Press, 2013), 2–3, 183.
34. Diaries of C. E. DeLong, July 30, 1855; Wheat and De Long, "California's Bantam Cock," *California Historical Society Quarterly* 8, no. 4 (1929): 341, 348.
35. Erwin G. Gudde, *California Gold Camps: A Geographical and Historical Dictionary of Camps* (University of California Press: 2009), 120.
36. Diaries of C. E. DeLong, October 21–22, 1855.
37. [Untitled], *Morning Transcript* (Nevada City, CA), March 7, 1861; see also "Accidentally Shot," *Nevada Democrat*, March 23, 1859; "Translation of Nine Sections of the Foreign Miner's Law into Chinese," *Sacramento Daily Union*, April 16, 1853.
38. "Return of Chinese," *Nevada Journal* (Nevada City, CA), November 2, 1855.
39. Wheat and De Long, "California's Bantam Cock," *California Historical Society Quarterly* 11, no. 1 (1932): 47–64.
40. [Untitled], *Nevada Journal* (Nevada City, CA), November 23, 1855.
41. Grand Jury Reports, Tuolumne County [1855–1871], June 1858, February 1859, Court of Sessions, CFA, 77, 80.
42. Kanazawa, "Immigration, Exclusion, and Taxation," 779–805; "State Controller's Reports," in Coolidge, *Chinese Immigration*, 37.
43. Diaries of C. E. DeLong, September 22, 1855.
44. Diaries of C. E. DeLong, October 23, 1855.
45. "Foreign Miner's Tax—New Mode of Collection," *Sacramento Daily Union*, April 29, 1853.
46. Diaries of C. E. DeLong, November 15, 1855.
47. California Legislature, "Report of the Joint Select Committee Relative to the Chinese Population," 13th sess., 1862, appendix to *Journals of the Assembly and Senate*, Report No. 23, 7.
48. On road taxes, see Edward Leo Lyman, "The Beginnings of Anglo-American Local Government in California," *California History* 81, no. 3/4 (2003): 199–223. In Ah Fook v. John Conners, case file no. 386 (1862), County Court, PC, the plaintiff (unsuccessfully) sued the collector for demanding poll tax and road tax in addition to foreign miner's tax.
49. People v. Williams, case file no. 2983, WPA no. 9054 (1860), CSA/CSC; People v. Williams, 17 Cal 142 (1860).
50. People v. Williams, 17 Cal 142 (1860).
51. People v. Ah Fa[n] & Ah Chow, case file no. 737, Court of Sessions, Tuolumne County (1858), CFA/TCR. ("Ah Fa" is sometimes recorded as "Ah Fan.")
52. "John Chinaman in Siskiyou," *Shasta Courier* (Redding, CA), May 14, 1853. See also Leigh Bristol-Kagan, "Chinese Migration to California, 1851–1882: Selected Industries of Work, the Chinese Institutions and the Legislative Exclusion of a Temporary Labor Force" (PhD diss., Harvard University, 1982).
53. "Denounce Action at Briggsville," *Shasta Courier* (Redding, CA), May 21, 1853. See also Hudson N. Janisch, "The Chinese, the Courts, and the Constitution: A Study of Legal Issues Raised by Chinese Immigration to the United States, 1850–1902" (JD thesis, University of Chicago, 1971), 228.
54. For more on *huìguǎn* (會館), see Lawrence Douglas Taylor Hansen, "The Chinese Six Companies of San Francisco and the Smuggling of Chinese Immigrants Across the U.S.-Mexico Border, 1882–1930," *Journal of the Southwest* 48,

no. 1 (2006): 37–61, at 41; Yucheng Qin, "A Century-Old 'Puzzle': The Six Companies' Role in Chinese Labor Importation in the Nineteenth Century," *Journal of American–East Asian Relations* 12, no. 3 / 4 (2003): 225–254, 230; Him Mark Lai, "Historical Development of the Chinese Consolidated Benevolent System / Huiguan System," *Chinese America: History and Perspectives* (Chinese Historical Society of America) (1987): 13–50, at 13–14.

55. "Report of the Committee on Mines," in *Journal of the Assembly . . . 4th Session . . . State of California* (State Printer, 1853), 7–12.
56. "Report of the Committee on Mines," 7–12.
57. For similar strategies in the Black community, see Camille Walsh, *Racial Taxation: Schools, Segregation, and Taxpayer Citizenship, 1869–1973* (University of North Carolina Press, 2018); Kate Masur, *An Example for All the Land: Emancipation and the Struggle over Equality in Washington, D.C.* (University of North Carolina Press, 2010), 133.
58. "Report of the Committee on Mines," 9–10.
59. Lai Chun-Chuen, "Remarks of the Chinese Merchants of San Francisco upon Governor Bigler's Message, and Some Common Objections" (Printed at the office of the "Oriental" by Whitton, Towne & Co., 1855), 4–5, https://oac.cdlib.org/ark:/13030/hb367n993g/?brand=oac4.
60. "Return of the Chinese," *The Oriental: Or, Tung-Ngai San-Luk* (San Francisco), October 19, 1855.
61. "John Chinaman—What of Him?," *Shasta Courier* (Redding, CA), November 24, 1855; "A New Swindle," *Empire County Argus*, November 17, 1855.
62. "Receipt [in Chinese] for $1.00 donation [ca. 1892]," 1989-142-2, HSJ, http://www.oac.cdlib.org/ark:/13030/kt3xonc5xs/?layout=metadata&brand=oac4, cited by Alexander Jin, "'No Chinese Should Obey It': A Trans-Pacific History of the Geary Act," *Pacific Historical Review* (forthcoming Winter 2026).
63. Michael L. Stahler, "William Speer: Champion of California's Chinese, 1852–1857," *Journal of Presbyterian History* 48, no. 2 (1970): 113–129.
64. As quoted in William Speer, "A Humble Plea . . . In Behalf of the Immigrants from the Empire of China . . . ," (Sterett & Co., 1856), 33.
65. Speer, "A Humble Plea," 34.
66. "A Humble Plea for the Chinese," *San Joaquin Republican* (Stockton, CA), February 29, 1856; "The Chinese," *Georgetown News*, March 13, 1856.
67. "Majority Report of the Committee on Mines and Mining Interests," *Journal of the Senate During the 7th Session of the Legislature of the State of California* (1856): 399–400, 414, 567, https://hdl.handle.net/2027/mdp.39015067103641?urlappend=%3Bseq=400. Repealed Saturday, March 22, 1856.
68. *Journal of the Senate . . . of the State of California* (1856): 460–464.
69. "Foreign Miner's Tax," *Sacramento Daily Union*, March 22, 1856; "Matters at the Capital," *San Joaquin Republican* (Stockton, CA), March 29, 1856.
70. "Matters at the Capital," *Sacramento Daily Union*, April 17, 1856. The law was repealed on March 21 in the Senate and April 16 in the Assembly. *Journal of the Assembly . . . 7th Session . . . State of California* (1856): 784, https://hdl.handle.net/2027/uc1.b2988766?urlappend=%3Bseq=788.
71. Stevens, "Brokers Between Worlds," 165–168.

72. Wheat and De Long, "California's Bantam Cock," *California Historical Society Quarterly* 8, no. 3 (1929): 195, 276.
73. Wheat and De Long, "California's Bantam Cock," *California Historical Society Quarterly* 8, no. 3 (1929): 282.
74. "Constitutionality of the Anti-Chinese Immigration Act," *Sacramento Daily Union*, July 29, 1858.
75. "News Items," *Nevada Democrat* (Nevada City, CA), January 19, 1859. For Oregon restrictions on Black migration and foreigners ineligible for citizenship, see the Appendix.
76. *Journal of the Assembly . . . 10th Session . . . State of California* (State Printers, 1859), 401–406, https://hdl.handle.net/2027/uc1.31175026651011?urlappend=%3Bseq=408.
77. *Journal of the Assembly . . . 10th Session . . . State of California* (1859), 401–406; "Mob Law in Shasta County," *Daily National Democrat* (Marysville, CA), March 5, 1859; "The Chinese," *Daily National Democrat*, February 9, 1859; "The Chinese Question," *Placer Herald* (Auburn, CA), February 19, 1859.
78. Act of April 28, 1860; repealed, 1864 Cal. Stats. (1863–1864) 493; "A Fishy Bill," *Sacramento Daily Union*, March 15, 1860; Stevens, "Brokers Between Worlds," 168.
79. "Senate," *Sacramento Daily Union*, March 26, 1862; "Laws of California," *Sacramento Daily Union*, May 28, 1862.
80. Lin Sing v. Washburn, case file no. 3630, WPA no. 7501 (1862), CSA/CSC; Sing v. Washburn, 20 Cal. 534 (Cal. 1862). The court made a similar ruling in People v. Downer, 7 Cal. 169 (1857), regarding a law that required $50 from shipmasters landing Chinese laborers.
81. Hee v. Crippen, 19 Cal. 491 (Cal. 1861). See also Ah Ok et al. v. McClighty et al., case file no. 10511, box 384 (1865), Sacramento District Court Civil, CSH.
82. Act of May 31, 1870 [Force Act], 16 Stat. 140 (1870); *U.S. Statutes at Large*, vol. 18 (1875), 43rd Congress; *Revised Statutes in Force, Relating to D.C., and Post Roads; Public Treaties in Force, United States*, https://www.loc.gov/item/llsl-v18/.
83. Janisch, "The Chinese, the Courts," 228–232.

Chapter 2. The "Criminal" and the Fear of a Chinese Underclass

1. "Murder of M.V.B. Griswold, by Five Chinese Assassins" (T. A. Springer & Co., Printers, 1858), VAULT BIOG G889m, CHS, 15–25. Fou Sin left behind four accounts of the murder, three in nearly fluent English and one in Chinese. "Trial of Fousin and Chou Yee," *Argus Weekly*, February 27, 1858.
2. "Murder of M.V.B. Griswold," 15–25.
3. "Murder of M.V.B. Griswold," 1, 6, 13.
4. California Census of 1852, schedule 2, vol. 1, CSA.
5. Jail Book, 1856–1866, Sheriff, Tuolumne County, CFA.
6. Robert J. Gordon, "Vernacular Law and the Future of Human Rights in Namibia," *Acta Juridica/African Customary Law* 1991 (1991): 86–103; Sally

Engle Merry, "Legal Pluralism," *Law & Society Review* 22, no. 5 (1988): 869–896.
7. "Departure of Chinamen," *Daily Alta California* (San Francisco), February 17, 1852; "Difficulties with the Chinese," *Daily Alta California*, May 15, 1852; "Chinese," *Nevada Journal* (Nevada City, CA), December 9, 1853.
8. Kelly Lytle Hernandez, *City of Inmates: Conquest, Rebellion, and the Rise of Human Caging in Los Angeles, 1771–1965* (University of North Carolina Press, 2017), 36–44.
9. *Report of Joint Select Committee Relative to Chinese Population of the State of California* (State Printer, 1862), 7.
10. "The Terrible Chinese," *Sacramento Daily Union*, December 24, 1869; "The Chinese in California," *Sacramento Daily Union*, November 27, 1869; San Francisco Board of Supervisors, *San Francisco Municipal Reports, 1873–1874* (Spaulding and Barto Printers, 1874), 118–119.
11. Hubert Howe Bancroft, *Popular Tribunals* (History Company, 1887), 562, 534–535.
12. Bancroft, *Popular Tribunals*, 567, 569–570, 643. See also *Prairie City*, November 12, 1861, as quoted in John R. Wunder, *Gold Mountain Turned to Dust: Essays on the Legal History of the Chinese in the Nineteenth-Century American West* (University of New Mexico Press, 2018), 201.
13. People v. Ah Ki, case file no. 3467/8395 (1862), CSA/CSC; People v. Ah Ki, 20 Cal. 177 (1862).
14. People v. Ah Put and Ah Hin (Two Chinaman), case file no. 1154 (1866), Tuolumne County, CFA/TCR.
15. People v. Ah Kim, case file no. 1445/2834 (1867), CSA/CSC.
16. "Ah Fat," Death Inquest, case no. 431 (1872), Nevada County, SHL/NCC. See also "Ah Tong," Death Inquest case no. 50 (1865), CFA/TCR.
17. Adam McKeown, *Chinese Migrant Networks and Cultural Change: Peru, Chicago, Hawaii, 1900–1936* (University of Chicago Press, 2001), 181.
18. US Congress, *Report of the Joint Special Committee to Investigate Chinese Immigration* (Government Printing Office, 1877), 209–215; see also People v. Ah Quong, case file no. 1021 (1877), PCC; *Chinese Immigration: Report to the California State Senate of Its Special Committee on Chinese Immigration; Its Social, Moral, and Political Effect* (F. P. Thompson, State Printing, 1878), 11, 13–14.
19. Lily Siu Kagawa, "Gambling and the Law: A Study of the Utility of Gambling and Its Prohibition in an American Chinatown" (PhD diss., University of Illinois at Urbana-Champaign, 1983), 160–171; Mark Kanazawa, "Immigration, Exclusion, and Taxation: Anti-Chinese Legislation in Gold Rush California," *Journal of Economic History* 65, no. 3 (2005): 779–805; McKeown, *Chinese Migrant Networks*, 183–184.
20. Philip C. C. Huang, "Between Informal Mediation and Formal Adjudication: The Third Realm of Qing Civil Justice," in *The History and Theory of Legal Practice in China: Toward a Historical-Social Jurisprudence,* ed. Philip C. C. Huang and Kathryn Bernhardt (Brill, 2014), 175–214; Guangyuan Zhou, "Beneath the Law: Chinese Local Legal Culture During the Qing Dynasty" (PhD diss., University of California, Los Angeles, 1995), 208; Zhengyang Jiang, "The

System of 'Turning Oneself In' in Qing and Contemporary China: Some Reflections of Legal Modernism," in Huang and Bernhardt, *The History and Theory*, 271–305.
21. *Chinese Immigration . . . Its Social, Moral, and Political Effect*, 135–140.
22. There was considerable difference between Chinese formal law and legal practice in rural settings. Zhou, "Beneath the Law," 163–191, 208–213; Philip C. C. Huang, *Chinese Civil Justice, Past and Present* (Rowman and Littlefield, 2009), 3–6, 21–23; Huang, *Civil Justice in China: Representation and Practice in the Qing* (Stanford University Press, 1996), 61–68. On the dangers of applying Western standards to Chinese law, see Teemu Ruskola, "Legal Orientalism," *Michigan Law Review* 101, no. 1 (2002): 179–234.
23. People v. Chew Sing Wing, case file no. 9491 (1890), CSA/CSC.
24. "The Rockwell Raid on the Chinese," *Daily Alta California* (San Francisco), February 3, 1870.
25. "The Chinese Question: Report of the Special Committee on Assembly Bill No. 13," in *Appendix to the Journals of Senate and Assembly, of the Eighteenth Session of the Legislature of the State of California*, vol. 2 (D. W. Gelwicks, State Printer, 1870), 3–4.
26. Sing v. Washburn, 20 Cal. 534 (1862); Alina Das, "Inclusive Immigrant Justice: Racial Animus and the Origins of Crime-Based Deportation," *UC Davis Law Review* 52, no. 1 (2018): 171–195, at 183; Hidetaka Hirota, *Expelling the Poor: Atlantic Seaboard States and the Nineteenth-Century Origins of American Immigration Policy* (Oxford University Press, 2017), 70–99; William J. Novak, "Police Power and the Hidden Transformation of the American State," in *Police and the Liberal State*, ed. Markus D. Dubber and Mariana Valverde (Stanford University Press, 2008), 54–73.
27. As quoted in D. Michael Bottoms, *An Aristocracy of Color: Race and Reconstruction in California and the West, 1850–1890* (University of Oklahoma, 2013), 55–56, 75.
28. Act of March 18, 1870, chap. 230, 1870 Cal. Stat. 330–331; "Acts Amendatory of the Codes, Passed at the Twentieth Session of the Legislature, 1873–1874," secs. 69–73, *The Statutes of California* (1874). See also Kerry Abrams, "Polygamy, Prostitution, and the Federalization of Immigration Law," *Columbia Law Review* 105, no. 3 (2005): 641–714.
29. On opium laws, see State v. Ah Chew, 16 Nev. 50 (1881); State v. Ah Gonn, 16 Nev. 61 (1881); State v. Ching Gang, 16 Nev. 62 (1881); *1883 Washington Territorial Statutes*, chap. 2073, sec. 30 (1883); Ah Lim v. Washington, 1 Wash. 156 (1890); Ex parte Yung Jon, 28 F. 308, 311–312 (D. Ore. 1886).
30. "Mayor Bryant's Address," *San Francisco Municipal Reports, 1875–1876* (Spaulding and Barto Printers, 1876), 591.
31. *Chinese Immigration . . . Its Social, Moral, and Political Effect*, 9–10, 13–14.
32. *Chinese Immigration . . . Its Social, Moral, and Political Effect*, 32, 56.
33. *Chinese Immigration . . . Its Social, Moral, and Political Effect*, 28.
34. Page Act, 43 Cong., sess. 2, chap. 141 (1875).
35. *Report of Joint Select Committee*, i–viii.
36. Sucheng Chan, "Against All Odds: Chinese Female Migration and Family Formation on American Soil During the Early Twentieth Century," in *Chinese*

American Transnationalism: The Flow of People, Resources, and Ideas Between China and America During the Exclusion Era, ed. Sucheng Chan (Temple University Press, 2006), 34–135.
37. Charles A. Tracy, "Race, Crime and Social Policy: The Chinese in Oregon, 1871–1885," *Crime and Social Justice*, no. 14 (1980): 11–25, at 16–18.
38. In this study, the violent crimes included rape and sexual assault, battery, robbery, assault, and murder. Tracy, "Race, Crime and Social Policy," 16–18. Clarinèr Freeman Boston, "A Historical Perspective of Oregon's and Portland's Political and Social Atmosphere in Relation to Legal Justice System as It Pertained to Minorities" (MA thesis, Portland State University, 1997), 55, 99, 112–114, 124–139, 197, 205–208, appendix 4; US Census Bureau, "Oregon, Number of Inhabitants," in *1910 US Census* (Government Printing Office, 1912).
39. Tracy, "Race, Crime and Social Policy," 16–18.
40. "Rules for the Government of the Police Force of the City of Portland (August 2, 1886)," rule 43, in Boston, "Historical Perspective," appendix 23, p. 8.
41. Nayan Shah, *Contagious Divides: Epidemics and Race in San Francisco's Chinatown* (University of California Press, 2001).
42. Author database based on Sacramento Jail Registers, 1867–1872, 1872–1875, 1876–1878, 1879–1883, 1883–1886, 1887–1890, 1890–1896, 1896–1899, CSH.
43. Chinese Theatre Petition (1882) AD/10060; Complaint Regarding Chinese Inhabitants in Wash House (1882) AD/6968; Petition Against Chinese Theatre (1880) AD/6995; Petition Against Chinese Wash House (1892) AD/10072, City Auditor, City Recorder, Council Documents, CPA.
44. Petition to Suppress Chinese Prostitution (1885) AD/10069, City Auditor, City Recorder, Council Documents, CPA.
45. Nuisance Complaints About Chinese Market (1887) AD/10070, City Auditor, City Recorder, Council Documents, CPA.
46. "The Chinese Companies," *Daily Alta California* (San Francisco), April 3, 1876.
47. See, for example, San Francisco, California, Police Court Ledgers, 1873–1875, boxes 1 and 2, BANC MSS 2006/104LOCAL, BL. For forced labor after an arrest for operating a wash-house without a license, see City of Port Townsend v. Gee Wah, case file no. 2-261, JEF-1305 (1879), Jefferson County, WA/NW.
48. For example, see Oregon Code of Civil Procedure, chap. 12, sec. 918 (October 12, 1862).
49. Marianne Constable, *The Law of the Other: The Mixed Jury and Changing Conceptions of Citizenship, Law, and Knowledge* (University of Chicago Press, 1994).
50. People v. Chin Mook Sow, case file no. 10232/8463 (1876), CSA/CSC; Chiou-Ling Yeh, "The Chinese 'Are a Race That Cannot Be Believed': Impaneling and Prejudice in Nineteenth-Century California," *Western Legal History* 24, no. 1 (Winter/Spring, 2011): 1–26, at 12–14.
51. People v. Sam Sing, case file no. 1-1060 (1878), Jefferson County Criminal Cases, WA/NW; People v. Ling Ying Toy, case file no. 1708, 1719 (1897), Sacramento Superior Court, CSH. See also People v. Ah Yute, case no. 12657

(1878), CSA/CSC, 17; People v. Ah Ching, case file no. 10710/11721 (1881), CSA/CSC, 38; People v. Chew Sing Wing, case file no. 9491 (1890), CSA/CSC, 37; People v. Ah Fat and Ah Week, case no. 375 (1873), Sacramento District Court, CSH.
52. "The Chinese," *Daily Alta California* (San Francisco), October 25, 1876. This is based on his estimate of the white and Chinese populations: 240,000 white and 30,000 Chinese.
53. John R. Wunder and Clare V. McKanna Jr., "The Chinese and California: A Torturous Legal Relationship," *California Superior Court Historical Society Yearbook* 2 (1995): 195–214.
54. John C. Lammers, "The Accommodation of Chinese Immigrants in Early California Courts," *Sociological Perspectives* 31, no. 4 (1988): 446–465; Wunder and McKanna, "The Chinese and California," 195–214.
55. Sometimes Chinese also faced lengthy jail time awaiting trial; for example, see People v. John Doe (Ah Hong), case file no. 2151.5 (1895), Superior Court, PCC. US Census Office, 7th–12th Census, 1850, 1860, 1870, 1880, 1890, 1900 (Government Printing Office). At the time, Mexican immigrants and Mexican Americans were legally classified as "white," making it difficult to estimate their rate of incarceration. In her study of Los Angeles, Kelly Lytle Hernandez found that individuals with Hispanic surnames did not face disproportionately high levels of arrest until the 1910s; African Americans began to be targeted in the 1920s. Hernandez, *City of Inmates*, 56–57, 159.
56. Sarah Haley, *No Mercy Here: Gender, Punishment, and the Making of Jim Crow Modernity* (University of North Carolina Press, 2019); Kidada Williams, *They Left Great Marks on Me: African American Testimonies of Racial Violence from Emancipation to World War* (NYU Press, 2012).
57. Compendium of the Tenth Census, table 23, "Population by Race and by Counties"; table 143, "Prisoners by Sex, Nativity and Race," US Census Office, 10th Census, 1880, pt. 1 (Government Printing Office, 1885), 335, 1876. Lammers, "Accommodation of Chinese Immigrants," 452; W. E. Burghardt Du Bois, ed., *Some Notes on Negro Crime Particularly in Georgia* (Atlanta University Press, 1904), 11.
58. "Vancouver Barracks in the 1880s: Incarceration of the Tukudika," National Parks Service, https://www.nps.gov/articles/000/1880svancouverincarceration .htm; Margaret Werner Cahalan, *Historical Corrections to the Statistics in the United States, 1850–1984* (Westat, 1986), 151, 160.
59. Du Bois, *Some Notes on Negro Crime*.
60. Du Bois focused on state prisons and penitentiaries, whereas my estimates include inmates in county and city jails. Du Bois, *Some Notes on Negro Crime*; US Census Office, "Report on Crime, Pauperism, and Benevolence in the United States," 11th Census, 1890 (Government Printing Office, 1896), pt. 1: 125, 131, 132, 135; pt. 2: 99, 451, 489. These statistics only include Native people living within white society, known as "civilized Indians" or "taxed Indians."
61. Brianna Nofil, *The Migrant's Jail: An American History of Mass Incarceration* (Princeton University Press, 2024), 27. For other uncounted immigrant detainees, see Records of Prisoners Received at U.S. Penitentiary on McNeil Island, 1875–1892, vol. 1–3, RG 129, NARA/S.

62. For an album missing a key, see "Criminal Album," (no date), ACS.
63. Sacramento Police Department Mug Book, 1870–1883, CSH, 98. See also Yuba County Jail Mug Shot Photographs of Chinese Miners, BANC PIC 2002.174-PIC, BL; San Francisco Police Department Records, 1870–1983, SFH 61, vol. 6, Chinese San Francisco key no. 3 (#875-1474), SFHC; Photograph Album of Chinese Men and Women in Sierra County, 1890–1930 (Vault 184), CHS.
64. See, for example, "Criminal Album," (no date), ACS.
65. Photograph Album of Chinese Men and Women in Sierra County, 1890–1930.
66. Sacramento Police Department Chinese Mug Book, 1873–1880, 55, CSH. For more on Ah Joe and Ah Lee, see Alexander Jin, "Heathen Intimacy: Chinese Migrants and Criminal Sexualities in Turn of the Century California" (PhD diss., Princeton University, 2024).
67. Ah Ben, California Governor Pardons Collection, file 64, box 16, CSA.
68. San Quentin Inmate Photograph Album (1922–1931), CSA.
69. Sacramento Police Department Chinese Mug Book, 1873–1880, 37.

Chapter 3. The "Alien" and the Reconstruction of Chinese Rights

1. Mark Twain, "The Treaty with China—Its Provisions Explained," *New York Tribune*, August 4, 1868.
2. Lucy E. Salyer, "Reconstructing the Immigrant: The Naturalization Act of 1870 in Global Perspective," *Journal of the Civil War Era* 11, no. 3 (2021): 382–405, at 387.
3. Emphasis added. US Const. amend. XIV, sec. 2.
4. "Additional Articles to the Treaty Between the United States of America and the Ta-Tsing Empire, of June 18, 1858. Concluded at Washington, July 28, 1868," Library of Congress, https://www.loc.gov/item/2020783770/.
5. Twain, "The Treaty with China"; John Schrecker, "'For the Equality of Men—For the Equality of Nations': Anson Burlingame and China's First Embassy to the United States, 1868," *Journal of American–East Asian Relations* 17, no. 1 (2010): 9–34.
6. Previously most scholars have focused on what rights the Chinese were due, whereas in this chapter I will focus on what rights the Chinese managed to exercise. Charles J. McClain, *In Search of Equality: The Chinese Struggle Against Discrimination in Nineteenth-Century America* (University of California Press, 1994); John R. Wunder, *Gold Mountain Turned to Dust: Essays on the Legal History of the Chinese in the Nineteenth-Century American West* (University of New Mexico Press, 2018).
7. California State Assembly, "An Act Concerning Crimes and Punishments," *First Session of the Legislature, Statutes of California*, chap. 99, sec. 14, 229; Alfred Avins, "Right to Be a Witness and the Fourteenth Amendment," *Missouri Law Review* 31, no. 4 (1966): 471–504; J. A. C. Grant, "Testimonial Exclusion Because of Race: A Chapter in the History of Intolerance in California," *UCLA Law Review* 17, no. 192 (1969): 192–201; Wunder, *Gold Mountain*.
8. Gabriel J. Chin, "'A Chinaman's Chance' in Court: Asian Pacific Americans and Racial Rules of Evidence," *UC Irvine Law Review* 3 (2013): 965–990; McClain, *In Search of Equality*, 21; People v. Hall, 4 Cal. 399 (1854); Ian Haney

Lopez, *White by Law: The Legal Construction of Race* (NYU Press, 2006), 27–35.
9. Pun Chi, "A Chinese Merchant's Appeal to Congress [1860]," in William Speer, *The Oldest and the Newest Empire: China and the United States* (National Publishing Co., 1870), 588–601. It was the California Supreme Court that ruled in *People v. Hall*.
10. Lai Chun-chuen, "Remarks of the Chinese Merchants of San Francisco upon Governor Bigler's Message, and Some Common Objections" (San Francisco: Printed at the Offices of the "Oriental" by Whiton, Towne & Co., 1855), 5; Hsuan L. Hsu, *Sitting in Darkness: Mark Twain, Asia, and Comparative Racialization* (NYU Press, 2015), 27–52. On anti-Blackness as a form of Asian resistance, see Claire Jean Kim, *Asian Americans in an Anti-Black World* (Cambridge University Press, 2023), 49–52.
11. "An Act to Regulate Proceedings in Civil Cases in the Courts of Justice in This State," passed April 29, 1851, and amended May 18, 1853; May 18, 1854; April 28, May 4, and May 7, 1855; February 20, 1857; March 24, and April 15, 1858; February 21, March 28, April 2, and April 12, 1859; April 28, 1860. Also "An Act Concerning the Courts of Justice of This State, and Judicial Officers," passed May 19, 1853; Speer v. See Yup Co., 13 Cal. 73 (1859); Speer v. See Yup Co., case file no. 2245, WPA no. 3070 (1859), CSA/CSC.
12. Hubert Howe Bancroft, *History of Nevada, Colorado, and Wyoming, 1540–1888* (History Company, 1890), 160.
13. Act of March 16, 1863, chap. 68; Grant, "Testimonial Exclusion," 197; for Arizona, see Chin, "'A Chinaman's Chance,'" 969; "Negroes or Chinamen in Actions or Proceedings to Which a White Person Is Party," *Laws of Washington*, chap. 32, sec. 330, 66. See also Kellen Richard Funk, "The Lawyers' Code: The Transformation of American Legal Practice, 1828–1938" (PhD diss., Princeton University, 2018), 281–284.
14. People v. Downer, 7 Cal. 169 (1857); Sing v. Washburn, 20 Cal. 534 (Cal. 1862); Lin Sing v. Washburn, case file no. 3630, WPA no. 7501 (1862), CSA/CSC. There is one notable exception: courts agreed that the federal government, rather than the states and territories, held the constitutional power to regulate foreign commerce.
15. Territory v. Charles Birch, case file no. 1-204 (1860), Jefferson County Court files, WA/NW.
16. People v. Otto Johnson et al., case file no. 238 (1859), PCC.
17. *Statutes of Oregon*, chap. 4, title 1, sec. 6(3), in 1854; Clarinèr Freeman Boston, "A Historical Perspective of Oregon's and Portland's Political and Social Atmosphere in Relation to Legal Justice System as It Pertained to Minorities" (MA thesis, Portland State University, 1997), appendix 13.
18. In the Matter of the Inquisition upon the Body of Yun Dip, no. 6-694 (1868), Nevada County, SHL/NCC. See also Ah Mun, Coroner's Inquest no. 508 (1862), Tuolumne County, CFA/TCR. See also Unknown Chinaman, Coroner's Inquest no. 666 (1852), CFA/TCR; Unknown Chinaman, Coroner's Inquest no. 349 (1871), CFA/TCR; Ah Tong, Coroner's Inquest no. 50 (1865), CFA/TCR; In the Matter of the Inquisition upon the Body of Ah Fat, no. 6-431 (1872), SHL/NCC.

19. In the Matter of the Inquisition upon the Body of Ah Fon, no. 6-609 (1870), SHL/NCC.
20. Guangyaun Zhou, "Beneath the Law: Chinese Local Legal Culture During the Qing Dynasty" (PhD diss., UCLA, 1995), 45. In turning to private prosecution, Chinese were relying on a process that had been the norm in the United States. Laura F. Edwards, *The People and Their Peace: Legal Culture and the Transformation of Inequality in the Post-Revolutionary South* (University of North Carolina Press, 2009); Allen Steinberg, *The Transformation of Criminal Justice: Philadelphia, 1800–1880* (University of North Carolina Press, 1989); Steinberg, "From Private Prosecution to Plea Bargaining: Criminal Prosecution, the District Attorney, and American Legal History," *Crime & Delinquency* 30 (1984): 568–592.
21. Achunn v. Lyman, case file no. 1864 (1852), box 355, Sacramento County Courts, CSH. See also Chang v. Fritz Hollander et al., no 2-1179 (1859), SHL/NCC.
22. Lung Lee & Co v. John Perkinpine, no. 4-3180 (1868), SHL/NCC. For later examples of private prosecution, see Ah Long v. W. H. Gardner, case file no. 980 (1876), PCC. See also Ah Fooh vs. John Street, case file no. 1-941 (1875), WA/NW; Ah Mow v. Wm. L. Lewis, case file no. CC55 (1909), CCC.
23. Victor Bascara, "In the Future to Any Third Power: Most Favored Nations, Personhood, and an Emergent World Order in *Yick Wo v. Hopkins*," *Asian American Law Journal* 21, no. 1 (2014): 177–208.
24. [The Angell Treaty], Treaty signed at Peking November 17, 1880, modifying treaties of June 18, 1858, and July 28, 1868.
25. Washington Territory reacted by repealing discriminatory laws; see "An Act to Repeal All Police Tax Discriminating Against Chinese, Mongolians and Kanakas," approved November 25, 1869, *Statutes of the Territory of Washington* (James Rodgers Printer, 1869). John Hayakawa Torok, "Reconstruction and Racial Nativism: Chinese Immigrants and the Debates on the Thirteenth, Fourteenth, and Fifteenth Amendments and Civil Rights Laws," *Asian Law Journal* 3 (1996): 55–104.
26. As we will see in Chapter 5, they had less success in matters of education, residential segregation, and public accommodation. Kate Masur, *Until Justice Be Done: America's First Civil Rights Movement, from the Revolution to Reconstruction* (W. W. Norton, 2021), 327–341; Eric Foner, *Reconstruction: America's Unfinished Revolution, 1863–1877* (Harper and Row, 1988), 355–356.
27. People v. Washington, 36 Cal. 658 (1869); People v. Washington, case file no. 1531, WPA no. 1569 (1868), CSA/CSC. The dissenting judges believed the Civil Rights Act to be unconstitutional, but agreed that the Chinese were "a degraded, brutal and vicious race, peculiarly addicted to crime and vice, and demanding more stringent regulations for their government than are required for the general mass of citizens."
28. People v. Brady, 40 Cal. 198, 6 A.M. Rep. 604 (1870).
29. Emphasis added. Act of April 9, 1866 (Civil Rights Act), Public Law 39–26, 14 STAT 27; US Const. amend. XIV, sec. 2; Act of May 31, 1870 (Force Act), 16 Stat. 140 (1870); *U.S. Statutes at Large*, vol. 18 (1873–1875): 43rd Congress; Section 1977, US Congress. *U.S. Statutes at Large*, vol. 18, 1875, 43rd Con-

gress; *Revised Statutes in Force, Relating to D.C., and Post Roads; Public Treaties in Force,* https://www.loc.gov/item/llsl-v18/; McClain, *In Search of Equality,* 39. With codification in 1875, the law became known as Section 1977 of the Revised Statutes. On Stewart's opposition to naturalization, see Salyer, "Reconstructing the Immigrant," 398.

30. James H. Deering, ed., *The Penal Code of California, Enacted in 1872* (Bancroft-Whitney, 1899).
31. People v. Ah Ching, case file no. 10710/11721 (1881), CSA/CSC, 21–22. See also State of Oregon v. Mar Jim [Mah Jim], case file no. 11565, Multnomah County Circuit Court, MC; State v. Mah Jim, 13 Ore 235 at 236–237 (1886); State v. Ching Ling, 16 Ore 419 (1888). This case is mischaracterized in John R. Wunder, "Chinese in Trouble: Criminal Law and Race on the Trans-Mississippi West Frontier," *Western Historical Quarterly* 17, no. 1 (1986): 25–41, at 37–38.
32. Huang, "Between Informal Mediation and Formal Adjudication," 175–214; Zhou, "Beneath the Law," 208; Zhengyang Jiang, "The System of 'Turning Oneself In' in Qing and Contemporary China: Some Reflections of Legal Modernism," in *The History and Theory of Legal Practice in China,* ed. Philip C. C. Huang and Kathryn Bernhardt (Brill, 2014), 271–305.
33. Bias against Chinese testimony was also written into Chinese exclusion laws. After 1893, Chinese exclusion laws required "at least one credible white witness" to establish previous residency in the United States. Chin, "'A Chinaman's Chance,'" 970–973. The Oregon Supreme Court reversed course in State v. Lem Woon, 107 P. 974, 978 (Or. 1910). Lucy E. Salyer, *Laws Harsh as Tigers: Chinese Immigrants and the Shaping of Modern Immigration Law* (University of North Carolina Press, 1995).
34. Act of April 28, 1860; repealed, 1864 Cal. Stats. (1863–1864), 493; "A Fishy Bill," *Sacramento Daily Union,* March 15, 1860. For an example of an arrest for illegal fishing, see People v. Chow, Lee, et al., case file no. CC203 (1910), Criminal Records, CCC; In re Ah Chong, 2 F. 733 (1880).
35. As quoted by Hudson N. Janisch, "The Chinese, the Courts, and the Constitution: A Study of the Legal Issues Raised by Chinese Immigration to the United States, 1850–1902" (JSD diss., University of Chicago, 1971), 303. Sacramento also passed a law in 1870. "Board of Health," *Sacramento Daily Union,* July 20, 1870. See also Nayan Shah, *Contagious Divides: Epidemics and Race in San Francisco's Chinatown* (University of California Press, 2001). On police powers, see William J. Novak, "Police Power and the Hidden Transformation of the American State," in *Police and the Liberal State,* ed. Markus D. Dubber and Mariana Valverde (Stanford University Press, 2008), 54–73.
36. San Francisco, California, Police Court ledgers, 1873–1875, boxes 1–2, BL; "Chinese Obstinacy," *San Francisco Bulletin,* May 22, 1873; Ho Ah Kow v. Nunan, 12 F. Cas. 252 (C.C.D. Cal. 1879).
37. Janisch, "The Chinese, the Courts"; City of Portland, An Ordinance for Preservation of Health and the Prevention of Disease, 19 June 1878, no. 1347, in Boston, "Historical Perspective," appendix 23, p. 21.
38. McClain, *In Search of Equality,* 65–73. The Chinese-language newspaper *The Oriental (Hua Fan Hui Bao),* which was published only for a short time in

1876, should not be confused with the bilingual newspaper *The Oriental (Tung-Ngai San-Luk)* published from 1855 to1857.
39. *Report of Joint Select Committee Relative to Chinese Population of the State of California* (State Printer, 1862), 199, appendix D, 1116.
40. *Report of Joint Select Committee Relative to Chinese Population*, 199. Eng Ying Gong and Bruce Grant, *Tong War! The First Complete History of the Tongs in America; Details of the Tong Wars and Their Causes* (N. L. Brown, 1930), 57–58.
41. Mary Roberts Coolidge, *Chinese Immigration* (Henry Holt, 1909), 451.
42. Yucheng Qin, *The Diplomacy of Nationalism: The Six Companies and China's Policy Toward Exclusion* (University of Hawai'i Press, 2009), 88; "The Cubic Air Law," *Daily Alta California* (San Francisco), April 16, 1878, and February 28, 1878.
43. In re Chin Ah Win[g], case file no. 1880 (1878), RG 21, Old Circuit court, Civil Cases, NARA/SB; McClain, *In Search of Equality*, 69.
44. McClain, *In Search of Equality*, 69, 73.
45. "A Note from the Envoy to the U.S. Gong to the U.S. Minister of Foreign Affairs Which Requested No Mistreatment of Chinese Workers. The First Month of the Lunar Year, 29, the Sixth Year of Guangxu Emperor" [1878]; Prince Gong to Minister Seward, doc. no. 16 (July 31, 1879), in *American Diplomatic and Public Papers: The United States and China*, ser. 2, vol. 13, ed. Jules Davids (Scholarly Resources, 1979).
46. Ho Ah Kow v. Nunan, 12 F. Cas. 252 (C.C.D. Cal. 1879).
47. "Health and Police," *Daily Alta California* (San Francisco), September 12, 1878.
48. Laundry ordinances were ultimately struck down in People v. Soon Kung (1874); In re Quong Woo, 7 Saw. 526 (C.C.D. Cal. 1882); In re Tie Loy [The Stockton Laundry Case], 26 F. 611 (C.C.D. Cal. 1886); In re Wan Yin [The Laundry License Case], 22 F. 701 (D. Ore. 1885); In re Sam Kee, 31 F. 680 (C.C.N.D. Cal. 1887); Ex parte Sing Lee, 96 Cal. 354 (1892); Ex parte Hung Hang, 108 U.S. 552 (1883); In re Yick Wo, 68 Cal. 294 at 299 (1885).
49. Victor Bascara, "In the Future to Any Third Power."
50. Yick Wo v. Hopkins, 118 U.S. 356 (1886). Here I differ in interpretation from Gabriel J. Chin, who sees the case as primarily based on treaty rights. Chin, "Unexplainable on Grounds of Race: Doubts About Yick Wo," *University of Illinois Law Review* (2008): 1359–1392.
51. Struck down in In re Triburcio Parrott, 1 F. 481 (1880).
52. In re Tiburcio Parrott, 1 F. 481; Ex parte Case, 116 P. 1037, 1037–1038 (Idaho 1911).
53. In re Sam Kee, 31 F. 680 (C.C.N.D. Cal. 1887).
54. Ex parte Sing Lee, 96 Cal. 354 (1892). See also In re Wan Yin [The Laundry License Case], 22 F. 701 (D. Or. 1885); In re Tie Loy [The Stockton Laundry Case], 26 F. 611 (C.C.D. Cal. 1886).
55. For a failed challenge to exhumation law, see In re Wong Yung Quy, 6 Saw. 237 (C.C.D. Cal. 1880). For failed challenges to laws regulating laundry hours, see Barbier v. Connolly, 113 U. S. 27, 5 Sup. Ct. Rep. 357, Soon Hing v. Crow-

ley, 113 U. S. 703, 5 Sup. Ct. Rep. 730. For a failed challenge to law regulating laundry locations, see Ex parte San Chung, 11 Cal. App. 511, 105 P. 609 (Cal. Ct. App. 1909).

56. For failed challenges to opium laws, see Ah Lim v. Washington, 1 Wash. 156 (1890); In re Hang Kie, 69 Cal. 149 (1886). For failed challenges to gambling laws, see People v. Chue Fan, 42 F. 865 (C.C.N.D. Cal. 1890); In Re Ah Kit (C.C. N.D. Cal. 1890), 45 Fed. 793.

57. For a failed challenge to educational segregation, see Tape v. Hurley, 66 Cal. 473, 6 P. 129 (Cal. 1885). For failed challenges to anti-miscegenation laws, see In re Paquet's Est., 101 Or. 393, 400, 200 P. 911, 914 (1921); Naim v. Naim, 197 Va. 80, 90, 87 S.E.2d 749, 756, vacated, 350 U.S. 891, 76 S. Ct. 151, 100 L. Ed. 784 (1955).

58. "An Act to Create an Irrigation District" (1875), *Statutes of California* (State Printing Office, 1876), chap. 491, sec. 46; "An Act Authorizing the Board of Supervisors of the County of Mono to Issue Bonds for the Construction of a Wagon Road" (1877), *Statutes of California* (State Printing Office, 1878), chap. 305, sec. 11; "An Act to Create an Irrigation District," March 25, 1878, *Statutes of California* (State Printing Office, 1878), chap. 345, sec. 46.

59. "The Mayor and Council are prohibited from entering into any contract for public works." Revised Charter and Compiled Ordinances and Resolutions of the City of Los Angeles (Evening Express Steam Printing Establishment, 1878); Eliot Grinnell Mears, *Resident Orientals on the American Pacific Coast: Their Legal and Economic Status* (University of Chicago Press, 1928), 318–334.

60. For alien public works laws, see Gabriel J. Chin, "A Nation of White Immigrants: State and Federal Racial Preferences for White Noncitizens," *Boston University Law Review* 100 (2020): 1271–1313.

61. Noah Pickus, *True Faith and Allegiance: Immigration and American Civic Nationalism* (Princeton University Press, 2005).

62. Hiroshi Motomura, *Americans in Waiting: The Lost Story of Immigration and Citizenship in the United States* (Oxford University Press, 2006); Kevin Kenny, *The Problem of Immigration in a Slaveholding Republic: Policing Mobility in the Nineteenth-Century United States* (Oxford University Press, 2023); Hardeep Dhillon, "The Making of Modern US Citizenship and Alienage: The History of Asian Immigration, Racial Capital, and US Law," *Law and History Review* 41, no. 1 (2023): 1–42.

63. Masur, *Until Justice Be Done*, 303–341; Cybelle Fox and Irene Bloemraad, "Beyond 'White by Law': Explaining the Gulf in Citizenship Acquisition Between Mexican and European Immigrants, 1930," *Social Forces* 94, no. 1 (2015): 181–207.

64. Slayer, "Reconstructing the Immigrant," 382–405; Kate Masur, *Until Justice Be Done*, 338; Deenesh Sohoni, "Unsuitable Suitors: Anti-Miscegenation Laws, Naturalization Laws, and the Construction of Asian Identities," *Law and Society Review* 41, no. 3 (2007): 587–618; An Act to Execute Certain Treaty Stipulations Relating to Chinese, 22 Stat. 58, chap. 126 (May 6, 1882); The Naturalization Act of 1790 (1 Stat. 103, enacted March 26, 1790); Johnson, "Additional Articles"; The Naturalization Act of 1870 (16 Stat. 254).

65. United States v. Wong Kim Ark, 169 U.S. 649 (1898).
66. "An Act Relating to Elections," *Statutes of the Territory of Washington* (1854), chap. 1, sec. 1; Oregon Constitution, art. 2, sec. 2 (1857); *California Constitution*, art. 2, sec. 1 (1879). Long excluded from the electorate, Chinese migrants have also been largely ignored in the history of American political development.
67. Alexander Keyssar, *The Right to Vote: The Contested History of Democracy in the United States* (Basic Books, 2000), 114.
68. "Shall Chinamen Vote?," *Chicago Daily Tribune*, October 19, 1874.
69. The unknown third man was Chin Tin. McClain, *In Search of Equality*, 72; *Report to the California State Senate of Its Special Committee on Chinese Immigration; Its Social, Moral, and Political Effect* (F. P. Thompson, State Printing, 1878), 179.
70. "John's Vote: How Many Chinamen Desire Naturalization Papers," *San Francisco Chronicle*, April 25, 1878. Ah Yup could have claimed Blackness as a route toward naturalization but did not. This shows an understanding that the disadvantages of Blackness extended beyond formal law. Kim, *Asian Americans in an Anti-Black World*, 115.
71. In re Ah Yup, 1 F. Cas. 223, 5 Sawy. 155 (1878). Previously historians have assumed that this ruling was applied nationally. Haney-López, *White by Law*; John S. W. Park, *Elusive Citizenship: Immigration, Asian Americans, and the Paradox of Civil Rights* (NYU Press, 2004); McClain, *In Search of Equality*; Gloria J. Browne Marshall, *Race, Law and American Society: 1607–Present* (Routledge, 2013), 190.
72. McClain, *In Search of Equality*, 72.
73. Yung Wing (1852) and Ah Chung (1868), Index to New England Naturalization Petitions, 1791–1906, M1299, roll 38, 57, ANC.
74. *Washington Post*, December 22, 1885; "John Chinaman at Last," *New York Times*, April 11, 1875, 6. U.S., *Naturalization Records Indexes, 1794–1995*, ANC; 1900, 1910, 1920, 1930, 1940 US Census, Population Schedule, ANC.
75. Steven Ruggles, Catherine A. Fitch, Ronald Goeken, J. David Hacker, Matt A. Nelson, Evan Roberts, Megan Schouwiler, and Matthew Sobek, IPUMS Ancestry Full Count Data: Version 3.0 [dataset], https://doi.org/10.18128/D014 .V3.0. If the schedules of the 1890 census had survived, they might have shown additional naturalized Chinese. For further discussion of Chinese naturalization and denaturalization, see Beth Lew-Williams, "Chinese Naturalization, Voting, and Other Impossible Acts," *Journal of the Civil War Era* 13, no. 4 (2023): 515–536.
76. On the vulnerability of the Reconstruction-era federal government, see Gregory P. Downs and Kate Masur, eds., *The World the Civil War Made* (University of North Carolina Press, 2015), 7–11.
77. Harry Lum in the Kansas, U.S., County Marriage Records, 1811–1911, *Kansas, U.S., County Marriage Records, 1811–1911*, ANC; Kristine Schmucker, "'Our Good Laundryman:' Harry Lum," https://hchm.org/our-good-laundryman -harry-lum/.
78. *Newton Daily Republican*, February 12, 1886; Harry Lum, *U.S., Naturalization Records Indexes, 1794–1995, Passport Applications, 1795–1925*, ANC.

For the power of assimilation in citizenship claims, see Stephen Kantrowitz, *Citizens of a Stolen Land: A Ho-Chunk History of the Nineteenth-Century United States* (University of North Carolina Press, 2023).
79. 1910 US Census, Harvey County, Kansas, population schedule, Newton City, 2nd Ward, ANC.
80. Marian L. Smith, "Race, Nationality, and Reality: INS Administration of Racial Provisions in U.S. Immigration and Nationality Law Since 1898," *Prologue: Quarterly of the National Archives and Records Administration* 34, no. 2 (2002), https://www.archives.gov/publications/prologue/2002/summer/immigration-law-1.
81. Salyer, "Reconstructing the Immigrant," 388.
82. In 2015 Hong Yen Chang was posthumously admitted to the bar. "First to the Bar: Chinese Immigrant Granted Posthumous Law License," *The Guardian*, March 16, 2015; In re Hong Yen Chang, 84 Cal. 163, 24 P. 156 (Cal. 1890). See also In re Gee Hop, 71 F. 274 (N.D. Cal. 1895); Mears, *Resident Orientals*, 318.
83. "Cannot Vote in US but Is Entitled to Pension," *Colusa Daily Sun*, August 20, 1909.
84. See, for example, Sonia Gomez, "'Yankee, Why Does a Big Man Like You Fear My Baby?': The Politics of the Anti-Japanese Movement, 1908–1924," *Amerasia Journal* 46, no. 2 (2020): 162–179; Eric J. Pido, "Property Relations: Alien Land Laws and the Racial Formation of Filipinos as Aliens Ineligible to Citizenship," *Ethnic and Racial Studies* 39, no. 7 (2016): 1205–1222; Deenesh Sohoni, "Unsuitable Suitors: Anti-Miscegenation Laws, Naturalization Laws, and the Construction of Asian Identities," *Law and Society Review* 41, no. 3 (2007): 587–618; Brendan A. Shanahan, *Disparate Regimes: Nativist Politics, Alienage Law, and Citizenship Rights in the United States, 1865–1965* (Oxford University Press, 2025).
85. Daniel Kanstroom, *Deportation Nation: Outsiders in American History* (Harvard University Press, 2010); Adam Goodman, *The Deportation Machine: America's Long History of Expelling Immigrants* (Princeton University Press, 2021).
86. Mears, *Resident Orientals*, 192, 219, 224, 284, 332.
87. For a similar strategy among African Americans, see Martha S. Jones, *Birthright Citizens: A History of Race and Rights in Antebellum America* (Cambridge University Press, 2018), 10.

Chapter 4. The "Chinawoman" and the Search for Runaways

1. "The People vs. Loo Sing," May 20, 1884, In Re Yun Gee, case file no. 3204 (1884), box 40, HL/LACC. Yun Gee is also referred to as "Loo Sing." I have used "Yun Gee," which appears on her own affidavit.
2. In Re Yun Gee, case file no. 3204 (1884).
3. Lucie Cheng Hirata, "Free, Indentured, Enslaved: Chinese Prostitutes in Nineteenth-Century America," *Signs* 5, no. 1 (Autumn 1979): 3–29. In this chapter, I tend to use the word "woman" rather than "female," but in fact many of these migrants were underage.

4. Eithne Luibhéid, *Entry Denied: Controlling Sexuality at the Border* (University of Minnesota Press, 2002), 31–54; Huping Ling, *Surviving on the Gold Mountain: A History of Chinese American Women and Their Lives* (SUNY Press, 1998); Sucheng Chan, "The Exclusion of Chinese Women, 1870–1943," in *Entry Denied: Exclusion and the Chinese Community in America, 1882–1943*, ed. Sucheng Chan (Temple University Press, 1991), 94–97; Peggy Pascoe, *The Search for Female Moral Authority in the American West, 1874–1939* (Oxford University Press, 1990); Kerry Abrams, "Polygamy, Prostitution, and the Federalization of Immigration Law," *Columbia Law Review* 105, no. 3 (2005): 641–714; Sucheng Chan, "Against All Odds: Chinese Female Migration and Family Formation on American Soil During the Early Twentieth Century," in *Chinese American Transnationalism: The Flow of People, Resources, and Ideas Between China and America During the Exclusion Era*, ed. Sucheng Chan (Temple University Press, 2006), 34–135. On the problem of sources on prostitution in China, see Gail Hershatter, *Dangerous Pleasures: Prostitution and Modernity in Twentieth-Century Shanghai* (University of California Press, 1997), 3–33.

5. For discussion of the "Chinese slave girl," see Alexander Jin, "Heathen Intimacy: Chinese Migrants and Criminal Sexualities in Turn of the Century California" (PhD diss., Princeton University, 2024).

6. On fugitive mobility, see Stephen Lucasi, "William Wells Brown's 'Narrative' and Traveling Subjectivity," *African American Review* 41, no. 3 (2007): 521–539. Running away was also a key strategy for Chinese women in bad or abusive domestic relations in China (especially because they lacked a means to initiate divorce). It was a crime to desert a husband, however. Philip C. Huang, "Women's Choices Under the Law: Marriage, Divorce, and Illicit Sex in the Qing and the Republic," in *The History and Theory of Legal Practice in China: Toward a Historical Social Jurisprudence*, ed. Philip C. Huang (Brill, 2014), 58.

7. No doubt some Chinese women worked within the established trafficking system to advance their own social and economic status, but in this chapter I will focus on those who found ways to disrupt, disobey, and escape the system itself. Stephanie M. H. Camp, *Closer to Freedom: Enslaved Women and Everyday Resistance in the Plantation South* (University of North Carolina Press, 2004); James C. Scott, *Weapons of the Weak: Everyday Forms of Peasant Resistance* (Yale University Press, 1987).

8. César López, "Lost in Translation: From *Calle de los Negros* to Nigger Alley to North Los Angeles Street to Place Erasure, Los Angeles 1855–1951," *Southern California Quarterly* 94, no. 1 (2012): 25–90.

9. "The People vs. Loo Sing," May 20, 1884, In Re Yun Gee.

10. "An Ordinance Prohibiting Houses of Prostitution and Ill-Fame in the City of Los Angeles," approved November 13, 1882, in *Compiled Ordinances and Resolutions of the City of Los Angeles*, ed. William Wilcox Robinson (Marley and Freeman, printers, 1884); Page Act, 43 Cong., sess. 2, chap. 141 (1875). It is not clear whether the Page Act regulated only entry or also presence.

11. Sucheng Chan, *This Bittersweet Soil: The Chinese in California Agriculture, 1860–1910* (University of California Press, 1986), 62–63, 392–393. Benson

Tong, *Unsubmissive Women: Chinese Prostitutes in Nineteenth Century San Francisco* (University of Oklahoma Press, 1994), 16–24, 94–102.
12. George A. Peffer, *If They Don't Bring Their Women Here: Chinese Female Immigration Before Exclusion* (University of Illinois Press, 1996), 11, 91. Peffer argues that these numbers have been overstated, but still maintains that 50 percent of all Chinese females in San Francisco in 1870 were prostitutes. On the sociolegal construction of the difference between "wife" and "prostitute," see Luibhéid, *Entry Denied*, 38–50.
13. Matthew H. Sommer, *Polyandry and Wife-Selling in Qing Dynasty China: Survival Strategies and Judicial Interventions* (University of California Press, 2015), 12, 25, 92. See also Huang, "Women's Choices."
14. Susan L. Mann, *Gender and Sexuality in Modern Chinese History: New Approaches to Asian History* (Cambridge University Press, 2011), 3.
15. Hirata, "Free, Indentured, Enslaved," 4–7; Ling, *Surviving on the Gold Mountain*, 52–61. For the economics of split households, see Madeline Hsu, *Dreaming of Gold, Dreaming of Home: Transnationalism and Migration Between the United States and South China, 1882–1943* (Stanford University Press, 2000), 90–123.
16. Hirata, "Free, Indentured, Enslaved," 14–15.
17. Matthew Sommer, *Sex, Law and Society in Late Imperial China* (Stanford University Press, 200), 260–274.
18. For anti-prostitution sentiment within the Chinese community, see Gordon H. Chang, *Ghosts of Gold Mountain* (Houghton Mifflin Harcourt, 2019), 175–181; Judy Yung, Gordon H. Chang, and Him Mark Lai, eds., *Chinese American Voices: From the Gold Rush to the Present* (University of California Press, 2006), 23–24, 43–47.
19. Elizabeth Sinn, *Pacific Crossing: California Gold, Chinese Migration, and the Making of Hong Kong* (Hong Kong University Press, 2013), 226–235. For discussion of the widespread trafficking within China, see Huang, "Women's Choices," 54, 65; Mann, *Gender and Sexuality*, 57.
20. Kazuhiro Oharazeki, *Japanese Prostitutes in the North American West, 1887–1920* (University of Washington Press, 2016), 97–99; Laura Woodworth-Ney, *Women in the American West* (ABC-CLIO, 2008), 163.
21. See Julia Flynn Siler, *The White Devil's Daughters: The Women Who Fought Slavery in San Francisco's Chinatown* (Knopf, 2019). Only one known case makes a Thirteenth Amendment argument in regard to a Chinese woman. In Ah Sou v. United States, 200 U.S. 611 (1905), a lower court vacated an order for deportation because sending the defendant to China amounted to "a life of perpetual slavery" and the Thirteenth Amendment prohibited slavery. This legal logic was ultimately rejected by the appellate court, United States v. Ah Sou, 138 F. 775 (9th Cir. 1905).
22. Johanna S. Ransmeier, *Sold People: Traffickers and Family Life in North China* (Harvard University Press, 2017), 8.
23. With the exception of a handful of conversion confessionals and testimony from Chy Lung v. Freeman, 92 U.S. 275 (1875), scholars have written the history of Chinese women in America without benefit of women's "voices."
24. Sommer, *Polyandry and Wife-Selling*, 8; Ransmeier, *Sold People*, 3–8.

25. As quoted by Hirata, "Free, Indentured, Enslaved," 15–16. This resembles "coolie" labor contracts in Cuba; see Lisa Yun, *The Coolie Speaks: Chinese Indentured Laborers and African Slaves in Cuba* (Temple University Press, 2009).
26. For similar contracts, see *Report of the Committees of the Senate of the United States for the Second Session of the Forty-Fourth Congress, 1876–1877* (Government Printing Office, 1877), 147; Judy Yung, *Unbound Feet: A Social History of Chinese Women in San Francisco* (University of California Press, 1995), 27.
27. "Chinese Kidnapping," *Daily Alta California* (San Francisco), December 26, 1875. For Chinese women's fear of kidnapping, see "Hearing," February 27, 1873, People v. Ah Son, case file no. 1184 (1873), HL/LACC; People v. Pong Suey et al., case file no. 2637 (1910), CFA/TCR.
28. People v. Ah Quong, case file no. 1021 (1877), PCC. See related cases, nos. 1021, 1032.
29. On night watchmen, see US Congress, *Report of the Joint Special Committee to Investigate Chinese Immigration* (Government Printing Office, 1877), 209–219; People v. Chin Yeun and Yee Hung [San Francisco County], case file no. 1126, WPA no. 23885 (1904), CSA/CSC, 35–57.
30. See also People v. Chuey Ying Git et al., case file no. 21013 [Kern County] (California Sup. Crt., 1893), 30–37, CSA/CSC.
31. People v. Cum-Chow & Ah-pe-o, case no. 1240 (1867), CFA/TCR.
32. *Report of the Joint Special Committee*, 229.
33. Willard B. Farwell, *The Chinese at Home and Abroad: Together with the Report of the Special Committee of the Board of Supervisors of San Francisco on the Condition of the Chinese Quarter of that City* (A. L. Bancroft and Co., 1885), 14.
34. "The People vs. Loo Sing," 21 May 1884, In Re Yun Gee.
35. In 1860 there were 681 Chinese females recorded in San Francisco. Tong, *Unsubmissive Women*, 94. Newspapers reported in the early 1860s that the Chinese Six Companies and the police were cooperating in the deportation of Chinese prostitutes. "Small Feet and High Caste," *Daily Alta California* (San Francisco), June 11, 1860; "Sending Home the Chinese Females," *Daily Alta California*, April 27, 1864; Hudson N. Janisch, "The Chinese, the Courts, and the Constitution: A Study of the Legal Issues Raised by Chinese Immigration to the United States, 1850–1902" (JSD diss., University of Chicago, 1971), 111.
36. Nayan Shah, *Contagious Divides: Epidemics and Race in San Francisco's Chinatown* (University of California Press, 2001), 81.
37. Luibhéid, *Entry Denied*, 33.
38. *San Francisco Municipal Reports, 1865–1866* (Towne and Bacon, 1866), 125–126.
39. Chan, "The Exclusion of Chinese Women," 97–98; In re Ah Fong, 1 F. Cas. 213 (CCD Cal. 1874), No. 102. At a time when Chinese testimony was routinely excluded, early prostitution and kidnapping laws (in an effort to facilitate the prosecution of white brothel owners and traffickers) included sections specifically allowing Chinese to serve as "competent witnesses." Act of March 21, 1866, chap. 505, 1866 Cal. Stat. 641. David Beasley, "More than People v. Hall:

Chinese Immigration and American Law in a Sierra Nevada County, 1850–1920," in *Chinese Immigrants and American Law,* ed. Charles McClain (Routledge, 1994), 125–139.

40. "Act to prevent the kidnapping and importation of Mongolian, Chinese and Japanese females, for criminal or demoralizing purposes," March 18, 1870, chap. 230, 1870 Cal. Stat. 330; Abrams, "Polygamy, Prostitution," 674–677; Acts Amendatory of the Codes, Passed at the Twentieth Session of the Legislature, 1873–1874, sec. 69–73, *The Statutes of California* (1874).
41. "Chinese Women Arrested," *Daily Alta California* (San Francisco), August 26, 1874; "A Cargo of Infamy," *San Francisco Chronicle,* August 28, 1874; "The Case of the Chinese Women," *San Francisco Chronicle,* August 30, 1874; "Enforcing the Law," *Trinity Journal,* September 5, 1874.
42. On traffickers coaching Chinese female migrants, see Sinn, *Pacific Crossings,* 233.
43. As quoted in Abrams, "Polygamy, Prostitution," 685; Transcript of Record, Chy Lung v. Freeman, case no. 478 (1875), U.S. Supreme Court, *Making of Modern Law: Primary Sources, 1620–1970.*
44. Abrams, "Polygamy, Prostitution," 685; Chy Lung v. Freeman (1875).
45. Peffer, *If They Don't Bring Their Women Here,* 33.
46. In Re Ah Fong, 1 F. Cas. 213 (1874).
47. Chy Lung v. Freeman (1875); Abrams, "Polygamy, Prostitution," 644; Sarah Cleveland, "Powers Inherent in Sovereignty: Indians, Aliens, Territories, and the Nineteenth Century Origins of Plenary Power in Foreign Affairs," *Texas Law Review* 81, no. 1 (2002): 108.
48. Page Act, 43 Cong., sess. 2, chap. 141 (1875).
49. Abrams, "Polygamy, Prostitution," 690, 703.
50. Peffer, *If They Don't Bring Their Women Here,* 27, 44.
51. Oharazeki, *Japanese Prostitutes,* 18.
52. "An Ordinance to Prohibit Houses of Ill fame and Prostitution in Certain Parts of the City of Los Angeles," approved May 25, 1874, amended September 26, 1882, in *Compiled Ordinances and Resolutions of the City of Los Angeles,* ed. William Wilcox Robinson (Marley and Freeman, 1884); "An ordinance prohibiting houses of prostitution and ill-fame in the city of Los Angeles," approved November 13, 1882, *Compiled Ordinances and Resolutions of the City of Los Angeles.*
53. The lack of records may also result from extortion by the police or the informal practice of delivering Chinese prostitutes to missions rather than jails.
54. "Statement on Appeal to County Court," May 11, 1876, People v. Ah Hoy et al., case file no. 201 (1876), HL/LACC.
55. *Report of the Joint Special Committee,* 192, 1142–1143.
56. On the operation of female cooperative brothels in British Malay, see Sandy F. Chang, "Intimate Itinerancy: Sex, Work, and Chinese Women in Colonial Malaya's Brothel Economy, 1870s–1930s," *Journal of Women's History* 33, no. 4 (2021): 92–117.
57. People v. Ah Son et al., case file no. 136 [1184] (1873), Justices Court, HL/LACC.

58. Petition to Suppress Chinese Prostitution, City Council Documents, AD/10069, CPA; see also Employment of Women in Chinese Theatre, Council Documents, AD/10074, CPA.
59. Charles A. Tracy, "Race, Crime and Social Policy: The Chinese in Oregon, 1871–1885," *Crime and Social Justice,* no. 14 (1980): 15. Japanese arrests for prostitution peaked in the first decade of the twentieth century. Oharazeki, *Japanese Prostitutes;* Norman S. Hayner, "Social Factors in Oriental Crime," *American Journal of Sociology* 43, no. 6 (1938): 908–919.
60. Janisch, "The Chinese, the Courts," 115; Chan, "Against All Odds," 56.
61. Some of these men had first wives back in China and took Chinese prostitutes as second wives. A few Chinese men entered polyandrous arrangements, sharing one woman with multiple men. Huping Ling, "Family and Marriage of Late-Nineteenth and Early-Twentieth Century Chinese Immigrant Women," *Journal of American Ethnic History* 19, no. 2 (2000): 43–63; Sue Fawn Chung, "Their Changing World: Chinese Women in the Comstock, 1860–1910," in *Comstock Women: The Making of Mining Community,* ed. Ronald M. James and C. Elizabeth Raymond (University of Nevada Press, 1997).
62. Regina G. Kunzel, *Fallen Women, Problem Girls: Unmarried Mothers and the Professionalization of Social Work, 1890–1945* (Yale University Press, 1993), 2, 12.
63. Aye Ling Writ of Habeas Corpus, case file no. 402 (1855), Tuolumne County, CFA/TCR. For another successful petition, see also Gim Chong, Writ of Habeas Corpus, no. 1315 (1868), Tuolumne County, CFA/TCR. Tian Atlas Xu, "Chinese Women Migrants, Habeas Petitions, and the Search for a Freer Life in California, 1857–1882," *Journal of the Civil War Era* 13, no. 4 (2023): 515–536.
64. See also "Portland," *Marysville Daily Appeal,* May 10, 1871.
65. For another example of hiding on trains, see "A Chinawoman Boxed Up and Shipped as Freight," *Sentinel,* June 15, 1878.
66. Lilac Chen as quoted in Victor G. Nee and Brett De Bary Nee, *Longtime Californ': A Documentary Study of an American Chinatown* (Pantheon, 1973), 83–90.
67. As quoted by Peggy Pascoe, "Gender Systems in Conflict: The Marriages of Mission-Educated Chinese American Women, 1874–1939," *Journal of Social History* 22, no. 4 (1989): 631–652, 643. At times Chinese women found simultaneous support from both their Chinese suitors and American missionaries. Ah Quin, who served as a translator in San Diego courts, recounts a case against Low Lee, who was "under charge by Mrs. McKinsy and Mrs. Noble" and "help[ed]" by Kim Fung, "her sweetheart." Ah Quin, "Diary," July 6, 1891, as translated by Susie Lan Cassel (unpublished, used with permission).
68. Chen as quoted in Nee and Nee, *Longtime Californ',* 83–90.
69. People v. Fong Ah Tuck, case file no. 10327, WPA no. 8228 [Sacramento County] (1878), CSA/CSC, 7–8. "For Sentence," *Sacramento Daily Union,* July 20, 1877.
70. "Transcript on Appeal," 1878, People v. Fong Ah Tuck, 3–6. Other cases detail the physical abuse and confinement of Chinese women; see People v. Chow et al., case no. 1240 (Tuolumne Justice Court, 1867), CFA/TCR; People v. Chin

Yeun and Yee Hung [San Francisco County], case file no. 1126, WPA 23885 (1904), CSA/CSC, 35–57; People v. Richard Kerren, case file no. 1101 (1872), HL/LACC; People v. Henry Searls, case file no. 6-138 (1862), SHL/NCC.

71. "Transcript on Appeal," 1878, People v. Fong Ah Tuck, 43. The California Supreme Court upheld the verdict a year later.

72. Japanese women also escaped brothels, using the courts, marriages, and rescue missions. Oharazek, *Japanese Prostitutes*, 121.

73. "The People vs. Loo Sing," May 21, 1884, In Re Yun Gee.

74. "Affidavit of John Godfrey," May 26, 1884, "Affidavit of John C. Morgan," May 23, 1884, "Affidavit of M. L. Statton," May 22, 1884, In Re Yun Gee.

75. "Investigate the Charges Against Chief of Police King," *Los Angeles Times*, July 8, 1882. See also "The Council and the Gamblers," *Los Angeles Times*, July 17, 1888; "Abbott in Court," *Los Angeles Times*, June 23, 1888. On the extent of bribery, see Peffer, *If They Don't Bring Their Women Here*, 31–32.

76. California Legislature, *California Investigation of Chinese Immigration: Its Social, Moral, and Political Effect* (State Printing Office, 1876), 12, 202, 207–208. See also John C. Lammers, "The Accommodation of Chinese Immigrants in Early California Courts," *Sociological Perspectives* 31, no. 4 (1988): 446–465, at 454.

77. "Points and Authorities of Appellant," November 4, 1880, People v. Ah Fook, case file no. 10589, WPA no. 10861 [Sonoma County] (1880), CSA/CSC.

78. "Bill of Exceptions," December 15, 1880, People v. Ah Fook.

79. The press reported that "the kidnapping of Chinese women through sham prosecutions for offences never committed is a matter of almost everyday occurrence in California." "Women Kidnapping," *Daily Alta California* (San Francisco), October 11, 1864, as quoted in Janisch, "The Chinese, the Courts," 116. See also "A Victim of Persecution," *Daily Alta California*, November 12, 1857; "A Case of China Kidnapping," *Daily Alta California*, December 10, 1858; "Highbinders' Methods," *Daily Alta California*, November 27, 1884; "City Intelligence," *Sacramento Daily Union*, December 21, 1858.

80. People v. Ah Fook, case file no. 10589, WPA no. 10861 [Sonoma County] (1880), CSA/CSC.

81. The telegraphs were preserved by the telegraph operator and eventually published as a "queer queue tale." Albert Dressler, *California Chinese Chatter* (Albert Dressler, 1927). The original telegrams can be found in the Albert Dressler Collection, box 756, CSL.

82. Marriage contracts could be used to escape prostitution or to traffic women; see "Kidnapping Chinese Women," *Morning Union*, April 10, 1885.

83. The telegrams suggest that Gan Que temporarily resided in at least four California counties (San Francisco, Sierra, Nevada, and Placer), but she does not appear in the records of any of them.

84. Kelly Lytle Hernandez, *City of Inmates: Conquest, Rebellion, and the Rise of Human Caging in Los Angeles, 1771–1965* (University of North Carolina Press, 2017), 54–56.

85. Mr. T. J. K. McGowen interviewed by Catharine Holt, August 18, 1924, Major Documents no. 30-298, HI/SRR, 4.

Chapter 5. The "Invader" and the Entrenchment of Chinese Segregation

1. J. I. Seiter, M. J. Worthington, B. L. Voss, et al., "Carving Chopsticks, Building Home: Wood Artifacts from the Market Street Chinatown in San Jose, California," *International Journal of Historical Archaeology* 19 (2015): 664–685. On the San Jose Chinese community, see Connie Young Yu, *Chinatown, San Jose, USA* (San Jose Historical Museum Association, 1991).
2. Beth Lew-Williams, *The Chinese Must Go: Violence, Exclusion, and the Making of the Alien in America* (Harvard University Press, 2018).
3. "After the Fire," *Evening Herald* (San Jose), May 5, 1887. (With thanks for the newspaper records of the Market Street Chinatown Archaeological Project under the direction of Barbara Voss; https://marketstreet.stanford.edu/).
4. Lew-Williams, *The Chinese Must Go*, 28–29.
5. C. Vann Woodward, *The Strange Career of Jim Crow*, commemorative ed. (Oxford University Press, 2001); Sarah Haley, *No Mercy Here: Gender, Punishment, and the Making of Jim Crow Modernity* (University of North Carolina Press, 2016).
6. Claire Jean Kim, *Asian Americans in an Anti-Black World* (Cambridge University Press, 2023); Benjamin H. Pollak, "'A New Ethnology': The Legal Expansion of Whiteness Under Early Jim Crow," *Law and History Review* 39, no. 3 (2021): 513–538; Edlie L. Wong, *Racial Reconstruction: Black Inclusion, Chinese Exclusion, and the Fictions of Citizenship* (NYU Press, 2015); Devon Carbado, "Racial Naturalization," *American Quarterly* 57, no. 3 (2005): 633–658; Natalia Molina, *How Race Is Made in America: Immigration, Citizenship, and the Historical Power of Racial Scripts* (University of California Press, 2014), 6–9; Tomás Almaguer, *Racial Fault Lines: The Historical Origins of White Supremacy in California* (University of California Press, 1994); Najia Aarim-Heriot, *Chinese Immigrants, African Americans, and Racial Anxiety in the United States, 1848–82* (University of Illinois Press, 2003); D. Michael Bottoms, *An Aristocracy of Color: Race and Reconstruction in California and the West, 1850–1890* (University of Oklahoma Press, 2013).
7. Clarinèr Freeman Boston, "A Historical Perspective of Oregon's and Portland's Political and Social Atmosphere in Relation to Legal Justice System as It Pertained to Minorities" (MA thesis, Portland State University, 1997), appendix 4; Lynn M. Hudson, *West of Jim Crow: The Fight Against California's Color Line* (University of Illinois Press, 2020), 5. US Census Bureau, "Population by Race, Sex, and Nativity," *Population in the U.S. in 1880* (Government Printing Office, 1880).
8. Similarly, the Jim Crow regime emerged through experimentation; see Stephanie Cole and Natalie J. Ring, eds., *The Folly of Jim Crow: Rethinking the Segregated South* (Texas A&M University Press, 2012). Scholars have acknowledged that Black segregation was a form of inclusion; see Howard N. Rabinowitz, "From Exclusion to Segregation: Southern Race Relations, 1865–1890," *Journal of American History* 63, no. 2 (1976): 325–350.
9. Hannah M. Postel, "At the Margins of Gold Mountain? Chinese Immigrant Segregation in 19th Century California," unpublished manuscript. See also

Charlotte Brooks, *Alien Neighbors, Foreign Friends: Asian Americans, Housing, and the Transformation of Urban California* (University of Chicago Press, 2009); Nayan Shah, *Contagious Divides: Epidemics and Race in San Francisco's Chinatown* (University of California Press, 2001).
10. John R. Logan and Matthew J. Martinez, "The Spatial Scale and Spatial Configuration of Residential Settlement: Measuring Segregation in the Postbellum South," *American Journal of Sociology* 123, no. 4 (2018): 1161–1203. Northern cities were not as segregated at the time; see Angelina Grigoryeva, "The Historical Demography of Racial Segregation," *American Sociological Review* 80, no. 4 (2015): 814–842.
11. Postel, "At the Margins of Gold Mountain?"
12. Kenneth H. Marcus and Yong Chen, "Inside and Outside Chinatown: Chinese Elites in Exclusion Era California," *Pacific Historical Review* 80, no. 3 (2011): 369–400; Brookes, *Alien Neighbors, Foreign Friends*, 23; Shah, *Contagious Divides*, 76.
13. Megan S. Kane with contributions by Barbara L. Voss, "Reconstructing Historical and Archaeological Context of an Orphaned Collection: Report on Archival Research and Feature Summaries for the Market Street Chinatown Archaeology Project," Market Street Chinatown Archaeological Project (MSCAP) Technical Report no. 1, August 2011, https://marketstreet.stanford.edu/2011/08/.
14. Kane, "Reconstructing Historical and Archaeological Context"; Barbara L. Voss, "Between the Household and the World System: Social Collectivity and Community Agency in Overseas Chinese Archaeology," *Historical Archaeology* 42, no. 3 (2008): 37–52.
15. "Ordinances Regulating Chinese Burials and the Removal of Chinatown," *Sacramento Daily Union*, January 12, 1886; City Council Minutes, September 30, 1865, Accession no. AF/177076, CPA; In re Lee Sing, 43 F. 359 (Circuit Court, N.D. Cal. 1890).
16. City Council Minutes, September 30, 1865, Accession no. AF/177076, CPA. In a sample of 45 townships, Hannah Postel found that 19 passed laws attempting to limit the location of Chinese residences or businesses (e.g., laundries) via identity-based or behavior-based laws. Postel, "At the Margins of Gold Mountain?," 34.
17. California Constitution, art. 19, sec. 4.
18. [Untitled], *San Jose Herald*, April 27, 1880; "A Warning," Daily Alta California, May 26, 1880.
19. Sacramento also considered an ordinance against the exhumation of remains. "Ordinances Regulating Chinese Burials and the Removal of Chinatown," *Sacramento Daily Union*, January 12, 1886.
20. "The Chinese Question," *Chico Weekly Enterprise*, January 15, 1886; "Fighting the Chinese," *San Jose Herald*, January 21, 1886; "News," *San Jose Herald*, January 14, 1886.
21. "Fighting the Chinese," *San Jose Herald*, January 21, 1886.
22. In re Lee Sing, 43 F. 359 (Circuit Court, N.D. Cal. 1890). Sawyer's opinion "left the matter of framing a new ordinance a very difficult task." "Coolie Influence," *San Jose Herald*, November 15, 1890.

23. Buchanan v. Warley, 245 U.S. 60 (1917); Harmon v. Tyler, 273 U. S. 668 (1927); Michael Jones-Correa, "The Origins and Diffusion of Racial Restrictive Covenants," *Political Science Quarterly* 115, no. 4 (2000–2001): 541–568.
24. "Petition of the Anti-Chinese Club," November 5, 1885, San Jose Common Council, Accession no. 1976-176, HSJ.
25. "The Bond Ordinance," *Evening Herald* (San Jose), March 26, 1887; "To Whom It May Concern," *Evening Herald*, April 1, 1887.
26. "To Condemn Chinatown," *Evening Herald* (San Jose), April 4, 1887; "Removing Chinatown," *Evening Herald*, April 5, 1887. In a Portland case, Chinese sued after their leased building was condemned and destroyed; see Lee Tung v. Burkhart, 59 Or. 194, 116 P. 1066 (1911); Lee Tung v. Burkhart, case file no. 968 (1911), OSA/OSC.
27. "A Doomed Quarter," *Evening Herald* (San Jose), March 9, 1887.
28. "Chinatown Trouble," *Morning Times* (San Jose), April 21, 1887.
29. "An Excellent Site. A New City Hall in Place of Chinatown," *San Jose Herald*, February 11, 1887.
30. "Help Remove It," *Morning Times* (San Jose), April 12, 1887; "Should Be Cleaned," *Morning Times*, April 13, 1887.
31. "Reclaimed," *Morning Times* (San Jose), May 5, 1887; "Among the Ruins," *Morning Times*, May 6, 1887.
32. "Reclaimed," *Morning Times* (San Jose), May 6, 1887; Seiter et al., "Carving Chopsticks, Building Home."
33. "Here Is the Opportunity," *Evening Herald* (San Jose), May 5, 1887; "Looking to San Jose," *Evening Herald*, May 9, 1887.
34. "The Market Plaza," *San Jose Herald*, June 10, 1887; "Attacking Titles," *San Jose Herald*, April 20, 1887; "Chinatown Trouble," *Morning Times* (San Jose), April 21, 1887.
35. "City Affairs," *San Jose Mercury-News*, July 2, 1887.
36. Gandolfo v. Hartman, case file no. 199 (1890), Civil Law Case Files, 1887–1911, U.S. Circuit Court for the Southern District of California, RG21, box 35, folder 199, NARA/R; Ventura County Deeds, March 22, 1886, vol. 16, Ventura County Clerk-Recorder Office, Ventura, CA, 162–163; Jones-Correa, "The Origins and Diffusion."
37. Santa Clara Leases, June 14, 1884, Leases Book D, SCCA, 516–519.
38. "Celestial Exodus," *Ventura Signal*, February 14, 1885.
39. "Chinese Legislation," *Humboldt Times*, March 17, 1886.
40. Gandolfo v. Hartman, case file no. 199 (1890); Ventura County Deeds, March 22, 1886.
41. Gandolfo v. Hartman, 49 F. 181 (C. C. S. D. Cal. 1892).
42. Maureen E. Brady, "Turning Neighbors into Nuisances," *Harvard Law Review* 134, no. 5 (2021): 1611–1682; Jones-Correa, "The Origins and Diffusion."
43. Corrigan v. Buckley, 271 U.S. 323 (1926).
44. For example, see "Segregated Seattle," Seattle City Rights and Labor History Project, University of Washington, n.d., https://depts.washington.edu/civilr/segregated.htm. In the 1930s, redlining would become another powerful seg-

regationist tool. Richard Rothstein, *The Color of Law: A Forgotten History of How Our Government Segregated America* (Liveright, 2017).

45. "Heinlen's Grab," *San Jose Mercury-News*, June 22, 1887; "Removal of the Chinese," *San Jose Herald*, June 3, 1887; "Two Chinatowns," *San Jose Herald*, June 20, 1887.

46. "No Chinese," *San Jose Mercury-News*, June 23, 1887.

47. "Indignation," *San Jose Mercury-News*, June 11, 1887; "A Protest," *San Jose Herald*, June 9, 1887; "The Prevailing Topic," *San Jose Mercury-News*, June 24, 1887.

48. John Heinlen to Wing Chung Yuen et al., July 1887, Record Number 125, Book G, leases, 622, SCCA. Similar racial language is included in Truckee deeds for a "new Chinatown" in 1879; see Charles Crocker to E. J. Brickell et al., March 25, 1879, Deed Book 56, Nevada County Recorder's office, Nevada City, California, 252–253; Calvin Cheung-Miaw and Roland Hsu, "Before the 'Truckee Method': Race, Space, and Capital in Truckee's Chinese Community, 1870–1880," *Amerasia Journal* 45, no. 1 (2019): 68–85.

49. "Segregation," box 27, folder 1, HI/SRR.

50. "Segregation," box 27, folder 1, HI/SRR. A 1940 survey of Los Angeles found that 8 out of 10 housing districts were closed to "Orientals." Charles Kasreal Ferguson, "Political Problems and Activities of Oriental Residents in Los Angeles and Vicinity" (MA thesis, UCLA, 1938). On racial capitalism, see Cedric J. Robinson, *Black Marxism: The Making of the Black Radical Tradition* (University of North Carolina Press, 2005).

51. James A. Clayton to Harry B. Allen, March 1, 1927, in "Segregation," box 27, folder 1, HI/SRR.

52. Willard B. Farwell, *Chinese at Home and Abroad: Together with the Report of the Special Committee of the Board of Supervisors of San Francisco, on the Condition of the Chinese Quarter of the City* (A. L. Bancroft & Co., 1885), appendix 1, p. 58.

53. Tape v. Hurley, 66 Cal. 473 (1885). For an excellent study of the Tape family, see Mae Ngai, *The Lucky Ones: One Family and the Extraordinary Invention of Chinese America* (Houghton Mifflin Harcourt, 2010).

54. Act of March 24, 1866, California Laws [1865–1866], chap. 342, p. 398, as cited in Hudson Janisch, "The Chinese, the Courts, and the Constitution: A Study of the Legal Issues Raised by Chinese Immigration to the United States, 1850–1902" (JSD diss., University of Chicago, 1971), 151n3.

55. It appears there was one exception: the courts ordered a handful of Chinese "inmates" to live and study at the city industrial school for delinquent youths. Board of Supervisors, "San Francisco Municipal Reports for the Fiscal Year 1883–84" (W. A. Woodward, Alta Printing House, 1884), 96.

56. Ward v. Flood, 48 Cal. 49–52 (1874); Albert S. Broussard, *Black San Francisco: The Struggle for Racial Equality in the West, 1900–1954* (University Press of Kansas, 1993), 18–19.

57. Board of Supervisors, "San Francisco Municipal Reports for the Fiscal Year 1879–80" (W. M. Hinton, Printers, 1880), 655.

58. Joyce Kuo, "Excluded, Segregated and Forgotten: A Historical View of the Discrimination of Chinese Americans in Public Schools," *Asian American Law*

Journal 5, no. 1 (1998): 181–212, 194. On petitioning as political practice, see Daniel Carpenter, *Democracy by Petition: Popular Politics in Transformation, 1790–1870* (Harvard University Press, 2021).

59. "To the Honorable Senate and the Assembly of the State of California" (ca. 1878), Accession no. xfF870.C5C15, California Chinese Population, BL.
60. Act to Amend Section 1662 approved April 7, 1880, 23 sess., chap. 44, p. 38, "The Acts Amendatory of the Codes of California Passed at the Twenty-Third Session of the Legislature, 1880" (State Printing Office, 1880), 38; James D. Anderson, *The Education of Blacks in the South, 1860–1935* (University of North Carolina Press, 1988).
61. Act to Amend Section 1662, approved April 7, 1880.
62. Tape v. Hurley, case file no. 9916, WPA no. 18443 (1884) CSA/CSC.
63. Tape v. Hurley, case file no. 9916.
64. Tape v. Hurley, case file no. 9916. Later, in 1905, San Francisco would attempt to segregate Japanese schoolchildren, an action that set off an international incident and helped lead to the Gentleman's Agreement. Chris Suh, *The Allure of Empire: American Encounters with Asians in the Age of Transpacific Expansion and Exclusion* (Oxford University Press, 2023), 55–89.
65. Tape v. Hurley, case file no. 9916.
66. Tape v. Hurley, 66 Cal. 473 (1885).
67. Act of March 12, 1885, Ca. 27th sess., chap. 117, pp. 99–100.
68. "Chinese Mother's Letter," *Daily Alta California* (San Francisco), April 16, 1885.
69. Wong Him v. Callahan, 119 F. 381 (C.C.N.D. Cal. 1902).
70. Charles Wollenberg, *All Deliberate Speed: Segregation and Exclusion in California Schools, 1855–1975* (University of California Press, 1978).
71. Suh, *The Allure of Empire*, 55–89.
72. As quoted in Victor G. Nee and Brett De Bary Nee, *Longtime Californ': A Documentary Study of an American Chinatown* (Pantheon, 1973), 73, 78, 84. For casual mention of integrated classrooms in Placer County, see People v. Wong Tung, case file 4866 (1913), Superior Court, PC.
73. Nellie Chung interview, no. 8, folder 3, October 25, 1979, 6 no. 1979, UCLA/SC.
74. Wollenberg, *All Deliberate Speed*. In Oregon, the first and only known case of a segregated school was in Portland for Black children in 1867–1872. Ethan Johnson and Felicia Williams, "Desegregation, Multiculturalism and Portland Schools," *Oregon Historical Quarterly* 111, no. 1 (2010): 6–37.
75. Philippa Strum, *Mendez v. Westminster: School Desegregation and Mexican-American Rights* (University Press of Kansas, 2010); Rand Quinn, *Class Action: Desegregation and Diversity in San Francisco Schools* (University of Minnesota Press, 2020). The situation differed considerably in the South, where Black school segregation was more widespread, rigid, and enduring. In Gong Lum v. Rice, 275 U.S. 78 (1927), the Supreme Court endorsed the rejection of a Chinese child from a white school in Mississippi, as long as she was admitted into a "colored" school. School segregation for Chinese in the South also varied by locality. See Stephanie Hinnershitz, *A Different Shade of Justice: Asian American Civil Rights in the South* (University of North Carolina

Press, 2017); Robert Seto Quan in collaboration with Julian B. Roebuck, *Lotus Among the Magnolias: The Mississippi Chinese* (University Press of Mississippi, 1982); James W. Loewen, *The Mississippi Chinese: Between Black and White*, 2nd ed. (Waveland Press, 1988); Robert W. O'Brien, "Status of Chinese in the Mississippi Delta," *Social Forces* 19, no. 3 (1941): 386–390.

76. Ruby Tsang v. Reno Amusement Co., case file no. 12134 (1916), Second Judicial District Court, Washoe County; "Refused Seat in Theatre, Chinese Girl Sues," *Reno Gazette-Journal*, December 16, 1916.
77. "Ruby Tsang," *1900 United States Federal Census*, ANC.
78. "Ruby Tsang," in *1910 United States Federal Census*, ANC.
79. "Little Chinese Musicians," *New York Tribune*, February 21, 1909; "Eight Little Chinese Visitors to Buffalo," *Buffalo Times*, December 5, 1908; "Chinese Children," *Colton Daily Courier* (Colton, California), March 19, 1909; "Little Chinese at White House," *New York Tribune*, November 6, 1908.
80. "Becoming Americanized; Second Chinese Woman in America to Get Divorce," *Topeka State Journal*, February 3, 1910; "Oriental Public School," *San Francisco Call*, December 21, 1912.
81. "Chinese Ejected from Reno Theater; Bring Heavy Damage Suit," *Honolulu Star-Bulletin*, January 2, 1917; "Race Question Raised in Reno," *Sacramento Daily Union*, December 18, 1916.
82. A. K. Sandoval-Strausz, "Travelers, Strangers, and Jim Crow: Law, Public Accommodations, and Civil Rights in America," *Law and History Review* 23, no. 1 (2005): 53–94.
83. Ruby Tsang v. Reno Amusement Co., case file no. 12134 (1916); "Refused Seat in Theatre."
84. Sandoval-Strausz, "Travelers, Strangers, and Jim Crow."
85. *Session Laws of the State of Washington Enacted by the First State Legislature, Session of 1889–90* (O. C. White, State Printer, 1890), 524.
86. "Charlie Lui Life History," box 27, folder 189, HI/SRR; "Life History and Social Document of S. C. Eng," box 29, folder 21, HI/SRR.
87. "Clarence R. Anderson," *Cayton's Weekly* (Seattle), September 29, 1917; *Cayton's Weekly*, December 1, 1917; "Purely Personal," *Cayton's Weekly*, May 22, 1920; *Cayton's Weekly*, September 29, 1917.
88. Sarah Gonzalez, "One Theater, Many Names," February 2, 2017, https://sites.uw.edu/gonzalsa/2017/02/02/one-theater-many-names/.
89. Nicholas Deshais, "How One Spokane Couple Desegregated the Pantages Chain of Vaudeville Theaters," *Spokesman-Review* (Spokane), August 18, 2019.
90. Kate Masur, *Until Justice Be Done: America's First Civil Rights Movement, from the Revolution to Reconstruction* (W. W. Norton, 2021), 327–341.
91. Anderson v. Pantages Theatre Co., 194 P. 813 (Wash. 1921).
92. Errol Jones, A Minor, Etc., Respondent, V. Oliver Kehrlein, Jr., et al., 49 Cal. App. 646 (Cal. Ct. App. 1920).
93. Joseph C. Rhine and Stanley A. Zimmerman, "The Unruh Civil Rights Act as Applied to Real Estate Brokers," *Hastings Law Journal* 13, no. 120 (1961): 120–140; Ronald P. Klein, "The California Equal Rights Statutes in Practice," *Stanford Law Review* 10, no. 2 (1958): 253–273.

94. Rhine and Zimmerman, "The Unruh Civil Rights Act"; Klein, "California Equal Rights Statutes."
95. Nai-Ming Ginn, interview no. 69, folder 8, n.d., UCLA/SC.
96. Lansing Lee, interview no. 118, folder 20, October 27, 1980, UCLA/SC.
97. "Lew Kay Life History," box 27, folder 19, HI/SRR. On the effect of socioeconomic status on Chinese segregation, see Marcus and Chen, "Inside and Outside Chinatown."
98. "Life History of Hung Kei Lui," box 32, folder 11, HI/SRR; Look Ting Tom, interview no. 57, folder 6, May 22, 1979, UCLA/SC; Kit Quan, interview no. 88 f. 14, March 8, 1980, UCLA/SC; James W. Fing, interview no. 45 f. 5, August 30, 1979, UCLA/SC. For Black and Asian segregation in a Pasadena public pool, see Hudson, *West of Jim Crow*, 208–242.
99. "Life History of Chin Cheung," box 27, folder 187, HI/SRR.

Chapter 6. The "Predator" and the Problem of Interracial Intimacy

1. May's legal name was Engelina and Hattie's was Hallie. 1900 US Census, Placer County, California, population schedule, Township 9, E.D. 64, roll 96, page 2A, ANC. People v. Ah Lung, case file no. 3507 (Placer County Dist. Ct., 1905), PCC, 7, 12; Loomis Basin Historical Society, *Images of America: Loomis* (Arcadia, 2009), 7, 15.
2. "Mortgage of Ah Dick," folder Placer Co., Chinese Chattel Mortgages, box 3, Sucheng Chan Papers, Immigration History Research Center Archives, University of Minnesota.
3. Vivian A. Zelizer, *Pricing the Priceless Child: The Changing Social Value of Children* (Princeton University Press, 1985), 77; Linda Gordon, *Pitied but Not Entitled: Single Mothers and the History of Welfare 1890–1935* (Harvard University Press, 1994), 24. For examples of Chinese employing or managing whites, see Sucheng Chan, *This Bittersweet Soil: The Chinese in California Agriculture, 1860–1910* (University of California Press, 1989), 364; Lisa See, *On Gold Mountain* (Penguin Random House, 1995), 47–58; Richard Steven Street, *Beasts of the Field: A Narrative History of California Farm Workers, 1769–1913* (Stanford University Press, 2004), 353.
4. Neil R. McMillen, *Dark Journey: Black Mississippians in the Age of Jim Crow* (University of Illinois Press, 1990), 24–28; J. Williams Harris, "Etiquette, Lynching and Racial Boundaries in Southern History: A Mississippi Example," *American Historical Review* 100, no. 2 (1995): 387–410, at 390–392; Albert Camarillo, "Navigating Segregated Life in America's Racial Borderhoods, 1910s–1950s," *Journal of American History* 100, no. 3 (2013): 645–652, at 649–650.
5. This chapter was first published in 2017. In that version, I placed more emphasis on what was unknown about the terms of Chinese inclusion. Here, I have updated the essay and answered some of my own questions. Beth Lew-Williams, "'Chinamen' and 'Delinquent Girls': Intimacy, Exclusion and a Search for California's Color Line," *Journal of American History* 104, no. 5 (2017): 632–655. "A Case Where Hanging Would Be Too Good," *Placer Her-*

ald (Auburn, CA), December 17, 1904; "Superior Court," *Placer Herald*, March 11, 1905; 1910 US Census, San Francisco Assembly District 32, San Francisco, California, population schedule, E.D. 38, roll T624–96, p. 2A, ANC.

6. For example, see Rachel F. Moran, "Love with a Proper Stranger: What Anti-Miscegenation Laws Can Tell Us About the Meaning of Race, Sex and Marriage," *Hofstra Law Review* 32, no. 4 (2004): 1663–1679, 1667; Sucheng Chan, *Asian Americans: An Interpretive History* (Twayne, 1991), 57; Charlotte Brooks, *Alien Neighbors, Foreign Friends: Asian Americans, Housing, and the Transformation of Urban California* (University of Chicago Press, 2009), 23; Nayan Shah, *Contagious Divides: Epidemics and Race in San Francisco's Chinatown* (University of California Press, 2001), 76; Peggy Pascoe, *What Comes Naturally: Miscegenation Law and the Making of Race in America* (Oxford University Press, 2009), 79–93.

7. On "toleration," see Martha Hodes, *White Women, Black Men: Illicit Sex in the 19th-Century South* (Yale University Press, 1997), 3; D. Michael Bottoms, *An Aristocracy of Color: Race and Reconstruction in California and the West* (University of Oklahoma Press, 2013), 19–38.

8. Daniel T. Rodgers, "In Search of Progressivism," *Reviews in American History* 10, no. 4 (1982): 113–132; Thomas C. Leonard, *Illiberal Reformers: Race, Eugenics, and American Economics in the Progressive Era* (Princeton University Press, 2016); Ann Laura Stoler, *Haunted by Empire: Geographies of Intimacy in North American History* (Duke University Press, 2006), 15; Ian F. Haney-López, "The Social Construction of Race: Some Observations on Illusion, Fabrication, and Choice," *Harvard Civil Rights–Civil Liberties Law Review* 29, no. 1 (1993): 7; Michael Omi and Howard Winant, *Racial Formation in the United States* (Routledge, 1994).

9. Lawrence Stone, "The Revival of Narrative: Reflections on a New Old History," *Past and Present* 85 (November 1979): 3–24. For policing of urban female delinquency, see Catherine Cocks, "Rethinking Sexuality in the Progressive Era," *Journal of the Gilded Age and Progressive Era* 5, no. 2 (2006): 93–118, at 110–111; Ruth M. Alexander, *The "Girl Problem": Female Sexual Delinquency in New York, 1900–1930* (Cornell University Press, 1995), 35; Gordon, *Pitied but Not Entitled*, 35; Zelizer, *Pricing the Priceless Child*, 77.

10. Karen Leong, "'A Distinct and Antagonistic Race': Constructions of Chinese Manhood in the Exclusion Debates, 1869–1878," in *Across the Great Divide: Cultures of Manhood in the American West*, ed. Matthew Basso, Laura McCall, and Dee Garceau (Routledge, 2001); Martha Mabie Gardner, "Working on White Womanhood: White Working Women in the San Francisco Anti-Chinese Movement, 1877–1890," *Journal of Social History* 33, no. 1 (1999): 73–95, at 83–84.

11. Maggie Bruck and Stephen J. Ceci, "The Suggestibility of Children's Memory," *Annual Review of Psychology* 50, no. 1 (1999): 419–439; Judith Herman, *Trauma and Recovery: The Aftermath of Violence—From Domestic Abuse to Political Terror* (Basic Books, 1992).

12. Emma Woo Louie, *Chinese American Names: Tradition and Transition* (McFarland, 1998).

13. Chan, *This Bittersweet Soil*, 80–81, 258–259; "Biographical Sketch of Prisoners Eligible to Parole," Ah Lung, Corrections case file no. 21440 (1905), San Quentin State Prison Records, CSA.
14. For similar practices in Santa Clara County, see Cecilia Tsu, *Garden of the World: Asian Immigrants and the Making of Agriculture in California's Santa Clara Valley* (Oxford University Press, 2013), 40; "Letter from Loomis," *Placer Herald* (Auburn, CA), February 13, 1886; 1900 US Census, Placer County, California, population schedule, Township 9, E.D. 64, roll 96, p. 2A, ANC.
15. Allison Brownell Tirres, "Ownership Without Citizenship: The Creation of Noncitizen Property Rights," *Michigan Journal of Race and Law* 19, no. 1 (2013): 1–52.
16. Early examples include the 1857 Oregon constitution and an 1879 Nevada law that allowed all nonresident aliens "except subjects of the Chinese empire" the right to hold real property or land. On alien land laws, see Mark L. Lazarus II, "An Historical Analysis of Alien Land Law: Washington Territory & State 1853–1889," *University of Puget Sound Law Review* 12, no. 2 (1989): 197–246; Bruce A. Castleman, "California's Alien Land Laws," *Western Legal History: Journal of the Ninth Judicial Circuit Historical Society* 7, no. 1 (1994): 25–68; Masao Suzuki, "Important or Impotent? Taking Another Look at the 1920 California Alien Land Law," *Journal of Economic History* 64, no. 1 (2004): 125–143; Eiichiro Azuma, "Japanese Immigrant Farmers and California Alien Land Laws: A Study of the Walnut Grove Japanese Community," *California History* 73, no. 1 (1994): 14–29; Polly J. Price, "Alien Land Restrictions in the American Common Law: Exploring the Relative Autonomy Paradigm," *American Journal of Legal History* 43, no. 2 (1999): 152–208; Mary Szto, "From Exclusion to Exclusivity: Chinese American Property Ownership and Discrimination in Historical Perspective," *Journal of Transnational Law and Policy* 25 (2015–2016): 33–99.
17. Brooks, *Alien Neighbors, Foreign Friends*, 3, 58. Many Japanese and Chinese believed the law meant they could not own residential property, and realtors used this perception to dissuade Asian buyers. Although this broad interpretation was never tested in court, California's attorney general appeared to endorse it. Keith Aoki, "No Right to Own: The Early Twentieth-Century 'Alien Land Laws' as a Prelude to Internment," *Boston College Third World Law Journal* 19, no. 1 (2022), 37–72; Eliot Grinnell Mears, *Resident Orientals on the American Pacific Coast* (University of Chicago Press, 1928), 169, 179, 187, 201.
18. Gabriel J. Chin, "A Nation of White Immigrants: State and Federal Racial Preferences for White Noncitizens," *Boston University Law Review* 100, no. 1271 (2020): 1294–1295.
19. Tsu suggests that many of these white women were widows or fatherless adult daughters. Tsu, *Garden of the World*, 31–46.
20. 1900 US Census, Placer County, California, population schedule; Sucheng Chan found that Chinese made up 26.2 percent of farm laborers in Placer County; 8.2 percent were identified as Japanese, 54.4 percent were American, 11.1 percent were European immigrants, 0.1 percent were Mexican. Chan, *This Bittersweet Soil*, 81, 231, 263, 314, 404. See also "Chinese Farmers in

the Sacramento-San Joaquin Delta, California," boxes 2–3, Sucheng Chan Papers.
21. People v. Ah Lung case file; Andrew Urban, *Brokering Servitude: Migration and the Politics of Domestic Labor During the Long Nineteenth Century* (NYU Press, 2017); Henry Yu, "Mixing Bodies and Cultures: The Meaning of America's Fascination with Sex Between 'Orientals' and 'Whites,'" in *Sex, Race, Love: Crossing Boundaries in North American History*, ed. Martha Hodes (NYU Press, 1999), 44–63.
22. Stuart Creighton Miller, *Unwelcome Immigrant: American Image of the Chinese, 1785–1882* (University of California Press, 1969), 185; "Chinese Servants: Full Particulars of What a Chinese Servant Did to Pretty Lillie Leslie and How He Was Caught" (San Francisco, n.d. [circa 1880s]), 1, BL.
23. "Chinese Servants," 2, 4–5.
24. Robert Lee, *Orientals: Asian Americans in Popular Culture* (Temple University Press, 1999), 85; Susan Johnson, *Roaring Camp: The Social World of the California Gold Rush* (W. W. Norton, 2000), 245; Shah, *Contagious Divides*, 77–90; Nayan Shah, "Between 'Oriental Depravity' and 'Natural Degenerates': Spatial Borderlands and the Making of Ordinary Americans," *American Quarterly* 57, no. 3 (2005): 703–725, at 719–720; Victor Jew, "'Chinese Demons': The Violent Articulation of Chinese Otherness and Interracial Sexuality in the U.S. Midwest, 1885–1889," *Journal of Social History* 37, no. 2 (2003): 389–410; Viet Thanh Nguyen, "The Remasculinization of Chinese America: Race, Violence, and the Novel," *American Literary History* 12, no. 1-2 (2000): 130–157, at 133; Peggy Pascoe, *Relations of Rescue: The Search for Female Moral Authority in the American West* (Oxford University Press, 1990), 121; Najia Aarim-Heriot, *Chinese Immigrants, African Americans and Racial Anxiety* (University of Illinois Press, 2003), 74, 136; Tomás Almaguer, *Racial Fault Lines: The Historical Origins of White Supremacy in California* (University of California Press, 1994), 160–162; Leti Volpp, "American Mestizo: Filipinos and Anti-Miscegenation Laws in California," *UC Davis Law Review* 33, no. 795 (Summer 2000): 795–835, 798, 809–810; "Chinese Servants," 1–3.
25. For the sexual predator stereotype in exclusion propaganda, see Workingmen's Party of California, *The Labor Agitators, or the Battle for Bread* (Geo. W. Green, 1879), 25; Samuel Gompers and Herman Gutstadt, *Meat vs. Rice. American Manhood Against Asiatic Coolieism; Which Shall Survive?* (Asiatic Exclusion League, 1908), 18–19, 25–26; Emma Jihuan Teng, *Eurasian: Mixed Identities in the United States, China, and Hong Kong, 1842–1943* (University of California Press, 2013), 35–46; Miller, *Unwelcome Immigrant*, 183–189; Krystyn R. Moon, *Yellow Face: Creating the Chinese in American Popular Music and Performance, 1850s–1920s* (Rutgers University Press, 2005), 30–56; Karen Leong, "'A Distinct and Antagonistic Race'"; Gardner, "Working on White Womanhood," 80.
26. People v. Ah Lung case file, 13, 32.
27. People v. Ah Lung case file, 9, 23, 27–28.
28. People v. Ah Lung case file, 37.
29. People v. Ah Lung case file, 33, 56; Vivian Rasmussen, *Yesteryear: Loomis and the Surrounding Area*, vol. 1 (Rasmussen, 1994), 44. For cases of Chinese

giving children food or gifts, see Chan, *Bittersweet Soil*, 361–363; People v. Ah Soon, case file no. 5572 (Sacramento County Sup. Ct., 1915), Sacramento County Court Records, CSH. Comparative racial regimes rarely made exceptions based on class and age; see Ann Laura Stoler, *Carnal Knowledge and Imperial Power: Race and the Intimate in Colonial Rule* (University of California Press, 2002), 74; Jennifer Lynn Ritterhouse, *Growing Up Jim Crow: How Black and White Southern Children Learned Race* (University of North Carolina Press, 2006), 201; Estelle Freedman, *Redefining Rape: Sexual Violence in the Era of Suffrage and Segregation* (Harvard University Press, 2013), 90. On Progressive Era regulation of working-class adolescent females, see Alexander, *The "Girl Problem,"* 33–66; Mary Ting Yi Lui, *The Chinatown Trunk Mystery: Murder, Miscegenation, and Other Dangerous Encounters in Turn-of-the-Century New York* (Princeton University Press, 2007), 92; Michael A. Rembis, *Defining Deviance: Sex, Science, and Delinquent Girls, 1890–1960* (University of Illinois Press, 2011), 35–41.

30. Pascoe, *What Comes Naturally*; Heather Miyano Kopelson, *Faithful Bodies: Performing Religion and Race in the Puritan Atlantic* (NYU Press, 2014).

31. In 1935 Maryland banned "Malays" but not Chinese or Mongolians. Deeneshi Sohoni, "Unsuitable Suitors: Anti-Miscegenation Laws, Naturalization Laws, and the Construction of Asian Identities," *Law and Society Review* 41, no. 3 (2007): 587–618; Pascoe, *What Comes Naturally*, 79–93. California statute prohibited the issuance of marriage licenses authorizing a marriage of "a white person with a negro, mulatto, or Mongolian." Cal. Stats., 1880 Code Amendments, chap. 41, sec. 1, 3. Hrishi Karthikeyan and Gabriel J. Chin, "Preserving Racial Identity: Population Patterns and the Application of Anti-Miscegenation Statutes to Asian Americans, 1910–1950," *Asian American Law Journal* 9, no. 1 (January 2002): 1–40. Racial hierarchies were created not only through the sexual exclusion of Chinese men, but also through white men's access to Chinese women through prostitution.

32. People v. Ah Lung case file, 22; Rodger Daniels, *Asian America: Chinese and Japanese in the United States Since 1850* (University of Washington Press, 1988), 97; 1900 US Census, Placer County, California, population schedule. National estimate based on 5 percent sample of the 1900 census; Steven Ruggles, Katie Genadek, Ronald Goeken, Josiah Grover, and Matthew Sobek, Integrated Public Use Microdata Series, Version 6.0 (machine-readable database), University of Minnesota, 2015. Defendants sometimes appealed on the basis of language proficiency; see Territory v. Ah Lim, case file no. KNG-6479 (1889), King County, WA/PS.

33. People v. Ah Lung case file, 44; John M. Fulweiler to W. D. Sturtevant, October 19, 1909, Ah Lung, Corrections case file no. 21440.

34. People v. Ah Woon, case file no. 3508.

35. Mary E. Odem, *Delinquent Daughters: Protecting and Policing Adolescent Female Sexuality in the United States, 1885–1920* (University of North Carolina Press, 1995), 8–9; People v. Ah Woon case file.

36. People v. Ah Woon case file; Megumi Dick Osumi, "Asians and California's Anti-Miscegenation Laws," in *Asian and Pacific American Experiences: Women's Perspectives*, ed. John Nabuya Tsuchida (University of Minnesota

Press, 1982), 1-37; "Refuses to Issue Marriage License," *San Francisco Call*, January 13, 1905; Eunhye Kwon, "Interracial Marriages Among Asian Americans in the U.S. West, 1880-1954," (PhD diss., University of Florida, 2011), 122-126. Newspaper reports reveal uneven enforcement: for approved licenses, see "An Anglo-Chinese Wedding," *Daily Alta California* (San Francisco), December 23, 1888; "Will Marry Miss Ah Fong," *San Francisco Call*, September 18, 1893; for denied licenses, see "Love's Young Dream," *San Francisco Call*, October 21, 1891; for an out-of-state wedding, see "Chinese Weds a White Woman," *San Francisco Call*, February 26, 1901.

37. People v. Ah Woon case file.
38. Lui, *Chinatown Trunk Mystery*, 68-70; "Dragged Girls to Ruin," *Sacramento Daily Union*, August 19, 1896, and June 7, 1896. For anti-cohabitation laws regulating white/Black relationships, see Pascoe, *What Comes Naturally*, 252-253; People v. Ah Woon case file; John E. B. Meyers, *Child Protection in America: Past, Present, and Future* (Oxford University Press, 2006), 45-46.
39. Shah, *Contagious Divides*, 6; "Petition," December 16, 1904, People of the State of California vs. Hattie Lucas and May Lucas, Dependent Children, case file no. 3499 (1905), Placer County District Court, PCC.
40. It is possible that some sexual assault accusations arose from white prostitution. For a description of an offer of payment during an alleged assault, see Territory v. Hip (a Chinaman), case file no. PRC-1301 (1884), WA/PS.
41. People v. Ah Lung case file, 38; Untitled Examination of Daniel Healy, circa 1905, People v. Ah Lung case file, 1-2; Gardner, "Working on White Womanhood," 83-84; People v. Ah Woon case file.
42. "Watsonville Cupid Erred," *Madera Tribune*, August 22, 1928.
43. Stoler, *Haunted by Empire*, 13-15. Harris, "Etiquette, Lynching, and Racial Boundaries," 391.
44. People v. Ah Lung case file; People v. Ah Woon case file.
45. People v. Ah Lung case file.
46. Odem, *Delinquent Daughters*, 65, 76-77.
47. People v. Ah Yek, case file no. 820 (1866), CSA/CSC; People v. Ah Yek, 29 Cal. 575 (1866).
48. John M. Fulweiler to W. D. Sturtevant, October 19, 1909, Ah Woon, Corrections case file no. 21094; Bonni Kay Cermak, "In the Interest of Justice: Legal Narratives of Sex, Gender, Race and Rape in Twentieth Century Los Angeles, 1920-1960" (PhD diss., University of Oregon, 2005), 47-49, 53-54; Hal Goldman, "'A Most Detestable Crime': Character, Consent and Corroboration in Vermont's Rape Law, 1850-1920," in *Sex Without Consent: Race and Sexual Coercion in America*, ed. Merril D. Smith (NYU Press, 2001), 178-203. See also Pablo Mitchell, *Coyote Nation: Sexuality, Race, and Conquest in Modernizing New Mexico, 1880-1920* (University of Chicago Press, 2005), 52-80.
49. People v. Ah Lung case file, 3, 12. See also People v. Ah Soon, case file no. 5572 (1915), Sacramento County, CSA/CSC.
50. Jacob A. Riis, *How the Other Half Lives: Studies Among the Tenements of New York* (Charles Scribner's Sons, 1890), 96-99; Jew, "'Chinese Demons,'" 389-390, 405. "Defendant's Proposed Bill of Exceptions and Statement on Motion for New Trial," January 18, 1905, People v. Ah Lung case file, 5; Lui,

Chinatown Trunk Mystery, 68–69. For other sexual assault cases that involve Chinese spaces, see "A Lecherous Chinee," *Los Angeles Times*, November 11, 1895; "Lee Gun Had to Leave," *New York Times*, January 13, 1888; People v. Sing (A Chinaman), case file no. 1243 (1905), CSA/CSC; "A White Girl Gave Accusation Against Her Chinese Employer," *San Francisco Chronicle*, September 10, 1887.

51. Beth Lew-Williams, *The Chinese Must Go: Violence, Exclusion, and the Making of the Alien in America* (Harvard University Press, 2018); James Paddison, *American Heathens: Religion, Race and Reconstruction in California* (University of California Press, 2012), 1; Moon Ho-Jung, *Coolies and Cane: Race, Labor and Sugar in the Age of Emancipation* (Johns Hopkins University Press, 2006), 4–38. [Untitled], *San Francisco Call*, September 10, 1887; "Lee Gun Had to Leave," *New York Times*, January 13, 1888; "At the Courthouse," *Los Angeles Times*, July 3, 1894; "Charged with Rape," *Los Angeles Times*, July 15, 1894; "Ah Sam Said to Be an Old Offender and Insulter of Women," *Los Angeles Times*, September 30, 1895; "Police Record," *Los Angeles Times*, July 23, 1899; Lui, *Chinatown Trunk Mystery*, 68–70; Jew, "'Chinese Demons,'" 389–410; People v. Fong Chung, 5. Cal. 587 (1907), 101–102; People v. Sing (A Chinaman), case file no. 1243 (1905). For a parallel pattern in cultural representations, see Lee, *Orientals*, 113–136.

52. A. K. Robinson to W. D. Sturtevant, August 16, 1909, Ah Lung, Corrections case file no. 21440.

53. Lui, *Chinatown Trunk Mystery*, 176–180; "Ah Sam Jumps His Bond and Goes in Hiding," *Los Angeles Times*, October 9, 1895; "Police Record," *Los Angeles Times*, July 23, 1899. See also "A Case Where Hanging Would Be Too Good," *Placer Herald* (Auburn, CA), December 17, 1904; "A White Girl's Grave Accusation Against Her Chinese Employer," *San Francisco Chronicle*, September 10, 1887.

54. "Exceptions Taken by Defendant on Trial," circa 1905, People v. Ah Lung case file, 11.

55. Third Appellate District Finding, Ah Lung, Corrections case file no. 21440 (1905).

56. The Qing dynasty, and the practice of wearing a queue, ended in 1912. Ah Woon Corrections case file no. 21094 (1905).

57. Stewart E. Tolnay and E. M. Beck, *A Festival of Violence: An Analysis of Southern Lynchings, 1882–1930* (University of Illinois Press, 1995), 48–50, 269; Freedman, *Redefining Rape*, 220–239; Lisa Lindquist Dorr, *White Women, Rape and the Power of Race in Virginia, 1900–1960* (University of North Carolina Press, 2004); Hodes, *White Women, Black Men*, 176–208; Christopher Walden, *The Many Faces of Judge Lynch: Extralegal Violence and Punishment in America* (Palgrave Macmillan, 2002), 90, 105–106; Diane Miller Sommerville, *Rape and Race in the Nineteenth-Century South* (University of North Carolina Press, 2004), 223–257. Although Black-on-white rape was often cited as the motivation of lynching campaigns, Ida B. Wells noted that more lynchings of African Americans arose from other criminal accusations. Ida B. Wells, *Crusade for Justice: The Autobiography of Ida B. Wells*, ed. Alfreda M. Duster (University of Chicago Press, 1970), 47–52. Accusations

against Chinese could also elicit vigilantism; see Jew, "'Chinese Demons'"; People v. Hong Di (Ho Ah Heung), case file no. 1126 (1887), CCS.
58. Many accusations against Chinese men were dismissed. See People v. Ah Fook, case file no. 18300 (1900), Sacramento County, CSH; People v. Tom Hung, case file no. 1891 (1899), Sacramento County, CSH; People v. Fong Chung, 5 Cal. 587 (1907); People v. Ah Lean, 7 Cal. 626 (1908); Yee Chung, no. 1282 (1892), Alameda County Register of Actions, vol. 3, 298, ACC. "No Case," *Los Angeles Times*, July 19, 1894; "Assaulted a Child," *Los Angeles Times*, July 3, 1894; "Charged with Rape," *Los Angeles Times*, July 15, 1894; "Two White Men and a Chinaman Arrested on Suspicion as the Perpetrators," *Los Angeles Times*, June 14, 1895; "One Indictment Found Against Charlie Sui," *Los Angeles Times*, December 19, 1896; "Charley Sui Held to Answer in Superior Court," *Los Angeles Times*, January 10, 1897; "New Information," *Los Angeles Times*, December 31, 1895.
59. Freedman, *Redefining Rape*, 91–92, 101–103.
60. For images of the hypersexual Black man, see Winthrop Jordan, *White over Black: American Attitudes Toward the Negro, 1550–1812* (University of North Carolina Press, 1995), 35–38; Sommerville, *Rape and Race*, 223–257. On the racial uncertainty of the Chinese, see Gordon H. Chang, *Fateful Ties: A History of America's Preoccupation with China* (Harvard University Press, 2015), 79–84.
61. Leong, "'A Distinct and Antagonistic Race'"; Gardner, "Working on White Womanhood," 83–84. On transcalar analysis, see Lew-Williams, *The Chinese Must Go*, 10–12.

Chapter 7. The "Immigrant" and the Meaning of Chinese Exclusion

1. Carol Green Wilson, *Chinatown Quest: The Life Adventures of Donaldina Cameron* (Stanford University Press, 1931), 76; Yick Yook Lan case file no. 15597/19-26, box 1087, Immigration Services San Francisco, RG 85, NARA/SB; John A. Robinson papers pertaining to the U.S. Immigration Service, San Francisco, Calif., 1906–1936 (MS 1816), CHS (hereafter cited as Robinson Papers).
2. Wilson, *Chinatown Quest*, 76–77. Yick Yook Lan case file no. 15597/19-26. Her name appears in various transliterations, including Yick Yok Lan, Yick Yook Lan, Yuk Yuk Lan, Yick Yick Lan, and Yik Yoke Long.
3. Finding Guide to the John A. Robinson Papers, CHS; John Andrew Robinson, Personnel File no. 53000-117, box 1068, Justice Department, National Personnel Records Center, St. Louis.
4. I use her proper name and her father's proper name in order to distinguish them.
5. "Two Chinatowns," *San Jose Herald*, June 20, 1887.
6. Robert Caldwell, M.D., and Geo. W. Seifert, Affidavit, March 31, 1901, Yick Yook Lan case file.
7. Adam McKeown, "Ritualization of Regulation: The Enforcement of Chinese Exclusion in the United States and China," *American Historical Review* 108, no. 2 (2003): 377–403, at 396; Kitty Calavita, "The Paradoxes of Race, Class, Identity and 'Passing': Enforcing the Chinese Exclusion Acts, 1882–1910," *Law*

and *Social Inquiry* 25, no. 1 (2000): 1–40; Anna Pegler-Gordon, "Chinese Exclusion, Photography, and the Development of U.S. Immigration Policy," *American Quarterly* 58, no. 1 (2006): 51–77; Erika Lee, *At America's Gates: Chinese Immigration During the Exclusion Era, 1882–1943* (University of North Carolina Press, 2005), 9–11.

8. Ching Chao Wu, "Chinatown: A Study of Symbiosis and Assimilation" (PhD diss., University of Chicago, 1940), 96; Calavita, "The Paradoxes."
9. Yick Yook Lan, List or Manifest of Alien Passengers for the United States Immigration Officer at Port of Arrival, Arriving at Port of San Francisco, Cal., September 30, 1916, in *San Francisco, California, U.S., Chinese Arriving Passenger Arrivals and Disposition, 1903–1947*, ANC; Madeline Y. Hsu, *Dreaming of Gold, Dreaming of Home: Transnationalism and Migration Between the United States and South China, 1882–1943* (Stanford University Press, 2000).
10. Yick Yook Lan, List or Manifest of Alien Passengers, September 30, 1916; William Theiss to Commissioner of Immigration, October 11, 1916, In re: No. 15597/19–26, Yick Yook Lan case file.
11. Erika Lee and Judy Yung, *Angel Island: Immigrant Gateway to America* (Oxford University Press, 2010), 77.
12. Judy Yung, *Unbound Feet: A Social History of Chinese Women in San Francisco* (University of California Press, 1995); Lee, *At America's Gates*; Statement of Applicant, October 5, 1916, Yick Yook Lan case file.
13. William Theiss to Commissioner of Immigration, October 11, 1916.
14. As cited by Lee and Yung, *Angel Island*, 101, 104; Him Mark Lai, Genny Lim, and Judy Yung, eds., *Island: Poetry and History of Chinese Immigrants on Angel Island, 1910–1940*, 2nd ed. (University of Washington Press, 2014).
15. Pegler-Gordon, "Chinese Exclusion," 51–77; Chas. W. Pierce, Memorandum for the Commissioner, In re: Yick Yook Lan, native, October 24, 1916, Yick Yook Lan case file.
16. Lee, *At America's Gates*, 12.
17. As quoted by McKeown, "Ritualization of Regulation," 400; Lee and Yung, *Angel Island*, 93.
18. Beth Lew-Williams, *The Chinese Must Go: Violence, Exclusion, and the Making of the Alien in America* (Harvard University Press, 2018), 197–209; Paul A. Kramer, "Imperial Openings: Civilization, Exemption, and the Geopolitics of Mobility in the History of Chinese Exclusion, 1868–1910," *Journal of the Gilded Age and Progressive Era* 14, no. 3 (2015): 317–347, at 322; McKeown, "Ritualization of Regulation," 377–403.
19. McKeown, "Ritualization of Regulation," 402.
20. Yick Yook Lan case file.
21. "Efficiency Report," January 25, 1909, May 15, 1910, John Andrew Robinson, Personnel File no. 53000-117.
22. John A. Robinson, Notebook, April 5, 1909, vol. 1, Robinson Papers.
23. Lorelei Lee, "The Roots of 'Modern Day Slavery': The Page Act and the Mann Act," *Columbia Human Rights Law Review* 52, no. 3 (2021): 1199–1239.
24. Robinson, Notebook, May 1, 1909, vol. 1, Robinson Papers; see also Notebook, October 1, 1914, vol. 5; Notebook, October 7, 1914, vol. 5; Notebook, March 2, 1917, vol. 5.

25. Robinson, Notebooks, vols. 1–5, Robinson Papers.
26. Chy Lung v. Freeman, 92 U.S. 275 (1875); Briana Nofil, *The Migrant's Jail: An American History of Mass Incarceration* (Princeton University Press, 2024), 13–18; Ana Raquel Minian, *In the Shadow of Liberty: The Invisible History of Immigrant Detention in the United States* (Viking, 2024), 18.
27. Fong Yue Ting v. United States, 149 U.S. 698 (1893).
28. On the concept of extra-constitutional absolute or "plenary power" over immigration matters, see Natsu Taylor Saito, "The Enduring Effect of the Chinese Exclusion Cases: The Plenary Power Justification for On-Going Abuses of Human Rights," *Asian Law Journal* 10, no. 13 (2003): 13–36.
29. "Twenty Two Chinese Women," *Sacramento Daily Union*, September 5, 1874; "San Francisco," *Los Angeles Times*, September 1, 1874.
30. Minian, *In the Shadow of Liberty*, 78–81. Therefore, local jails, mission homes, and ships (not federal penitentiaries) were the western birthplace of immigration incarceration. This is in contrast with Elliott Young, *Forever Prisoners: How the United States Made the World's Largest Detention System* (Oxford University Press, 2021), 23–34.
31. Lew-Williams, *The Chinese Must Go*, 53–88, 197–199. Elliott Young, "Caging Immigrants at McNeil Island Federal Prison, 1880–1940," *Pacific Historical Review* 88, no. 1 (2019): 48–85; Elliott Young, *Forever Prisoners*, 23–24.
32. Alameda Jail Register Index, January 1892–May 1893, and January 1907–April 1909, ACS.
33. Nofil, *The Migrant's Jail*, 16–33, 39, 55.
34. Punctuation added for clarity. Robinson, Notebooks, February 17, 1917, vol. 1, Robinson Papers.
35. Later deportation files did not survive government culling in the 1960s. Of more than 35,000 previously existing files, now only 846 remain, and these are from later decades. National Archives at San Francisco, RG 85, *Immigration and Naturalization Service Inventory*, 25. On deportation and voluntary exit, see Adam Goodman, *The Deportation Machine: America's Long History of Expelling Immigrants* (Princeton University Press, 2021).
36. Emma Teng, "Chinese Elites and U.S. Gatekeeping: Racial Discrimination and Class Privilege in Boston's 1905 King Incident," *Modern American History* 4, no. 1 (2021): 1–24; Brianna Nofil, "Policing, Profits, and the Rise of Immigration Detention in New York's 'Chinese Jails,'" *Law and History Review* 39, no. 4 (2021): 649–677. Robinson focused his work on prostitution, but surviving records from other Chinese inspectors suggest that Chinese men were targeted for narcotics violations. See, for example, Chin Chung Jew (alias Sam Kee, Portland file 1017/75), NARA/S.
37. *Annual Report of the Commissioner-General of Immigration* (Government Printing Office, 1906), 90.
38. Julia Flynn Siler, *The White Devil's Daughters: The Women Who Fought Slavery in San Francisco's Chinatown* (Knopf Doubleday, 2019); Peggy Pascoe, *Relations of Rescue: The Search for Female Moral Authority in the American West, 1874–1939* (Oxford University Press, 1990); Mildred Crowl Martin, *Chinatown's Angry Angel: The Story of Donaldina Cameron* (Pacific Books, 1977); Wilson, *Chinatown Quest*.

39. Pascoe, *Relations of Rescue*, 55, 96–103.
40. Pascoe, *Relations of Rescue*, 55, 96–103; Alexander Jin, "Heathen Intimacy: Chinese Migrants and Criminal Sexualities in Turn of the Century California" (PhD diss., Princeton University, 2024).
41. Pascoe, *Relations of Rescue*, 121, 129; An interview with Donaldina Cameron, letter to Miss Cameron from Office of the Commissioner, Angel Island, box no. 26, folder no. 39, HI/SRR.
42. Register of Inmates, March 22, 1897, box 5, folder 10, SCSU/MM.
43. Miss M. Culbertson, *Eighteenth Annual Occidental Board Report*, 1891, box 18, folder 4, SCSU/MM; see also *Missionary Assistant Report*, 1895, box 18, folder 4, SCSU/MM, 53; *Assistant Missionary Vroonman Report*, 1896, box 18, folder 4, SCSU/MM, 70.
44. *Assistant Missionary Vroonman Report*, 1896, box 18, folder 4, SCSU/MM, 70.
45. *Missionary Assistant Report*, 1895, box 18, folder 4, SCSU/MM, 53.
46. Immigration Cases, n.d., box 4, folder 13, SCSU/MM. See also 1935 Report, section B, "Exodus from '920' to China" [1932], box 4, folder 13, SCSU/MM.
47. Sometimes spelled "Sue Ching." John A. Robinson to Commissioner of Immigration, July 16, 1919, Yick Yook Lan immigration file.
48. Wendy Rouse Jorae, *The Children of Chinatown: Growing Up Chinese American in San Francisco, 1850–1920* (University of North Carolina Press, 2009), 146.
49. "Local News Notes," *San Francisco Chronicle*, June 11, 1891; "Chinese Girls Saved," *Philadelphia Times*, April 23, 1893.
50. "Chinese Girls Saved."
51. In re Woman's N. Pac. Presbyterian Bd. of Missions, 18 Or. 339, 22 P. 1105 (1890); Ah Wah & Ah Tie vs. Boys & Girls Aid Society, case file no. 4084, box 85, OSA/OSC.
52. Lilac Chen as quoted in Victor G. Nee and Brett De Bary Nee, *Longtime Californ': A Documentary Study of an American Chinatown* (Pantheon, 1973), 83–90.
53. Donaldina Cameron, "Native Workers and the Presbyterian Mission Home," January 1912, *The Assembly Herald* (Philadelphia: General Assembly, 1912), 395–397.
54. Nee and De Bary Nee, *Longtime Californ'*, 83–90.
55. "Miss Yoke Lon Lee, Graduate of the Presbyterian Hospital in Philadelphia, United States," *Funü zazhi* (The ladies' journal), March 5, 1915; "Interesting Personalities," *Pittsburgh Press*, February 16, 1914; "Interesting Personalities," *Kentucky Post*, February 10, 1914; "First Chinese Girl a Graduate Nurse," *Evansville Courier*, February 8, 1914.
56. Yoke Lon Lee, *San Francisco Examiner*, November 11, 1975, 30.
57. United States Immigration Service translation, February 28, 1917, Yick Yook Lan immigration file; John Robinson to Commissioner of Immigration, April 18, April 26, 1917, Yick Yook Lan immigration file.
58. Wilson, *Chinatown Quest*, 81.
59. Robinson to Commissioner, April 18, 1917, Yick Yook Lan immigration file; Wilson, *Chinatown Quest*, 77–81; John Manion, "Lo Mo: Mother of Chinatown," *Women and Missions* 8 (January 1932): 387–389.

60. "Knights Templar Lay Plans for Conclave Here in 1917," *Sacramento Daily Union,* July 10, 1916; "Knights Templar Conclave Meets," *Riverside Daily Press,* April 19, 1917.
61. Wilson, *Chinatown Quest,* 79.
62. Yick Yoke Long no. 211, April 19, 1917, Sacramento Police Department Mug Book, 1916–1918, CSH.
63. Wilson, *Chinatown Quest,* 81.
64. "Sergeant Cook's Case," *San Francisco Call,* June 27, 1895.
65. "A New Chinese Squad Chosen," *Daily Alta California* (San Francisco), February 21, 1889.
66. "The Chinatown Detail," *San Francisco Call,* November 13, 1902; "Changes Are Made in Police Department," *San Francisco Call,* January 1, 1904; "Every Corner Has Its 'Cop,'" *San Francisco Call,* December 2, 1904; Darren A. Raspa, *Bloody Bay: Grassroots Policing in Nineteenth-Century San Francisco* (University of Nebraska Press, 2020), 181–216.
67. "Interesting Westerners," *Sunset Magazine,* November 1925, 51; "Sargent Manion Five Years in Chinatown," *Douglas 20 Police Journal,* 1926; "White Man Rules Chinatown for 20 Years," *Police and Peace Officers Journal,* January 1941.
68. "Tongs Now Arbitrate in Peace Temple," *San Pedro Daily News,* June 17, 1926.
69. John Manion, "Chinese Writings," [November 1927], John J. Manion Papers, BL; "Chinatown in Frisco Quiet in Tong Wars," *San Pedro Daily News,* November 24, 1925.
70. Manion, "Lo Mo"; "Slave Girls Rescued in Raids on Chinese Dens," *Press Democrat* (Santa Rosa, CA), March 18, 1924.
71. It seems likely he was conflating two court proceedings: a Juvenile Court hearing regarding guardianship and a criminal court proceeding charging Hom Wah Bow. Manion, "Lo Mo."
72. Manion, "Lo Mo"; "Slave Girls Rescued in Raids on Chinese Dens."
73. "Manion Would End Tong Wars," *Santa Cruz Evening News,* August 19, 1926; Manion, "Lo Mo." See also "China Tong War Causes Police Search Here," *San Francisco Call,* May 17, 1921.
74. Manion, "Chinese Writings."
75. Frank Wong no. 3969, Chinese San Francisco Key, vol. 9, San Francisco Police Department Records, 1870–1983 (SFH 61), SFHC. See also Santa Clara Sheriff's Office Wanted Fliers Index, HSJ.
76. Risa Goluboff, *Vagrant Nation: Police Power, Constitutional Change, and the Making of the 1960s* (Oxford University Press, 2016).
77. Lum Gong no. 3986, Chinese San Francisco Key, vol. 9, San Francisco Police Department Records, 1870–1983 (SFH 61), SFHC.
78. Charles Mayer, Memorandum for Immigration Division, June 20, 1917, Yick Yook Lan Immigration file.
79. John A. Robinson to Commissioner of Immigration, July 16, 1919, Yick Yook Lan immigration file.
80. McKeown, "Ritualization of Regulation"; Mae M. Ngai, "Legacies of Exclusion: Illegal Chinese Immigration During the Cold War Years," *Journal of*

American Ethnic History 18, no. 1 (1998): 3–35; Lee, *At America's Gates,* 12; Erika Lee, *The Making of Asian America: A History* (Simon and Schuster, 2015), 95.
81. Beth Lew-Williams, "Paper Lives of Chinese Migrants and the History of the Undocumented in America," *Modern American History* 4, no. 2 (2021): 109–130. Estelle T. Lau, *Paper Families: Identity, Immigration Administration, and Chinese Exclusion* (Duke University Press, 2006), 115–116, 132; Xiaojian Zhao, *Remaking Chinese America: Immigration, Family, and Community, 1940–1965* (Rutgers University Press, 2002), 30–35; Madeline Hsu, "Gold Mountain Dreams and Paper Son Schemes: Chinese Immigration Under Exclusion," *Chinese America: History & Perspectives* 11 (1997): 46–61; Lee, *At America's Gates,* 189–220.
82. Alicia Schmidt Camacho, *Migrant Imaginaries: Latino Cultural Politics in the U.S.-Mexico Borderlands* (NYU Press, 2008), 840; Cecilia Menjívar, "Liminal Legality: Salvadoran and Guatemalan Immigrants' Lives in the United States," *American Journal of Sociology* 111, no. 4 (2006): 999–1037.
83. Elsewhere I have argued for a broad definition for the term "undocumented" to include all people whose territorial presence within the nation has been criminalized by the state. Lew-Williams, "Paper Lives of Chinese Migrants."

Epilogue

1. Beth Lew-Williams, *The Chinese Must Go: Violence, Exclusion, and the Making of the Alien in America* (Harvard University Press, 2018); US Census Bureau, *Population of the United States in 1920* (Government Printing Office, 1922), https://www.loc.gov/item/22026371/.
2. Eliot Grinnell Mears, *Resident Orientals on the American Pacific Coast* (University of Chicago Press, 1928), 179, 191–206, 224–234, 284.
3. Mears, *Resident Orientals,* 330–334.
4. Nayan Shah, *Contagious Divides: Epidemics and Race in San Francisco's Chinatown* (University of California Press, 2001), 208–224.
5. Mears, *Resident Orientals,* 295, 300, 357, 372; "Segregation, United States," Subject File 21-1, HI/SRR.
6. Ching Chao Wu, "Chinatowns: A Study of Symbiosis and Assimilation" (PhD diss., University of Chicago, 1928), 3.
7. M.L.L., Life History and Social Document, October 13, 1924, Major Documents, box 23, folder 233, HI/SRR.
8. Fred Wong, Life History and Social Document, August 29, 1924, Major Documents, box 27, folder 195, HI/SRR.
9. Jane H. Hong, *Opening the Gates to Asia: A Transpacific History of How America Repealed Asian Exclusion* (University of North Carolina Press, 2019); Abby Budiman and Neil G. Ruiz, "Asian Americans Are the Fastest-Growing Racial or Ethnic Group in the U.S.," April 9, 2021, Pew Research Center, https://pewrsr.ch/3tbjILO; "Asian Americans: A Survey Data Snapshot," Pew Research Center, n.d., https://www.pewresearch.org/race-and-ethnicity/2024/08/06/asian-americans-a-survey-data-snapshot/.

10. Madeline Y. Hsu and Ellen D. Wu, "'Smoke and Mirrors': Conditional Inclusion, Model Minorities, and the Pre-1965 Dismantling of Asian Exclusion," *Journal of American Ethnic History* 34, no. 4 (2015): 43–65; Keeanga-Yamahtta Taylor, *Race for Profit: How Banks and the Real Estate Industry Undermined Black Homeownership* (University of North Carolina Press, 2019), 8, 17–18.
11. Ellen D. Wu, *The Color of Success: Asian Americans and the Origins of the Model Minority* (Princeton University Press, 2015), 2–6; Cindy I-Fen Cheng, *Citizens of Asian America: Democracy and Race During the Cold War* (NYU Press, 2014), 1–14; Simeon Man, *Soldiering Through Empire: Race and the Making of the Decolonizing Pacific* (University of California Press, 2018); Eiichiro Azuma, "Race, Citizenship and the 'Science of Chick Sexing': The Politics of Racial Identity Among Japanese Americans," *Pacific Historical Review* 78, no. 2 (2009): 242–275, at 245.
12. Wu, *The Color of Success*, 2–6; David L. Eng and Shinhee Han, *Racial Melancholia, Racial Dissociation: On the Social and Psychic Lives of Asian Americans* (Duke University Press, 2019); Cathy Park Hong, *Minor Feelings: An Asian American Reckoning* (House Publishing Group, 2020).
13. William Groves, Account Books, 1859–1891, MM E.90, SHL.
14. Anne Anlin Cheng, *The Melancholy of Race: Psychoanalysis, Assimilation and Hidden Grief* (Oxford University Press, 2001); Eng and Han, *Racial Melancholia, Racial Dissociation;* Hong, *Minor Feelings*, 55–57, 202–203; Hua Hsu, "The Muddled History of Anti-Asian Violence," *New Yorker*, February 28, 2021; Jay Caspian Kang, *The Loneliest Americans* (Crown, 2022), 10–16; Anne Anlin Cheng, *Ordinary Disasters: How I Stopped Being a Model Minority* (Pantheon, 2024), 20–23.
15. For an example burial law, see Spokane City Charter, art. 11, sec. 147, September 13, 1891, 54. Elizabeth Sinn, *Pacific Crossing: California Gold, Chinese Migration, and the Making of Hong Kong* (Hong Kong University Press, 2013), 265–295; Sue Fawn Chung and Priscilla Wegars, eds., *Chinese American Death Rituals: Respecting Ancestors* (Rowman Altamira, 2005), 1–14.

Appendix

1. Mark Kanazawa, "Immigration, Exclusion, and Taxation: Anti-Chinese Legislation in Gold Rush California," *Journal of Economic History* 65, no. 3 (2005): 779–805.
2. Chap. 37, p. 84, May 4, 1852, *California Mining Statutes Annotated*, ed. J. W. Thompson (Government Printing Office, 1918), 36–37.
3. "A Meeting of the Miners of Columbia Mining District," October 1, 1853, CFA.
4. "An Act to Provide for Taxing Negroes, Chinamen, Kanakas and Mulattoes," October 15, 1862, The Code of Civil Procedure and Other General Statutes of Oregon, Sess. 1862 (Asahel Bush, State Printer, 1863), 76–77.
5. "An Act to Protect Free White Labor Against Competition with Chinese Coolie Labor, and to Discourage the Immigration of the Chinese into this Territory,"

January 23, 1864, *Statutes of the Territory of Washington*, Sess. 1863–1864 (Olympia: T. F. McElroy, Printer, 1864), 56–59.

6. *The Oregon Constitution and Proceedings and Debates of the Constitutional Convention of 1857*, ed. Charles Henry Carey (State Printing Department, 1926), 401–406, 427.
7. "The Constitution of the State of California," in *The Statutes of California*, 23rd Sess. (J. D. Young, Supt. State Printer, 1880), xxiii–xxv, xli–xlii.
8. *Act of March 24, 1866, California Laws*, chap. 342, p. 398.
9. Act of April 4, 1870, *General Laws of California*, 824.
10. *Act to Amend Section 1662 Approved April 7, 1880*, 23rd sess., chap. 44, p. 38.
11. *Act of March 12, 1885*, Ca. 27th Sess., chap. 117, pp. 99–100.
12. Deeneshi Sohoni, "Unsuitable Suitors: Anti-Miscegenation Laws, Naturalization Laws, and the Construction of Asian Identities," *Law and Society Review* 41, no. 3 (2007): 587–618.
13. *Oregon Criminal Code*, chap. 8, sec. 689, 690 (October 24, 1866), 440.
14. In re Triburcio Parrott, 1 F. 481 (1880).
15. Act of February 13, 1880, Acts Amendatory of the Penal Code (California 1880), chap. 3, sec. 178, pp. 1–2.
16. "An Act to Prohibit the Employment of Chinese and Mongolians in Certain Cases," March 6, 1879, sec. 4947, *The General Statutes of the State of Nevada in Force from 1861–1885* (Josiah C. Harlow, Supt. State Printing, 1885), 1097.
17. *Charter of the City of Oakland*, March 8, 1818, sec. 200 (Tribune, 1909).
18. "An Act to Enforce Section 5, of Article 13, of the Constitution, Prohibiting the Employment of Aliens on State or Municipal Works," March 14, 1891, General Laws of the State of Idaho, 1st sess. (Statemen Printing, 1891), 233.
19. "Declaring What Are Public Nuisances and providing for Their Abatement," October 6, 1879, Ordinance no. 156, *Charter and Ordinances of the City of Sacramento*, ed. R. M. Clarken (D. Johnston & Co., 1896), 211.
20. "Regulating the Establishment and Maintenance of Public Laundries and Public Wash-Houses Within the City and County of San Francisco," October 10, 1887, Order no. 1930, *General Orders of the Board of Supervisors*, 215–217.
21. "An Ordinance Concerning Offenses and Disorderly Conduct," June 19, 1878, Ordinance no. 3983, *Laws of Portland, Charter of the City of Portland, General Ordinances in Force September 1886* (Schwab, 1886), 325–338.
22. "An Ordinance to Prohibit the Discharge of Cannon, Anvils, Firearms and Fireworks," May 15, 1891, Ordinance no. 1143, *General Municipal Ordinances of the City of Oakland* (Enquirer Pub. Co., Printers, 1895), 333–334.

ACKNOWLEDGMENTS

My thanks must first go to the archivists, librarians, and other guardians of old paper. I owe a debt of gratitude to the amazing collections and staff at the Bancroft Library, California State Archive, California State Library, UCLA Special Collections, and Huntington Library. Thank you to the staff and volunteers at History San José, Contra Costa County Historical Society, Tuolumne County Historical Society, El Dorado County Museum, Washington State Historical Society, Columbia State Historic Park, Marshall Gold Discovery Park, Chinese American Museum of Northern California, Nevada Historical Society, and City of Monterey Museums. Somewhere along the way, I started taking a photo of every archive door I entered. Without question, the award for Best Archive Door goes to the City of Monterey with its camera-ready, heist-proof, stainless-steel bank vault door.

Thank you to librarians at the San Francisco History Center, Doris Foley Library, Loomis Library, and Tacoma Public Library. I am grateful to the staff at the Wiley W. Manuel Courthouse, Multnomah County Courthouse, Sierra County Superior Court, Ventura County Clerk-Recorder, and Colusa County Superior Court. All of the courthouse staff had more timely matters to deal with than nineteenth-century records, but they still dug up the old cases.

Some archivists went above and beyond, helping me to navigate the intricacies of their collections. I sincerely appreciate Kim Hayden (Center for Sacramento History), Ben Stone (Stanford University Special Collections), Frances Kaplan (California Historical Society), Andy Mattos (Carlo M. De Ferrari Archive), Dale Toussaint (Alameda County Sheriff's Office Archive), Pat Chesnut (Searls Historical Library), Charles Miller (National Archives at San Bruno), Kelsey Monahan (Placer County Archives), Midori Okazaki (Puget Sound Regional Branch of the Washington State Archives), Alison Costanza (Northwest Regional Branch of the Washington State Archives), Madeline Moya (Portland City Archives), and Gary Halvorson (Oregon State Archives). I won't name those of you who let me walk right into the stacks, but I do want to thank you.

I also want to acknowledge the archives I could not visit, but that helped me from afar, including the Washoe County Second Judicial District Court, Santa Clara County Archives, National Archives at Riverside, Harvey County Historical Museum, Antioch Historical Society, and National Archives at St. Louis. When I could not travel and many archives closed to outsiders, I got help from Tammy Grier in San Jose and Lily Amelia Susman at Stanford.

I owe a special debt to other researchers who were generous enough to share their work and wisdom, including Kim Bui, Susie Lan Cassel, Donald Kohrs, and Marilou West Ficklin. In particular, I would like to express my sincere gratitude to Clarinèr Freeman Boston. Thank you for going back to school, writing your incredible master's thesis, and entrusting me with the only copy of your 670-page appendices (for the half hour it took to scan it at FedEx).

I was lucky enough to have a truly extraordinary editor, Emily Silk. It has been a gift to be in conversation with you about this book. I would also like to thank the team at Harvard University Press and beyond, including Jillian Quigley, Stephanie Vyce, Sana Mohtadi, Wendy Nelson, and Isabelle Lewis (who produced the maps and infographics).

I am deeply grateful to Hannah Postel. I learned a lot from you when you were a graduate student and even more when you became a collaborator. I would like to thank Hannah for doing the legwork to obtain and process charters, ordinances, and statutes from 133 municipalities and three states. To help turn these manuscripts into machine-readable text, we also hired wonderful student research assistants, including Lauren Almstead, Lilly Bay, Sam Bisno, Marina Carlucci, Julie Chen, Lucy Chuang, Andrew Hernandez, Caroline Hochman, Amy Jeon, Jack Kilgallon, Jennifer Lee, Cary Marz, Linh Nguyen, Megan Pan, Nick Kim Sexton, Cy Watsky, and Alis Yoo. As part of her computer science senior thesis, Kathryn Chou created a great search tool for the Survey of Race Relations.

Funding and childcare made this work possible. At Princeton, I want to acknowledge the University Committee on Research in the Humanities and

Social Sciences, Philip and Beulah Rollins Bicentennial Preceptorship, and the Department of History. A fellowship from the National Endowment for the Humanities gave me additional time to devote to this book. I am indebted to the Princeton Public Schools and, when those schools shut, to Makenna May and Ella Norman.

I was grateful to have opportunities to share my work. Thank you to the generous colleagues I encountered (far too many to name here) at Yale Law School, Penn Law School, Michigan Law School, UC Davis, Penn State, Cal State San Bernadino, Brown University, Huntington Library, Wake Forest University, Bates College, Dartmouth University, Smith College, University of Delaware, Stanford University, New York University, Boston University, the Tobin Project, and UC Berkeley.

I would like to thank my chair, Angela Creager, for suggesting and funding a manuscript workshop. Lori Flores, Ariela Gross, and Mary Lui gave the gift of a close reading and great insight. Maia Silber read along and took excellent notes. After all these years, Gordon Chang is still an endlessly generous mentor. Daniel Rodgers read the full manuscript and produced a revelatory reader report. Richard White saved me from overstating my point in Chapter 2. Maggie Blackhawk, Calvin Cheung-Miaw, John Cisternino, Laura Edwards, Sally Gordon, Naomi Lamoreaux, Bernadette Perez, Lucy Salyer, Chris Suh, Judith Surkis, Karen Tani, Timothy Thomlinson, Cecilia Tsu, and Keith Wailoo all made time to comment on sections of the manuscript.

Portions of Chapter 3 were first published in "Chinese Naturalization, Voting, and Other Impossible Acts," *Journal of the Civil War Era* 13, no. 4 (2023): 515–536. Thank you to *JCWE* editors Greg Downs and Kate Masur, and special edition editor Hidetaka Hirota. Chapter 6 includes portions of text first published in "'Chinamen' and 'Delinquent Girls': Intimacy, Exclusion, and a Search for California's Color Line," *Journal of American History* 104, no. 5 (2017): 632–655. Thank you to the *JAH* editor, Alex Lichtenstein. In addition, I know I'm indebted to anonymous colleagues who read this work in the context of peer review, fellowship applications, or promotion. Thank you for your knowledge, labor, and goodwill.

I also want to give thanks to friends, inside and outside the academy. I'm lucky to have many of them as colleagues, including He Bian, Michael Blaakman, Margot Canaday, Anne Cheng, Michael Gordin, Matt Karp, Reg Kunzel, Mike Laffan, Rosina Lozano, Erika Milam, Paul Nadal, Emily Thompson, and Natasha Wheatley. I am grateful to have Jake Brenner, Kathryn DeLonga, Lori Flores (again), Lee James, Aly Kassam-Remtulla, Greg Miller, Lara Miller, Leila Moustafa, Vinay Shamasundara, Moulie Vidas, and Ilana Witten in my life. Ken Norman, Liz Lempert, and Adele Goldberg made sure I celebrate every milestone. Lisa Margulis, Martin

Miller, and their children, Alexander, Nikolai, and Hugo, bring me joy. Allen Gillers has brightened countless family holidays. Wendy Warren helped me make it through those pandemic days and beyond. Christine O'Malley is always there, for thirty years now.

I'm lucky to have a fiercely supportive family. My parents, Marion Franck and Bob Lew, have given me unconditional love, astute advice, use of their car, and occasional company on my travels. Mom also lent her writer's eye to the entire manuscript. Sue and Keith Williams outgrew the term "in-laws" long ago. I am especially grateful that they watched the kids so that I could drive around California. My brother, Daniel Lew, and his family, Lindsay Quass and Everett Quass-Lew, bring me comfort and delight. I must thank Sutter, Atropa, and my brothers-in-law Seth Williams and Victor Zarour Zarzar, who know it's a big compliment to be listed alongside beloved dogs. I give thanks to the whole Lew family, especially Kristi Ng, who shares my love of this history. Thank you to my uncle, Ron Franck, who isn't a professional copy editor, but wow, coulda fooled me.

My children-turned-teenagers, Carson and Dane, do an excellent job of getting my mind to the immediate present. Thank you for teasing me every time I start a sentence, "Well, historically. . . ." And thank you for giving me so much life.

I dedicate this book to Casey Lew-Williams, my love and my reader. Whatever I encounter in the archive or the world outside, all I want is to come home to you.

INDEX

Page numbers in italics refer to photos and illustrations

Achunn v. Lyman (1864), 106–107
Act Concerning Crime and Punishment (1850), 101
Act for the Government and Protection of Indians (1850), 32, 66
Act for the Protection of Children (1878), 254
Act for the Suppression of Chinese Houses of Ill Fame (1866), 143
Act to Enforce Contracts and Obligations to Perform Work and Labor or Contracts for Foreign Laborers (1852), 32
Act to Prevent the Kidnapping and Importation of Mongolian, Chinese and Japanese Females, for Criminal or Demoralizing Purposes (1870), 76, 144
Act to Protect Free White Labor Against Competition with Chinese Coolie Labor, and to Discourage the Immigration of the Chinese into this Territory (1894), 75
Act to Provide for Taxing Negroes, Chinamen, Kanakas and Mulattoes (1862), 52
Act to Provide for the Protection of Foreigners and to Define Their Liabilities and Privileges (1852), 33, 54, 284
Act to Tax and Protect Chinamen Mining in Oregon (1857), 36

African Americans, 14, 47, 167, 202, 211, 275, 285; anti-Blackness, 5, 7–8, 76, 133, 183, 279; Black citizenship, 121–123; Black freedom struggle, 98, 99; Black legal testimony, 100–102, 104, 108; Black miners, 38–39; Black population in Pacific West, 19, 77, 169, 269, 271; Black rapist stereotype, 230, 231; Black students, 8, 189–190, 195; free Blacks, 34–35; incarceration of, 88-89; low status in American racial regime, 13, *101*; in mug books, 92, *95*; Negro Exclusion Bill, 52, 53; segregation of, 169, 170, 175–176, 183, 189–190, 195, 199–202, 204, 207, 287
agricultural land, limiting Chinese access to, 211–212, 269–270
Ah Hee v. Crippen (1861), 56
Alameda, city of, 91, 118
Alameda county, 224, 244, 246
aliens, regulation of, 176, 270, 289; alienage, 15, 17, 111, 120, 128–129; alien land laws, 16, 185, 211–212; in California Constitution, 285, 286–287; criminal aliens, deportation of, 243, 249; identity-based laws, regulation via, 129, 283

Ambery, C., 69
Anderson, Clarence R., 199–201, 202
Angell Treaty (1880), 107
Anti-Chinese League, 173, 176, 182
anti-Chinese stereotypes. *See* stereotypes
anti-Chinese violence, 14, 67, 104, 105, 168, 211, 278, 279; anti-Chinese laws, violence behind, 7, 10; mob violence against the Chinese, 67, 81; of police force, 29, 64, 68; of tax collectors, 27, 41–43
Arizona, 102, 103, 212, 217, 289
Auburn, CA, 20, 140, 160, 161, 223

Bancroft, George, 67
Bee, Frederick A., 125
behavior-based laws, 8, 15, 83, 120, 176; basket laws as, 8, 77, 83, 120; burial and exhumation laws as, 12, 77; cultural practices, as targeting, 77, 121, 283; discriminatory intent behind, 111–113; firecracker laws as, 8, 77, 270; gong laws as, 77, 82; as health and safety ordinances, 129, 292–293; laundry ordinances, 8, 118, 291; police regulation of, 8–9
Berkeley, CA, 196, 244, 248
Bigler, John, 30, 33, 48
Bingham Ordinance, 175
Birch, Charles, 103
birthright citizenship, 98, 122, 123–124, 267
Blacks. *See* African Americans
border control, 3, 18, 25, 65, 166, 234–235, 244, 248, 267, 279
Breyfogle, Charles, 176
Bryant, Andrew Jackson, 78
burial practices, 12, 77, 79, 120, 236, 280
Burlingame Treaty (1868), 15, 16, 115, 116, 123, 129, 146; Fourteenth Amendment and, 98, 147; most favored nation status under, 99, 107, 112, 145

Calaveras county, 87, 135
California Constitution, 119, 120, 124, 174, 195, 285–286, 286–287
California Mining Committee, 47, 48, 50
California statutes and laws, 53, 65, 66, 80, 101, 119, 146, 188; alien land laws, 212; anti-miscegenation laws, 216–217, 220, 289; behavior-based laws, 77; civil rights laws, 202; coolies, lawmakers responding to perceived threat of, 32, 57, 80, 129; cubic air policy, 112–113, 116; employment laws, 290; fishing laws, targeting Chinese with, 55, 111; Foreign Miner's Act, 35–36, 48, 51, 109, 284; identity-based laws, 131, 143, 144, 283; lodging house laws, 120; school laws, 190–195, 287–288; segregation laws, 201, 271; testimony laws, 102; vagrancy laws, 61
California Supreme Court, 44–45, 53, 56, 75, 76, 101, 108, 119, 128, 145, 159, 189, 191, 192, 195
Cameron, Donaldina: Lonnie Lee as interpreter for, 233, 235, 247, 257; Presbyterian Mission Home, as manager, 233, 249–252, 256–257; rescue work, 235, 248, 253, 262–263; Yick Yok Lan and, 233–234, 247, 254, 258, 259, 265–267
Cantrell, Thomas, 86
Catlin, Amos, 175
Chen, Lilac, 154, 156, 256–257
Chewey, Ah, 96
Chico, CA, 118, 119, 175
Chin, Cheung, 203
Chin, Leland, 194
Chinaman: burials of John Chinaman, 277–280; cuisine of John Chinaman, 262; deceased, declaring John Doe Chinaman as, 4; Charles Delong as shooting a Chinaman, 27, 42; disturbance of the peace, John Chinaman arrested for, 64; inquest into the body of a Chinaman, 69; insanity, John Chinaman arrested for, 64; John Doe Chink, 5; liquor-selling, John Chinaman arrested for, 64; nuisance, Chinaman no. 7 declared as a, 64; Otto Johnson, John Doe Chinaman assaulted by, 103; placemaker, term used as, 225; as a racial term, 3, 4–5, 63, 237; robbery of a sluice, John Chinaman accused of, 67; Sacramento jail cell, John Doe Chinaman held in, 4; San Jose, John Doe Chinamen as property owners in, 181; San Jose Home Protection Society, as target of, 184; shave, John Doe Chinaman receiving, 43; vagrancy, John Chinaman arrested for, 59, 60, 64. *See also* Chinawoman
Chinatown, general, 13, 16, 137, 140, 226; abandonment of, 269, 271; over-policing of, 64–65
Chinatown Eureka, 178
Chinatown Heinlenville, 184, 237, 254
Chinatown Loomis, 210, 212
Chinatown Los Angeles, 133, 149, 157, 164

INDEX   351

Chinatown San Francisco, 137, 171, 177, 187, 188, 263; collage of baby boys from, 1–3, 23; Inspector Manion as policing, 261, 262; lodging house laws of, 113, 115; as the original Chinatown, 169–170; police raids in, 233, 235, 248; Ruby Tsang, as home of, 196, 197; special police as serving, 65, 71

Chinatown San Jose, 155, 170; calls for the end of, 173, 184; fire in, 166, 167, 169, 172, 178–179, 185, 187, 204, 237; Market Street center, 172–173, 175, 176, 179, 181, 183, 204, 237

Chinatown Squad, 270; Jesse Brown Cook as heading, 1, 2, 6, 260, 262; Inspector Manion as leading, 260–265; raids and rescues of, 248, 253; white men as populating, 83–84

Chinawoman: burials of Mary Chinaman, 278–280; China Mary, referenced as, 5; Chinese slave girl, referenced as, 132; Mary Chinaman, as referred to, 237, 267–268; as a racial term, 4, 22, 132. *See also* Chinaman

Chinese criminal activity, 59; anti-Chinese bias of juries, 85–87; arrest statistics, 81–85, 87; campaign for exclusion due to, 75–81; Chinese vernacular law and, 70–75; incarceration statistics, 88–89, 90, 93; mug books of Chinese criminals, 90–92, 94–96, 163, 263, 264; stereotypes of Chinese criminality, 61, 62, 64, 66. *See also* prostitution

Chinese death inquests, 69–70, Ah Fan, 105; Ah Fat, 70; Yun Dip, 104–105

Chinese defendants. *See under* defendants and respondents

Chinese exclusion, 29, 35, 48, 267, 268, 278; anti-Chinese expulsions, 16, 17, 166–167, 172, 173, 174, 181, 182; anti-Chinese laws as aiming for, 7–8; Charles Delong as calling for, 55, 58; Chinese criminalization and the campaign for exclusion, 65, 75–81; Chinese Exclusion Act, 16, 17, 53, 167–168, 216, 278; Chinese exclusion laws, 3, 6, 10, 13, 17, 25, 49, 53–54, 89; documentation, Chinese using to arm against, 237–238; immigrant detention in early days of, 245–246; Immigration Service, role in, 234–236, 249; Inspector Robinson as an agent of, 234, 235, 242, 248; mining laws and, 36, 53–54; population numbers, as limiting, 269, 271; repeal of Chinese exclusion, 240–241, 275; resistance to, 129, 241; taxation, exclusion attempts via, 55–56. *See also* conditional inclusion

Chinese incarceration, 73, 93, 131, 251; arrest statistics, 64, 81–82; deportation, detention of Chinese migrants awaiting, 90, 246; mug books as artifacts of, 90–92, 94–96, 163, 263, 264; racial discrepancies and, 87–89

Chinese laundries, 8, 129, 226; Harry Lum as operating, 126–127; laundry laws, 11, 16, 118, 119, 120, 290–292

Chinese life histories, self-recordings of, 272–275, 277

Chinese litigants. *See* litigants and complainants

Chinese names: absence of personal names, 3–5, 277–278, 280; transliteration difficulties, 21

Chinese police taxes, 55, 75, 284, 285

Chinese removal laws, 11, 16, 176, 181. *See also* racial zoning laws

Chinese Restriction Act (1882), 16, 237; Chinese migration, as slowing, 167–168; Chinese naturalization, as barring, 123, 127; deportation of Chinese immigrants under, 245–246; Japanese female migration, leading to increase in, 147–148; seeking admission after passage of, 218, 240–241; U.S. entry to new Chinese laborers, restricting, 15, 81

Chinese Six Companies (Chinese Consolidated Benevolent Association), 49, 70–71, 72, 75, 113, 125, 136, 260

Chinese vernacular law, 65, 70–75, 110

Chinese witness testimony. *See* witness testimonies

Ching, Chao Wu, 271

Chung, Nellie, 195

Chy Lung v. Freeman (1875), 146

civil rights, 13, 15, 56, 112, 190, 202, 275; Chinese workers, civil rights claims of, 22, 98, 129; legislation and court cases for Chinese civil rights, 99–100; *Tape v. Hurley* as emblematic of Chinese fight for, 188. *See also* queues; voting

Civil Rights Act (1866), 108, 122

Civil Rights Act (1870), 146, 147

Civil Rights Act (1875), 198, 199

Civil Rights Cases (1883), 198

Civil War, 14, 16, 56, 98, 108, 128, 217

Clarke, William, 103–104

Clayton, James B., 187

Columbia Mining Laws (1853), 35, 284

Colusa County, 20, 109, 135, 160, 161, 162
conditional inclusion, 58, 100, 164, 248; Chinese criminality fears as influencing, 65, 81–96; conditional inclusion and, 17, 271; cultural terms of, 11, 14, 99, 273, 278, 283; describing and defining, 10–11; economic terms of, 14, 99, 102, 269–270, 278, 283; exclusion repeal, continuing after, 10, 275, 277, 278; Immigration Service, power over, 234–236; political terms of, 11, 14, 99, 102, 270, 278, 283; racial elements of, 13, 129; resistance to, 21–22, 129; segregation as a form of, 168, 208; shifts in terms of, 14, 231–232, 276; social control through, 17–18; spatial terms of, 14, 99, 172, 271, 278, 283; taxation as a form of, 36, 47, 50; unequal access resulting from, 71–72. *See also* foreign miner's tax; Lodging House Laws; witness testimonies
Consolidated School Acts, 287–289
Cook, Jesse Brown, 1, 2, 3, 5, 6, 260, 262
coolies, 22, 58, 180; Coolie Bill, 32–33; human slavery, coolieism declared a form of, 285–286, 287; as temporary laborers, 6–7, 29; white wariness toward, 28, 30, 57, 66, 129
Corrigan v. Buckley (1926), 183
Crippen, Joshua, 56
Cubic Air Acts, 112, 114, 176. *See also* Lodging House Laws
Culbertson, Margaret, 249–250, 251–252, 254–255

Davidson, G. H., 140
Dawes Act (1887), 122–123
decolonization, 275–276
defendants and respondents, 85–86, 209; Ah Ben, 92–93; Bow, China, 263; Chan Chun, 243; Ah Chewey, 92, 93, 96; Ah Ching, 110; Chin Jong, 92, 94; Chin Mook Sow, 86; Chiu Sing Wing, 74; Chon Tong, 233–234; On Chou, 155–156; Chou Yee, 60, 62; Choy, Sam, 182; Coon See, 60–61; Cum Chow, 141; Ah Fa, 45–46; Fong Ah Tuck, 155–156; Fong Yet, 182; Ah Fook, 158–159; Fou Sin, 59–61, 62, 64; Gim Ying, Sue, 248; Gook Nai, 150; Ah Hoo, 105; Ah Hoy, 149; Ah Joe, 91, 92; Ah Ki, 68–69; Ah Kin, 91; Ah Lee (arrested for prostitution), 149; Ah Lee (arrested for sodomy), 91, 92; Ah Lee (arrested on immigration charges), 246; Lee, S. K., 248; Leong Dong, 252; Leong Ling, 227; Lim Mon, 243; Low, Chris, 150; Low Shu, 233–234, 247; Lum Gong, 263, 265; Me Fook, 158; Ah Pe-o, 141; Ah Quong, 139–140; Ah Sam, 227; Ah Sing (arrested for cohabitation), 222; Ah Sing (attempted kidnapping, 140; Sing Chow, 45–46; Ah Son, 150; Sue Gim Ying, 248; Sui, Charlie, 230; Tue Ying, 244; Wah Hing, 256; Whalebone (murder suspect), 67; Wong Fook, Jim, 227–228; Yim Gim, 139–140
DeLong, Charles Egbert, 26–29, 36–44, 51–58
deportation, 18, 25, 52, 128, 145, 235, 236, 245; Chinese women as subject to, 131, 132; incarceration of migrants awaiting deportation, 90, 246; Inspector Robinson and deportation cases, 243, 248, 249, 263; missionaries' role in, 251–253; threat of deportation as ever-present, 251, 268, 271
Dick, Ah, 206
Downieville, CA, 20, 91, 159–160, 161, 162, 163
Duffield, George, 71
Duffy, Hugh, 86
Dwinelle, Samuel H., 85–86

El Dorado County, 31, 35, 42–44, 56, 135, 210
Ellis, Henry Hiram, 78, 80, 83, 87
Ellis Island, 241
Enforcement Act (1870), 57, 109, 111, 115, 119
Eng, S. C., 199
equal protection, 86, 108, 111, 116, 117, 199, 235, 247; Burlingame Treaty and, 98, 112; bypassing attempts, 15, 129, 131, 147; Chinese litigants as pursuing, 99, 115, 121; constitutional guarantees of, 15, 17, 167; Enforcement Act and, 109, 119; of the Fourteenth Amendment, 146, 182, 192, 198; under racial liberalism, 276; *Yick Wo v. Hopkins* as guaranteeing, 100, 118–119
Errol Jones v. Kehrlein et al. (1920), 201
Eureka, CA, 121, 178, 182
exhumation laws, 79, 120. *See also* burial practices
Ex parte Ah Pong (1861), 56
Ex parte Case (1911), 121
Ex parte Sing Lee (1892), 121

Fallamine, Mary, 104
fan tan game, 8, 83, 270, 292, 293
federalism, 10, 32, 146, 244; equal protection guarantees, bypassing, 147, 167; exclusion and inclusion, simultaneous pursuit of, 278; federal and state law, contrast between, 122, 235; political inclusion, terms of, 270
Feeney, Hugh, 69–70
Fellows, H., 69
Ferguson, A. A., 140
Field, Stephen, 117, 118, 146
Fing, James W., 203
firecracker and fireworks regulation, 8, 12, 77, 270, 292, 293
fires, 80, 173, *180*, 196, 248, 267, 270. *See also under* Chinatown San Jose
fishing laws, 8, *11*, *16*, 55, 111, 128, 270
Fong Yue Ting v. United States (1893), 244–245
Fook, Ah (Ung Fook), 173
Fook, Sing, 159–160, 162
foreigners, perpetual fear of, 39, 122
Foreign Miner's Act (1852), 26–27, 35, 55, 109, 283, 284
foreign miner's tax, 9, 37, 42, 49, 50, 54, 55, 284; California state dependence on, 28, 41; Chinese, as targeting, *16*, 39–40; Chinese elites, endorsement of, 46, 48; indirect exclusion, as a means of, 53; lawsuits as challenging, 56–57; revisions of, 33–36
Fourteenth Amendment, 15, 16, 129, 145, 183, 193; birthright citizenship, recognizing, 122–124, 267; Burlingame Treaty and, 98, 99; Chinese litigants, evoking, 147, 174; Chinese right to testify not granted by, 108–109; equal protection under, 146, 182, 192, 198
Fresno, CA, 185, 201, 202, 203
Froklick, Louis, 142, 148
Fronk, John, 148–149
Fulweiler, John, 224–225

Gan, Que, 20, 159–162, *163*
Gandolfo, Alexander, 182–183
Gandolfo v. Hartman, Fong Yet, and Sam Choy (1890), 182–183
Gano, George M., 260
Geary Act (1892), *16*, 17, 167–168, 237
gender, 208, 221, 232; gender-normative behavior, 215; gender ratio, 81, 89, 90; gender taboos, 216

general-outcast laws: Chinese, as targeting, 8, 176; Chinese behavior, as regulating, 129, 144, 283; disease and quarantine laws as, 9, 77; as health and safety ordinances, 292–293; Jim Crow, as elements of, 9–10; local and state applications, 15, 77, 121; nuisance laws as, 9; peddling laws as, 121; prostitution laws as, 143, 149; sanitation laws as, 9; vagrancy laws as, 9, 77
Gentleman's Agreement, 194
Gibbs, Frederick A., 115
Ginn, Nai-Ming, 202
Godfrey, John F., 157
gold, 106; bonds paid in, 144–145; Chinese gold miners, 14, 30, 57; gold jewelry, 151, 153, 156; gold mining towns, 20, 26, 33, 60, 61, 97, 205; stealing gold, 60, 67, 68, 141; tax collection on, 27, 29, 40, 55, 56. *See also* foreign miner's tax
gongs, ordinances against playing, 77, 82
Griffin, John W., 151, 152–153, 156, 157
Griswold, Martin Van Buren, 60–61, 62
Groves, William, 277–278

Haight, Henry H., 76
Hall, George W., 101
Harris, N. R., 155
Hartman, Fredolin, 182
Hayes, David, 45–46
Healy, Daniel, 221–222, 223
Hecht, Treu Ergeben, *171*
Heinlen, John, 183–184
Herrington, D. W., 176, 178
Hickok, O. H., 43
Higgins, Ethel, 254, 259
Hill, A. M., 68–69
Ho Ah Kow v. Nunan (1878), 117, 118, 119
Hoeffler, L. M., 184
Holmes, W. H., 173
Hom, Wah Bow, 233–234, 247, 257, 262
Hong Kong, 59, 136, 137, 144, 147, 253, 257, 288
Hossack, Joseph, 53
How, V. E. J., 164
How the Other Half Lives (Riis), 226
Huang, Philip C. C., 73
huiguan (district associations), 73, 74, 78, 84, 110; foreign miner's tax, support for, 48–49; four Chinese companies as leading, 46–48; Sam Yup Company, 125; Six Companies as peace-keepers for, 70–71, 72; Sun On Company, 46; Sze Up Association, 46, 102; Yeong Wo Company, 46

"Humble Plea for the Chinese" (Speer), 49–50
Hurley, Jennie, 188, 192, 193

Idaho, 102, 106, 119, 121, 212, 217, 289, 290
identity-based laws, 131, 167, 173, 175, 289; Chinese behavior, as constricting, 14, 28–29; Chinese race, directly targeting, 8, 9, 172; citizenship, as a requirement for public office, 270; identity-based immigration restriction, 144; identity-based mining laws, 36, 55, 283–284; identity-based taxes, 28, 39, 55; litigation challenges, 55, 99, 100–102, 110, 129; local targeting of Chinese via, 15, 76–77; poll taxes as identity-based laws, 284–285; private prosecution strategy against, 105–107; public office, barring Chinese from, 120–121, 270, 289–290; testimony laws and, 20–21, 47, 85, 102–105, 108, 109, 111
Immigration Service: at Angel Island, 238–239, 240, 241, 243, 244, 246, 248, 253, 267; Detention Shed as a processing center, 244, 246, 251; Inspector Robinson as an immigration inspector, 242–249; police cooperation with, 235, 251, 263, 265; in Yick Yok Lan case, 233–234, 239, 258–259
index of dissimilarity, 170
Indian Citizenship Act (1924), 122–123
Indians. *See* Native Americans
In re Ah Fong (1874), 145–146
In re Ah Wing (1878), 120
In re Ah Yup (1878), 100, 125–126, 127
In re Lee Sing (1890), 175
In re Rodriguez (1898), 122
In re Sam Kee (1887), 121
In re Tiburcio Parrott (1880), 121
In re Yun Dip (1868), 104
integration, 14, 193, 214, 228; dissimilarity index findings on, 170; in racial liberalism, 276; student integration, 8, 189, 190, 194
interracial relations, 92, 208, 212, 213; interracial encounters, 207, 208, 226; interracial households, 219, 221; interracial intimacy, 206, 218, 222. *See also* miscegenation

Jackson, John, 57
Jackson, O. C., 157
Jansen, F. H, 215
Japanese Americans, 76, 92, 121, 144, 185, 215; alien land laws as targeting, 212; anti-miscegenation laws applied to, 220; Japanese prostitution, 147–148, 247; naturalization restrictions on, 126, 128; population growth, 18, 19, 120, 269, 271; schooling of Japanese children, 192, 194, 195; segregation of Japanese theatergoers, 201, 202
Jeong, John, 194, 196
Johnson, Otto, 103
Jones, Errol, 201, 202

Keely, Frank, 212, 225
Keely, Ida, 212–213, 226
Kehrlein, Oliver, 201
Kelly, Geo. F., 79
kidnapping, 144, 154, 159, 162, 258; anti-kidnapping laws, 76, 80, 162; Loui How, attempted kidnapping of, 139–140; of potential sex workers, 136, 150
Know Nothings party, 51–52
Knox, Shannon L., 43–44

Lai, Chun-chuen, 101–102
Lake, William, 104
Lee, Charley, 213, 214
Lee, Erika, 241
Lee, Kwang, 128
Lee, Lansing, 202
Lee, Lonnie, 233, 235, 247, 248, 254–260, 266
Lee, Robert George, 214
legal history, 7; approach to, 20–23; customary laws, 54, 73; formal laws, 8, 22, 67, 73, 74, 100, 144, 278, 279
Leslie, Lillie, 213, 214
Lew, Kay, 202–203
Li, Po Tai, 173
Lin, Quay, 91, *163*
Ling, Robert A., 151, 152, 156
Ling, Sing, 101
Ling Sing v. Washburn (1862), 55, 75–76
litigants and complainants, 15, 21, 99–100, 106–107, 111, 129, 147; Aye-Ying, 152; Charley John, 158; Chin Ah Win, 115, 122; Chong Wock, 125; Ah Chow, 141; Ah Choy, 141, 149, 150; Ah Fong, 145; Ah Fook, 145; Fun Dai, 253; Ah Gan, 104–105; Ah Hee, 56; Ah Hoi, 152, 156; Hong Chung, 125; Hong Yen Chang, 128; Ah Koo, 56–57, 109; Lai Hock Yan, 6; Leong Lan, 125; Ah Li, 141; Li Huang, 127;

INDEX

Loui How, 139–140; Ah Pong, 56; Sam Sing, 103; Si Choy, 150; Sing Yuke, 104; Tin Sing, 155–156; Ah Wang, 110; Wong Chin Way, 256; Yick Wo, 118–119; Ah Yup, 125
Lodging House Laws, 9, 16, 112–121. *See also* Cubic Air Acts
Look, Ting Tom, 203
Loomis, CA, 205, 207–209, 210, 212, 214–218, 219–222, 223, 227–228, 231
Los Angeles. *See* Chinatown Los Angeles
Lowe, Pany, 23–25
Lowe, Ralph, 181–182
Lucas, Charley, 206, 210, 212, 215, 218
Lucas, Elizabeth, 205, 210, 215, 222, 225; interracial marriage plans, sanctioning, 220, 224; Ah Lung as tenant farmer under, 206, 207, 209; parental rights, as stripped of, 221, 228; Ah Woon, turning to for housing assistance, 218, 219, 227
Lucas, Grace, 206, 214
Lucas, Hattie, 205, 206, 218, 219, 221; interracial relations with Ah Lung, 212–215, 217, 225–226; rape allegations against Ah Lung, 207–208, 215–216, 222, 223, 228
Lucas, James, 205
Lucas, May, 205, 206, 221, 228; interracial marriage plans, 219–220, 224; rape allegations against Ah Woon, 207–208, 222; testimony on sister's interracial relations, 214, 215
Lui, Charlie, 199
Lui, Hung Kei, 203
Lui, Mary Ting Yi, 227
Lum, Harry, 126–127
Lung, Ah, 206–208, 209–218, 221–222, 223–230
Lyman, Ackley, 106
lynching, 67, 68, 88, 133, 230, 231

Manion, John (Jack), 233, 235, 247, 248, 258, 260–265
Mann Act (1910), 243
marriage laws. *See* miscegenation
Marysville, CA, 57, 92, 93, 160, 161, 162
McAllister, M. H., 53
McFadden, John, 148–149
McFadden, Patrick, 103–104
McGowen, T. J. K., 164
McHardy, Alexander, 226

McKeown, Adam, 241–242
McMahon, A., 155
McMillen, Neil, 207
McNeil Island Corrections Center, 89–90, 246
Mead, W. H., 158–159
Mexicans and Mexican Americans, 67, 77, 127, 202; citizenship for, 122, 123; foreign miner's tax, applying to, 33; as segregated, 185, 195, 201
miscegenation, 16, 25; limited marriage prospects for Chinese men, 135, 152; interracial cohabitation, 221–222; interracial marriage, 120, 207, 217, 220, 289; white women, distancing from Chinese men, 13, 216–217, 271
missions, 48, 51, 227, 259, 278; Chinese women fleeing from, 132, 165; guardianship and, 234, 247, 254, 256, 258, 266; immigration cases, missionary involvement in, 235, 252; Methodist missions, 196, 197, 244; missionary impressions of the Chinese, 132, 139, 203, 214; Presbyterian missions, 49, 244, 256; private missionary schools, 188, 189–190; rescue work, 137, 154, 250–252, 255, 262; runaways, turning to, 154, 165, 250. *See also* Presbyterian Chinese Mission Home
Montana, 102, 217, 289
Monterey, CA, 20, 24, 180
Moore, Samuel Simon, 200
Moral Squad, 233, 247, 260
Morgan, John C., 157, 163–164
Morris, Hazel, 222
most favored nation, 99, 107, 112, 119, 145
Motomura, Hiroshi, 122
mug books, 91–96, 94–96, 163, 263, 264
Murasky, Frank, 258
"Murder of M. V. B. Griswold by Five Chinese Assassins" (pamphlet), 61, 62

Nager, Clara, 226
Napa, CA, 118, 119
Native Americans, 8, 13, 19, 67, 77, 180; anti-miscegenation laws, applying to, 217, 289; dispossession of, 6, 18, 122–123, 279; forced indenture of Native children, 32–33; foreign miner's tax, applying to, 33, 284; incarceration of, 66, 88–89; school laws and, 188–189, 287, 288; testimony laws and, 100–102, 103–104

naturalization, 30, 33, 98, 123, 213, 270, 275; Blacks, naturalization laws constraining, 121–122; Harry Lum as a naturalized citizen, 126–127; naturalization rights, 126–127, 275, 286; public works, non-citizens barred from, 12, 121, 271, 289–290; racial bars on, 8, 36, 100, 108, 125, 129, 158, 211; *U.S. v. Wong Kim Ark* case as opposing, 123–124
Naturalization Act (1790), 122
Naturalization Act (1870), 122, 124, 126
Negro Exclusion Bill (1858), 52–53
Nelson, James, 68
Nelson Mining Company, 68
Nevada City, CA, 20, 69, 161, 162, 174, 277, 279
Nevada county, 31, 68, 69, 101, 105, 135
Nevada statutes and laws, 77, 102, 121, 198, 217, 289, 290
Nofil, Briana, 246

Oakland, CA, 20, 118, 195, 242, 243, 244, 248, 290, 292, 293
Odem, Mary E., 224
opium, 11, 59, 82, 83, 159, 244, 262; behavior-based laws as regulating, 8, 9, 77, 121, 293; opium den laws, 16, 176; recreational opium smoking, 12, 71, 120, 270
Oregon Constitution, 36, 285, 286
Oregon Poll Tax (1862), 284–285
Oregon statutes and laws, 36, 55, 77, 103, 120, 211, 212, 217, 256, 270, 283, 289
Oriental, The (*Tang Fan Gonghao*), 113
Oriental, The (*Tung-Ngai San-Luk*), 48, 49, 125
Oriental School, 194, 197

Page Act (1875), 16, 265; Asian female migrants, as targeting, 15, 146–147, 216; Chinese women, associating with prostitution, 239, 243; U.S. entrance, banning for "immoral women," 80, 147, 245
Palmer, J. G., 69
Pantages Theatre chain, 199, 200–201
Parker, Judge, 258
Passenger Cases (1848), 76
People v. Ah Ching (1881), 111
People v. Ah Fa & Sing Chow (1858), 45
People v. Ah Fook (1880), 160
People v. Ah Hoy et al. (1876), 148
People v. Ah Ki (Chinaman) [1861], 68
People v. Ah Lung, A Chinaman (1881), 223
People v. Ah Son et al. (1873), 149–150

People v. Ah Woon, a Chinaman (1898), 223
People v. Ah Yek (1865), 224
People v. Brady (1870), 110
People v. Chew Sing Wing (1890), 74
People v. Chin Mook Sow (1876), 85
People v. Hall (1854), 100, 101
People v. John Doe Chinaman (1862), 4
People v. Otto Johnson et al. (1859), 103
People v. Sing (A Chinaman) [1905], 226, 227
People v. Washington (1869), 110
People v. Williams (1860), 43, 44
Petty, Mary, 104
Pierce, Charles W., 240
Pigtail Order, 115, 116. *See also* queues
Placer County, 31, 37, 103, 135, 139, 206, 212, 222, 283
Placerville, CA, 20, 26
Plessy, Homer, 188
Plessy v. Ferguson (1896), 188, 201–202
Pockman, J. M., 221
police powers, 15, 53, 76–77, 112, 117, 119, 120, 144–146
Police Tax Law (1894), 75
policing, 79, 88, 90, 132, 144, 246, 279; aggressive policing of the Chinese, 29, 80, 81, 94; border control and, 18, 234–235, 244; of Chinatown, 83, 178, 180, 184, 262; Chinese self-policing, 65, 71, 81; of Chinese sex workers, 148, 247; immigration control, coordination with, 263, 264; to maintain Chinese segregation, 172, 208; over-policing and under-protecting, 64–65; racialized policing, 22, 64, 77, 82, 84, 149, 221; regulation of Chinese activities, 12, 65–70
poll taxes, 16, 34, 55, 284–285
Portland, OR, 31, 121; Chinatown Portland, 84; local policing in, 81, 84, 150–151; Portland ordinances, 82–83, 112, 118, 292; segregation in, 24, 173–174, 186–187; white-on-Chinese crime in, 103–104
Postel, Hannah, 7, 170
Presbyterian Chinese Mission Home, 154, 244, 270; detainees held at, 154, 234, 245, 251; Donaldina Cameron as managing, 249–250, 253, 258, 263; Lonnie Lee as translator for, 233, 255, 257; Yick Yok Lan, presence at, 234, 254, 259–260, 265–266
Prewett, J. E., 228
private acts of discrimination, 168, 181

Progressive Era reforms, 208, 216
progressive reformers, 221, 270
property rights, 11–12, 176, 184, 211, 252, 285, 286
prostitution, 16, 61, 71, 159, 221, 222; arrests for prostitution offenses, 82, 176; Chinese women as associated with, 239, 243; contracts for Chinese prostitutes, 138–139, 141; immigration of sex workers as criminalized, 144–147; laws regulating, 12, 77, 111, 120, 121, 162, 207, 292; limited agency of Chinese sex workers, 164–165; Inspector Manion and, 260, 262, 263; Inspector Robinson and, 247, 248, 266; in Los Angeles, 130–131, 133, 142, 148–150, 152; Mission Home as a refuge for sex workers, 250, 254, 257; Page Act and, 80, 239, 243; Portland ordinances against, 83, 84, 293; robbery and assault as linked with, 140–141, 155–156; in San Francisco, 135, 137, 142–143, 148, 154; selling of women into, 130, 134, 136, 137–138, 141, 142, 151, 252.; trafficking of Chinese women, 131–132, 136–137, 139–142, 144, 145, 150, 153, 156, 157, 159, 162, 164–165, 243, 248, 250, 252–254, 256–258, 262, 265, 268
public employment laws, 16, 83, 121, 289, 290
public office-holding, 11, 12, 83, 270, 289, 290
public-private collaboration in discrimination, 17, 168, 187
Pun, Chi, 101

Quan, Kit, 203
queues, 9, 11, 67, 92, 105, 213; jails, queues cut in, 114–118, 228, 229; Qing Court, hairstyle as honoring, 42, 115, 210; tax collectors as removing, 20, 41–42, 43; voluntary removal to Americanize, 192, 219

racial etiquette, 11, 70, 203, 204, 207, 209, 230, 271; Chinese behavior, constraining, 14, 132, 269, 278–279; Chinese litigants as attempting to shift, 129; huiguan, objections to, 84–85; in rural spaces, 216, 221, 223; as shifting over time, 13; white poverty as breaking down, 206, 219; white supremacists as enforcing, 169
racial liberalism, 10, 276

racial reconstruction, 14, 16, 17, 99, 144, 198; anti-Chinese regime, Chinese litigants challenging, 15, 111, 129, 279; backlash as provoked by, 15, 167; identity-based laws and, 120–121, 131–132
racial retrenchment, 14, 16, 17, 167, 168, 207
racial zoning laws, 8, 173–175, 185–186
Radical Republicans, 14–15, 98, 107–108, 123, 124, 198
Reconstruction, 15, 56, 76, 98, 122, 128, 147, 247, 285. *See also* racial reconstruction
Reno, NV, 195, 197–198, 202, 204
Riis, Jacob, 226
Ripley, Jacob, 104
Roberts, Julietta, 227–228
Robinson, A. K., 225–227
Robinson, John Andrew, 233–235, 242–249, 257, 258, 263, 265–267
Rocca, Andrew, 141
Rockwell, E. A., 75, 76
Rodgers, J. J., 105
Rogers, James R., 115, 142
Roosevelt, Theodore, 194, 197
Roth, Angeline, 103

Sacramento, 20, 31, 121, 159, 194, 219, 221, 259; as capital city, 174, 259; Sacramento county, 87, 135, 195; Sacramento jail system, 4, 91, 259; Sacramento ordinances, 112, 118, 174–175, 290–291; Sacramento police, 96, 155, 158; Sacramento Valley, 135, 212
Safford, A. P. K., 103
Sam Yup Company, 46, 125
San Francisco. *See* Chinatown San Francisco
San Joaquin county, 87
San Jose. *See* Chinatown San Jose
San Quentin State Prison, 92, 95, 207, 209, 218, 228, 229, 244
Santa Clara County, 20, 211
Santa Rosa, CA, 118, 158
Sawyer, Lorenzo, 125–126, 175
Schaum, Lem, 73
school laws, 190–193, 194, 287–289
Scott, William, 69–70
Seattle, 20, 23, 31, 186, 199–201, 202, 273
See Yup Company (Siyi huiguan). *See* Sze Yup Association

segregation, 58, 136, 206, 208, 250; Black segregation, 176, 183, 189, 190, 204, 231; Jim Crow laws, 6, 7–8, 17, 168, 174, 198, 207, 211, 230, 279; public accommodations for, 13, 168, 169, 198–199, 201, 202; racial restrictive covenants and, 8, 16, 172, 181–183; residential segregation, 13, 168, 169–170, 172, 175, 184–187, 207, 210, 275; rural areas, relaxed segregation practices in, 212, 222; school segregation, 8, 11, 120, 187–195, 199, 203, 204, 207, 271, 287; segregated detention, 240, 241; segregated mug books, 95, 263; segregated theaters, 195–204; separate but equal doctrine, 17, 168, 199, 201; western segregationists as anti-Chinese, 168–169, 175
Shah, Nayan, 214
Sharp, Solomon A., 85–86
Shasta County, 31, 53–54
Sierra City, CA, 91, 161, 162, 163
Sin, Fou, 59–61, 62, 64
Sin, Wing, 74
Sing, Kee: as beating Yun Gee, 130–131, 133, 140; as buying Yun Gee, 130, 133, 138; escape from, Yun Gee attempting, 152–153, 156; return of Yun Gee, petitioning court for, 130–131, 157, 163, 164; as a sex trafficker, 130, 142, 148, 151, 152
Sing, Lung, 160, 162
Slattar, J., 104
slavery, 6, 15, 22, 30, 34, 122, 217; chattel slavery, 5, 14; Chinese prostitution viewed as, 136–137, 142, 143, 155, 165, 259; Chinese "slave girls," 132, 250, 252, 255, 262–263; coolieism as a form of human slavery, 30, 33, 76, 286, 287; Negro Exclusion Bill and, 52–53; testimony from the enslaved as restricted, 100–101; White-Slave Traffic bill, 243
Smith, Joseph, 103
social control, 34, 65, 70, 91, 208, 270, 271; in California, 19, 35, 142; exclusion laws as a form of, 17, 36, 77, 236; local systems of, 10, 168
Sonora, CA, 4, 20, 33, 61, 152
Speer, James F., 102
Speer, William, 48, 49–50
state rights of Chinese regulation: in California, 53, 76–77, 117, 144, 285; general welfare laws, right to enact, 76, 112; police power, states' right of, 15, 53, 76–77, 117, 120, 144–146

stereotypes, 92, 110, 169; of Chinese criminality, 61, 62, 64, 66; of Chinese false testimony, 110–111; of Chinese predators, 213, 214, 223, 225, 227–228, 230–231; racial stereotypes, 14, 86, 131, 224–225
Stevens, E. N., 155
Stewart, Marvin, 182
Stewart, William, 111
Stockton, CA, 87, 118, 239, 258, 259
Stockton, H. C., 54
Strauss, Gaston, 155
Sun On Company, 46
Swadler, Beckie, 126
Sze Yup Association, 46, 102

Tape, Joseph, 188, 191–192
Tape, Mamie, 188, 190–193, 204
Tape, Mary, 188, 191, 193
Tape v. Hurley (1885), 188, 193
taxation. *See* foreign miner's tax
Thiess, William, 239
Tie, Ah, 256
Tingley, George, 33
tongs (sworn brotherhood societies), 74, 84, 92, 136, 262, 263; criminal activity associated with, 75, 78, 110, 262; Hop Sing Tong, 72–73; tong war mug books, 94, 264
Tracy, Charles A., 81
Tsang, Pearl, 196–197
Tsang, Ruby, 20, 195–199, 204
Tsang, Won, 196
Tsang, Wong Kiew, 196
Tsu, Cecilia M., 211
Tuolumne County, 31, 35, 40, 45, 61, 63, 68, 87, 135, 141, 152, 283
Twain, Mark, 97–98, 99, 100
Tyler, F. W., 153

unauthorized immigration: false documentation, assembling, 238; Inspector Robinson as investigating, 235, 247–248; paper sons/daughters as invented kin, 267–268
U.S. v. Wong Kim Ark (1898), 123–124, 267

Virginia Act (1779), 122
Virginia Town, 160, 161
voting, 9, 11, 257; Chinese as barred from, 12, 29, 270, 290; by naturalized citizens, 127, 128; voting rights, 124, 286

Ward, Mary Frances, 189
Washington, George, 110
Washington statutes and laws, 199, 201, 211, 212, 246

Washington Territory, 31, 55, 77, 86, 102, 124, 169, 245, 283, 284, 285
Weller, John B., 54
Westmoreland, Charles, 50
white supremacy, 5–6, 17, 100, 167, 168–168, 279
Williams, Fountain, 42–43
witness testimonies, 11, 12, 15, 20–22, 44, 47, 74, 85, 100–111; He Hoo, 105; Ah How, 156; Kam Jip Wing, 102; Liu Him, 74; Liu Jing, 74; Liu Tang Fook, 74; minors, testimony from, 209; Ah Sing (husband of Yun Gee), 151–153; Ah Sing (murder witness), 70; Ah Tie, 256; Ah Wah, 256; women, testimony from, 132, 138–141; Wong Woon, Frank, 256; Woo, Flora, 195, 197; Yum Lee, 195, 197
Women and Missions (periodical), 262
Wong, Fred Chew, 273–275
Woon, Ah, 207–208, 218–222, 223–230
Wu, Tingfang, 197
Wy, Kee, 181
Wyoming, 217, 289

Xin, Jin, 138–139

Yeong Wo Company, 46
Yick, Ki Wing, 236–239, 258, 259, 265, 267
Yick, Yok Lan, 163, 242, 243, 248; application as denied and appealed, 239–240; departure from U.S., preparing for, 236–238; at the Presbyterian Mission, 234, 258, 259–260; rescue raid, as the subject of, 233–234, 247, 254; as Suey Ching, 235, 257–258, 265–268
Yick Wo v. Hopkins (1886), 100, 118–120
Yuba City, CA, 91, 93
Yuba County, 26, 31, 37, 52, 106, 135
Yum, Gee, 263
Yun, Gee, 139, 140; escape attempt, 130, 152–154, 156, 157, 163; habeas corpus, filing a writ of, 163–164; marriage, escaping sex work via, 151–152, 154; mobility restraints, 131, 132; as a sold woman, 130, 133, 134, 136, 138
Yung, Wing, 118